THE ENGLISH SERMON 1650-1750

General editors

C. H. Sisson
Val Warner
Michael Schmidt

THE ENGLISH SERMON
volume II: 1650-1750

an anthology

C. H. SISSON

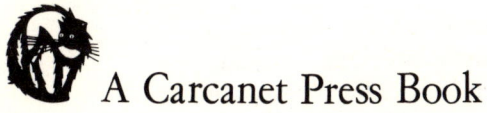 A Carcanet Press Book

SBN 85635 094 X

Copyright © C. H. Sisson 1976

All Rights Reserved

First published in 1976
by Carcanet Press Limited
266 Councillor Lane
Cheadle Hulme, Cheadle
Cheshire SK8 5PN

Printed in Great Britain
by Unwin Brothers Limited
The Gresham Press, Old Woking, Surrey.

Contents

CALENDAR 7
INTRODUCTION 11

JEREMY TAYLOR
(c. 1613-67)
    Apples of Sodom: or, the Fruits of Sin 20

ISAAC BARROW
(1630-77)
    Of a Peaceable Temper and Carriage 64
    Of Industry in Our Particular Calling, as Scholars 88

ROBERT SOUTH
(1634-1716)
    A Discourse against Long and Extempore Prayers: in Behalf of the Liturgy of the Church of England 105
    Obedience for Conscience-sake, the Duty of Good Subjects 126

EDWARD STILLINGFLEET
(1635-99)
    [Preached at Whitehall] 145

THOMAS KEN
(1637-1711)
    At the Funeral of the Right Hon. the Lady Margaret Mainard 168

JOHN TILLOTSON
(1630-94)
    The Advantages of Religion to Particular Persons 191

WILLIAM SHERLOCK
(1641-1707)
    The Charity of Lending without Usury 206

JOSEPH BINGHAM
(1668-1723)
    On the Trinity 220

FRANCIS ATTERBURY
(1662-1732)
    On the Martyrdom of King Charles I 242
    A Discourse Occasioned by the Death of the Right Hon. the Lady Cutts 257

THOMAS WILSON
(1663-1755)
    The Lord's Supper the Medicine of the Soul 275

JONATHAN SWIFT
(1667-1745)

GEORGE BERKELEY
(1685-1753)

JOSEPH BUTLER
(1692-1752)

On Brotherly Love   286
Doing Good   297
On Mutual Subjection   306

A Sermon Preached before the
  Incorporated Society for the
  Propagation of the Gospel
  in Foreign Parts   315

Upon the Government of the
  Tongue   333
Preached in the Parish Church
  of Christ-Church, London 344

Calendar

1651	Scots crown Charles II at Scone
	Cromwell defeats Charles who flees to France
	Hobbes: *Leviathan*
1652	English declare war on Dutch
	Williams: *The Hireling Ministry None of Christ's*
1653	Parliament resigns, Protectorate established (Cromwell as Protector)
	Rise of 'Fifth Monarchy' men
	Walton: *The Compleat Angler*
1655	Cromwell forbids Anglican service
	Jews readmitted to England
1656	Pascal: *Lettres Provinciales*
1658	Death of Cromwell; succeeded as Protector by Richard Cromwell, his son
	Birth of Purcell
1659	Richard Cromwell resigns; Commonwealth re-established
1660	Restoration of Charles II
	Pepys begins his *Diary*
	Patents granted for re-opening London theatres
	Birth of George I
1662	Royal Society receives its charter
	Book of Common Prayer: final text approved and enforced by Act of Uniformity
1663	Leibniz: *De principio individui*
1665	Great Plague of London
	La Rochefoucauld: *Maximes*
1666	Great Fire of London
1667	Milton: *Paradise Lost*
1669	Death of Rembrandt
1670	Pascal: *Pensées* (posthumous)
	Spinoza: *Tractatus Theologico-Politicus*
1671	Bunyan: *A Confession of My Faith, and a Reason of My Practice*
	Milton: *Paradise Regained; Samson Agonistes*
1674	Boileau: *L'Art poétique*
1675	Greenwich Observatory established
	Wycherley: *The Country Wife*
1677	Spinoza: *Ethics*
	Death of Spinoza

1678	Titus Oates reveals Popish Plot
	Bunyan: *The Pilgrim's Progress* (I)
	Dryden: *All for Love*
1679	First use of the terms 'Tory' and 'Whig'
1680	Wren: St. Clement Dane's Church, London
	Purcell appointed organist at Westminster Abbey
1681	Marvell: *Miscellaneous Poems* (posthumous)
1682	Ashmolean Museum, Oxford, founded
	Wren: Chelsea Hospital
1683	Rye House Plot to assassinate Charles II and his brother James is discovered
1684	Bunyan: *The Pilgrim's Progress* (II)
1685	Accession of James II
	Monmouth's Rebellion
	Massive emigration of Huguenots from France following the revocation of the Edict of Nantes
	Birth of Handel
	Birth of Bach
1686	Browne: *Works* (posthumous)
1687	Newton: *Principia Mathematica*
1688	William of Orange invited by Whig Lords to England
	James II escapes to France
	Birth of Pope
	Death of Bunyan
1689	Bill of Rights
	Coronation of William and Mary
	Locke: *Two Treatises on Civil Government*
	Purcell: *Dido and Aeneas*
1690	Locke: *An Essay Concerning Human Understanding*
1691	Death of George Fox
1692	Massacre of highlanders at Glencoe after MacDonald's refusal to swear allegiance to William III
1693	The National Debt established in England
	La Fontaine: *Fables*
1694	*Dictionnaire de l'Académie française*
	Birth of Voltaire
1695	Ending of press censorship in England
	Congreve: *Love for Love*
	Death of Purcell
1699	Death of Racine
1700	Congreve: *The Way of the World*
1702	Death of William III; succession of Queen Anne

1703	Death of Pepys
1704	Bach writes first cantata
	Swift: *A Tale of a Tub*
1705	Vanburgh: Blenheim Palace
1706	Farquhar: *The Recruiting Officer*
	Birth of Benjamin Franklin
1707	Union of England and Scotland
	Birth of Fielding
	Birth of Wesley
1708	Birth of Pitt
1709	First issue of *The Tatler*
	Birth of Johnson
1710	Berkeley: *A Treatise Concerning the Principles of Human Knowledge*
	Leibniz: *Théodicée*
1711	Shaftesbury: *Characteristics of Men, Manners, Opinions and Times*
	First issue of *The Spectator*
1712	Pope: *The Rape of the Lock*
	Birth of Rousseau
1713	Scriblerus Club founded in London (by Pope, Gay, Swift, Congreve and others)
1714	Death of Queen Anne; succession of George I
	Leibniz: *Monadologie*
1715	Jacobite rising, 'The Fifteen', in Scotland
	Handel: *Water Music*
1719	Defoe: *Robinson Crusoe*
	Death of Addison
1720	'South Sea Bubble' bursts
	Charles Edward Stuart ('the Young Pretender') born
1722	Defoe: *A Journal of the Plague Year; Moll Flanders*
1723	Death of Wren
1724	Birth of Kant
1725	Pope: translation of *The Odyssey*
1726	First circulating library opened in Edinburgh
	Swift: *Gulliver's Travels*
1727	Death of George I; succession of George II
	John Wood, the elder: *Plans for Bath*
	Death of Newton
1728	Law: *A Serious Call to Devout and Holy Life*
	Gay: *Beggar's Opera*
	Pope: *The Dunciad* (I-III)

1728	Birth of Goldsmith
1729	Bach: *St Matthew Passion*
	Swift: *A Modest Proposal*
	Birth of Burke
	Death of Congreve
1730	Thomson: *The Seasons*
	Death of Defoe
	Birth of Cowper
1732	Franklin: *Poor Richard's Almanack* begun
	Birth of Washington.
	Birth of Haydn
1733	Bach: B Minor Mass
	Pope: *Essay on Man*
	Voltaire: *English Letters*
1735	Hogarth: *Rake's Progress*
1737	Wesley: *Psalms and Hymns*
1738	Handel: *Israel in Egypt; Saul*
1739	Hume: *A Treatise on Human Nature*
	Dick Turpin hanged
1740	Richardson: *Pamela*
	Birth of Boswell
1741	Handel: *Messiah*
1743	Hogarth: *Marriage à la Mode*
	Birth of Jefferson
1744	Death of Pope
1745	Charles Edward Stuart advances as far south as Derby where he is forced to retreat
	Death of Swift
	Death of Walpole
1746	Jacobite defeat at Culloden
	Edwards: *A Treatise Concerning the Religious Affections*
1748	Klopstock: *The Messiah*
	Richardson: *Clarissa*
	Smollett: *The Adventures of Roderick Random*
1749	Fielding: *The History of Tom Jones, a Foundling*
1750	'Capability' Brown lays out Warwick Castle gardens
	Johnson starts *The Rambler*
	Death of Bach

Introduction

ONE OF the profound differences between England and France is that in France the Revolution followed a century of widespread amusement at the mysteries of the Christian faith, while the English revolution took place after a century of reformation and counter-reformation, and while the language of Christianity was still the language of political and social aspiration, as of more intimate reflections. In France as in England, of course, many of the ideas in play in the revolutionary movements had a theological origin or colour—there is in the west no complete escape from the Church—but the process of laicization had gone much further, and bitten much deeper, in the Paris of 1789 than in the London of 1649. 1649 was still a long way from Locke, whose ideas, and those of the empirical rationalism that went with him, were popularized in France by Voltaire.

At the starting-point of this volume, in the mid-seventeenth century, the public disarray of this country was inextricably at once political and religious. The movement from Episcopacy to Presbyterianism, from Presbyterianism to Independency and so to chaos, marks the political progress, or declension, of those times. There are many shifts, in the century that follows, to 1750, and by that time we are in another world. Theological arguments have become frivolities, as far as politics is concerned. The Whig bishops and the Whig landowners overlay the country like a plateful of cold porridge. In 1650 things were not like that. The king had been put to death by a revolutionary tribunal. The bishops had been pushed out; the use of the Book of Common Prayer, privately as well as publicly, had been made a criminal offence punishable by fine or imprisonment; thousands of the parochial clergy had been deprived of their functions and their means of livelihood; there had been a great smashing of church ornaments, under parliamentary direction. The Church was, politically, a defeated and illegal opposition. No doubt it learned something from that, and it is worth reflection that a great century of Anglican divinity included this period in the wilderness.

When the revolutionary movement had played itself out, and Charles II came back in 1660 without serious dissent, the English Church was restored with him, and the remnant was swollen by many who were less sure of their bearings. There was some vindictiveness and much mutual incomprehension, but the Church was again there, visibly, in every diocese and in every parish, ministering the sacraments in accordance with a Prayer Book which was certainly not less Catholic than its proscribed predecessor. The bishops had a part to play on the public stage. It was a transitory phase. The moment of their greatest political—and only popular—triumph came in 1688 when seven of their number took a public stand against James II's Declaration of Indulgence (see note on Ken, p. 166 below). It was the last time the hierarchy played a significant public role in England. The settlement of 1689 meant, in the long run, the resurgence, in more sedate guise, of the forces behind the revolution of 1649 and their integration with the new forces of scientific rationalism. The outcome was the Whig oligarchy which, so to speak, had its licence from the financial enterprise of the City of London and has hardly relaxed its grip since; Certainly the prosperity of the High Church party in the last years of Anne's reign was a flash-in-the-pan. Ever since, Toryism in the sense defined by Dr Johnson —a Tory, says the *Dictionary*, is 'One who adheres to the ancient constitution of the state, and the apostolical hierarchy of the church of England'—has been no more than an obscure opposition doctrine, held more or less ironically by a few scattered people who persist in thinking that it has a bearing on the orientation of the country, however unhandy politicians may find it. That Toryism, which was that of Swift and of Johnson himself, has nothing whatever to do with the present-day political party which sometimes appropriates the name.

The strand of political involvement can never be lost sight of for long by any reader of the sermons of this period. It shows up most clearly in this volume in Atterbury's sermon *On the Martyrdom of King Charles I* and in the sermons of South, but it is present also in Swift and Barrow, to name no others. Atterbury's subject was common to the divines of the age; the Prayer Book provided a form of service to be used on 30 January, the day Charles was beheaded. The word 'martyrdom' was used because of the King's final stand for episcopacy. It must always have been distasteful to many, and the service fell into disuse— not without protest from such men as Swift—as the Whig oligarchy tightened its grip. These remote political quarrels have to be accepted as part of the scene of the times.

The related, but more general, political theme which recurs with a frequency which is likely to surprise the casual reader of the literature of the age is that of passive obedience. This meant the duty of obeying civil authorities—the king and the king's government—whether one liked what they were doing or not. South's treatment of this subject will be found in his sermon on Romans 13:5, 'Wherefore he must needs be subject, not only for wrath, but also for conscience sake' (see p. 126 below). But the subject was not one only for party men. No one was ever less that than Berkeley, and he gave a series of discourses on the subject, in the most conciliatory vein, in the chapel of Trinity College, Dublin. It is a way of thinking remote from any that is now current, but there is a theological issue to be understood. The classic application of the doctrine, in this period, was to the difficult question of allegiance to James II after he had fled the country and William and Mary had come in. It was possible to maintain, and many, like Stillingfleet, did maintain—after more or less hesitation—that obedience was due to the *de facto* government, whatever it might be. But many of the most sensitive churchmen of the time felt, with Sancroft, the Archbishop of Canterbury, and Ken, that they could not rescind the oath of allegiance they had given to James II and so could not take the oath to William and Mary.

These events are important for an understanding of sermon literature of the age, not merely because they echo through it, but because those who felt they could not take the oath were an important group and the fact that they were turned out affected the character of the subsequent literature. For the Non-Jurors, who were catholic-minded and had strong affinities with the earlier Caroline divines, had no access to pulpits and delivered no more sermons. A valuable stream of Anglican thought went underground, re-emerging in various ways with Wesley and Newman. There was Jeremy Collier, whose *Short View of the Immorality and Profaneness of the English Stage* is less absurd than it is often made out to be and who was the author of a number of other works, including a most readable *Ecclesiastical History of Great Britain*. The greatest name is undoubtedly that of William Law, of whom every student of eighteenth-century literature should read at least *A Serious Call to a Devout and Holy Life* and the *Three Letters to the Bishop of Bangor*—charming and elegant masterpieces, the latter an ironic onslaught on the Erastianism of Hoadly. The chill on the English pulpit, as the century advances, would have been less if these men had had their say.

With the political involvement of the Church from 1650 to

1750 there developed another characteristic, a relative neglect of dogma, what seems a lack of curiosity as of passion in relation to the fundamental tenets of the Christian religion. This neglect is far from being general, or absolute, but there is enough of it to make a contrast with the preceding period, when the quarrels of the Reformation still reverberated. This is not to say that the essentials of doctrine were not kept alive by the more Catholic part of the clergy—a Bingham or a Wilson, even Swift. But there is, undoubtedly, an orientation towards questions of conduct, which is marked from the very beginning of the period. Before the mid-point of the century Henry Hammond had published his *Practical Catechism*, a lucid, deeply considered work aimed at the 'heightening of Christian practice'. The book is uncompromising in its claims for the apostolic church of England, but one senses in the prominent attention given to conduct a desire to lay weight on those matters in which reconciliation between Christian opinions seemed least hopeless. There is something of this even in Jeremy Taylor, with whom this volume opens. *Holy Living* and *Holy Dying* are, after all, manuals of conduct, and in the latter part of his life what Taylor most valued among his works was the casuistry of *Ductor Dubitantium*. The sermon given in this volume, which belongs to his best period as a writer, shows a most delicate psychological insight. While one may miss, in this period, the doctrinal expositions of an Andrewes, one cannot make light of the longing for peace which must have been partly responsible for turning men's minds in the direction of practice. There was, however, also a more sinister motive for this development, which can be felt in France as well as in England. This is the movement towards deism, not to say atheism, which accompanied the fading of the imagination of the seventeenth century and the growth of the sort of rationalism which founded itself on empirical and mechanical philosophies. This movement did produce some direct theological reaction, of which a notable monument is Bingham's sermon given on p. 220 below. But there is still more of an attempt to meet the new prejudices on their own ground, one common sense against another, which leads only to the complacency and worldliness of the time-servers (see below the notes on Tillotson, p. 190). Butler, with talents and a personal forbearance which put him in quite a different class, is really a last serious bid to answer the eighteenth century on its own terms (see p. 331 below).

*

14

The form and style of the sermon alters during the period, in the same way as the form and style of literature at large. The great poem of 1650 is Marvell's 'Horatian Ode', which looks backwards to the Metaphysicals and forwards to the clarities of the Augustan age. The reform of the heroic couplet had already begun with Denham and Waller, but the way was so far only obscurely open to the ages of Dryden and Pope. By 1750 this aesthetic was in decline, though 'The Deserted Village', which would not have been possible without it, was still to come. The movement in prose style is well exemplified in this volume. Jeremy Taylor, born seventeen years before any other divine here represented, belongs wholly to the world before the formation of the Royal Society, which however happened before his death. His abstractions are not the abstractions of science, and the new conception of rationality, as of eloquence, which marks the latter part of the seventeenth century and becomes dominant in the eighteenth, hardly shows itself. It is more marked in Barrow, who was a mathematician, and in Stillingfleet, yet they still drag their feet a little in the old rhythms. The watershed is marked by Tillotson, a man of much less ability than any of them. Tillotson was born in the same year as Barrow, and before South, but he was a man with his ear, as well as his eye, on the present, and perhaps had less strong attachments than they. He saw what was needed for the worldly success of the Church—if that is not a contradiction in terms—and it is he, more than anyone, who grasped what sort of thing decent people in that age would listen to, without feeling that they were in any danger of being disturbed in their complacencies. He set the tone of the eighteenth-century pulpit. This is not to say that there were not, in the first half of the eighteenth century, powerful minds among the clergy who had absorbed all the new elegances—to a degree, indeed, far beyond Tillotson's capacities—and were capable of using them to convey orthodox and disturbing messages. Swift's tongue was rough as well as elegant, and, under all his armour of irony against the world of the Whigs, he was a Caroline High Churchman. Berkeley, one of the most brilliant minds in the Europe of his age, was not the man to throw away the imagination of the seventeenth century. Finally there is Butler, a man of the eighteenth century certainly, and speaking the language of his opponents, but holding fast to his orthodoxy in a world of deism.

No one can take the study of seventeenth-century literature

very far without some acquaintance with the works of the Anglican divines who were among its greatest prose writers. So much of the intellect and imagination of the age went into these channels. Even if one considers that Hobbes, Locke and Hume swept the board, and that the science which followed them has made all theology a useless dream—which is a common enough assumption, even conclusion, in our own day—it is still necessary to know what it was they swept away. Moreover, the reader of Vaughan and Traherne will not be very near their poetry unless he has some knowledge of the world of Jeremy Taylor. The deficiency of Christian teaching in the latter part of the twentieth century has made the approach more difficult, for many readers, and this deficiency has to be made up for somehow, whether or not one thinks Christianity superannuated. This book at least contains a number of clues to what was involved in the transition from the seventeenth to the eighteenth century, and might well be found of value by any student or general reader within whose field of interest that large subject falls for one reason or another. It is not and does not pretend to be a comprehensive guide to the subject.

The sermons have been chosen both for their intrinsic interest and to give an indication of the drift of the times. To the newcomer to this branch of literature—which, because of the widespread suspicion, in our time, of theological writers, as if they were the only repositories of superstition, has been comparatively neglected—these sermons will at least indicate what variety there is, and what sort of entertainment is to be found. There is at any rate a massive amount of good prose, written by men passionately concerned for the truth of what they were saying and perfectly primed in the intellectual difficulties of their contemporaries which are, of course, no more than more or less our own.

In the seventeenth and eighteenth centuries the clergy, as a matter of course, attracted to its numbers a high proportion of the ability which, in the twentieth century, would be more likely to find its way into ordinary academic work, the civil service, or any one of a variety of professional and business pursuits; and that can be said without aspersion on the able men in orders now. Moreover, a variety of literary talent, which would now be more likely to find vent in imaginative or analytical writing of an entirely lay character, then found an outlet in the pulpit and in other forms of theological writing. So the mind of those times is not to be known without some acquaintance with the sermons, nor can any comparison of our own with the older literature be made without it.

*

In accordance with the general plan of the three volumes of *The English Sermon*, the notes prefixed to each of the sermons selected give some account of the author and enough additional material to give the reader his bearings in the matter before him. The notes are indicative rather than comprehensive and, in the case of the biographies, if the authors the reader is unfamiliar with are brought a little alive, and the more familiar figures—a Swift or a Berkeley—put in context as the authors of sermons, their purpose will have been served.

I would like to thank Paris Leary for a number of helpful suggestions he made while this volume was being put together.

*

Acknowledgement is due to Dr William's Library for permission to copy the Library's 1682 pamphlet edition of the sermon by Ken, on which the modernized text is based.

*

Note: The spelling has been modernized throughout; in other matters of style the best editions have been followed. Greek quotations in the sermons have been retained where essential to the meaning, but otherwise omitted (omissions indicated by square brackets and marks of ellipsis).

Jeremy Taylor

TAYLOR WAS born in Cambridge in or about 1613. His father was a barber; Heber and others have tried to make out that he must have been at least a *surgeon*-barber, but those who are anxious to prove the respectability of the bishop could rest content with his own life and works. He was admitted to Gonville and Caius College, Cambridge, in 1626, having been to school in the same town. He was elected a fellow of Caius, and ordained, in 1633. He spent little time in the college, however. He went to London to preach at St Paul's in place of a Cambridge friend, and made impression enough for news of his performance to reach the ears of Laud, who was attentive to such matters. He was invited to preach before the Archbishop at Lambeth. Laud's only adverse remark afterwards was that he was too young, a fault Taylor is said to have promised to cure, if he lived. In 1635 he was nominated to a fellowship at All Souls, Oxford, by Laud, who expressed the hope that the fact that he had been educated at Cambridge would 'be no prejudice to him'. Taylor thus started his ecclesiastical career under the most favourable auspices.

He stayed at All Souls no more than three years, and then became rector of Uppingham in Rutlandshire, and married. Shortly afterwards he became chaplain to Charles I, and it is probably that which took him back to Oxford in 1642. He became a chaplain in the Royalist army. Naturally his house in Uppingham was 'plundered, his estate seized, and his family driven out of doors'. He seems to have been taken prisoner in the struggle around Cardigan Castle, and the same year—1645—was released and went to live as chaplain to the Earl of Carbery, at Golden Grove in Carmarthenshire. Carbery seems hardly to have been a hero; after some initial gestures for the royal cause he apparently preferred to stay at home drinking, and not to imperil his estate. It was this circumstance which gave Taylor the safe seclusion in which much of his best work was produced. At Golden Grove he wrote not only many of his best sermons but *The Liberty of Prophesying* and *Holy Living* and *Holy Dying*.

In 1655 Taylor was imprisoned for a time in Chepstow Castle. After that he did not go back to Golden Grove. Royalists were by then forbidden to keep chaplains, or tutors for their children. After some comings and goings among Royalists in London and elsewhere, Taylor went to northern Ireland in 1658, under the protection of Lord Conway. He was back in London in 1660 and able to declare his support for Monk. With the Restoration he was appointed Bishop of Down and Connor and Vice-Chancellor of Trinity College, Dublin. It was perhaps a mark of distrust due to literary ability that he was not offered an English bishopric; 'a man of dangerous temper,' as Sheldon said later, 'apt to break out into extravagances.' His Irish see brought him troubles; it was full of Scottish Presbyterians who could not be pacified. Taylor's work at Trinity College was, however, a success. He found 'a heap of men and boys' and set the place on its feet as a university. He died in 1667.

Despite adversities—which were hardly to be avoided by anyone who took a firm stand in the internal struggles of the seventeenth century—Taylor had a fortunate life, if anything too much under the protection of great men. His writings are among the most seductive in the great literature produced by the Anglican clergy of the period. *Holy Living* and *Holy Dying* are full of wisdom, charm and eloquence; no one should let a prejudice against works of piety stop him from exploring them. *The Worthy Communicant* is a book for the practising Christian, but can be read with pleasure and other advantages by anyone who wants to understand the temper of Anglicanism.

APPLES OF SODOM: OR, THE FRUITS OF SIN
Romans 6:21.
What fruit had ye then in those things whereof ye are now ashamed? For the end of those things is death.

OF ALL the sermons in this book, these of Taylor have in them most of the flavour of an earlier period. Charles I was dead; the Restoration was still some years off. Taylor was one of those who was keeping a candle alight. It must have felt like that, in view of the public state of the Church, and from the relative seclusion in which he lived. But Taylor was no mere continuer of old fashions. 'Sermons are not like curious *Inquiries* after *New-Nothings*', as he said in the dedication to the Earl of Carbery. They were 'pursuances of *Old-truths*', but Taylor pursued them, not merely with silvery eloquence but, when he was not too far carried away, with a good deal of psychological exactness. He has a kind of imagination which the twentieth century has been more inclined to look for—and more likely to find, if at all—in works of fiction than in sermons, and more in such half-lit work as Forrest Reid's than in anything more blatant and explicit. Yet of course there is in the sermons only an occasional approximation to such work. Taylor is a preacher and a theologian, speaking in and through the language of the Church.

The issue of his analyses and directions is in prayer, and he came to the sermons at Golden Grove from the composition of *Holy Living* and *Holy Dying*, where this turn of mind is repeatedly made explicit. And he was moving towards the sort of casuistical analyses of his later years, the *Ductor Dubitantium*. Coleridge, for whom the writings of Jeremy Taylor were 'a perpetual feast', said he was 'an excellent author for a young man to study, for the purpose of imbibing noble principles, and at the same time learning to exercise caution and thought in detecting his numerous errors.' Theologians have found some fault with his work. Certainly the closest reasoning is not evident there, and some have found in him too much blandness and optimism about human nature. There is a highly personal tone, a certain imaginative kindness. Taylor, who married a second time after his first wife's death, in an age when prelates were not uncommonly unmarried, and who preached a splendid sermon on *The Marriage Ring; or the Mysteriousness and Duties of Marriage*, did not live beyond the reach of Eros.

The ethical theory of Taylor, in this sermon—so far as he may be said to have one—is really not at all unlike that elucidated, more abstractly and much more coherently, by Butler nearly a century later. Butler thought that a man should act in accordance with his whole nature, and not on the impulse of the moment. For Taylor the pleasures of sin 'are at best so little, that they are limited to one Sense, not spread upon all the Faculties like the pleasures of virtue.' But there is a sort of hedonism about Taylor. 'If by Experience' men 'feel Sin Pleasant, it is certain also by Experience, that most sins are in their own nature Sharpnesses and Diseases.' He is conscious of his own skin: 'nothing but the skin for its organ or instrument,' he says, 'an Artery, or something not more considerable than a Lute-string.' He is, of course, not concerned only with sins directly related to sex, but with a whole catalogue,

> every one of which is a Disease, a trouble in its very constitution and its nature: such are *loathing of spiritual things, bitterness of spirit, rage, greediness, confusion of mind* and *irresolution, cruelty and despite, slothfulness* and *distrust,*

unquietness and *anger, effeminacy* and *niceness, prating* and *sloth, ignorance* and *inconstancy, incogitancy* and *cursing, malignity* and *fear, forgetfulness* and *rashness, pusillanimity* and *despair, rancour* and *superstition*.

This sermon as we have it is in three parts. In Part II, Taylor touches on a theory of the relationship of sin and knowledge. All that the Devil offered to Adam and Eve was *'the experience of evil'*, for 'they knew good before.' But evil cannot properly speaking be known. Whatever is knowable is true; 'all the Knowledge a man gets by Sin is to feel Evil', and the feel of it is a *smart*. Part III deals with shame and other consequences of sin. There is forgiveness, but not impunity. 'Christ hath redeemed our Souls, and if we repent we shall not die eternally, yet he hath no where promised we shall not be smitten.'

THE SON of *Sirach* did prudently advise concerning making judgments of the felicity or infelicity of men: *Judge none blessed before his death; for a man shall be known in his children.* Some men raise their fortunes from a cottage to the chairs of Princes, from a sheep-cote to a throne, and dwell in the circles of the Sun, and in the lap of prosperity; their wishes and success dwell under the same roof, and providence brings all events into their design, and ties both ends together with prosperous successes; and even the little conspersions and intertextures of evil accidents in their lives, are but like a feigned note in music, by an artificial discord making the ear covetous, and then pleased with the harmony into which the appetite was enticed by passion, and a pretty restraint; and variety does but adorn prosperity, and make it of a sweeter relish, and of more advantages; and some of these men descended into their graves without a change of fortune, *Eripitur persona, manet res.* Indeed they cannot longer dwell upon the estate, but that remains unrifled, and descends upon the heir, and all is well till the next generation: but if the evil of his death, and the change of his present prosperity for an intolerable danger of an uncertain eternity, does not sour his full chalice; yet if his children prove vicious, or degenerous, cursed, or unprosperous, we account the man miserable, and his grave to be strewed with sorrows and dishonours. The wise and valiant *Chabrias* grew miserable by the folly of his son *Ctesippus*; and the reputation of brave *Germanicus* began to be ashamed, when the base *Caligula* entered upon his scene of dishonourable crimes. *Commodus* the wanton and feminine son of wise *Antoninus* gave a check to the great name of his Father; and when the son of *Hortensius Corbius* was prostitute, and the heir of *Q. Fabius Maximus* was disinherited by the sentence of the City *Praetor*, as being unworthy to enter into the fields of his glorious Father, and young *Scipio* the son of *Africanus* was a fool and a prodigal; posterity did weep afresh over the monuments of their brave Progenitors, and found that infelicity can pursue a man, and overtake him in his grave.

This is a great calamity when it falls upon innocent persons: and that *Moses* died upon *Mount Nebo* in the sight of *Canaan*, was not so great an evil, as that his sons *Eliezer* and *Gerson* were unworthy to succeed him; but that *Priesthood* was devolved to his *Brother*, and the *Principality* to his *servant*: And to *Samuel*, that his sons proved corrupt, and were exauthorated for their unworthiness, was an allay to his honour and his joys, and such as proclaims to all the world, that the measures of our felicity are not to be taken by the lines of our own person, but of our relations too; and he that is cursed in his children, cannot be reckoned among the fortunate.

This which I have discoursed concerning families in general, is most remarkable in the retinue and family of sin; for it keeps a good house, and is full of company and servants, it is served by the possessions of the world, it is courted by the unhappy, flattered by fools, taken into the bosom by the effeminate, made the end of human designs, and feasted all the way of its progress: wars are made for its interest, and men give or venture their lives that their sin may be prosperous; all the *outward senses* are its handmaids, and the *inward senses* are of its privy chamber; *the understanding* is its counsellor, *the will* its friend, *riches* are its ministers, *nature* holds up its train, and *art* is its emissary to promote its interest and affairs abroad: and upon this account, all the world is enrolled in its taxing tables, and are subjects or friends of its kingdom, or are so kind to it as to make too often visits, and to lodge in its borders; because all men stare upon its pleasures, and are enticed to taste of its wanton delicacies. But then if we look what are the children of this splendid family, and see what issue sin produces, it may help to untie the charm. Sin and concupiscence marry together, and riot and feast it high, but their fruits, the children and production of their filthy union, are *ugly* and *deformed, foolish* and *ill-natured*; and the Apostle calls them by their names, *shame* and *death*. These are *the fruits of sin, the apples of* Sodom, fair outsides, but if you touch them they turn to ashes and a stink; and if you will nurse these children, and give them whatsoever is dear to you, then you may be admitted into the house of feasting, and chambers of riot where sin dwells; but if you will have the mother, you must have the daughters; the tree and the fruits go together; and there is none of you all that ever entered into this house of pleasure, but he left the skirts of his garment in the hands of shame, and had his name rolled in the chambers of death. What fruit had ye then? That's the Question.

In answer to which question we are to consider, 1. What is the sum total of the pleasure of sin? 2. What fruits and relishes it leaves behind by its natural efficiency? 3. What are its consequents by its demerit, and the infliction of the superadded wrath of God, which it hath deserved? Of the first St. *Paul* gives no account, but by way of upbraiding asks, what they had? that is, *nothing* that they dare own, *nothing* that remains: and where is it? show it; what's become of it? Of the second he gives the sum total; all its natural effects are *shame* and its appendages. The third, or the superinduced evils by the just wrath of God, he calls *death*, the worst name in it self, and the greatest of evils that can happen.

1. Let us consider what pleasures there [are] in sin; *most of them are very punishments*. I will not reckon nor consider concerning *envy*, which one in *Stobaeus* calls *the basest spirit and yet very just*, because it punishes the delinquent in the very act of sin, doing as *Aelian* says of the *Polypus*, when he wants his prey, he devours his own arms; and the leanness, and the secret pangs, and the perpetual restlessness of an envious man feed upon his own heart, and drink down his spirits, unless he can ruin or observe the fall of the fairest fortunes of his neighbour. The fruits of this tree are mingled and sour, and not to be endured in the very eating. Neither will I reckon the horrid afrightments and amazements of murder, nor the uneasiness of impatience, which doubles every evil that it feels, and makes it a sin, and makes it intolerable; nor the secret grievings, and continual troubles of peevishness, which makes a man incapable of receiving good, or delighting in beauties and fair entreaties in the mercies of God and charities of men.

It were easy to make a catalogue of sins, every one of which is a disease, a trouble in its very constitution and its nature: such are *loathing of spiritual things, bitterness of spirit, rage, greediness, confusion of mind*, and *irresolution, cruelty* and *despite, slothfulness* and *distrust, unquietness* and *anger, effeminacy* and *niceness, prating* and *sloth, ignorance* and *inconstancy, incogitancy* and *cursing, malignity* and *fear, forgetfulness* and *rashness, pusillanimity* and *despair, rancour* and *superstition*: if a man were to curse his enemy, he could not wish him a greater evil than these; and yet these are several kinds of sin which men choose, and give all their hopes of heaven in exchange for one of these diseases. Is it not a fearful consideration that a man should rather choose eternally to perish, than to say his prayers heartily, and affectionately? but so it is with very many men; they are driven to their devotions by custom, and shame, and reputation, and civil compliances; they sigh and look sour when they are called to it, and abide there as a man under the Surgeon's hands, smarting and fretting all the while; or else he passes the time with *incogitancy*, and hates the employment, and suffers the torments of prayers which he loves not; and all this, although for so doing it is certain he may perish: what fruit, what deliciousness can he fancy in being weary of his prayers? There is no pretence or colour for these things. Can any man imagine a greater evil to the body and soul of a man, than madness, and furious eyes, and a distracted look, paleness with passion, and trembling hands and knees, and furiousness, and folly in the heart and head? and yet this is the pleasure of anger, and for this pleasure men choose damnation. But it is a great truth, that *there are but very few sins that pretend to pleasure*: although a man be weak and soon deceived, and the Devil is crafty, and sin is false and impudent, and pretences are too many, yet most kinds of sins are *real* and *prime troubles* to the very body, without all manner of deliciousness, even to the sensual, natural, and carnal part; and a man must put on something of a *Devil* before he can choose such sins, and he must love mischief because it is a sin; for in most instances there is no other reason in the world. Nothing pretends to pleasure but *the lusts of the lower belly, ambition,* and *revenge*; and although the catalogue of sins is numerous as the production of fishes, yet these three only can be apt to cozen us with a fair outside; and yet upon the survey of what fruits they bring, and what taste they have, in the *manducation*, besides the filthy relish they leave behind, we shall see how miserably they are abused and fooled, that expend any thing upon such purchases.

2. For a man cannot take pleasure *in lusts of the flesh*, in *gluttony*, or *drunkenness*, unless he be helped forward with *inconsideration* and *folly*. For we see it evidently that grave and wise persons, men of experience and consideration are extremely less affected with lust and loves, than the hare-brained boy; the young gentleman that thinks nothing in the world greater than to be free from a Tutor, he indeed courts his folly and enters into the possession of lust without abatement; consideration dwells not there; but when a sober man meets with a temptation, and is helped by his natural temper, or invited by his course of life; if he can consider, he hath so many objections and fears, so many difficulties and impediments, such sharp reasonings and sharper jealousies concerning its event, that if he does at all enter into folly, it pleases him so little, that he is forced to do it in despite of himself; and the pleasure is so allayed, that he knows not whether it be wine or vinegar; his very apprehension and instruments of relish are filled with fear and contradicting principles, and the deliciousness does but *affricare cutem*, it went but to

the skin; but the allay went further; it kept a guard within, and suffered the pleasure to pass no further. A man must resolve to be a fool, a rash, inconsiderate person, or he will feel but little satisfaction in the enjoyment of his sin: indeed he that stops his nose, may drink down such corrupted waters, and he understood it well who chose rather to be a fool, *'Dum mala delectent mea me, vel denique fallant, / Quam sapere et ringi—'* so that his sins might delight him, or deceive him, than to be wise and without pleasure in the enjoyment. So that in effect a man must lose his discerning faculties, before he discerns the little fantastic joys of his concupiscence; which demonstrates how vain, how empty of pleasure that is, that is beholding to folly and illusion, to a juggling and a plain cozenage, before it can be fancied to be pleasant. For it is a strange beauty that he that hath the best eyes cannot perceive, and none but the blind or blear-eyed people can see; and such is the pleasure of lust, which by every degree of wisdom that a man hath is lessened and undervalued.

3. For the pleasures of intemperance, they are nothing but the relics and images of pleasure, after the nature hath been feasted; For so long as she needs, that is, so long as temperance waits, so long pleasure also stands there. But as temperance begins to go away, having done the ministries of Nature, every morsel, and every new goblet is still less delicious, and cannot be endured but as men force nature by violence to stay longer than she would: How have some men rejoiced when they have escaped a cup! and when they cannot escape, they pour it in, and receive it with as much pleasure as the old women have in the *Lapland* dances; they dance the round, but there is a horror and a harshness in the Music; and they call it pleasure, because men bid them do so: but there is a *Devil* in the company, and such as is his pleasure, such is theirs: he rejoices in the thriving sin, and the swelling fortune of his darling drunkenness, but his joys are the joys of him that knows and always remembers that he shall infallibly have the biggest damnation; and then let it be considered how forced a joy that is, that is at the end of an intemperate feast. *'Non bene mendaci risus componitur ore, / Nec bene sollicitis ebria verba sonant.'* Certain it is, intemperance takes but nature's leavings; when the belly is full and nature calls to take away, the pleasure that comes in afterwards is next to loathing: it is like the relish and taste of meats at the end of the third course, or the sweetness of honey to him that hath eaten till he can endure to take no more; and in this, there is no other

difference of these men from them that die upon another cause, than was observed among the *Phalangia* of old, some of these serpents make men die laughing, and some to die weeping: so does the intemperate, and so does his brother that languishes of a consumption; this man dies weeping, and the other dies laughing: but they both die infallibly, and all his pleasure is nothing but the sting of a serpent, *immixto liventia mella veneno*, it wounds the heart, and he dies with a *Tarantula* dancing and singing till he bows his neck, and kisses his bosom with the fatal noddings and declensions of death.

4. In these pretenders to pleasure which you see are but few, and they not very prosperous in their pretences, there is mingled so much trouble to bring them to act and enjoyment, that the appetite is above half tired before it comes; It is necessary a man should be hugely *patient* that is *ambitious, Ambulare per Britannos, Scythicas pati pruinas*; no man buys death and damnation at so dear a rate, as he that fights for it, and endures cold and hunger,—'*Patiens liminis atque solis*,' The heat of the Sun, and the cold of the threshold; the dangers of war, and the snares of a crafty enemy; he lies upon the ground with a severity greater than the penances of a Hermit, and fasts beyond the austerity of a rare penitent; with this only difference, that the one does it for heaven, the other for an uncertain honour, and an eternity of flames. But however, by this time that he hath won something, he hath spent some years, and he hath not much time left him to rest in his new purchase, and he hath worn out his body, and lessened his capacity of feeling it; and although it is ten to one he cannot escape all the dangers he must venture at, that he may come near his trifle, yet when he is arrived thither, he can never long enjoy, nor well perceive or taste it; and therefore there are more sorrows at the gate, than there can dwell comforts in all the rooms of the houses of pride and great designs. And thus it is in *revenge*, which is pleasant only to a devil, or a man of the same cursed temper. He does a thing which ought to trouble him, and will move him to pity what his own vile hands have acted; but if he does not pity, that is, be troubled with himself and wish the things undone, he hath those affections by which the Devil doth rejoice in destroying souls; which affections a man cannot have, unless he be perfectly miserable, by being contrary to God, to mercy, and to felicity; and after all, the pleasure is *false, fantastic*, and *violent*; it can do him no good, it can do him hurt: 'tis odds but it will; and on him that takes revenge, revenge

shall be taken; and by a real evil he shall dearly pay for the goods that are but *airy* and *fantastical*; It is like a rolling stone, which when a man hath forced up a hill, will return upon him with a greater violence, and break those bones whose sinews gave it motion. The pleasure of revenge is like the pleasure of eating chalk and coals; a foolish disease made the appetite, and it is entertained with an evil reward; it is like the feeding of a *Cancer* or a *Wolf*, the man is restless till it be done, and when it is, every man sees how infinitely he is removed from satisfaction or felicity.

5. These sins when they are entertained with the greatest fondness from without, it must have but extreme little pleasure, because there is a strong faction, and the better party against them: something that is within contests against the entertainment, and they sit uneasily upon the spirit when the man is vexed, that they are not lawful. The *Persian King* gave *Themistocles* a goodly pension, assigning *Magnesia* with the revenue of 50 talents for his bread, *Lampsacum* for his wine, and *Myos* for his meat; but all the while he fed high and drunk deep, he was infinitely afflicted that every thing went cross to his undertaking, and he could not bring his ends about to betray his Country; and at last he mingled poison with his wine, and drank it off, having first entreated his friends to steal for him a private grave in his own Country. Such are the pleasures of the most pompous and flattering sins: their meat and drink are good and pleasant at first, and it is *plenteous* and *criminal*; but its employment is base, and it is so against a man's interest, and against what is and ought to be dearest to him, that he cannot persuade his better parts to consent, but must fight against them and all their arguments. These things are *against a man's conscience*, that is, *against his reason* and *his rest*; and something within makes his pleasure sit uneasily. But so do violent perfumes make the head ache, and therefore wise persons reject them; and the eye refuses to stare upon the beauties of the Sun, because it makes it weep itself blind; and if a luscious dish please my palate, and turns to loathing in the stomach, I will lay aside that evil, and consider the danger and the bigger pain, not that little pleasure. So it is in sin, it pleases the senses, but diseases the spirit, and wounds that; and that it is as apt to smart as the skin, and is as considerable in the provisions of pleasure and pain respectively: and the pleasures of sin to a contradicting reason, are like the joys of wine to a condemned man, '—*Difficile est imitare gaudia falsa, / Difficile est tristi fingere mente jocum.*' It will be very hard to delight

freely in that which so vexes the more tender and most sensible part; so that, what *Pliny* said of the Poppies growing in the river *Caicus*, it brings a stone instead of a flower or fruit; so are the pleasures of these pretending sins; the flower at the best is stinking, but there is a stone in the bottom, it is gravel in the teeth, and a man must drink the blood of his own gums when he manducates such unwholesome, such unpleasant fruit. '—*Vitiorum gaudia vulnus habent.*' They make a wound, and therefore are not very pleasant. It is a great labour, and travail to live a vicious life.

6. The pleasure in the acts of these few sins that do pretend to it, is a little limited nothing, confined to a single faculty, to one sense, having nothing but the skin for its organ, or instrument, an artery, or something not more considerable than a Lute-string; and at the best it is but the satisfaction of an appetite which reason can cure, which time can appease, which every diversion can take off; such as is not perfective of his nature, nor of advantage to his person; it is a desire to no purpose, and as it comes with no just cause, so can be satisfied with no just measures; it is satisfied before it comes to a vice, and when it is come thither, all the world cannot satisfy it: a little thing will weary it, but nothing can content it. For all these *sensual desires are nothing but an impatience of being well and wise, of being in health, and being in our wits*; which two things if a man could endure (and it is but reasonable, a man would think, that we should) he would never lust to drown his heart in seas of wine, or oppress his belly with loads of undigested meat, or make himself base as the mixtures of a harlot, by breaking the sweetest limits, and holy festivities of marriage. *Malum impatientia est boni*, said *Tertullian*, it is nothing else; to please the sense, is but to do a man's self mischief; and all those lusts tend to some direct dissolution of a man's *health*, or his *felicity*, his *reason*, or his *religion*; it is an enemy that a man carries about him, and as the spirit of God said concerning *Babylon, Quantum in deliciis fuit, tantum dat illi tormentum et luctum*. Let her have torment and sorrow according to the measure of her delights; is most eminently true in the pleasing of our senses; the *lust* and *desire* is a torment; the *remembrance* and the *absence* is a torment, and the *enjoyment* does not satisfy, but disables the instrument, and tires the faculty; and when a man hath but a little of what his sense covets, he is not contented, but impatient for more; and when he hath loads of it, he does not feel it; for he that

swallows a full goblet does not taste his wine: and this is the pleasure of the sense; nothing contents it but that which he cannot perceive: and it is always restless, till he be weary; and all the way unpleased, till it can feel no pleasure; and that which is the instrument of sense is the means of its torment; by the faculty by which it tastes, by the same it is afflicted; for so long as it can taste, it is tormented with desire: and when it can desire no longer, it cannot feel pleasure.

7. Sin hath little or no pleasure in its very enjoyment; because its very manner of entry and production is by a curse and a contradiction; it comes into the world like a viper through the sides of its mother by means unnatural, violent, and monstrous. *Men love sin only because it is forbidden; Sin took occasion by the Law,* saith St. *Paul,* it could not come in upon its own pretences, but men rather suspect a secret pleasure in it because there are guards kept upon it; '*Sed quia caecus inest vitiis amor, omne futurum / Despicitur, suadentque brevem praesentia fructum, / Et ruit in vetitum damni secura libido.*' Men run into sin with blind affections, and against all reason despise the future, hoping for some little pleasure for the present; and all this is only because they are forbidden: Do not many men sin out of spite? some out of the spirit of disobedience, some by wildness, and indetermination, some by impudence, and because they are taken in a fault, '*—Frontemque a crimine sumunt,*' Some because they are reproved, many by custom, others by importunity: '*Ordo fuit crevisse malis—*' It grows upon crab-stocks, and the lust itself is sour and unwholesome; and since it is evident, that very many sins come in wholly upon these accounts, such persons and such sins cannot pretend pleasure; but as Naturalists say of *pulse, cum maledictis et probris serendum praecipiunt, ut laetius proveniat;* the country people were used to curse it and rail upon it all the while that it was sowing, that it might thrive the better; 'tis true with sins, they grow up with curses, with spite and contradiction, peevishness and indignation, pride and cursed principles; and therefore pleasure ought not to be the inscription of the box; for that's the least part of its ingredient and constitution.

8. The pleasures in the very enjoying of sin are infinitely trifling and inconsiderable, because they pass away so quickly; if they be in themselves little, they are made less by their volatile and fugitive nature. But if they were great, then their being so transient does not only lessen the delight, but changes it into a torment, and loads the spirit of the sinner with impatience and

indignation. Is it not a high upbraiding to the watchful adulterer, that after he hath contrived the stages of his sin, and tied many circumstances together with arts and labour, and these join and stand *knit*, and *solid* only by contingency, and are very often borne away with the impetuous torrent of an inevitable accident, like *Xerxes'* bridge over the *Hellespont*, and then he is to begin again, and sets new wheels agoing; and by the arts, and the labour, and the watchings, and the importunity, and the violence, and the unwearied study, and indefatigable diligence of many months *he enters upon possession*, and finds them not of so long abode as one of his cares, which in so vast numbers made so great a portion of his life afflicted? *The enjoying of sin for a season*, St. *Paul* calls it; he names no pleasures; our English translation uses the word of *enjoying pleasures*; but if there were any, they were but *for that season*, that *instant*, that very transition of the act, which dies in its very birth, and of which we can only say as the minstrel sung of *Pacuvius* when he was carried dead from his supper to his bed: A man can scarce have time enough to say *it is alive*, but that *it was: nullo non se die extulit*, it died every day, it lived never unto life, but lived and died unto death, being its mother and its daughter: The man died before the sin did live, and when it had lived, it consigned him to die eternally.

Add to this, that it so passes away, that nothing at all remains behind it, that is pleasant: it is like the path of an arrow in the air; the next morning no man can tell what is become of the pleasures of the last night's sin: they are no where but in God's books, deposited in the conscience, and sealed up against the day of dreadful accounts; but as to the man, they are as if they never had been; and then let it be considered, what a horrible aggravation it will be to the miseries of damnation, that a man shall for ever perish for that, which if he looks round about he cannot see, nor tell where it is. *He that dies, dies for that which is not*; and in the very little present he finds it an unrewarding interest, to walk seven days together over sharp stones only to see a place from whence he must come back in an hour. If it goes off presently, it is not worth the labour; if it stays long, it grows tedious: so that it cannot be pleasant, if it stays; and if it does stay, it is not to be valued: *Haec mala mentis gaudia*. It abides too little a while to be felt, or called *pleasure*; and if it should abide longer, it would be troublesome as *pain*, and loathed like the tedious speech of an Orator pleading against the life of the innocent.

9. Sin hath in its best advantages but *a trifling inconsiderable pleasure*: because not only *God* and *reason, conscience* and *honour, interest* and *laws*, do sour it in the sense and gust of pleasure, but even the Devil himself either being over-ruled by *God*, or by a strange insignificant malice makes it *troublesome* and *intricate, entangled* and *involved*; and one sin contradicts another, and vexes the man with so great variety of evils, that if in the course of God's service he should meet with half the difficulty, he would certainly give over the whole employment. Those that St. *James* speaks of who *prayed that they might spend it upon their lusts*, were *covetous* and *prodigal*, and therefore must endure the torments of one to have the pleasure of another; and which is greater, *the pleasure of spending*, or *the displeasure that it is spent* and does not still remain after its consumption, is easy to tell: certain it is, that this lasts much longer. Does not the Devil often tempt men to despair, and by that torment put bars and locks upon them, that they may never return to God? Which what else is it but a plain *indication* that it is intended, the man should feel the images and dreams of pleasure, no longer but till he be without remedy? *Pleasure* is but like *centres* or wooden frames, set under arches, till they be strong by their own weight and *consolidation* to stand alone; and when by any means the Devil hath a man sure, he takes no longer care to cozen you with pleasures, but is pleased that men should begin *an early hell*, and be *tormented before the time*. Does not *envy* punish or destroy *flattery*; and self-love sometimes torment the drunkard; and intemperance abate the powers of lust, and make the man impotent; and laziness become a hindrance to ambition; and the desires of man wax impatient upon contradicting interests, and by crossing each others' design on all hands lessen the pleasure, and leave the man tormented?

10. Sin is of so little relish and gust, so trifling a pleasure, that it is always greater in expectation than it is in the possession. But if men did beforehand see, what the utmost is, which sin ministers to please the beastly part of man, it were impossible it should be pursued with so much earnestness and disadvantages. It is necessary it should promise more than it can give; Men could not otherwise be cozened. And if it be enquired, why men should sin again, after they had experience of the little and great deception? It is to be confessed, it is a wonder they should; but then we may remember that men sin again, though their sin did afflict them; they will be drunk again, though they were sick; they will

again commit folly, though they be surprised in their shame, though they have needed an hospital; and therefore there is something else that moves them, and not the pleasure; for they do it *without* and *against* its interest; but either they still proceed, hoping to supply by numbers what they find not in proper measures; or God permits them to proceed as an instrument of punishment; or their understandings and reasonings grow cheaper; or they grow in love with it, and take it upon any terms; or contract new appetites, and are pleased with the baser and the lower reward of sin: but whatsoever can be the cause of it, it is certain by the experience of all the world, that the fancy is higher, the desires more sharp, and the reflection more brisk, at the door and entrance of the entertainment, than in all the little and shorter periods of its possession: for then it is but limited by the natural measures, and abated by distemper, and loathed by enjoying, and disturbed by partners, and dishonoured by shame and evil accidents; so that as men coming to the river *Lucius*, and seeing waters pure as the tears of the spring, or the pearls of the morning, expect that in such a fair promising bosom, the inmates should be fair and pleasant, but finds the fishes black, filthy, and unwholesome; so it is in sin, its face is fair and beauteous, [. . .] Softer than sleep, or the dreams of wine, tenderer than the curds of milk, *et Euganea quamtumvis mollior agna*; but when you come to handle it, it is filthy, rough as the Porcupine, black as the shadows of the night, and having promised a fish it gives a scorpion, and a stone instead of bread.

11. The fruits of its present possession, the pleasures of its taste are less pleasant, because no sober person, no man that can discourse does like it long,—*'Breve sit quod turpiter audes.'* But he approves it in the height of passion, and in the disguises of a temptation; but at all other times he finds it ugly and unreasonable; and the very remembrances must at all times abate its pleasures, and sour its delicacies. In the most parts of a man's life he wonders at his own folly, and prodigious madness, that it should be ever possible for him to be deluded by such trifles; and he sighs next morning, and knows it over night; and is it not therefore certain that he leans upon a thorn, which he knows will smart, and he dreads the event of tomorrow? But so have I known a bold Trooper fight in the confusion of a battle, and being warm with heat and rage received from the swords of his enemy, wounds open like a grave; but he felt them not, and when by the streams of blood he found himself marked for pain, he refused to consider

then, what he was to feel tomorrow: but when his rage had cooled into the temper of a man, and a clammy moisture had checked the fiery emission of spirits, he wonders at his own boldness, and blames his fate, and needs a mighty patience to bear his great calamity. So is the bold and merry sinner, when he is warm with wine and lust, wounded and bleeding with the strokes of hell, he twists with the fatal arm that strikes him, and cares not; but yet it must abate his gaiety, because he remembers that when his wounds are cold and considered, he must roar or perish, repent or do worse; that is, be miserable or undone. The Greeks call this the felicity of condemned slaves feasted high in sport. *Dion Prusaeus* reports that when the *Persians* had got the victory, they would pick out the noblest slave, [. . .] They make him a King for three days, and clothe him with royal robes, and minister to him all the pleasures he can choose, and all the while he knows he is to die a sacrifice to mirth and folly. But then let it be remembered what checks and allays of mirth the poor man starts at, when he remembers the axe and the altar where he must shortly bleed; and by this we may understand what that pleasure is, in the midst of which the man sighs deeply, when he considers what opinion he had of this sin, in the days of counsel and sober thoughts, and what reason against it, he shall feel tomorrow when he must weep or die. Thus it happens to sinners according to the saying of the Prophet, *Qui sacrificant hominem osculabuntur Vitulum, He that gives a man in sacrifice shall kiss the calf*, that is, shall be admitted to the seventh chapel of *Moloch* to kiss the Idol: a goodly reward for so great a price, for so great an iniquity.

After all this I do not doubt but these considerations will meet with some persons that think them to be *protestatio contra factum*, and fine pretences against all experience; and that for all these severe sayings, sin is still so pleasant as to tempt the wisest resolution. Such men are in a very evil condition: and in their case only I come to understand the meaning of those words of *Seneca; Malorum ultimum est mala sua amare, ubi turpia non solum delectant, sed etiam placent.* It is the worst of evils when men are so in love with sin that they are *not only delighted with them but pleased also*; not only feel the relish with too quick a sense, but also feel none of the objections, nothing of the pungency, the sting, or the lessening circumstances. However, to these men say this only, that if by experience they feel sin pleasant, it is as certain also by experience, that most sins are in their own nature sharpnesses and diseases; *and that very few do pretend to pleasure; *That a man cannot feel any deliciousness in them, but when he is helped by folly and inconsideration; that is, a wise man cannot, though a boy or a fool can be pleased with them: *That they are but relics and images of pleasure left upon Nature's stock, and therefore much less than the pleasures of natural virtues: *That a man must run through much trouble before he brings them to act and enjoyment: *That he must take them in despite of himself, against reason and his conscience, the tenderest parts of man and the most sensible of affliction: *They are at the best so little, that they are limited as one sense, not spread upon all the faculties like the pleasures of virtue, which make the bones fat by an intellectual rectitude, and the eyes sprightly by a wise proposition, and pain itself to become easy by hope and a present rest within: *It is certain (I say) by a great experience, that the pleasures of sin enter by cursings and a contradictory interest, and become pleasant not by their own relish, but by the viciousness of the palate, by spite and peevishness, by being forbidden and unlawful; *And that which is its sting is at some times the cause of all its sweetness it can have; *They are gone sooner than a dream; *They are crossed by one another, and their Parent is their Tormentor, *and when sins are tied in a chain, with that chain they dash one another's brains out, or make their lodging restless. *It is never liked long; *and promises much and performs little; *it is great at distance, and little at hand, against the nature of all substantial things; *And after all this, how little pleasure is left, themselves have reason with scorn and indignation to resent. So that if experience can be pretended against experience, there is nothing to be said to it but the words which *Phryne* desired to be writ on the gates of *Thebes*, *Phryne the harlot built it up, but Alexander digged it down*; the pleasure is supported by little things, by the experience of fools and them that observed nothing, and the relishes tasted by artificial appetites, by art and cost, by violence and preternatural desires, by the advantage of deception and evil habits, by expectation and delays, by dreams and inconsiderations, these are *the harlot's hands* that build *the fairy castle*, but the hands of reason and religion, sober counsels and the voice of God, experience of wise men, and the sighings and intolerable accents of perishing or returning sinners dig it down, and sow salt in the foundations, that they may never spring up in the accounts of men that delight not in the portion of fools and forgetfulness. *Neque enim*

Deus ita viventibus quicquam promisit boni, neque ipsa per se mens humana talium sibi conscia quicquam boni sperare audet. To men that live in sin God hath promised no good, and the conscience itself dares not expect it.

PART II

We have already opened this *dunghill covered with snow*, which was indeed on the outside white as the spots of leprosy, but it was no better; and if the very colours and instruments of deception, if the *fucus* and *ceruse* be so spotted and sullied, what can we suppose to be under the wrinkled skin, what in the corrupted liver, and in the sinks of the body of sin? That we are next to consider; But if we open the body, and see what a confusion of all its parts, what a rebellion and tumult of the humours, what a disorder of the members, what a monstrosity or deformity is all over, we shall be infinitely convinced, that no man can choose a sin, but upon the same ground on which he may choose a *fever*, or long for *madness* or the *gout*. Sin in its natural efficiency hath in it so many evils, as must needs afright a man, and scare the confidence of every one that can consider.

When our blessed Saviour shall conduct his Church to the mountains of glory, he shall *present it to God without spot or wrinkle*, that is, pure and vigorous, entirely freed from the power, and the infection of sin. Upon occasion of which expression it hath been spoken, that sin leaves in the soul a *stain* or *spot*, permanent upon the spirit, discomposing the order of its beauty, and making it appear to God *in sordibus* in such filthiness, that he who *is of pure eyes cannot behold*. But concerning the nature or proper effects of this *spot* or *stain*, they have not been agreed. Some call it an obligation or a guilt of punishment; so *Scotus*. Some fancy it to be an *elongation from God*, by a dissimilitude of conditions; so *Peter Lombard*. *Alexander* of *Ales* says it is a privation of the proper beauty and splendour of the soul, with which God adorned it in the creation and superaddition of grace; and upon this expression they most agree, but seem not to understand what they mean by it; and it signifies no more, but as you describing *sickness*, call it *a want of health*, and folly *a want of wisdom*; which is indeed to say, what a thing is not, but not to tell what it is: But that I may not be hindered by this consideration, we may observe that the *spots* and *stains* of sin are metaphorical significations of the *disorder* and evil consequents of sin; which it leaves partly upon the soul, partly upon the state and condition of a man, as *meekness* is called *an ornament*, and *faith a shield*, and *salvation a helmet*, and *sin* itself *a wrinkle, corruption, rottenness, a burden, a wound, death, filthiness*: so it is *a defiling of a man*, that is, as the body contracts *nastiness* and *dishonour* by impure contacts, and adherencies, so does the soul receive such a change, as must be taken away before it can enter into the eternal regions, and house of purity. But it is not a distinct thing, *not an inherent quality*, which can be separated from other evil effects of sin, which I shall now reckon by their more proper names; and St. *Paul* comprises under the scornful appellative of *shame*.

1. The first *natural fruit* of sin is *ignorance*. Man was first tempted by the promise of knowledge; he fell into darkness by believing the Devil holding forth to him a new light. It was not likely good should come of so foul a beginning; that the woman should believe the Devil putting on no brighter shape than a snake's skin, she neither being afraid of sin, nor afrighted to hear a beast speak, and he pretending so weakly in the temptation, that he promised only that they should *know evil*; for they knew good before; and all that was offered to them was *the experience of evil*: and it was no wonder that the Devil promised no more; for sin never could perform any thing but *an experience of evil*, no other knowledge can come upon that account; but the wonder was, why the woman should sin for no other reward, but for that which she ought to have feared infinitely; for nothing could have continued her happiness, but *not to have known evil*. Now this knowledge was the introduction of ignorance. For when *the understanding* suffered itself to be so baffled as to study evil, *the will* was as foolish to fall in love with it, and they conspired to undo each other. For when *the will* began to love it, then *the understanding* was set on work to commend, to advance, to conduct and to approve, to believe it, and to be factious in behalf of the new purchase. I do not believe the understanding part of man received any natural decrement or diminution. For if to the Devils their naturals remain entire, it is not likely that the lesser sin of man should suffer a more violent and effective mischief. Neither can it be understood how the reasonable soul being immortal both in itself and its essential faculties, can lose or be lessened in them, any more than it can die. But it received impediment, by new propositions: It lost and willingly

forgot what God had taught, and went away from the fountain of truth, and gave trust to the father of lies, and it must without remedy grow foolish; and so a man came to *know evil*, just as a man is said to *taste of death*: for in proper speaking, as death is not to *be felt*, because it takes away all sense; so neither can evil *be known*, because whatsoever is truly *cognoscible*, is *good* and *true*; and therefore all the knowledge a man gets by sin is to feel evil: he knows it *not by discourse, but by sense*; not by *proposition*, but by *smart*; The Devil doing to man as *Aesculapius* did to *Neoclides*, [. . .] he gave him a formidable collirium to torment him more: the effect of which was [. . .] : the Devil himself grew more quick-sighted to abuse us, but we became more blind by that opening of our eyes. I shall not need to discourse of the Philosophy of this mischief, and by the connection of what causes ignorance doth follow sin: but it is certain, whether a man would fain be pleased with sin, or be quiet, or fearless when he hath sinned, or continue in it, or persuade others to it, he must do it by false propositions, by lyings and such weak discourses as none can believe but such as are born fools, or such as have made themselves so, or are made so by others. Who in the world is a verier fool, a more ignorant wretched person than he that is an Atheist? A man may better believe there is no such man as himself, and that he is not in being, than that there is no God: for himself can cease to be, and once was not, and shall be changed from what he is, and in very many periods of his life knows not that he is; and so it is every night with him when he sleeps: but none of these can happen to God; and if he knows it not, he is a fool. Can any thing in this world be more foolish than to think that all this rare fabric of heaven and earth can come by chance, when all the skill of art is not able to make an Oyster? To see rare effects and no cause; an excellent government and no Prince; a motion without an immoveable; a circle without a centre; a time without eternity; a second without a first; a thing that begins not from itself, and therefore not to perceive there is something from whence it does begin, which must be without beginning; these things are so against Philosophy, and natural reason, that he must needs be a beast in his understanding that does not assent to them, This is the Atheist: *the fool hath said in his heart, there is no God*. That's his character: the thing framed says that nothing framed it; the tongue never made itself to speak, and yet talks against him that did; saying, that which is made, *is*, and that which made it, *is not*. But this folly is as infinite as hell, as much without light or bound, as the *Chaos* or the *primitive nothing*. But in this, the Devil never prevailed very far; his Schools were always thin at these Lectures: some few people have been witty against God, that taught them to speak before they knew to spell a syllable; but either they are monsters in their manners, or mad in their understandings, or ever find themselves confuted by a thunder or a plague, by danger or death.

But the Devil hath infinitely prevailed in a thing that is almost as senseless and ignorant as Atheism, and that is *idolatry*; not only making *God after man's image*, but in the likeness of a calf, of a cat, of a serpent; making men such fools as to worship a quartan ague, fire and water, onions and sheep. This is the skill man learned, and the Philosophy that he is taught by believing the Devil. *What wisdom can there be in any man, that calls good evil, and evil good; to say *fire is cold*, and the *Sun black*, that fornication can make a man happy, or drunkenness can make him wise? And this is the state of a sinner, of every one that delights in iniquity; he cannot be pleased with it if he thinks it evil; he cannot endure it, without believing this proposition, that *there is in drunkenness, or lust, pleasure enough, good enough to make him amends for the intolerable pains of damnation*. But then if we consider upon what *nonsense principles* the state of an evil life relies, we must in reason be impatient, and with scorn and indignation drive away the fool; such as are: *sense is to be preferred before reason, interest before religion, a lust before heaven, moments before eternity, money above God himself*; that, *a man's felicity consists in that which a beast enjoys*; that, *a little in present* uncertain, fallible possession, *is better than the certain state of infinite glories hereafter*; what child, what fool can think things more weak, and more unreasonable? And yet if men do not go upon these grounds, upon what account do they sin? sin hath no wiser reasons for itself than these: [. . .], the same argument that a fly hath to enter into a candle, the same argument a fool hath, that enters into sin; it looks prettily, but rewards the eye, as burning basons do, with intolerable circles of reflected fire. Such are the principles of a sinner's Philosophy. And *no wiser are his hopes*; all his hopes that he hath is, that *he shall have time to repent* of that which he chooses greedily; that he whom he every day provokes will save him, whether he will or no; that he can in an instant, or in a day make amends for all the evils of 40 years; or else that he shall be saved whether he does or no; that heaven is to be had for a sigh, or a short prayer, and yet hell shall not be consequent to the affections, and labours, and hellish services of a whole life; he goes on and cares not, he hopes without a promise, and refuses to believe all the threatenings of God; but believes he shall have a mercy for which he never had a revelation. If this be knowledge or wisdom, then there is no such thing as folly, no such disease as madness.

But then consider, that there are some sins whose very formality is a lie. Superstition could not be in the world, if men did believe God to be good and wise, free and merciful, not a tyrant, not an unreasonable exactor: no man would dare do in private, what he fears to do in public, if he did know that God sees him there, and will bring that work of darkness into light. But he is so foolish as to think, that if he sees nothing, nothing sees him; for if men did perceive God to be present, and yet do wickedly, it is worse with them than I have yet spoke of; and they believe another lie; that to be seen by man will bring more shame, than to be discerned by God; or that the shame of a few men's talk is more intolerable than to be confounded before Christ, and his army of Angels, and Saints, and all the world. *He that excuses a fault by telling a lie, believes it better to be guilty of two faults, than to be thought guilty of one; and every hypocrite thinks it not good to be holy, but to be accounted so, is a fine thing; that is, that *opinion is better than reality*, and that there is in virtue nothing good, but the fame of it. *And the man that takes revenge, relies upon this foolish proposition; that *his evil that he hath already suffered grows less if another suffers the like*; that his wound cannot smart, if by my hand he dies that gave it, [...], the sad accents and doleful tunes are increased by the number of mourners, but the sorrow is not at all lessened.

I shall not need to thrust into this account the other evils of mankind that are the events of ignorance, but introduced by sin; such as are our being moved by what we see strongly, and weakly by what we understand; that men are moved rather by a fable than by a syllogism, by parables than by demonstrations, by examples than by precepts, by seeming things than by real, by shadows than by substances; that men judge of things by their first events, and measure the events by their own short lives, or shorter observations; that they are credulous to believe what they wish, and incredulous of what makes against them, measuring truth or falsehood by measures that cannot fit them, as foolishly as if they should judge of a colour by the dimensions of a body, or feel music with the hand; they make general conclusions from particular instances, and take account of God's actions by the measures of a man. Men call that justice that is on their side, and all their own causes are right, and they are so always; they are so when they affirm them in their youth, and they are so when they deny them in their old age; and they are confident in all their changes; and their first error which they now see, does not make them modest in the proposition which they now maintain; for they do not understand that what was may be so again: *So foolish and ignorant was I* (said *David*) *and as it were a beast before thee*. *Ambition* is *folly*, and *temerity* is *ignorance*, and *confidence* never goes without it, and *impudence* is worse, and *zeal* or *contention* is *madness*, and *prating* is *want of wisdom*, and *lust* destroys it, and makes a man of a weak spirit, and a cheap reasoning; and there are in the Catalogue of sins very many, which are directly, kinds and parts, and appendages of ignorance; such as are *blindness of mind, affected ignorance*, and *wilful neglect of hearing the word of God, resolved incredulity, forgetfulness of holy things, lying and believing a lie*; this is the fruit of sin, this is the knowledge that the Devil promised to our first parents as the rewards of disobedience; and although they sinned as weakly and fondly, upon as slight grounds and trifling a temptation and as easy a deception as many of us since, yet the causes of our ignorance are increased by the multiplication of our sins; and if it was so bad in the green tree, it is much worse in the dry; and no man is so very a fool as the sinner, and none are wise but the servants of God [...]. The wise *Chaldeans* and the wiser *Hebrews* which worship God chastely and purely, they only have a right to be called wise; all that do not so are fools and ignorants, neither knowing what it is to be happy, nor how to purchase it: ignorant of the noblest end, and of the competent means towards it; they neither know God nor themselves, and no ignorance is greater than this or more pernicious. What man is there in the world that thinks himself covetous or proud? and yet millions are, who like *Harpaste* think that the house is dark, but not themselves. Virtue makes our desires temperate and regular, it observes our actions, condemns our faults, mortifies our lusts, watches all our dangers and temptations: but sin makes our desires infinite, and we would have we cannot tell what; we strive that we may forget our faults; we labour that we may neither remember nor consider; we justify our errors, and call them innocent, and that which is our shame we miscall honour; and our whole life hath in it so many weak discourses and trifling propositions, that the whole world of sinners is like the Hospital of the *insensati*, madness and folly possesses the greater part of mankind. What greater madness is there than to spend the price of a whole farm in contention for three sheaves of corn? and yet *tantum pectora caecae noctis habent*, this is the wisdom of such as are contentious, and love their own will more than their happiness, their humour more than their peace.—'*Furor est post omnia perdere naulum.*' Men lose their reason, and their religion, and themselves at last for want of understanding; and all the wit and discourses by which sin creeps in, are but frauds of the tongue, and consultations of care: but in the whole circle of sins there is not one wise proposition, by which a man may conduct his affairs, or himself become instructed to felicity. This is the first natural fruit of sin: It makes a man a fool, and this hurt sin does to the understanding, and this is shame enough to that in which men are most apt to glory.

Sin naturally makes a man weak; that is, unapt to do noble things: by which I do not understand a *natural disability*: for it is equally ready for a man to will good as evil, and as much in the power of his hands to be lifted up in prayer to God as against his Brother in a quarrel; and between a virtuous object and his faculties there is a more apt proportion, than between his spirit and a vice; and every act of grace does more please the mind, than an act of sin does delight the sense; and every crime does greater violence to the better part of man, than mortification does to the lower; and oftentimes a duty consists in a negative, as *not to be drunk, not to swear*, and it is not to be understood that a man hath naturally no power *not to do*; if there be a *natural disability*, it is to action, not to *rest* or *ceasing*; and therefore in this case, we cannot reasonably nor justly accuse our *Nature*, but we have reason to blame our *manners* which have introduced upon us a *moral disability*; that is, not that *the faculty is impotent* and disabled, but that *the whole man is*; for *the will* in many cases desires to do good, and *the understanding* is convinced and consents, and *the hand* can obey, and *the passions* can be directed, and be instrumental to God's service: but because they are not used to it, *the will* finds a difficulty to do them so much violence, and *the understanding* consents to their lower reasonings, and the desires of the lower man do *will* stronger; and then *the whole man* cannot do the duty that is expected. *There is a law in the members*, and he that gave that law is *a tyrant*, and *the subjects* of that law are *slaves*, and oftentimes their ear is bored, and they love their fetters and desire to continue that bondage for ever; The law is *the law of sin, the Devil* is the *tyrant, custom* is the *sanction* or the *firmament* of the law; and every vicious man is a slave, and chooses the vilest master, and the basest of services, and the most contemptible rewards. *Lex enim peccati est violentia consuetudinis, qua trahitur et tenetur animus etiam invitus, eo merito quo in eam volens illabitur*, said St. *Austin; The law of sin is the violence of custom, which keeps a man's mind against his mind*, because he entered willingly, and gave up his own interest, which he ought to have secured for his own felicity, and for his service who gave for it an invaluable price: And indeed in questions of virtue and vice there is no such thing as *Nature*; or it is so inconsiderable, that it hath in it nothing beyond an inclination which may be reverted; and very often not so much; nothing but *a perfect indifferency*, we may if we will, or we may choose; but custom brings in a new Nature, and makes a *Bias* in every faculty. To a vicious man some sins become necessary; Temperance makes him sick; severity is death to him; it destroys his cheerfulness and activity; it is as his nature, and the desire dwells for ever with him, and his reasonings are framed for it and his fancy, and in all he is helped by example, by company, by folly, and inconsideration; and all these are a faction and a confederacy against the honour and service of God. And in this, *Philosophy is at a stand*, nothing can give an account of it but experience, and sorrowful instances; for it is infinitely unreasonable, that when you have discoursed wisely against *unchastity*, and told, that we are separated from it by a circumvallation of Laws of God and man, that it dishonours the body, and makes the spirit caitive, that it is fought against by arguments sent from all the corners of reason and religion, and the man knows all this, and believes it, and prays against his sin, and hates himself for it, and curses the actions of it; yet oppose against all this but a fable, or a merry story, a proverb or a silly saying, the sight of his mistress, or any thing but to lessen any one of the arguments brought against it, and that man shall as certainly and clearly be determined to that sin, as if he had on his side all the reason of the world. Custom does as much as Nature can do; it does sometimes more, and superinduces a disposition contrary to our natural temper. *Eudemus* had so used his stomach to so unnatural drinks, that, as himself tells the story, he took in one day two and twenty potions in which Hellebore was infused, and rose at noon, and supped at night, and felt no change. So are those that are corrupted with evil customs, nothing will purge them; if you discourse wittily, they hear you not; or if they do, they have twenty ways to answer, and twice twenty to neglect it: if you persuade them to promise to leave their sin, they do but show their folly at the next temptation, and tell that they did not mean it: and if you take them at an advantage when their hearts are softened with a judgment or a fear, with a shame or an indignation, and then put the *bars* and *locks* of vows upon them, it is all one; *one vow* shall hinder but *one action*, and the appetite shall be doubled by the restraint, and the next opportunity shall make an amends for the first omission: or else the sin shall enter by parts; the vow shall only put the understanding to make a distinction, or to change the circumstance, and under that colour the crime shall be admitted, because the man is resolved to suppose the matter so dressed was not vowed against. But then when that is done, the understanding shall open that eye that did but wink before, and see that it was the same thing, and secretly rejoice that it was so cozened: for now the lock is opened, and the vow was broken against his will, and the man is at liberty again, because he did the thing at unawares, still he is willing to believe the sin was not formal vow-breach, but now he sees he broke it materially, and because the band is broken, the yoke is in pieces, therefore the next action shall go on upon the same stock of a single iniquity without being afrighted in his conscience at the noise of perjury. I wish we were all so innocent as not to understand the discourse; but it uses to be otherwise. '*Nam si discedas, laqueo tenet ambitiosi / Consuetudo mali: —et in aegro corde senescit.*' Custom hath waxen old in his deceived heart, and made snares for him that he cannot disentangle himself; so true is that saying of God by the Prophet, *Can an Aethiop change his skin? then may ye learn to do well when ye are accustomed to do evil.* But I instance in two things, which to my sense seem great aggravations of the slavery and weakness of a customary sinner.

The first is, that *men sin against their interest.* They know they shall be ruined by it; it will undo their estates, lose their friends, ruin their fortunes, destroy their body, impoverish the spirit, load the conscience, discompose his rest, confound his reason, amaze him in all his faculties, destroy his hopes, and mischief enough besides; and when he considers this, he declares against it; but, *Cum bona verba erumpant, affectus tamen ad consuetudinem relabuntur,* the man gives good words, but the evil custom prevails; and it happens as in the case of the *Tyrinthians,* who to free their Nation from a great plague, were bidden only to abstain from laughter, while they offered their sacrifice: but they had been so used to a ridiculous effeminacy, and vain course of conversation, that they could not, though the honour and splendour of the Nation did depend upon it. *God of his mercy keep all Christian people from a custom in sinning*; for if they be once fallen thither, nothing can recover them but a miraculous grace.

2. The second aggravation of it is, that *custom prevails against experience.* Though the man hath already smarted, though he hath been disgraced, and undone, though he lost his relation and his friends, he is turned out of service, and disemployed, he begs with a load of his old sins upon his shoulders, yet this will not cure an evil custom: Do we not daily see how miserable some men make themselves with drunkenness, and folly? Have not we seen them that have been sick with intemperance, deadly sick, enduring for one drunken meeting, more pain than are in all the fasting days of the whole year? and yet do they not the very next day go to it again? Indeed some few are smitten into the beginning of repentance, and they stay a fortnight, or a month, and it may be resist two or three invitations; but yet the custom is not gone, '*Nec tu cum obstiteris semel, instantique negaris / Parere imperio, Rupi jam vincula, dicas.*' Think not the chain is off when thou hast once or twice resisted; or if the chain be broke, part remains on thee, like a cord upon a dog's neck, '*Nam et luctata canis nodum arripit; attamen illi / Cum fugit, a collo trahitur pars magna catenae.*' He is not free that draws his chain after him; and he that breaks off from his sins with greatest passion, stands in need of prosperous circumstances, and a strange freedom from temptation, and accidental hardness, and superinduced confidence, and a preternatural severity; *Opus est aliqua fortunae indulgentia adhuc inter humana luctanti, dum nodum illum exolvit et omne vinculum mortale,* for the knot can hardly be untied which a course of evil manners hath bound upon the soul; and every contingency in the world can entangle him that wears upon his neck the links of a broken chain. *Nam qui ab eo quod amat, Quam extemplo suaviis sagittatis percussus est, ilico res foras labitur, liquitur*; if he sees his temptation again he is ἐπικλωμενος ὑπ'ἐυνοίης, his kindness to it, and conversation

with his lust undoes him, and breaks his purposes, and then he dies again, or falls upon that stone that with so much pains he removed a little out of his way; and he would lose the spent wealth, or the health and the reputation over again, if it were in his power. *Philomusus* was a wild young fellow in *Domitian's* time, and he was hard put to it to make a large pension to maintain his lust and luxury, and he was every month put to beggarly arts to feed his crime. But when his father died and left him all, he disinherited himself; he spent it all though he knew he was to suffer that trouble always, which vexed his lustful soul in the frequent periods of his violent want.

Now this is such a state of slavery, that persons that are sensible ought to complain, that they serve worse lords than Egyptian task-masters, there is a lord within that rules and rages, *Intus et in jecore aegro pascuntur domini*; sin dwells there, and makes a man a miserable servant: and this is not only a Metaphorical expression, under which some spiritual and metaphysical truth is represented, but it is a physical, material truth, and a man endures hardship, he cannot move but at this command, and not his outward actions only, but his will and his understanding too are kept in fetters and foolish bondage: [...]; The two parts of a man are rent in sunder, and that that prevails is the life, it is the man, it is the eloquence persuading every thing to its own interest, said *Marcus Antonius*. *And now consider what is the effect of this evil. A man by sin is made a slave, he loses that liberty that is dearer to him than life itself; and like the dog in the fable, we suffer chains and ropes only for a piece of bread; when the Lion thought liberty a sufficient reward and price for hunger, and all the hardnesses of the wilderness. Do not all the world fight for liberty, and at no terms will lay down arms till at least they be cozened with the image and colour of it? and yet for the pleasure of a few minutes we give ourselves into bondage; and all the world does it, more or less. [...] Either men are slaves to fortune, or to lust; to covetousness, or tyranny; something or other compels him to usages against his will and reason; and when the laws cannot rule him, money can; *divitiae enim apud sapientem virum in servitute sunt, apud stultum in imperio*; for *money is the wise man's servant, and the fool's Master*: but the bondage of a vicious person, is such a bondage as the child hath in the womb, or rather as a sick man in his bed; we are bound fast by our disease, and a consequent weakness, we cannot go forth though the doors be open, and the fetters knocked off, and virtue and reason like St. *Peter's Angel* call us and beat us upon the sides, and offer to go before us, yet we cannot come forth from prison; for we have by our evil customs given hostages to the Devil, never to stir from the enemies' quarter; and this is the greatest bondage that is imaginable, the bondage of conquered, wounded, unresisting people: Virtue only is the truest liberty: *And if the Son of God make us free, then are we free indeed.*

3. Sin does naturally introduce a great baseness upon the spirit, expressed in Scripture in some cases by *the devil's entering into a man*, as it was in the case of *Judas, after he had taken the sop, Satan entered into him*; and St. *Cyprian* speaking of them that after Baptism lapsed into foul crimes, he affirms, that *spiritu immundo quasi redeunte quatiuntur, ut manifestum sit Diabolum in Baptismo fide credentis excludi, si fides postmodum defecerit regredi*; Faith, and the grace of Baptism turns the Devil out of possession: but when faith fails, and we loose the bands of Religion, then the Devil returns; that is, the man is devolved into such sins of which there can be no reason given, which no excuse can lessen, which are set off with no pleasure, advanced by no temptations, which deceive by no allurements and flattering pretences: such things which have a proper and direct contrariety to the good Spirit, and such as are not restrained by human laws; because they are *states of evil* rather than *evil actions*, principles of mischief rather than direct emanations; such as are, *unthankfulness, impiety, giving a secret blow, fawning hypocrisy, detraction, impudence, forgetfulness of the dead*, and *forgetting to do that in their absence which we promised to them in presence*; Concerning which sorts of unworthiness it is certain they argue a most degenerous spirit, and they are the effect, the natural effect of malice and despair, an unwholesome ill natured soul, a soul corrupted in its whole constitution. I remember that in the Apologues of *Phaedrus*, it is told concerning an ill natured fellow, that he refused to pay his Symbol, which himself and all the company had agreed should be given for every disease, that each man had; he denying his itch to be a disease; but the company taking off the refuser's hat for a pledge, found that he had a scaled head, and so demanded the money double; which he pertinaciously resisting, they threw him down, and then discovered he was broken-bellied, and justly condemned him to pay three Philippics:'—*Quae fuerat fabula, poena fuit.*'

One disease discovers itself by the hiding of another, and that being opened discovers a third; He that is almost taken in a fault, tells a lie to escape; and to protect that lie, he forswears himself; and that he may not be suspected of perjury, he grows impudent; and that sin may not shame him, he will glory in it, like the slave in the Comedy, who being torn with whips, grinned, and forced an ugly smile that it might not seem to smart. *There are some sins which a man that is newly fallen, cannot entertain. There is no crime made ready for a young sinner, but that which nature prompts him to. Natural inclination is the first tempter, then compliance, then custom, but this being helped by a consequent folly, dismantles the soul, making it to hate God, to despise Religion, to laugh at severity, to deride sober counsels, to flee from repentance, to resolve against it, to delight in sin without abatement of spirit or purposes. For it is an intolerable thing for a man to be tormented in his conscience for every sin he acts; that must not be; he must have his sin and his peace too, or else he can have neither long: and because true peace cannot come, (for *there is no peace, saith my God, to the wicked*) therefore they must make a fantastic peace by a studied cozening of themselves, by false propositions, by carelessness, by stupidity, by impudence, by sufferance, and habit; by conversation, and daily acquaintances; by doing some things as *Absalom* did when he lay with his father's concubines, to make it impossible for him to repent, or to be forgiven, something to secure him in the possession of hell; *Tute hoc intristi quod tibi exedendum est*, the man must through it now; and this is it that makes men fall into all baseness of *spiritual sins*, such as *malice* and *despite, rancour* and *impudence, malicious studied ignorance, voluntary contempt of all Religion, hating of good men and good counsels*, and *taking every wise man and wise action to be his enemy*. And this is that baseness of sin which *Plato* so much detested, that he said he should blush to be guilty of, though he knew God would pardon him, and that men should never know it, *propter solam peccati turpitudinem*, for the very baseness that is in it. A man that is false to God, will also, if an evil temptation overtakes him, betray his friend; and it is notorious in the covetous and ambitious, [. . .] They are an unthankful generation, and to please the people, or to serve their interest will hurt their friends. That man hath so lost himself to all sweetness and excellency of spirit, that is gone thus far in sin, that he looks like a condemned man, or is like the accursed spirits preserved in chains of darkness and impieties unto the Judgment of the great

Day, [. . .] this man can be nothing but evil; for these inclinations and evil forwardnesses, this discrasy and gangrened disposition does always suppose a long or a base sin for their parent; and the product of these is a wretchless spirit; that is, an aptness to any unworthiness, and an unwillingness to resist any temptation; a perseverance in baseness, and a consignation to all damnation, [. . .] If men do evil things, evil things shall be their reward. If they obey the evil spirit, an evil spirit shall be their portion; and the *Devil shall enter into them as he entered into* Judas, *and fill them full of iniquity.*

PART III

Although these are shameful effects of sin, and a man need no greater dishonour than to be a fool and a slave, and a base person, all which sin infallibly makes him; yet there are some sins which are directly shameful in their nature, and proper disreputation, and a very great many sins are the worst and basest in several respects; that is, every of them hath a venomous quality of its own, whereby it is marked and appropriated to a peculiar evil spirit. The *Devil's* sin was the worst, because it came from the greatest malice: *Adam's* was the worst, because it was of most universal efficacy and dissemination: *Judas's* sin the worst of men, because against the most excellent person; and *the relapses of the godly* are the worst, by reason they were the most obliged persons. But the *ignorance of the Law* is the greatest of evils, if we consider its danger, but *covetousness* is worse than it, if we regard its incurable and growing nature, *luxury* is most alien from spiritual things, and is the worst of all in its temptation and our proneness; but *pride* grows most venomous by its unreasonableness and importunity, arising even from the good things a man hath; even from graces, and endearments, and from being more in debt to God. *Sins of malice* and *against the Holy Ghost* oppugn the greatest grace with the greatest spite; but *Idolatry* is perfectly hated by God by a direct enmity. Some sins are therefore most heinous, because to resist them is most easy, and to act them there is the least temptation: such as are severally, *lying*, and *swearing*. There is a strange poison in the nature of sins, that of so many sorts, every one of them should be *the worst*. Every sin hath an evil spirit, a Devil of its own to manage, to conduct, and to embitter it: and although all these are God's enemies, and have an appendant *shame* in their retinue, yet to some sins *shame* is more appropriate, and a proper ingredient in their constitutions: such as are *lying*, and *lust*, and *vow-breach*, and *inconstancy*. God sometimes cures the pride of a man's spirit by suffering his evil manners, and filthy inclination to be determined upon lust; *lust* makes a man afraid of public eyes, and common voices; it is (as all sins else are, but especially) *a work of darkness*, it does debauch the spirit, and make it to decay and fall off from courage and resolution, constancy and severity, the spirit of government and a noble freedom; and those punishments which the nations of the world have inflicted upon it, are not *smart* so much as *shame*: Lustful souls are *cheap* and *easy, trifling* and *despised* in all wise accounts; they are so far from being fit to sit with Princes, that they dare not chastise a sinning servant that is private to their secret follies; It is strange to consider what laborious arts of concealment, what excuses and lessenings, what pretences and fig-leaves men will put before their nakedness and crimes; shame was the first thing that entered upon the sin of *Adam*, and when the second world began, there was a strange scene of shame acted by *Noah* and his sons, and it ended in slavery and baseness to all descending generations.

We see the event of this by too sad an experience. What arguments, what hardness, what preaching, what necessity can persuade men to confess their sins? they are so ashamed of them, that to be concealed they prefer before their remedy; and yet in penitential confession the shame is going off, it is like *Cato's* coming out of the *Theatre*, or the *Philosopher* from the *Tavern*; it might have been shame to have entered, but glory to have departed for ever; and yet ever to have relation to sin is so shameful a thing, that a man's spirit is amazed, and his face is confounded when he is *dressed* of so shameful a disease. And there are but few men that will endure it, but rather choose to involve it in excuses and denial, in the clouds of lying, and the white linen of hypocrisy: and yet when they make a veil for their shame, such is the fate of sin, the shame grows the bigger and the thicker; we lie to men, and we excuse it to God; either some parts of lying, or many parts of impudence, darkness, or forgetfulness, running away, or running further in, these are the covers of our shame, like menstruous rags upon a skin of leprosy: But so sometimes we see a decayed beauty besmeared with a lying *fucus*, and the chinks filled with *ceruse*; besides that it makes no real beauty, it spoils the face, and betrays evil manners; it does not hide old age, or the change of years, but it discovers pride or lust; it was not shame to be old, or wearied and worn out with age, but it is a shame to dissemble nature by a wanton vizor. So sin retires from blushing into shame; if it be discovered, it is not to be endured, and if we go to hide it, we make it worse. But then if we remember how ambitious we are for *fame* and *reputation*, for honour and a fair opinion, for a good name all our days, and when our days are done, and that no ingenuous man can enjoy any thing he hath, if he lives in disgrace, and that nothing so breaks a man's spirit as dishonour, and the meanest person alive does not think himself fit to be despised; we are to consider into what an evil condition sin puts us, for which we are not only disgraced and disparaged here, marked with disgraceful punishments, despised by good men, our follies derided, our company avoided, and hooted at by boys, talked of in fairs and markets, pointed at and described by appellatives of scorn, and *every body can chide us*, and we die unpitied, and lie in our graves eaten up by worms, and a foul dishonour; but after all this, at the day of Judgment we shall be called from our charnel houses, where our disgrace could not sleep, and shall in the face of God, in the presence of Angels and Devils, before all good men and all the evil, see, and feel the shame of all our sins written upon our foreheads: Here in this state of misery and folly we make nothing of it; and though we dread to be discovered to men, yet to God we confess our sins without a trouble or a blush; but tell an even story, because we find some forms of confession prescribed in our prayer books; and that it may appear how indifferent and unconcerned we seem to be, we read and say all, and confess the sins we never did, with as much sorrow and regret as those that we have acted a thousand times. But in that strange day of recompenses, we shall find the Devil to upbraid the criminal, Christ to disown them, the Angels to drive them from the seat of mercy; and shame to be their smart, the consigning them to damnation; they shall then find, that they cannot dwell where virtue is rewarded, and where honour and glory hath a throne; there is no veil but what is rent, no excuse to any but to them that are declared as innocent; no circumstances concerning the wicked to be considered, but them that aggravate; then the disgrace is not confined to the talk of a village, or a province, but is scattered to all the world, not only in one age shall the shame abide, but the men of all generations shall see and wonder at the vastness of that evil that is spread upon the souls of sinners for ever and ever; [. . .] No night shall then hide it, for in those regions of darkness where the dishonoured man shall dwell for ever, there is nothing visible but the *shame*; there is light enough for *that*, but darkness for all things else: and then he shall reap the full harvest of his shame; all that for which wise men scorned him, and all that for which God hated him; all that in which he was a fool, and all that in which he was malicious; that which was public, and that which was private; that which fools applauded, and that which himself durst not own; the secrets of his lust, and the criminal contrivances of his thoughts; the base and odious circumstances, and the frequency of the action, and the partner of his sin; all that which troubles his conscience, and all that he willingly forgets, shall be proclaimed by the trumpet of God, by the voice of an Archangel in the great Congregation of spirits and just men.

There is one great circumstance more of the shame of sin, which extremely enlarges the evil of a sinful state, but that is not consequent to sin by a natural emanation, but is superinduced by the just wrath of God: and therefore is to be considered in the third part, which is next to be handled.

3. When the *Boeotians* asked the Oracle, by what they should become happy? the answer was made, *wicked and irreligious persons are prosperous*: and they taking the Devil at his word, threw the inspired Pythian, *the ministering witch*, into the sea, hoping so to become mighty in peace and war. The effect of which was this, The Devil was found a liar, and they fools at first, and at last felt the reward of irreligion. For there are to some crimes such events, which are not to be expected from the connection of natural causes, but from secret influences and undiscernible conveyances; *that a man should be made sick for receiving the holy Sacrament unworthily, and blind for resisting the words of an Apostle, a Preacher of the Laws of Jesus, and die suddenly for breaking of his vow, and committing sacrilege, and be under the power and scourge of an exterminating Angel, for climbing his Father's bed, these are things beyond the world's Philosophy. But as in Nature, so in Divinity too there are *Sympathies* and *Antipathies*, effects which we feel by experience, and are forewarned of by revelation, which no natural reason can judge, nor any providence can prevent but by living innocently, and complying with the Commandments of God. *The rod of God, which cometh not into the lot of the righteous*, strikes the sinning man with *sore strokes of vengeance*.

1. The first that I shall note is that which I called *the aggravation of the shame of sin*; and that is, an impossibility of being concealed in most cases of heinous crimes, [. . .] let no man suppose that he shall for ever hide his sin: a single action may be conveyed away under the covert of an excuse or a privacy, escaping as *Ulysses* did the search of *Polyphemus*, and it shall in time be known that it did escape, and shall be *discovered* that *it was private*; that is, that *it is so no longer*. But no wicked man that dwelt and delighted in sin, did ever go off from his scene of unworthiness without a filthy character; The black veil is thrown over him before his death, and by some contingency or other he enters into his cloud, because few sins determine finally in the thoughts; but if they dwell there, they will also enter into action, and then the thing discovers itself; or else the injured person will proclaim it, or the jealous man will talk of it fore it's done, or curious people will inquire and discover, or the spirit of detraction shall be let loose upon him, and in spite shall declare more than he knows, not more than is true. The ancients, especially the Scholars of *Epicurus*, believed that no man could be secured or quiet in his spirit from being discovered. *Scelus aliqua tutum, nulla securum tulit*; They are not secure even when they are safe; but are afflicted with perpetual jealousies; and every whisper is concerning them, and all new noises, are arrests to their spirits; and the day is too light, and the night is too horrid, and both are the most opportune for their discovery; and besides the undiscernible connection of the contingencies of providence, many secret crimes have been published by dreams, and talkings in their sleep. It is the observation of *Lucretius*, '*Multi de magnis per somnum rebus loquuntur, / Indicioque sui facti persaepe fuere.*' And what their understanding kept a guard upon, their fancy let loose; fear was the bars and locks, but sleep became the key to open, even then when all the senses were shut, and God ruled alone without the choice and discourse of man. And though no man regards the wilder talkings of a distracted man, yet it hath sometimes happened that a *delirium* and a fever, fear of death, and the intolerable apprehensions of damnation have opened the cabinet of sin, and brought to light all that was acted in the curtains of night, '*Quippe ubi se multis per somnia saepe loquentes, / Aut morbo delirantes protraxe feruntur, / Et celata diu in medium peccata dedisse.*' But there are so many ways of discovery, and amongst so many, some one does so certainly happen that they are well summed up by *Sophocles*, by

saying, that *time hears all, and tells all,* [. . .] A cloud may be its roof and cover till it passes over, but when it is driven by a fierce wind, or runs fondly after the Sun, it lays open a deformity, which like an ulcer had a skin over it, and a pain within, and drew to it a heap of sorrows big enough to run over all its enclosures. Many persons have betrayed themselves by their own fears, and knowing themselves never to be secure enough, have gone to purge themselves of what no body suspected them; offered an Apology, when they had no accuser but one within; which like a thorn in the flesh, or like *a word in a fool's heart*, was uneasy till it came out; *Non amo se nimium purgitantes*, when men are over-busy in justifying themselves, it is a sign themselves think they need it. *Plutarch* tells of a young Gentleman that destroyed a swallow's nest, pretending to them that reproved him for doing the thing, which in their *superstition* the *Greeks* esteemed so *ominous*, that the little bird accused him for killing his Father. And to this purpose it was that *Solomon* gave counsel: *Curse not the King, no not in thy thought, nor the rich in thy bedchamber, for a bird of the air shall carry the voice, and that that hath wings shall tell the matter; Murder* and *treason* have by such strange ways been revealed, as if God had appointed an Angel president of the revelation, and had kept this in secret and sure ministry to be as an argument to destroy Atheism from the face of the earth, by opening the secrets of men with this key of providence. *Intercepting of letters, mistaking names, false inscriptions, errors of messengers, faction of the parties, fear in the actors, horror in the action, the majesty of the person, the restlessness of the mind, distracted looks, weariness of the spirit*, and all under the conduct of the Divine wisdom, and the Divine vengeance, make the covers of the most secret sin transparent as a net, and visible as the Chian wines in the purest Crystal.

For besides that God takes care of *Kings* and of the lives of men, [. . .] driving away evil from their persons, and watching as a Mother to keep gnats and flies from her dear boy sleeping in the cradle, there are in the machinations of a mighty mischief, so many motions to be concentred, so many wheels to move regularly, and the hand that turns them does so tremble, and there is so universal a confusion in the conduct, that unless it passes suddenly into act, it will be prevented by discovery, and if it be acted it enters into such a mighty horror, that the face of a man will tell what his heart did think, and his hands have done. And after all, it was seen and observed by him that stood behind the cloud, who shall also bring every work of darkness into light in the day of strange discoveries and fearful recompenses: and in the mean time certain it is, that no man can long put on a person and act a part, but his evil manners will peep through the corners of the white robe, and God will bring an hypocrite to shame even in the eyes of men.

2. A second superinduced consequent of sin brought upon it by the wrath of God, is *sin*; when God punishes *sin with sin* he is extremely angry; for then the punishment is not *medicinal*, but *final* and *exterminating*; God in that case takes no care concerning him, though he dies and dies eternally. I do not here speak of those sins which are naturally consequent to each other, as evil words to evil thoughts, evil actions to evil words, rage to drunkenness, lust to gluttony, pride to ambition; but such which God suffers the man's evil nature to be tempted to by evil opportunities: [. . .] This is the wrath of God, and the man is without remedy. It was a sad calamity, when God punished *David's* adultery by permitting him to fall to murder, and *Solomon's* wanton and inordinate love, with the crime of idolatry, and *Ananias* his sacrilege with lying against the Holy Ghost, and *Judas* his covetousness with betraying his Lord, and that betraying with despair, and that despair with self-murder. [. . .] One evil invites another, and when God is angry and withdraws his grace, and the holy Spirit is grieved and departs from his dwelling, the man is left at the mercy of the merciless enemy, and he shall receive him only with variety of mischiefs; like *Hercules* when he had broken the horn of *Achelous*, he was almost drowned with the flood that sprung from it; and the evil man when he hath passed the first scene of his sorrows, shall be enticed or left to fall into another. For it is a certain truth, that he who resists, or that neglects to use God's grace, shall fall into that evil condition, that when he wants it most, he shall have least. It is so with every man; he that hath the greatest want of the grace of God shall want it more; if this great want proceeded once from his own sin. *Habenti dabitur*, said our blessed Lord, *to him that hath shall be given, and he shall have more abundantly; from him that hath not shall be taken, even that which he hath*. It is a remarkable saying of *David, I have thought upon thy Name, O Lord in the night season, and have kept thy Law; this I had because I kept thy Commandments*: keeping God's Commandments, was rewarded with keeping God's Command-

ments; And in this world God hath not a greater reward to give; for so the soul is nourished unto life, so it grows up with the increase of God, so it passes on to a perfect man in Christ, so it is consigned for heaven, and so it enters into glory; for glory is the perfection of grace, and when our love to God is come to its state and perfection, then we are within the circles of a Diadem, and then we are within the regions of felicity. And there is the same reason in the contrary instance.

The wicked person falls into sin, and this he had because he sinned against his maker. *Tradidit Deus eos in desideria cordis eorum*: and it concerns all to observe it; and if ever we find that a sin succeeds a sin in the same instance, it is because *we refuse to repent*; but if a sin succeeds a sin in another instance, as if lust follows pride, or murder drunkenness; it is a sign that *God will not give us the grace of repentance*: he is angry at us with a destructive fury, he hath dipped his arrows in the venom of the serpent, and whets his sword in the forges of hell; then it is time that a man withdraw his foot, and that he start back from the preparations of an intolerable ruin: For though men in this case grow insensible, and that's part of the disease, [. . .] it is the biggest part of the evil that the man feels it not, saith *Chrysostom*, yet the very *antiperistasis* or the contrariety, the very horror and bigness of the danger may possibly make a man to contend to leap out of the fire; and sometimes God works a miracle, and besides his own rule delights to reform a dissolute person, to force a man from the grave, to draw him against the bent of his evil habits; yet it is so seldom, that we are left to consider, that such persons are in a desperate condition, who cannot be saved unless God is pleased to work a miracle.

3. Sin brings in its retinue, fearful plagues and evil angels, messengers of the displeasure of God, concerning which, [. . .] there are enough of dead; I mean the experience is so great, and the notion so common, and the examples so frequent, and the instances so sad, that there is scarce any thing new in this particular to be noted; but something is remarkable, and that is this, that God even when he forgives the sin, does reserve such [. . .] remains of punishment, and those not only to the less perfect, but to the best persons, that it makes demonstration, that every sinner is in a worse condition than he dreams of. For consider; can it be imagined that any one of us should escape better than *David* did? we have reason to tremble when we remember what he suffered, even when God had sealed his pardon. Did not God

punish *Zedekiah* with suffering his eyes to be put out in the house of bondage? was not God so angry with *Valentinian*, that he gave him into his enemies' hand to be flayed alive? Have not many persons been struck suddenly in the very act of sin, and some been seized upon by the Devil and carried away alive? These are fearful contingencies: but God hath been more angry yet; *rebellion* was punished in *Corah* and his company, by the gaping of the earth, and the men were buried alive; and *Dathan* and *Abiram* were consumed with fire for usurping the Priest's office: But God hath struck severely since that time; and for the prostitution of a Lady by the Spanish King, the Moors were brought in upon his Kingdom, and ruled there for 700 years. And have none of us known an excellent and good man to have descended, or rather to have been thrust into a sin, for which he hath repented, which he hath confessed, which he hath rescinded, and which he hath made amends for as he could, and yet God was so severely angry, that this man was suffered to fall in so big a calamity, that he died by the hands of violence, in a manner so seemingly impossible to his condition, that it looked like the biggest sorrow that hath happened to the sons of men? But then let us consider how many and how great crimes we have done; and tremble to think, that God hath exacted so fearful pains, and mighty punishments for one such sin which we, it may be, have committed frequently. Our sin deserves as bad as theirs; and God is *impartial*, and we have no privilege, no promise of exemption, no reason to hope it; what then do we think shall become of this affair? where must we suffer this vengeance? For that it is due, that it is just we suffer it, these sad examples are a perfect demonstration. We have done that, for which God thought *flaying alive* not to be too big a punishment: that for which God hath smitten Kings with formidable plagues; that for which governments have been changed, and Nations enslaved, and Churches destroyed, and the Candlestick removed, and famines and pestilences have been sent upon a whole Kingdom; and what shall become of us? why do we vainly hope it shall not be so with us? If it was just for these men to suffer what they did, then we are at least to expect so much; and then let us consider into what a fearful condition sin hath put us, upon whom a sentence is read, that we shall be plagued like *Zedekiah*, or *Corah*, or *Dathan*, or the King of *Spain*, or any other King, who were, for aught we know, infinitely more innocent and more excellent persons than any of us. What will become of us? For God is as just to us as to them; and Christ died for them as well as for us; and they have repented more than we have done; and what mercy can we expect, that they might not hope for, upon at least as good ground as we? God's ways are secret, and his mercies and justice dwell in a great abyss; but we are to measure our expectations by revelation and experience. But then what would become of us, if God should be as angry at our sin as at *Zedekiah's*, or King *David's*? Where have we in our body room enough for so many stripes, as our sin ought justly to be punished withal? or what security or probability have we that he will not so punish us?

For I did not represent this sad story, as a matter of possibility only, that we may fear such fearful strokes as we see God lay upon sinners; but we ought to look upon it as a thing that will come some way or other, and for aught we know we cannot escape it. So much, and more is due for the sin, and though Christ hath redeemed our souls, and if we repent we shall not die eternally, yet he hath nowhere promised we shall not be smitten. It was an odd saying of the Devil to a sinner whom he would fain have had to despair; *Me a Coelo ad Barathrum demisit peccatum, et vos ullum in terra locum tutum existimabitis?* Sin thrust me from heaven to hell, and do you think on earth to have security? Men use to presume that they shall go unpunished; but we see what little reason we have so to flatter and undo ourselves, [...] He that hath sinned must look for a Judgment, and how great that is, we are to take our measures by those sad instances of vengeance by which God hath chastised the best of men, when they have committed but a single sin; [...] sin is damnable and destructive: and therefore as the ass refused the barley which the fatted swine left, perceiving by it he was fatted for the slaughter; *'Tuum libenter prorsus appeterem cibum,/Nisi qui nutritus illo est, jugulatus foret'*; we may learn to avoid these vain pleasures which cut the throat after they are swallowed, and leave us in that condition that we may every day fear, lest that evil happen unto us, which we see fall upon the great examples of God's anger; and our fears cannot, ought not at all to be taken off, but by an effective, busy, pungent, hasty, and a permanent repentance; and then also but in some proportions, for we cannot be secured from temporal plagues, if we have sinned; no repentance can secure us from all that; nay God's pardon, or remitting his final anger, and forgiving the pains of hell, does not secure us here: [...]; but sin lies at the door ready to enter in, and rifle all our fortunes.

1. But this hath two appendages which are very considerable; and the first is, that there are some mischiefs which are the proper and appointed scourges of certain sins, and a man need not ask; *Cujus vulturis hoc erit cadaver?* what vulture, what death, what affliction shall destroy this sinner? The sin hath a punishment of its own which usually attends it, as giddiness does a drunkard. He that commits sacrilege, is marked for a vertiginousness and changeable fortune; *Make them, O my God, like unto a wheel*, of an unconstant state: and *we and our fathers have seen it*, in the change of so many families, which have been undone by being made rich: they took the lands from the Church, and the curse went along with it, and the misery and the affliction lasted longer than the sin. Telling lies frequently hath for its punishment to be *given over to believe a lie*, and at last, that no body shall believe it but himself; and then the mischief is full, he becomes a dishonoured and a baffled person. The consequent of *lust* is properly *shame*; and witchcraft is still punished with baseness, and beggary; and oppression of widows hath a sting, for the tears of the oppressed are to the *oppressor*, like the waters of jealousy, making the belly to swell, and the thigh to rot; the *oppressor* seldom dies in a tolerable condition: but is remarked toward his end with some horrible affliction. The sting of oppression is darted as a man goes to his grave. In these and the like, God keeps a rule of striking, *In quo quis peccat, in eo punitur*. The Divine Judgment did point at the sin, lest that be concealed by excuses, and protected by affection, and increased by passion, and destroy the man by its abode. For some sins are so agreeable to the spirit of a fool and an abused person, because he hath framed his affections to them, and they comply with his unworthy interest, that when God out of an angry kindness, smites the man and punishes the sin, the man does fearfully defend his beloved sin, as the serpent does his head which he would most tenderly preserve. But therefore God that knows all our tricks and devices, our stratagems to be undone, hath therefore apportioned out his punishments by analogies, by proportions, and entail: so that when every sin enters into its proper portion, we may discern why God is angry, and labour to appease him speedily.

2. The second appendage to this consideration is this, that there are some states of sin, which expose a man to all mischief, as it can happen by taking off from him all his guards, and defences; by driving the good Spirit from him, by stripping him of

the guards of Angels. But this is the effect of an habitual sin, a course of an evil life, and it is called in Scripture, *agrieving the good Spirit of God*. But the guard of Angels is in Scripture only promised to them that live godly; *The Angels of the Lord pitch their tents round about them that fear him, and delivereth them*, said *David*. [. . .] And the *Hellenists* use to call Angels [. . .] *watchmen*; which custody is at first designed and appointed for all, when by Baptism they give up their names to Christ, and enter into the covenant of Religion. And of this the Heathen have been taught something by conversation with the *Hebrews* and *Christians; unicuique nostrum dare paedagogum Deum*, said *Seneca* to *Lucilius, non primarium, sed ex eorum numero, quos Ovidius vocat ex plebe deos*. There is a guardian God assigned to every one of us, of the number of those which are of the second order; such are those of whom *David* speaks, *before the Gods will I sing praise unto thee*; and it was the doctrine of the Stoics, that to every one there was assigned a *Genius* and a *Juno:Quamobrem major coelitum populus etiam quam hominum intelligi potest, quum singuli ex semetipsis totidem Deos faciant, Junones geniosque adoptando sibi*, said *Pliny*. Every one does adopt Gods into his family, and get a *Genius* and a *Juno* of their own, *Junonem meam iratam habeam*; it was the oath of *Quartilla* in *Petronius*; and *Socrates* in *Plato* is said to swear by his *Juno*; though afterwards among the *Romans* it became the woman's oath, and a note of effeminacy; But the thing they aimed at was this, that God took a care of us below, and sent a ministering spirit for our defence; but that this is only upon the accounts of piety, they knew not. But we are taught it by the Spirit of God in Scripture. For, *the Angels are ministering spirits, sent forth to minister to the good of them who shall be heirs of salvation*; and concerning St. *Peter*, the faithful had an opinion, that it might be *his Angel*; agreeing to the Doctrine of our blessed Lord, who spake of Angels appropriate to his little ones, to infants, to those that belong to him. Now what God said to the sons of Israel is also true to us Christians; *Behold, I send an Angel before thee, beware of him and obey his voice, provoke him not, for he will not pardon your transgressions*. So that if we provoke the Spirit of the Lord to anger by a course of evil living, either the Angel will depart from us, or if he stays, he will strike us. The best of these is bad enough, and he is highly miserable, '*—Qui non sit tanto hoc custode securus*,' whom an Angel cannot defend from mischief, nor any thing secure him from the wrath of God. It was the description and character which the *Erythrean* Sibyl gave of God [...]. It is God's appellative to be a giver of excellent rewards to just and innocent persons: but to assign to evil men fury, wrath, and sorrow for their portion. If I should launch further into this Dead sea, I should find nothing but horrid shriekings, and the skulls of dead men utterly undone. Fearful it is to consider, that sin does not only drive us into calamity, but it makes us also impatient, and embitters our spirit in the sufferance: *It cries loud for vengeance, and so torments men before the time, even with such fearful outcries, and horrid alarms, that their hell begins before the fire is kindled. *It hinders our prayers, and consequently makes us hopeless and helpless. *It perpetually affrights the conscience, unless by its frequent stripes it brings a callousness and an insensible damnation upon it, *It makes us to lose all that which Christ purchased for us, all the blessings of his providence, the comforts of his Spirit, the aids of his grace, the light of his countenance, the hopes of his glory; it makes us enemies to God, and to be hated by him more than he hates a dog; and with a dog shall be his portion to eternal ages; with this only difference, that they shall both be equally excluded from heaven; but the dog shall not, and the sinner shall descend into hell; and which is the confirmation of all evil; for a transient sin God shall inflict an eternal Death. Well might it be said in the words of God by the Prophet, *ponam Babylonem in possessionem Erinacei, Babylon* shall be the possession of an Hedgehog: that's a sinner's dwelling; encompassed round with thorns and sharp prickles, afflictions and uneasiness all over. So that he that wishes his sin big, and prosperous, wishes his Bee as big as a Bull, and his Hedgehog like an Elephant; the pleasure of the honey would not cure the mighty sting; and nothing make recompense, or be a good, equal to the evil of an eternal ruin. But of this there is no end. I sum up all with the saying of *Publius Mimus, Tolerabilior est qui mori jubet quam qui male vivere*, He is more to be endured that puts a man to death, than he that betrays him into sin. *For the end of this is death* eternal.

Isaac Barrow

ISAAC BARROW was born in London in 1630. His father was Linen-draper to Charles I. He had an uncle who became Bishop of St Asaph. He was said to have been a pugnacious boy, and not attentive to school-work. He was thought to have done little good to himself at Charterhouse, but improved when afterwards he went to school at Felstead. His father 'often solemnly wished, that if it pleased God to take away any of his Children, it might be his son *Isaac*.' This opinion changed, and Thomas Barrow, who outlived his son by some years, regretted the loss to his old age. He also found it 'so small mitigation' to his sorrow, that while his son lived 'he was not unprofitable to the world', and he himself published his son's collected works. It cannot have taken Isaac long to settle down to his studies, for he did well at Felstead and was thought fit for Cambridge at the age of fifteen.

He was not well off at this time, his father being impoverished through his adherence to the King. Barrow apparently received some support from Henry Hammond, one of the chaplains of Charles I, who was in due course deprived and imprisoned. He took his B. A. in 1648 and became a Fellow of Trinity in 1649. He was a discreet and reasonable man, and managed to live with the Puritan authorities in spite of his Royalist connections and his own independence of mind. The Master of the college is said to have placed his hand on Barrow's head with the words: 'Thou art a good Lad, 'tis pity thou art a Cavalier.' His talents and industry were valued. For some years he took to the study of medicine, and thought of becoming a physician, but concluded that not to make divinity the end of his studies would be contrary to the oath he had taken when he became a Fellow.

In 1654 he sold his books and went abroad on the proceeds, though some other aids must have been found before he returned for his travels lasted till 1659 and he went as far as Constantinople. Off the coast of Italy he once manned a gun against pirates. He made notes on Mohammedanism, on Turkish proverbs and Turkish officials. He was a learned man when he went abroad, and he came back with numerous additions to his armoury.

At the Restoration he became Professor of Greek at Cambridge, then Professor of Geometry at Gresham College. In 1663 he became the first Lucasian Professor of Mathematics at Cambridge, and not the least sign of his unusual fitness for the post is that he recognized the superiority of Isaac Newton and gave way to him in 1669. His collected works were edited by Tillotson. They include, besides sermons and mathematical works, a treatise on the Pope's supremacy. Barrow died of a fever in 1677.

OF A PEACEABLE TEMPER AND CARRIAGE
Romans 12:18.
If it be possible, as much as lieth in you, live peaceably with all men.

BARROW'S SERMONS bear all the marks of his abilities and his charitable temper. A steady light glows from his pages. One's respect for him grows as one reads him. His is one of the best prosaic minds of the century. He was interested in many things, but all are pulled along by the central drift of his mind. The current is always towards the truth. It is by 'using his best faculties in the best manner' that a man comes upon faith. There is no obscurantism and no special pleading.

Barrow wrote a number of sermons and expositions on all the articles of the Apostles' Creed. He also wrote many which are primarily concerned with conduct. There is no gap between the two groups. When he speaks of conduct, what he says does indeed bear evidence of a great knowledge of the world and an intimate observation of how men behave. But it is by faith that 'we are informed concerning ourselves', according to Barrow, and the charity and insight which he has from that source give force to his commonest observation.

The sermon which follows was, as edited by Tillotson, the second of two on the same subject. Barrow had the reputation of preaching at length, even in those days when the tolerance of congregations was greater than it now is. It is therefore not unlikely that the two sermons may originally have been preached as one. Both are on the same text. In the first sermon, or part, which is not given here, Barrow defines what he means by 'a peaceable temper and carriage'. He does not mean merely doing no harm; he means 'a positive Amity, and disposition to perform such kind offices, without which good correspondence among men cannot subsist.' He notes the emphasis of his text on living in peace 'with *all* men', not with the party or people of your choice only, not with other Christians only.

Barrow's own experience of living with people with whom he disagreed was profound. The pressures put on the universities by the successive *de facto* authorities who opposed and then claimed to have taken over from the King were comparable to those exercised in our time by various totalitarian regimes. Barrow lived in Cambridge with all this till five years after the King's death. One cannot doubt that it is this experience which gives life to his observations. 'If we desire to live peaceably,' he says in the first sermon, 'we must restrain our pragmatical curiosity within the bounds of our proper business and concernment, not invading other men's provinces, and without leave or commission intermeddling with their affairs; not rushing into their closets, prying into their concealed designs, or dictating counsel to them without due invitation thereto.' One can almost see the busy, politically-minded fellows, darting about in their little games of power which were no doubt more exciting than learning. 'Quietness, and doing our own business', were the subject of two other sermons by Barrow, on a text from Thessalonians. It was not merely that Barrow had had experience of the need for proper caution, and seems to have been as outspoken as anyone when the occasion required. But he was one of those, less uncommon in his days than ours, who thought that submission to the authorities, in the ordinary way, was an element in the good life. It is interesting to note that Johnson's *Dictionary* still gives the name of 'pragmatic' simply as 'meddling; impertinently busy; assuming business without leave or invitation.'

In the second sermon *Of a Peaceable Temper and Carriage* given here, Barrow is less concerned with defining or describing what he means by peaceableness than with considering the grounds of this duty, *why* we ought to do what his text says we ought. The argument develops in a way which well illustrates the equability and rationality of the author's temper. The basis of the duty is our common humanity. 'All men are naturally kin, and friends to each other', he says, quoting Aristotle as well as Tertullian. 'We are but several streams issuing from one primitive source; several branches sprouting from the same stock; several stones hewed out of the same quarry.' His language so far is that of humanism, but for Barrow, characteristically, the reasons of reason and the reasons of faith are one. 'One element affords us matter, and one fire actuates it, kindled at first by the breath of God. One blood flows in all our veins; one nourishment repairs our decayed bodies, and one common air refreshes our languishing spirits. We are cohabitants of the same earth.' We 'are only distinguished by some accidental, inconsiderable circumstances of age, place, colour, stature, fortune and the like.' And he points out that, as we grow up and grow old, we differ as much from ourselves as we ever do from one another. It is a reflection worth some thought.

Nor will he have it that we are released from our duty by any dislike of persons or their opinions, or by the injuries they may do us, as 'no unkindness of a brother can wholly rescind that relation'. The involuntary pity we sometimes feel for another, the interest we take in others, demonstrate what we have in common. We are moved by the events of history, even by stories of imaginary events. 'Antipathies may be natural to wild beasts; but to rational creatures they are wholly unnatural.' We defeat the object of civil society if we do not live peaceably, that is honestly and helpfully to one another. Finally Barrow appeals to the example of Christ who, as he says in another sermon (*Of Faith*), lived on earth 'as a beggar and a vagrant, who died as a malefactor and a slave'. Here he is concerned to remind his listeners that Christ

> despised not the meanest, either in outward estate, or spiritual improvement. He invited all to him, repelled, or discouraged none; nor refused to any that came to him, his counsel, or his help. He was averse from no man's society (and if in any degree from any, chiefly from those, who confidently pretended to extraordinary sanctity, and proudly contemned others.)

No countenance here for any failure of patience with other people's boring habits or stupid opinions. Barrow is profoundly humane.

I HAVE very lately considered what it is to *live peaceably*, and what are the Duties included therein; and what Means conduce thereto.

II. I proceed now to consider the Object thereof, and why the Duty of living peaceably extends to *all men*, that is, why we are bound to bear good-will, and do good offices, and show civil respects to all men; and to endeavour, that all men reciprocally be well affected toward us. For it might with some colour of reason be objected, and said; Why should I be obliged heartily to love those, that desperately hate me, to treat them kindly, that use me despitefully; to help them, that would hinder me; to relieve them, that would plunge me into utter distress; to comfort them, that delight in my affliction; to be respective to and tender of their reputation, who despise, defame and reproach me: to be indulgent and favourable to them, who are harsh and rigorous in their dealings with me; to spare and pardon them, who with implacable malice persecute me? why should I seek their friendship, who disdainfully reject mine; why prize their favour, who scorn mine; why strive to please them, who purposely offend me? or why should I have any regard to men void of all faith, goodness or desert? And most of all, why should I be bound to maintain amicable correspondence with those, who are professed enemies to piety and virtue, who oppugn truth, and disturb peace, and countenance vice, error and faction? How can any love, consent of mind, or communion of good offices intercede between persons so contrarily disposed? I answer, they may and ought, and that because the obligation to these ordinary performances is not grounded upon any peculiar respects, special qualifications, or singular actions of men, (which are contingent and variable) but upon the indefectible score of common humanity. We owe them (as the Philosopher alleged, when he dispensed his alms to an unworthy person) [. . .] not to the men, but to human nature resident in them. There be indeed divers other sorts of love, in nature and object more restrained, built upon narrower foundations, and requiring more extraordinary acts of duty and respect (not competent to all men;) as a love of friendship, founded upon long acquaintance, suitableness of disposition, and frequent exchanges of mutual kindness; a love of gratitude due to the reception of valuable benefits; a love of esteem belonging to persons endued with worth and virtue; a love of relation resulting from kindred, affinity, neighbourhood and other common engagements. But the love of benevolence (which is precedent to these, and more deeply rooted in nature, more ancient, more unconfined, and more immutable) and the duties mentioned consequent on it, are grounded upon the natural constitution, necessary properties, and unalterable condition of humanity, and are upon several accounts due thereto.

1. Upon account of universal cognation, agreement and similitude of nature. For [. . .] *All men naturally are of kin, and friends to each other*, saith *Aristotle*. *Et fratres etiam vestri sumus jure naturae matris unius; We are also your brethren in the right of nature our common mother*, said *Tertullian* of old, in the name of the Christians to the Heathens. We are but several streams issuing from one primitive source; several branches sprouting from the same stock; several stones hewed out of the same quarry. One substance, by miraculous efficacy of the divine benediction diffused and multiplied. One element affords us matter, and one fire actuates it, kindled at first by the breath of God. One blood flows in all our veins; one nourishment repairs our decayed bodies, and one common air refreshes our languishing spirits. We are cohabitants of the same earth, and fellow-citizens of the same great Common-wealth; *Unam Rempublicam omnium agnoscimus mundum*, said the forementioned Apologist for Christianity. We were all fashioned according to the same original Idea (resembling God our common Father) all endowed with the same faculties, inclinations and affections; all conspire in the essential and more notable ingredients of our constitution; and are only distinguished by some accidental inconsiderable circumstances of age, place, colour, stature, fortune and the like; in which we differ as much from our selves in successions of time. So that what *Aristotle* said of a friend, is applicable to every man: Every man is [. . .] *Another our-self*; and he that hates another, detests his own most lively picture; he that harms another, injures his own nature; he that denies relief to another, starves a member of his own body, and withers a branch of his own tree. *The merciful man doeth good to his own soul; but he that is cruel troubleth his own flesh*. Neither can any personal demerit of vicious habit, erroneous opinion, enormous practice, or signal discourtesy towards us dissolve these bands: for as no unkindness of a brother can wholly rescind that relation, or disoblige us from the duties annexed thereto: so neither upon the faults or injuries of any man can we ground a total dispensation from the offices of humanity, especially if the injuries be not irreparable, nor the faults incurable.

2. We are indispensably obliged to these duties, because the best of our natural inclinations prompt us to the performance of them; especially those of pity and benignity, which are manifestly discernible in all, but most powerful and vigorous in the best natures; and which questionless by the most wise and good Author of our beings were implanted therein both as monitors to direct, and as spurs to incite us to the performance of our duty. For the same bowels, that in our want of necessary sustenance, do by a lively sense of pain inform us thereof, and instigate us to provide against it; do in like manner grievously resent the distresses of another, and thereby admonish us of our duty, and provoke us to relieve them. Even the stories of calamities, that in ages long since past have happened to persons no wise related to us, yea the fabulous reports of tragical events, do (even against the bent of our wills, and all resistance of reason) melt our hearts with compassion, and draw tears from our eyes: and thereby evidently signify that general sympathy which naturally intercedes between all men, since we can neither see, nor hear of, nor imagine another's grief without being afflicted ourselves. Antipathies may be natural to wild beasts; but to rational creatures they are wholly unnatural. And on the other side, as nature to eating and drinking, and such acts requisite to the preservation of our life, hath adjoined a sensible pleasure and satisfaction, enticing us to and encouraging us in the performance of them; so, and doubtless to the same end, hath she made relieving the necessities of others, and doing good offices to them, to be accompanied with a very contentful and delicious relish to the mind of the doer. *Epicurus*, that great Master of pleasure, did himself confess, that to bestow benefits was not only more brave, but more pleasant, than to receive them [. . .]. And certainly no kind of actions, a man can perform, are attended with a more pure, more perfect, more savoury delight, than those of beneficence are. Since nature therefore hath made our neighbour's misery our pain, and his content our pleasure; since with indissoluble bands of mutual sympathy she hath concatenated our fortunes and affections together; since by the discipline of our sense she instructs us, and by the importunity thereof solicits us to the observance of our duty, let us follow her wise directions, and conspire with her kindly motions; let us not stifle, or weaken by disuse, or contrary practice, but by conformable action cherish and confirm the good inclinations of nature.

3. We are obliged to these duties upon account of common

equity. We have all (the most sour and stoical of us all) implanted in us a natural ambition, and a desire (which we can by no means eradicate) of being beloved and respected by all; and are disposed in our need to demand assistance, commiseration of our misfortunes, and relief in our distress of all that are in capacity to afford them; and are apt to be vehemently displeased, to think ourselves hardly dealt with, and to complain of cruelty and inhumanity in those that refuse them to us: and therefore in all reason and equity we should readily pay the same love, respect, aid and comfort to others, which we expect from others; for, *Beneficium qui dare nescit, injuste petit*: Nothing is more unreasonable, or unequal, than to require from others those good turns, which upon like occasion we are unwilling to render to others.

4. We are obliged to these duties of humanity, upon account of common interest, benefit and advantage. The welfare and safety, the honour and reputation, the pleasure and quiet of our lives are concerned in our maintaining a loving correspondence with all men. For so uncertain is our condition, so obnoxious are we to manifold necessities, that there is no man, whose good-will we may not need, whose good word may not stand us in stead, whose helpful endeavour may not sometime oblige us. The Great *Pompey*, the glorious Triumpher over Nations, and admired darling of fortune, was beholden at last to a slave for the composing his ashes and celebrating his funeral obsequies. The honour of the greatest men depends on the estimation of the least, and the good-will of the meanest peasant is a brighter ornament to the fortune, a greater accession to the grandeur of a Prince, than the most radiant gem in his royal diadem. However the spite and enmity of one (and him the most weak otherwise and contemptible) person, may happen to spoil the content of our whole life, and deprive us of the most comfortable enjoyments thereof; may divert our thoughts from our delightful employments to a solicitous care of self-preservation and defence; may discompose our minds with vexatious passions; may by false reports, odious suggestions, and slanderous defamations blast our credit, raise a storm of general hatred, and conjure up thousands of enemies against us; may by insidious practices supplant and undermine us, prejudice our welfare, endanger our estate, and involve us in a bottomless gulf of trouble: it is but reasonable therefore, if we desire to live securely, comfortably and quietly, that by all honest means we should endeavour to

purchase the good-will of all men, and provoke no man's enmity needlessly; since any man's love may be useful, and every man's hatred is dangerous.

5. We are obliged to these duties by a tacit compact and fundamental constitution of mankind, in pursuance of those principal designs, for which men were incorporated, and are still contained in civil Society. For to this purpose do men congregate, cohabit, and combine themselves in sociable communion, that thereby they may enjoy a delightful conversation, void of fear, free from suspicion, and free from danger; promote mutual advantage and satisfaction; be helpful and beneficial each to other: abstracting from which commodities the retirements of a cloister, or the solitudes of a desert; the life of a recluse or of a wild beast, would perhaps be more desirable, than these of gregarious converse: For as men, being well pleased and affected to each other, are the most obliging friends, and pleasant companions; so being enraged, they are the most mischievous and dangerous neighbours, the most fierce and savage enemies. By neglecting therefore or contravening these duties of humanity, we frustrate the main ends of society, disappoint the expectations of each other, subvert the grounds of ordinary civility, and in the commonwealth deal as unpoliticly, as the members in the body should act unnaturally, in subtracting mutual assistance, or harming each other; as if the eye should deny to the hands the direction of sight, and the hands in revenge should pluck out the eyes.

6. We are by observing these rules to oblige, and render men well-affected to us, because being upon such terms with men conduceth to our living (not only delightfully and quietly, but) honestly and religiously in this world. How peace and edification, spiritual comfort and temporal quiet do concur and co-operate, we see intimated *Act. 9. v. 31. Then had the Churches peace throughout all Judaea, and Galilee, and Samaria, and were edified, and walking in the fear of the Lord, and in the comfort of the Holy Ghost were multiplied.* Saint *Paul* advised the Christians of his time, liable to persecution, *to make prayers for all men* (and *especially for those in eminent power,*) *that they might lead a quiet and peaceable life in all godliness and honesty*; to pray for them, that is, to pray that they might be disposed, as not to molest, interrupt or discourage them in the exercise of virtue, and practice of piety. For these by a tranquillity of mind, a sedateness of affections, a competency of rest and

leisure and retirement, a freedom from amazing fear, distracting care, and painful sense are greatly advanced; of which advantages by contentious broils and enmities we are deprived, and encumbered with the contrary impediments. They breed thorny anxieties, and by them choke the seeds of good intention: they raise dusky fumes of melancholy, by them intercepting the beams of spiritual light, and stifling the flames of devout affection. By them our thoughts are affixed upon the basest, and taken off from the most excellent objects; our fancies are disordered by turbulent animosities; our time is spent, and our endeavour taken up in the most ungrateful, and unprofitable employments, of defeating the attempts, resisting the assaults, disproving the calumnies, countermining the plots of adversaries; They bring us upon the stage against our will, and make us act parts in Tragedies, neither becoming nor delighting us. They disturb often our natural rest, and hinder us in the dispatch of our ordinary business; and much more impeach the steadiness of our devotion, and obstruct the course of religious practice. They tempt us also to omissions of our duty, to unseemly behaviour, and to the commissions of grievous sin; to harsh censure, envious detraction, unwarrantable revenge, repining at the good successes, and delighting in the misfortunes of others. Many examples occur in history, like those of *Hanno* the *Carthaginian*, and *Quintus Metellus* (*Pompey's* antagonist) who, in pursuance of some private grudges have not only betrayed their own interests, and sullied their own reputations; but notably disserved, and damnified the public weal of their country: And so will our being engaged in enmity with men cause us to neglect, if not to contradict, our dearest concernments: Whence we should carefully avoid the occasions thereof, and by an innocent and beneficent conversation oblige men to a friendly correspondence with us.

7. We are obliged to perform these duties of humanity, because by so doing we become more capable of promoting goodness in others, and so of fulfilling the highest duties of Christian Charity; of successfully advising and admonishing others; of instructing their ignorance, and convincing their mistakes; of removing their prejudices, and satisfying their scruples; of reclaiming them from vice, error, faction; and reconciling them to virtue, truth and peace. For by no force of reason, or stratagem of wit are men so easily subdued, by no bait so thoroughly allured and caught, as by real courtesy, gentleness and affability; as on the other side, by a sour and peevish humour, supercilious looks,

bitter language and harsh dealing men are rendered indocile and intractable, averse from better instruction, obstinate in their ways, and pertinacious in their conceits. Easily do men swallow the pill gilded with fair carriage, and sweetened by kind speech; readily do they afford a favourable ear to the advice seeming to proceed from good-will, and a tender care of their good; But the physic of wholesome admonition being steeped in the vinegar of reproach, and tempered with the gall of passion, becomes distasteful and loathsome to the patient; neither will men willingly listen to the reasonings of those, whom they apprehend disaffected to their persons, and more desirous to wound their reputations, than to cure their distempers. The slightest argument, the most simple and unpolished oration issuing from the mouth of a friend, is wonderfully more prevalent, than the strongest demonstration, than the most powerful eloquence of an enemy. For obliging usage and courteous speech unlock the affections, and by them insinuate into the reason of men; but surly deportment, and forward expressions dam up the attention with prejudice, and interclude all avenues to the understanding. An illustration of which discourse we have from comparing the different practice of the *Jews*, and the ancient *Christians*, with the contrary successes thereof. The *Jews*, by their seditious, and turbulent practices, by their insolent contempt, and implacable hatred of others (for you know what *Tacitus* saith of them: *Apud ipsos fides obstinata, misericordia in promptu, sed adversus omnes alios hostile odium*) by their perverse and unsociable humours, declining all intercourse, and refusing ordinary offices of humanity (so much as to show the way, or to direct the thirsty traveller to the fountain) to any not of their own sect, did procure an *odium*, scorn and infamy upon their religion, rendered all men averse from enquiring into, or entertaining any good opinion thereof, and so very little enlarged its bounds, and gained few proselytes thereto. But the *Christians* by a mild, patient and peaceable behaviour; by obedience to laws, and compliance with harmless customs: by perfect innocence, and abstinence from doing injury; by paying due respects, and performing civil offices and demonstrations of benevolence; by loving conversation, and friendly commerce with all, commended their doctrine to the regard of men: and by this only piece of Rhetoric (without terror of arms, or countenance of power, or plausibility of discourse, or promise of temporal reward) subdued the faith of men, and persuaded a great part of the world to embrace their excellent profession.

'We converse with you like men, we use the same diet, habit, and necessary furniture: We have recourse to your tribunals; we frequent your markets, your fairs, your shops, your stalls, your shambles, your baths: We cohabit, we sail, we war, we till, we trade, we maintain all manner of commerce with you'; saith the Christian Apologist, to the Pagans, in behalf of the ancient Christians. Which kind of practice they derived not only from the sweet temper and noble *Genius* of their Religion, but from the express institution of the first teachers thereof, and from their exemplary practice therein. For both by doctrine did the Apostles exhort, and by their example incite them to adorn the Gospel, and render the discipline of Christ amiable by their meek, gentle, compliant and inoffensive conversation; and thereby to allure others to a willing entertainment thereof. To this purpose are those exhortations, *Phil. 4. 5. Let your moderation ([. . .], your equity* or *gentleness) be known to all men:* and, *I Thess. 5. 14. — Comfort the afflicted, support the weak, be long-suffering toward all. Be ye all careful not to render evil for evil; but always pursue goodness toward each other, and toward all*: and *Gal. 6. 10. As we have opportunity, let us do good to all men*: and, *Tit. 3. 1. Put them in mind to be subject to principalities and powers, to be ready to every good work; to reproach no man; not to be contentious, but gentle, showing all meekness to all men*: and, *1 Tim. 2. 24 The Minister of the Lord must not strive, but be gentle unto all men, apt to teach, patient: In meekness instructing those that oppose themselves:* (or those that are otherwise disposed [. . .]) *if peradventure God will give them repentance to the acknowledgement of the truth*: where gentleness toward all, and meekness toward adversaries are oppositely conjoined, with aptness to teach and instruct; the one qualification so effectually predisposing to the other: and it is beside intimated, that gentle and meek treatment are suitable instruments ordinarily employed by God to convert men from error to truth.

8. We are bound hereto in compliance and conformity to the best patterns: God, Christ, the Apostles, the Primitive Saints: This illustrious Doctor of Christian Religion Saint *Paul* did not fail to second this his doctrine with his own example. For,*Give none offence* (saith he) *neither to the Jews, nor to the Gentiles, nor to the Church of God; Even as I please all men in all things, not seeking mine own profit, but the profit of many, that they may be saved: Please all men in all things* (1 Cor. 10); what could

Saint *Paul* say, or what do more? and again, *For though* (saith he) *I be free from all men, yet have I made myself a servant unto all, that I might gain the more: To the weak became I as weak, that I might gain the weak: I am made all things to all men, that by all means I might save some* (1 Cor. 19). See how far this charitable design of doing good to others transported him: He parted with his own freedom, that he might redeem them from the slavery of a wicked life; He denied his own present satisfaction that he might procure them a lasting content: he despised his own profit, that he might promote their spiritual advantage; He prostituted his own reputation, that he might advance them to a condition of true glory. He underwent grievous afflictions for their comfort; sustained restless pains for their ease, and hazarded his own safety for their salvation. He condescended to their infirmities, suited his demeanour to their tempers, complied with their various humours, and contrary customs: He differed from himself, that he might agree with them, and transformed himself into all shapes, that he might convert them into what they should be, reform their manners, and translate them into a happy estate. But above all is the practice of our Lord himself most remarkable to this purpose: and discovers plainly to him that observes an universally large and unrestrained Philanthropy. For having from a wonderful conspiracy of kindness and good will (between him and his eternal Father) toward the world of men, descended willingly from the throne of his celestial Majesty, and enveloped his divine glory in a cloud of mortal frailty, and *that* (as the Apostle saith) *he might reconcile all things in heaven and earth*, conjoin God and man by a nearer alliance, and unite men together by the more sacred bands of common relation to himself: Having assumed not only the outward shape and corporeal resemblance of man, but the inward frame, and real passions of human souls; he disdained not accordingly to obey the laws, to follow the inclinations, to observe the duties of the best and most perfect humanity; with an equal and imperial bounty imparting free admittance, familiar converse, friendly aid and succour unto all, even the worst of men in all appearance (and that so far, that some rigorous censurers thence presumed to tax him as *a glutton, and a good-fellow, a friend to publicans and sinners*) distributing liberally to all the incomparable benefits of his heavenly doctrine, of his holy example, of his miraculous power; instructing the ignorances, detecting the errors, dispossessing the devils; sustaining the weaknesses, overlooking the injuries, comforting the afflictions, supplying the necessities, healing the diseases, and remedying all the miseries of all, that did not wilfully reject their own welfare: *He went about* (saith Saint *Peter* in the *Acts*) *doing good, and healing all that were oppressed of the devil*: And, *He went about all the cities and villages teaching in their Synagogues, and preaching the Gospel of the Kingdom, and healing every sickness, and every disease among the people* (saith Saint *Matthew's* Gospel). He despised not the meanest, either in outward estate, or spiritual improvement. He invited all unto him, repelled, or discouraged none; nor refused to any that came unto him, his counsel, or his help. He was averse from no man's society (and if in any degree from any, chiefly from those, who confidently pretended to extraordinary sanctity, and proudly contemned others). Meek and gentle he was, mild and patient; courteous and benign; lowly and condescensive; tender and compassionate in his conversation unto all. And for a complement of his transcendent charity, and for an enforcement unto ours, he laid down his life for us all, as a common price to purchase remission of sins; a general ransom to redeem the human creation from the captivity of hell and slavery of corruption into the glorious liberty of the Sons of God; demolishing by his pacific death all partition walls, and laying open all enclosures of the divine favour; reconciling God to man, and combining man to himself by the fresh cement of his precious blood: so that now not only as fellow-creatures; but (which is exceedingly more) as partakers of the same common redemption, as objects of the same mercy, as obliged in the same common debt, and as capable of the same eternal happiness, by new and firmer engagements we are bound to all mutual kindness and benevolence toward all. For, *Destroy not* (saith Saint *Paul*, and by like reason I may say, harm not, vex not, be not unkind to) *him, for whom Christ died*.

Nay, farther, we have the example of Almighty God himself directing, and by our Saviour's express admonition obliging us to this universal beneficence, compassion and patience towards all. Who by express testimony of sacred writ, and by palpable signs of continual experience declareth himself to be a lover of mankind: to be good to all, and tenderly merciful over all his works: not to afflict willingly, nor grieve the children of men: to compassionate the miseries, and supply the needs, and relieve the distresses; to desire the salvation and to delight in the happiness of men. Who with an indifferent, unlimited munificence dispenseth his blessings, extends his watchful providence, and imparts his loving care unto all: Causing his Sun with comfortable beams to shine, and the refreshing showers to descend upon the earth to yield her pleasant fruits; the temperate seasons to recur, and all the elements to minister succour, joy and satisfaction even to the most impious and ingrateful toward him. Who with immense clemency and long-sufferance overlooks the sacrilegious affronts offered daily to his Majesty; the outrageous violations of his laws, and the contemptuous neglects of his unexpressible goodness: Who patiently waits for the repentance, and incessantly solicits the reconcilement, courts the amity, and in a manner begs the good-will of his most deadly enemies: whom he hath always in his hand, and can crush to nothing at his pleasure. For, *We are Ambassadors for Christ, as if God by us did entreat you: We beseech you in Christ's behalf; be reconciled to God* (saith Saint *Paul*).

Since therefore upon account of natural consanguinity, of our best inclinations, of common equity, and general advantage, and an implicit compact between men; of securing our, and promoting others' virtue and piety; from the exhortations of Scripture mentioned, and many more tending to the same purpose, from the example of the ancient Christians, the Leaders and Champions of our Religion, of the Apostles, the Masters and Patriarchs thereof, of our Blessed Redeemer, and of Almighty God himself, we are obliged to this Universal benevolence and beneficence toward all; No misapprehensions of judgment, no miscarriages in practice, no ill-dispositions of soul, no demerits in himself, no discourtesies toward us ought wholly to alienate our affections from, or to avert us from doing good, or to incline us to render evil for evil unto any person: especially considering, that the omissions of others, cannot excuse us from the performance of our duty; that no man is to be presumed incorrigible, nor (like the lapsed Angels) concluded in desperate impenitence; and that our loving and gentle demeanour toward them may be instrumental to their amendment, and the contrary may contribute to their progress and continuance in offences; that God hath promised to us a reward of our patience, and hath reserved to them a season of judgment and punishment, if they persist obstinate in their disorderly courses; that to avenge their trespasses belongs not to us, but to Almighty God, who is more nearly concerned in, and more injured by them, and is yet content to endure them, to prolong their lives, to continue his benefits to them, and to expect their conversion: That our differing from them is not to be attributed to ourselves, but wholly, or chiefly to the goodness of God; that we always were, are, and shall be liable to the same errors, vices and misdemeanours: that (lastly) the faults and follies of others, like the maims of body, distempers of soul, or crosses of fortune (being their own greatest unhappinesses) require rather our pity than our hatred, to be eased by our help, than aggravated by our unkindness. 'Tis too scant therefore and narrow a Charity that is limited by correspondence of courtesy, or by the personal merits of others. We are bound to live peaceably with, that is, to be innocent, beneficial, respective to all, and to seek the reciprocal good-will, love and amity of all. But I have insisted too long upon this particular, concerning the Object of this duty, and its extension.

III. I proceed briefly to consider whence it comes, that (as I before observed was intimated in these words, *If it be possible, as much as lieth in you*) though we do our parts, and perform carefully the duties incumbent on us, though we bear good-will, and do good offices, and yield due respects, and abstain from all not only injurious, but rigorous dealings toward all; though we revile none, nor censure harshly, nor presumptuously intermeddle with others' affairs; though we obey laws, and comply with received customs, and avoid all occasions of contention, though our tempers be meek, our principles peaceable, and our conversations inoffensive, we may yet prove successless in our endeavours to live peaceably, and may be hated, harmed and disquieted in our course of life. That it so happens, we find by plain experience, and manifold example. For *Moses, the meekest man upon earth*, and commended beside by all circumstances of divine favour, and human worth, was yet often envied, impugned and molested by those, whom by all manner of benefits he had most highly obliged. And we find *David* frequently complaining, that by those, whose good will by performing all offices of friendly kindness, and brotherly affection, he had studiously laboured to deserve, whose maladies and calamities he had not only tenderly commiserated, but had prayed and humbled his soul with fasting for their recovery and deliverance from them, was yet recompensed by their treacherous devices against his safety, by grievous reproaches, and scornful insultings over him in his affliction; as we see at large in *Psalms* the 35 and 69. And in *Psalm* 120 he thus lamentably bemoans his condition: *Woe is me that I sojourn in Mesech, that I dwell in the tents of Kedar: My soul hath long dwelt with him that hateth peace: I am for peace, but when I speak, they are for war*: And our Blessed Saviour himself, though in the whole tenor of his life he demonstrated an incomparable meekness and sweetness of disposition, and exercised continually all manner of kindness and beneficence toward all men, was notwithstanding loaded with all kinds of injuries and contumelies, was bitterly hated, ignominiously disgraced, and maliciously persecuted unto death: and the same lot befell his faithful Disciples, that although their design was benign and charitable, their carriage blameless and obliging toward all, they were yet pursued constantly both by the outrageous clamours of the people, and cruel usages from those in eminent power. Now though it seem strange and almost incredible, that they who are truly friends to all, and are ready to do to all what good they can; who willingly displease none, but industriously strive to acquire (not with glozing shows of popularity, but by real expressions of kindness) the good-will and favour of all, should yet be maligned, or molested by any; yet seeing it so happens, if we inquire into the reason, we shall find this miracle in morality, to proceed (to omit the neglect of the duties mentioned in our former discourse) chiefly from the exceeding variety, difference and contrariety of men's dispositions, joined with the morosity, aptness to mistake, envy, or unreasonable perverseness of some; which necessarily render the means of attaining all men's good-will insufficient, and the endeavours unsuccessful. For men seeing by several lights, relishing with diversly disposed Palates, and measuring things by different standards, we can hardly do or say anything, which if approved and applauded by some, will not be disliked and blamed by others; if it advance us in the opinion of some, will not as much depress us in the judgment of others; so that in this irreconcilable diversity and inconsistency of men's apprehensions, it is impossible not to displease many: Especially since some men either by their natural temper, or from the influence of some sour principles they have imbibed, are so morose, rigid, and self-willed; so impatient of all contradiction to, or discrepancy from their sentiments, that they cannot endure any to dissent in judgment, or vary in practice from them, without incurring their heavy disdain and censure. And, which makes the matter more desperate and remediless, such men commonly being least able either to manage their reason, or to command their passion, as guided wholly by certain blind impulses of fancy, or groundless prejudices of conceit, or by a partial admiration of some men's persons, examples and authorities, are usually most resolute and peremptory in their courses, and thence hardly capable of any change, mitigation or amendment. Of which sort there being divers engaged in several ways, it is impossible to please some without disgusting the other; and difficult altogether to approach any of these wasps, without being stung or vexed by them. Some also are so apt to misunderstand men's meanings, to misconstrue their words, and to make ill descants upon, or draw bad consequences from their actions, that 'tis not possible to prevent their entertaining ill-favoured prejudices against even those that are heartily their friends, and wish them the best. To others the good and prosperous estate of their Neighbour, that he flourishes in wealth, power or reputation, is ground sufficient of hatred and enmity against him; for so we see that *Cain* hated his innocent brother *Abel*, because his brother's works were more righteous, and his sacrifices better accepted than his own: that *Joseph's* brethren were mortally offended at him, because his father especially loved and delighted in him: that *Saul* was enraged against *David*, because his gallant deeds were celebrated with due praises and joyful acclamations of the people: and that the *Babylonian* Princes, upon no other score, maligned *Daniel*, but because he enjoyed the favour of the King, and a dignity answerable to his deserts: And who, that loves his own welfare, can possibly avoid such enmities as these? But the fatal rock, upon which peaceable designs are most inevitably split, and which by no prudent steering our course can sometimes be evaded, is the unreasonable perverseness of men's pretences, who sometimes will upon no terms be friends with us, or allow us their good-will, but upon condition of concurring with them in dishonest and unwarrantable practices; of omitting some duties to which by the express command of God, or evident dictates of right reason we are obliged, or performing some action repugnant to those indispensable rules. But though peace with men is highly valuable, and possessing their good-will in worth not inferior to any other indifferent accommodation of life, yet are these nothing comparable to the favour of God, or the internal satisfaction of conscience; nor though we were assured thereby to gain the entire love and favour of all men living, are we to purchase them at so dear a rate as with the loss of these. We must not, to please or gratify men, commit anything prohibited, or omit anything enjoined by God, the least glimpse of whose favourable aspect is infinitely more to be prized, than the most intimate friendship of the mightiest Monarchs upon earth: and the least spark of whose indignation is more to be dreaded, than the extremest displeasure of the whole world. In case of such competition, we must resolve with S. *Paul, Gal. 1. 10. Do I yet conciliate God, or do I endeavour to sooth men? for if I yet soothed* (or flattered) *men [. . .] I were not the servant of Christ*. Nor are we, that we may satisfy any man's pleasure, to contravene the dictates of Reason (that subordinate guide of our actions) to do any dishonourable or uncomely action, unworthy of a man, misbeseeming our education, or incongruous to our station in human society, so as to make ourselves worthily despicable to the most by contenting some; Nor are we bound always to desert our own considerable interest, or betray our just liberty, that we may avoid the enmity of such as would violently or fraudulently encroach upon them. Nor are we in the administration of justice, distribution of rewards, or arbitration of controversies to respect the particular favour of any, but the merits only of the cause, or the worth of the persons concerned. Nor are we by feeding men's distempered humours, or gratifying their abused fancies to prejudice or neglect their real good; to encourage them in bad practices, to foment their irregular passions, to applaud their unjust or uncharitable censures, or to puff up their minds with vain conceit, by servile flattery: but rather, like faithful Physicians, to administer wholesome, though unsavoury, advice; to reveal to them their mistakes, to check their intended progress in bad courses, to reprove their faults seasonably, and when it may probably do them good, though possibly thereby we may provoke their anger and procure their ill-will, and (as Saint *Paul* saith) become their enemies, for telling them the truth. Nor are we ever explicitly to assent to falsehoods (so apprehended by us,) to bely our consciences, or contradict our real judgments (though we may sometimes for peace-sake prudently conceal them:) Nor to deny the truth our defence and patronage, when in order to some good purpose it needs and requires them, though thereby we may incur the dislike, and forfeit the goodwill of some men. Nor are we by entertaining any extraordinary friendship, intimate familiarity, or frequent converse with persons notoriously dissolute in their manners, disorderly in their behaviour, or erroneous in weighty points of opinion, to countenance their misdemeanours, dishonour our profession, render our selves justly suspected, run the hazard of contagion, or hinder their reformation. And especially we are warily to decline the particular acquaintance of men of contentious dispositions, mischievous principles, and factious designs; a bare keeping company with whom looks like a conspiracy, an approving or abetting their proceedings; The refusing any encouragement, signification of esteem, or vouchsafing any peculiar respect to such, we owe to the honour of virtue, which they disgrace, to the love of truth which they oppugn, to the peace of the world which they disturb, and to the general good of mankind, which they impeach. And so S. *Paul* warns us not to Mingle or consort, not to *diet*, or *common* [. . .] with men of a dissolute and disorderly conversation: And, *to mark them which cause seditions, and scandals, contrary to Christian doctrine, and to shun, or decline them* [. . .] and to repudiate, deprecate the familiarity of Heretics [. . .]. And S. *John* forbids us to *wish joy*, or to allow the ordinary respects of civil salutation to Apostates and Imposters: *lest* (by such demonstration of favour) *we communicate with them in their wicked works*. None of which precepts are intended to interdict to us, or to disoblige us from bearing real good-will, or dispensing needful benefits to any, but to deter us from yielding any signal countenance to vice and impiety; and to excite to declare such dislike and detestations of those heinous enormities as may confer to the reclaiming of these, and prevent the seduction of others. So Saint *Paul* expressly, 2 *Thess.* 3. 14. *But if any man obeyeth not our injunction by epistle, do not consort with him, that he may by shame be reclaimed* [...] And, *account him not an enemy, but admonish him as a brother*. Nor ought lastly the love of peace, and desire of friendly correspondence with any men, avert us from an honest zeal, (proportionable to our abilities and opportunities) of promoting the concernments of truth and goodness, though against powerful and dangerous opposition: I say an honest zeal, meaning thereby not that blind, heady passion, or inflammation of spirit, transporting men beyond the bounds of reason and discretion, upon some superficially plausible pretences to violent and irregular practices; but a considerate and steady resolution of mind, effectually animating a man by warrantable and decent means vigorously to prosecute commendable designs; like that S. *Jude* mentions, of *striving earnestly for the faith once delivered to the Saints*. For this zeal may be very consistent with, yea greatly conducible to the designs of peace. And 'tis not a drowsiness, a slack remissness, a heartless diffidence, or a cowardly flinching from the face of danger and opposition, we discourse about, or plead for, but a wise and wary declining the occasions of needless and unprofitable disturbance to ourselves and others.

To conclude this point (which if time would have permitted, I should have handled more fully and distinctly) though to preserve peace, and purchase the good-will of men, we may and ought to quit much of our private interest and satisfaction, yet ought we not to sacrifice to them what is not our own, nor committed absolutely to our disposal, and which in value incomparably transcends them, the maintenance of truth, the advancement of justice, the practice of virtue, the quiet of our conscience, the favour of Almighty God. And if for being dutiful to God, and faithful to ourselves in these particulars, any men will hate, vex and despite us; frustrate our desires, and defeat our purposes of living peaceably with all men in this world: we may comfort ourselves in the enjoyment of eternal peace and satisfaction of mind, in the assurance of the divine favour, in the hopes of eternal rest and tranquillity in the world to come.

Now briefly to induce us to the practice of this duty of living peaceably, we may consider,

1. *How good and pleasant a thing it is* (as *David* saith) *for brethren* (and so we are all at least by nature) *to live together in unity.* How, that (as *Solomon* saith) *better is a dry morsel, and quietness therewith, than a house full of sacrifices with strife.* How delicious that conversation is, which is accompanied with a mutual confidence, freedom, courtesy and complacence: how calm the mind, how composed the reflections, how serene the countenance, how melodious the voice, how sweet the sleep, how contentful the whole life is of him that neither deviseth mischief against others, nor suspects any to be contrived against himself: and contrariwise, how ingrateful and loathsome a thing it is to abide in a state of enmity, wrath, dissension: having the thoughts distracted with solicitous care, anxious suspicion, envious regret; the heart boiling with choler, the face overclouded with discontent, the tongue jarring and out of tune, the ears filled with discordant noises of contradiction, clamour and reproach; the whole frame of body and soul distempered and disturbed with the worst of passions. How much more comfortable it is to walk in smooth and even paths, than to wander in rugged ways, overgrown with briars, obstructed with rubs, and beset with snares; to sail steadily in a quiet, than to be tossed in a

tempestuous Sea; to behold the lovely face of Heaven smiling with a cheerful serenity, than to see it frowning with clouds, or raging with storms; to hear harmonious consents, than dissonant janglings; to see objects correspondent in graceful symmetry, than lying disorderly in confused heaps; to be in health, and have the natural humours consent in moderate temper, than (as it happens in diseases) agitate with tumultuous commotions: How all senses and faculties of man unanimously rejoice in those emblems of peace, order, harmony and proportion. Yea, how nature universally delights in a quiet stability or undisturbed progress of motion; the beauty, strength and vigour of every thing requires a concurrence of force, co-operation, and contribution of help; all things thrive and flourish by communicating reciprocal aid, and the world subsists by a friendly conspiracy of its parts; and especially that political society of men chiefly aims at peace as its end, depends on it as its cause, relies on it as its support. How much a peaceful state resembles Heaven, into which neither *complaint, pain,* nor *clamour* [...] do ever enter; but blessed souls converse together in perfect love, and in perpetual concord; and how a condition of enmity represents the state of Hell, that black and dismal region of dark hatred, fiery wrath, and horrible tumult. How like a paradise the world would be, flourishing in joy and rest, if men would cheerfully conspire in affection, and helpfully contribute to each other's content: and how like a savage wilderness now it is, when, like wild beasts, they vex and persecute, worry and devour each other. How not only Philosophy hath placed the supreme pitch of happiness in a calmness of mind, and tranquillity of life, void of care and trouble, of irregular passions and perturbations; but that Holy Scripture itself in that one term of peace most usually comprehends all joy and content, all felicity and prosperity: so that the heavenly consort of Angels, when they agree most highly to bless, and to wish the greatest happiness to mankind, could not better express their sense, than by saying, *Be on earth peace, and good-will among men*.

2. That as nothing is more sweet and delightful, so nothing more comely and agreeable to human nature than peaceable living, it being (as *Solomon* saith) *an honour to a man to cease from strife*; and consequently also a disgrace to him to continue therein: That rage and fury may be the excellencies of beasts, and the exerting their natural animosity in strife and combat may become them; but reason and discretion are the singular

eminencies of men, and the use of these the most natural and commendable method of deciding controversies among them: and that it extremely misbecomes them that are endowed with those excellent faculties so to abuse them, as not to apprehend each other's meanings, but to ground vexatious quarrels upon the mistake of them: not to be able by reasonable expedients to compound differences, but with mutual damage and inconvenience to prorogue and increase them: not to discern how exceedingly better it is to be helpful and beneficial, than to be mischievous and troublesome to one another. How foolishly and unskilfully they judge, that think by unkind speech and harsh dealing to allay men's distempers, alter their opinions, or remove their prejudices; as if they should attempt to kill by ministering nourishment, or to extinguish a flame by pouring oil upon it. How childish a thing it is eagerly to contend about trifles, for the superiority in some impertinent contest, for the satisfaction of some petty humour, for the possession of some inconsiderable toy: yea how barbarous and brutish a thing it is to be fierce and impetuous in the pursuit of things that please us, snarling at, biting and tearing all competitors of our game, or opposers of our undertaking. But how divine and amiable, how worthy of human nature, of civil breeding, of prudent consideration it is, to restrain partial desires, to condescend to equal terms, to abate from rigorous pretences, to appease discords, and vanquish enmities by courtesy and discretion; like the best and wisest Commanders, who by skillful conduct, and patient attendance upon opportunity, without striking of stroke or shedding of blood, subdue their Enemy.

3. How that peace with its near alliance and concomitants, its causes and effects, love, meekness, gentleness and patience, are in Sacred Writ reputed the genuine fruits of the Holy Spirit, issues of Divine Grace, and offsprings of heavenly Wisdom; producing like themselves a goodly progeny of righteous deeds. But that emulation, hatred, wrath, variance and strife derive their extraction from fleshly lust, hellish craft, or beastly folly; propagating themselves also into a like ugly brood of wicked works. For so saith Saint *James, If ye have bitter zeal and strife in your hearts, glory not, nor be deceived untruly: This wisdom descendeth not from above, but is earthly, sensual, and devilish: For where emulation and strife are, there is tumult, and every naughty thing: but the wisdom that is from above is first pure, then peaceable, gentle, obsequious, full of mercy* (or beneficence)

and of good fruits, without partiality and dissimulation; And the fruit of righteousness is sowed in peace to those that make peace: and from whence are wars, and quarrels among you? Are they not hence, even from your lusts, that war in your members? Likewise, *He loveth transgression that loveth strife;* and *A fool's lips enter into contention, and his mouth calleth for strokes,* saith *Solomon.* That the most wicked and miserable of creatures is described by titles denoting enmity and discord: *the hater* (Satan) *the enemy [. . .] the accuser [. . .] the slanderer [. . .] the destroyer [. . .]* the furious dragon, and mischievously treacherous snake: and how sad it is to imitate him in his practices, to resemble him in his qualities: But that the best, most excellent, and most happy of Beings delights to be styled, and accordingly to express himself, *The God of love, mercy and peace;* and his blessed Son to be called, and to be, *the Prince of Peace,* the great *Mediator, Reconciler,* and *Peace-maker,* who is also said from on high to have visited us, *To give light to them that sit in darkness, and in the shadow of death, and to guide our feet in the ways of peace.* That lastly no devotion is pleasing, no oblation acceptable to God, conjoined with hatred, or proceeding from an unreconciled mind: For, *If thou bring thy gift to the altar, and there rememberest that thy brother hath aught against thee; Leave there thy gift before the altar, and go thy way; first be reconciled to thy brother, and then come and offer thy gift,* saith our Saviour.

I close up all with this *Corollary*: that if we must live lovingly, and peaceably with all men, then much more are we obliged to do so with all Christians: to whom by nearer and firmer bands of holy alliance we are related; by more precious communions in faith and devotion we are endeared; by more peculiar and powerful obligations of divine commands, sacramental vows, and formal professions we are engaged: Our spiritual brethren, members of the same mystical body, temples of the same holy Spirit, servants of the same Lord, subjects of the same Prince, professors of the same truth, partakers of the same hope, heirs of the same promise, and candidates of the same everlasting happiness.

Now Almighty God, the most good and beneficent Maker, gracious Lord, and merciful preserver of all things, infuse into our hearts those heavenly graces of meekness, patience and benignity, grant us and his whole Church, and all his Creation to serve him quietly here, and in a blissful rest to praise and magnify him for ever: To whom with his blessed Son, the great Mediator and Prince of peace, and with his holy Spirit, the ever-flowing Spring of all love, joy, comfort and peace, be all honour, glory and praise.

And

The peace of God which passeth all understanding keep your hearts and minds in the knowledge and love of God, and of his Son Jesus Christ our Lord: And the blessing of God Almighty, the Father, Son, and holy Ghost be among you, and remain with you for ever. Amen.

OF INDUSTRY IN OUR PARTICULAR CALLING, AS SCHOLARS
Romans 12:11.
Not slothful in business.

THIS IS one of a group of sermons Barrow wrote on the virtues of being industrious. The group starts with one *Of Industry in General*, on a text from Ecclesiastes: 'Whatsoever thy hand findeth to do, do it with all thy might.' It was the temper of the Puritan world, of which Barrow was prepared to recognize the good qualities, though his theology and politics were different. It was also very much Barrow's personal temper; the learning and activity of his forty-seven years were remarkable. There followed sermons on industry in our various callings—as Christians, as Gentlemen, and finally as Scholars. It is the last of these sermons which is given here.

God himself, in Barrow's system, is 'everlastingly busy'. He is 'immovably and infinitely happy', but what is most in Barrow's thought is his vigilance as the Father of mankind. 'He rested once from the great work of creation,' he says, 'but yet *my Father* (saith our Lord) *worketh still*; and he never will rest from his work of Providence, and of Grace. His eyes continue watchful over the World, and his hands stretched out in upholding it.' The creature should be careful after the pattern of the Creator. God 'hath a singular regard to every creature, supplying the needs of each, and *satisfying the desire of all*.' So should we try to do.

There is no room for frivolity in Barrow's way of thinking. This does not mean that he could not exercise his sharp wit, or that people were not to try to render life pleasant by pleasantries as by other social exchanges. There is a sermon on this topic too: *Against Foolish Talking and Jesting*, in which the matter is fully explored. Barrow's mind is serious because he sees man as bound 'to continual employment in respect of God'. He moves naturally within the circle of that belief.

The sermon *Of Industry in Our Particular Calling, as Scholars*, was no doubt preached in Cambridge to people who ought to consider the matter. Barrow had a high and practical view of this calling—practical in the sense that he knew fully what was involved in it, not in the sense that he thought scholars ought to concern themselves with matters of everyday utility. Quite the contrary. 'Our business is to attain knowledge, not concerning obvious and vulgar matters, but about sublime, abstruse, intricate and knotty subjects, remote from common observation and sense.' He is far from the indulgences of esotericism; his concern is that scholars should 'try the best forces in their minds with their utmost endeavours'.

He is far, too, from commending the mere specialist, for whom the twentieth century can offer so many excuses. 'There is such a connection of things, and dependence of notions,' he says, 'that one part of learning doth confer light to another' so that 'a man can hardly well understand anything without knowledge of divers other things.' 'He will be a lame Scholar, who hath not an insight into many kinds of knowledge, . . . he can hardly be a good Scholar, who is not a general one.' By this he meant that his scholar should study languages, rhetoric—'the art of conveying our thoughts to others by speech with advantages of clearness, force and elegancy'—, history, mathematics, natural and moral philosophy, and theology. Much has happened since Barrow's day to render this programme more difficult, but nothing that would render it less desirable. And one should not imagine that such a programme was easy, or could be complete, in the seventeenth century. Against the slothful, who eat the bread of Founders and benefactors (now including the taxpayer) but live in relative idleness, Barrow has an indignant peroration.

I PROCEED to the other sort of persons, whom we did propound, namely *Scholars*, and that on them particularly great engagements do lie to be industrious, is most evident, from various considerations.

The nature and design of this calling doth suppose industry; the matter, and extent of it doth require industry; the worth of it doth highly deserve industry. We are in special gratitude to God, in charity to men, in due regard to ourselves bound unto it.

1. First, I say, the nature and design of our calling doth suppose industry: *There is* (saith the divine *Preacher*) *a man, whose labour is in wisdom, in knowledge, and in equity*; Such men are Scholars; so that we are indeed no Scholars, but absurd usurpers of the name, if we are not laborious; for what is a Scholar, but one who retireth his person, and avocateth his mind from other occupations, and worldly entertainments, that he may [...] *vacare studiis*, employ his mind and leisure on study and learning, in the search of truth, the quest of knowledge, the improvement of his reason. Wherefore an idle Scholar, a lazy student, a sluggish man of learning is nonsense.

What is learning but a diligent attendance to instruction of Masters, skilled in any knowledge, and conveying their notions to us in word or writing?

What is study, but an earnest, steady, persevering application of mind to some matter, on which we fix our thoughts, with intent to see through it; what in *Solomon's* language are these *Scholastic* occupations, but *inclining the ear*, and *applying our heart to understanding*? than which commonly there is nothing more laborious, more straining nature, and more tiring our Spirits; whence it is well compared to the most painful exercises of body and soul.

The *Wise-man* advising men to seek wisdom, the which is the proper design of our calling, doth intimate that work to be like digging in the mines for silver, and like searching all about for concealed treasure; than which there can hardly be any more difficult and painful task, *If* (saith he) *thou seekest her as silver, and searchest for her as for hid treasures, then shalt thou understand*—Otherwise he compareth the same work to assiduous watching and waiting, like that of a guard or a client, which are the greatest instances of diligence, *Blessed* (saith he; or wisdom by him saith, blessed) *is the man that heareth me, watching daily at my gates, waiting at the posts of my doors*.

Wherefore if we will approve ourselves to be what we are

called, and what we pretend to be, if we will avoid being Impostors, assuming a name not due to us, we must not be slothful. Farther,

2. The matter and extent of our business doth require industry from us; the matter of it, which is truth and knowledge; the extent, which is very large and comprehensive, taking in all truth, all knowledge; worthy our study, and useful for the designs of it.

Our business is to find truth; the which (even in matters of high importance) is not easily to be discovered; being (as a vein of silver, encompassed with earth, and mixed with dross) deeply laid in the obscurity of things, wrapped up in false appearances, entangled with objections, and perplexed with debates; being therefore not readily discoverable; especially by minds clouded with prejudices, lusts, passions, partial affections, appetites of honour and interest; whence to descry it requireth the most curious observation, and solicitous circumspection that can be; together with great pains in the preparation and purgation of our minds toward the inquiry of it.

Our business is to attain knowledge, not concerning obvious and vulgar matters, but about sublime, abstruse, intricate and knotty subjects, remote from common observation and sense; to get sure and exact notions about which will try the best forces of our mind with their utmost endeavours; in firmly settling principles, in strictly deducing consequences, in orderly digesting conclusions, in faithfully retaining what we learn by our contemplation and study.

And if to get a competent knowledge about a few things, or to be reasonably skilful in any sort of learning, be difficult, how much industry doth it require to be well seen in many, or to have waded through the vast compass of learning, in no part whereof a Scholar may conveniently or handsomely be ignorant; seeing there is such a connection of things, and dependence of notions, that one part of learning doth confer light to another, that a man can hardly well understand anything without knowing divers other things; that he will be a lame Scholar, who hath not an insight into many kinds of knowledge, that he can hardly be a good Scholar, who is not a general one.

To understand so many Languages (which are the shells of knowledge,) to comprehend so many Sciences (full of various theorems and problems) to peruse so many Histories (of ancient and modern times;) to know the World, both natural and human;

to be acquainted with the various inventions, inquiries, opinions and controversies of learned men; to skill the arts of expressing our mind, and imparting our conceptions with advantage, so as to instruct or persuade others; these are works indeed, which will exercise and strain all our faculties (our reason, our fancy, our memory) in painful study.

The knowledge of such things is not innate to us; it doth not of itself spring up in our minds; it is not anywise incident by chance, or infused by grace (except rarely by miracle;) common observation doth not produce it; it cannot be purchased at any rate, except by that, for which it was said of old, *the gods sell all things*, that is for pains; without which the best wit and greatest capacity may not render a man learned; as the best soil will not yield good fruit or grain, if they be not planted or sown therein.

Consider, if you please, what a Scholar *Solomon* was; Beside his skill in *politics*, which was his principal faculty and profession, whereby he did with admirable dexterity and prudence manage the affairs of that great Kingdom, *judging his people, and discerning what was good and bad*; accurately dispensing justice; settling his Country in a most flourishing state of peace, order, plenty and wealth; largely extending his territory; so that his wisdom of this kind was famous over the earth; beside, I say, this civil wisdom, He had an exquisite skill in natural *Philosophy* and *Medicine*, for *He spake of trees* (or plants) *from the cedar that is in Lebanon, even unto the hyssop that springeth out of the wall; he spake also of beasts, and of fowl, and of creeping things, and of fishes*.

He was well versed in *Mathematics*; for it is said, *Solomon's wisdom excelled the wisdom of all the children of the East-country, and all the wisdom of Egypt*; the wisdom of which Nations did consist in those Sciences. And of his *Mechanic* skill he left for a monument the most glorious structure that ever stood on earth.

He was very skilful in Poetry and Music, for he did himself *compose above a thousand songs*; whereof one yet extant declareth the loftiness of his fancy, the richness of his vein, and the elegancy of his style.

He had great ability in Rhetoric; according to that in *Wisdom, God granted me to speak as I would*; and that in *Ecclesiastes, The Preacher sought to find out acceptable words*; a great instance of which faculty we have in that admirable Prayer of his composure, at the dedication of the Temple.

He did wonderfully excel in *Ethics*; concerning which *he spake three thousand Proverbs,* or moral Aphorisms; and *Moreover* (saith *Ecclesiastes) because the preacher was wise, he still taught the people knowledge; yea he gave good heed, and sought out, and set in order many proverbs;* the which did contain a great variety of notable observations, and useful directions for common life, couched in pithy expressions.

As for *Theology*, as the study of that was the chief study to which he exhorteth others (as to *the head*, or principal part *of wisdom*) so questionless he was himself most conversant therein; for proof whereof he did leave so many excellent theorems, and precepts of divinity to us.

In fine, there is no sort of knowledge, to which he did not apply his study; witness himself in those words, *I gave my heart to seek and search out by wisdom concerning all things, that are done under heaven.*

Such a Scholar was He; and such if we have a noble ambition to be, we must use the course he did; which was first in his heart to prefer wisdom before all worldly things; then to pray to God for it, or for his blessing in our quest of it; then to use the means of attaining it, diligent searching, and hard study; for that this was his method he telleth us, *I* (saith he) *applied my heart, to know, and to search, and to seek out wisdom, and the reason of things.*

Such considerations shew the necessity of industry for a Scholar; but

3. The worth, and excellency, and great utility, together with the pleasantness of his vocation, deserving the highest industry, do superadd much obligation thereto.

We are much bound to be diligent out of ingenuity, and in gratitude to God, who by his gracious providence hath assigned to us a calling so worthy, an employment so comfortable, a way of life no less commodious, beneficial and delightful to our selves, than serviceable to God, and useful for the World.

If we had our option and choice, what calling could we desire before this of any whereto men are affixed? how could we better employ our mind, or place our labour, or spend our time, or pass our pilgrimage in this World, than in scholastical occupations?

It were hard to reckon up, or to express the numberless great advantages of this calling, I shall therefore only touch some, which readily fall under my thought, recommending its value to us.

It is a calling, the design whereof conspireth with the general end of our being; the perfection of our nature in its endowments, and the fruition of it in its best operations.

It is a calling, which doth not employ us in bodily toil, in worldly care, in pursuit of trivial affairs, in sordid drudgeries; but in those angelical operations of soul, the contemplation of truth, and attainment of wisdom; which are the worthiest exercises of our reason, and sweetest entertainments of our mind; the most precious wealth, and most beautiful ornaments of our soul; whereby our faculties are improved, are polished and refined, are enlarged in their power and use by habitual accessions: the which are conducible to our own greatest profit and benefit, as serving to rectify our wills, to compose our affections, to guide our lives in the ways of virtue, to bring us unto felicity.

It is a calling, which being duly followed will most sever us from the vulgar sort of men, and advance us above the common pitch; endowing us with light to see farther than other men, disposing us to affect better things, and to slight those meaner objects of human desire, on which men commonly dote: freeing us from the erroneous conceits, and from the perverse affections of common people. It is said [. . .] *men of learning are double-sighted*; but it is true, that in many cases they see infinitely farther than a vulgar sight doth reach; and if a man by serious study doth acquire a clear and solid judgment of things, so as to assign to each its due weight and price; if he accordingly be inclined in his heart to affect and pursue them; if from clear and right notions of things a meek and ingenuous temper of mind, a command and moderation of passions, a firm integrity, and a cordial love of goodness do spring, he thereby becometh another kind of thing, much different from those brutish men (beasts of the people) who blindly follow the motions of their sensual appetite, or the suggestions of their fancy, or their mistaken prejudices.

It is a calling which hath these considerable advantages, that by virtue of improvement therein, we can see with our own eyes, and guide our selves by our own reasons, not being led blindfold about, or depending precariously on the conduct of others in matters of highest concern to us. That we are exempted from giddy credulity, from wavering levity, from fond admiration of persons and things, being able to distinguish of things, and to settle our judgments about them, and to get an intimate acquaintance with them, assuring to us their true nature and worth: that we are also thereby rescued from admiring our selves, and that overweening self-conceitedness, of which the *Wise-man* saith, *The sluggard is wiser in his own conceit, than seven men that can render a reason.*

It is a calling, whereby we are qualified and enabled to do God service; to gratify his desires, to promote his honour, to advance his interests; to render his name glorious in the World; by teaching, maintaining and propagating his truth; by persuading men to render their due love, reverence and obedience to him; than which we can have no more honourable or satisfactory employment; more like to that of the glorious and blessed Spirits.

It is a calling, the due prosecution whereof doth ingratiate us with God, and procureth his favour; rendering us fit objects of his love, and entitling us thereto in regard to our qualities, and recompense of our works; for *God loveth none but him that dwelleth with wisdom;* and, *So shalt thou find favour and good understanding in the sight of God and man.*

It is a calling, whereby with greatest advantage we may benefit men, and deserve well of the World; drawing men to the knowledge and service of God, reclaiming them from error and sin, rescuing them from misery, and conducting them to happiness; by clear instruction, by faithful admonition, by powerful exhortation; And what can be more noble, than to be the lights of the World, the guides of practice to men, the authors of so much good, so egregious benefactors to mankind?

It is a calling most exempt from the cares, the crosses, the turmoils, the factious jars, the anxious intrigues, the vexatious molestations of the World; its business lying out of the road of those mischiefs; wholly lying in solitary retirement, or being transacted in the most innocent, and ingenuous company.

It is a calling least subject to any danger or disappointment; wherein we may well be assured not to miscarry or lose our labour; for the Merchant indeed by manifold accidents may lose his voyage, or find a bad market; the husbandman may plow and sow in vain; but the student hardly can fail of improving his stock, and reaping a good crop of knowledge; especially if he study with a conscientious mind, and pious reverence to God, imploring his gracious help and blessing.

It is a calling, the industry used wherein doth abundantly

recompense it self, by the pleasure and sweetness which it carrieth in it; so that the more pains one taketh, the more delight he findeth, feeling himself proportionably to grow in knowledge; and that his work becometh continually more easy to him.

It is a calling the business whereof doth so exercise as not to weary, so entertain as not to cloy us; being not (as other occupations are) a drawing in a mill, or a nauseous (tedious) repetition of the same work; but a continued progress toward fresh objects; our mind not being staked to one or a few poor matters, but having immense fields of contemplation, wherein it may everlastingly expatiate, with great proficiency and pleasure.

It is a calling, which doth ever afford plentiful fruit, even in regard to the conveniences of this present, and temporal state; the which sufficiently will requite the pains expended thereon: for if we be honestly industrious we shall not want success; and succeeding we shall not want a competence of wealth, of reputation, of interest in the World: for concerning wisdom, which is the result of honest study, the *Wise-man* telleth us, *Riches and honour are with her, yea durable riches, and rightteousness: Length of days are in her right hand, and in her left hand riches and honour are with her, yea durable riches, and righteousness: bring thee to honour, when thou dost embrace her; she shall give to thine head an ornament of grace; a crown of glory shall she deliver to thee*; In common experience, the wealth of the mind doth qualify for employments, which have good recompenses annnexed to them; and neither God nor man will suffer him long to want, who is endowed with worthy accomplishments of knowledge; It was a ridiculous providence in *Nero* that if he should chance to lose his Empire, he might live by fiddling; yet his motto was good; and *Dionysius*, another Tyrant, found the benefit of it; [. . .] he that hath any good art, hath therein an estate, and land in every place; he is secured against being reduced to extremity of any misfortune: *Wisdom* (saith the *Wise-man*) *is a defence, and money is a defence; but the excellency of knowledge is, that wisdom giveth life to them that have it:* money is a defence, of which fortune may bereave us; but wisdom is beyond its attacks; being a treasure seated in a place inaccessible to external impressions.

And as a learned man cannot be destitute of substance; so he cannot want credit; having such an ornament, than which none hath a more general estimation; and which can be of low rate only among that sort of folk, to whom *Solomon* saith, *How long*, *ye simple ones, will ye love simplicity;—and fools hate knowledge?* It is that which recommendeth a man in all company, and procureth regard, every one yielding attention and acceptance to instructive, neat, apposite discourse (that which the *Scripture* calleth *acceptable, pleasant, gracious words*) men think themselves obliged thereby, by receiving information, and satisfaction, from it; and accordingly *Every man* (saith the *Wiseman*) *shall kiss his lips, that giveth a right answer;* and—*for the grace of his lips the King shall be his friend;* and, *The words of a wise-man's mouth are gracious.* It is that an eminency wherein purchaseth lasting fame, and a life after death, in the good memory and opinion of posterity; *Many shall commend his understanding, and so long as the world endureth, it shall not be blotted out, his memorial shall not depart away, and his name shall live from generation to generation.* A fame no less great, and far more innocent, than acts of chivalry and Martial prowess; for is not *Aristotle* as renowned for teaching the World with his Pen, as *Alexander* for conquering it with his Sword; is not one far oftener mentioned, than the other; do not men hold themselves much more obliged to the learning of the Philosopher, than to the valour of the Warrior? Indeed the fame of all others is indebted to the pains of the Scholar, and could not subsist but with and by his fame, *Dignum laude virum Musa vetat mori*; learning consecrateth it self and its subject together, to immortal remembrance.

It is a calling that fitteth a man for all conditions and fortunes; so that he can enjoy prosperity with moderation, and sustain adversity with comfort; He that loveth a Book will never want a faithful friend, a wholesome counsellor, a cheerful companion, an effectual comforter. By study, by reading, by thinking one may innocently divert, and pleasantly entertain himself, as in all weathers, so in all fortunes.

In fine, it is a calling, which *Solomon*, who had curiously observed, and exactly compared and scanned by reason and by experience all other occupations and ways of life, did prefer above all others; and we may presume would sooner have parted with his royal state, than with his learning; for *Wisdom* (saith he) *is the principal thing, therefore get wisdom, and with all thy getting get understanding;* and *Then I saw* (then, that is after a serious disquisition and discussion of things, I saw) *that wisdom exceedeth folly* (that is, knowledge excelleth ignorance) *as light excelleth darkness.*

These things and much more may be said of learning in general; but if more distinctly we survey each part and each object of it, we shall find, that each doth yield considerable emoluments, and delights; benefit to our soul, advantage to our life, satisfaction to our mind.

The observation of things, and collection of experiments how doth it enrich the mind with *Ideas*, and breed a kind of familiar acquaintance with all things, so that nothing doth surprise us, or strike our mind with astonishment and admiration? and if our *eye be not satisfied with seeing, nor our ear filled with hearing*, how much less is our mind satiated with the pleasures of speculating and observing that immense variety of objects subject to its view?

The exercise of our mind in rational discursiveness, about things, in quest of truth; canvassing questions, examining arguments for and against; how greatly doth it better us, fortifying our natural parts, enabling us to fix our thoughts on objects without roving, enuring us to weigh and resolve, and judge well about matters proposed; preserving us from being easily abused by captious fallacies, gulled by specious pretences, tossed about with every doubt or objection started before us?

Invention of any kind (in discerning the causes of abstruse effects, in resolving hard problems, in demonstrating theorems, in framing composures of witty description, or forcible persuasion) how much doth it exceed the pleasure of hunting for any game, or of combatting for any victory? do any man's children so much please him, as these creatures of his brain?

The reading of Books what is it, but conversing with the wisest men of all ages, and all countries, who thereby communicate to us their most deliberate thoughts, choicest notions, and best inventions, couched in good expression, and digested in exact method.

And as to the particular matters or objects of study, all have their use and pleasure. I shall only touch them.

The very initial studies of *Tongues* and *Grammatical* Literature are very profitable and necessary, as the inlets to knowledge, whereby we are enabled to understand wise men speaking their sense in their own terms and lively strain; whereby especially we are assisted to drink sacred knowledge out of the fountains, the divine Oracles.

Luther would not part with a little *Hebrew* he had for all the *Turkish* Empire.

Rhetoric, or the part of conveying our thought to others by speech with advantages of clearness, force and elegancy, so as to instruct, to persuade, to delight the auditors; of how great benefit is it, if it be well used? how much may it conduce to the service of God, and edification of men? what hath been a more effectual instrument of doing good, and working wonders not only in the World, but in the Church? how many souls have been converted from error, vanity and vice to truth, soberness and virtue, by an eloquent *Apollos*, a *Basil*, a *Chrysostome*?

The perusal of *History*, how pleasant illumination of mind, how useful direction of life, how spritely incentives to virtue doth it afford? how doth it supply the room of experience, and furnish us with prudence at the expense of others; informing us about the ways of action, and the consequences thereof by examples, without our own danger or trouble? how may it instruct and encourage us in piety, while therein we trace the paths of God in men, or observe the methods of divine providence, how the Lord and Judge of the World in due season protecteth, prospereth, blesseth, rewardeth innocence and integrity; how he crosseth, defeateth, blasteth, curseth, punisheth iniquity and outrage; managing things with admirable temper of wisdom to the good of mankind, and advancement of his own glory?

The *Mathematical* Sciences, how pleasant is the speculation of them to the mind, how useful is the practice to common life? how do they whet and excite the mind? how do they inure it to strict reasoning, and patient meditation?

Natural Philosophy, the contemplation of this great Theatre, or visible system presented before us; observing the various appearances therein, and inquiring into their causes; reflecting on the order, connection, and harmony of things; considering their original source, and their final design; how doth it enlarge our minds, and advance them above vulgar amusements, and the admiration of those petty things, about which men cark and bicker? how may it serve to work in us pious affections of admiration, reverence and love toward our great Creator, whose *eternal divinity is clearly seen*, whose *glory is declared*, whose transcendent perfections, and attributes of immense power, wisdom and goodness are conspicuously displayed, whose particular kindness toward us men doth evidently shine in those his works of nature?

The study of *Moral Philosophy* how exceedingly beneficial may it be to us, suggesting to us the dictates of reason concerning the nature and faculties of our soul, the chief good and end of our life, the way and means of attaining happiness, the best rules and methods of practice; the distinctions between good and evil; the nature of each virtue, and motives to embrace it; the rank wherein we stand in the World, and the duties proper to our relations; by rightly understanding and estimating which things we may know how to behave our selves decently and soberly toward our selves, justly and prudently toward our neighbours; we may learn to correct our inclinations, to regulate our appetites, to moderate our passions, to govern our actions, to conduct and wield all our practice well in prosecution of our end; so as to enjoy our being and conveniences of life in constant quiet and peace, with tranquillity and satisfaction of mind?

But especially the study of *Theology* how numberless unexpressible advantages doth it yield? for

It enlighteneth our minds with the best knowledge concerning the most high and worthy objects, in order to the most happy end, with the firmest assurance.

It certainly and perfectly doth inform us concerning the nature and attributes, the will and intentions, the works and providence of God.

It fully declareth to us our own nature, our original, our designed end, our whole duty, our certain way of attaining eternal life, and felicity.

It exactly teacheth us how we should demean our selves in all respects, piously toward God, justly and charitably toward our neighbour, soberly toward our selves; without blame in the World, with satisfaction of our conscience, with assured hope of blessed rewards.

It proposeth those encouragements, and exhibiteth assurances of those helps, which serve potently to engage us in all good practice.

It setteth before us a most complete and lively pattern of all goodness; apt most clearly to direct, most strongly to excite, most obligingly to engage us thereto; especially instructing and inclining to the practice of the most high and hard duties, meekness, humility, patience, self-denial, contempt of all worldly vanities.

It discovereth those sublime mysteries, and stupendous wonders of grace, whereby God hath demonstrated an incomprehensible kindness to mankind, and our obligation to correspondent gratitude.

It representeth manifold arguments and incentives to love God with most intense affection, to confide in him with most firm assurance, to delight in him continually *with joy unspeakable*; which are the noblest, the sweetest, the happiest operations of our soul.

It reareth our hearts from vain thoughts, and mean desires concerning these poor, transitory, earthly things to contemplations, affections, and hopes toward objects most excellent, eternal and celestial.

It engageth us to study the Book of God, the Book of Books, the richest mine of most excellent knowledge, containing infallible Oracles of truth, and heavenly rules of life; *which are able to make us wise to salvation, and perfect to every good work.*

And how can we otherwise be so well employed, as in meditation about such things? what occupation doth nearer approach to that of the blessed Angels? what Heaven is there upon Earth, like to that of constantly feasting our minds and hearts in the contemplation of such objects? Especially considering that this study doth not only yield private benefit to our selves, in forwarding our own salvation, but enableth us by our guidance and encouragement to promote the eternal welfare of others, and by our endeavours to people Heaven; according to that exhortation of St. *Paul* pressing on *Timothy* this study with diligence; *Meditate upon these things; give thy self wholly to them, that thy profiting may appear to all; take heed unto thy self, and unto the doctrine, continue in them; for in doing this, thou shalt both save thy self, and them that hear thee.*

So considerable is each part of learning, so extremely profitable are some parts of it; Indeed the skill of any liberal art is valuable, as a handsome ornament, as an harmless divertisement, as an useful instrument upon occasions; as preferable to all other accomplishments and advantages of person or fortune (beauty, strength, wealth, power, or the like;) for who would not purchase any kind of such knowledge at any rate; who would sell it for any price; who would not choose rather to be deformed or impotent in his body, than to have a mis-shapen and weak mind; to have rather a lank purse, than an empty brain; to have no title at all, than no worth to bear it out? if any would, he is not of *Solomon*'s mind; for of wisdom (by which he meaneth a comprehension of all knowledge, divine and human; into which the knowledge of natural things, of Mathematics, of Poetry, are reckoned ingredients) he saith, *The merchandise of it is better than the merchandise of silver, and the gain thereof than fine gold; she is more precious than rubies, and all the things thou canst desire, are not to be compared unto her: Her fruit is better than gold, yea than fine gold; and her revenue than choice silver.*

Now then, considering all these advantages of our calling, if we by our negligence or sluggishness therein do lose them, are we not very ungrateful to God, who gave them, as with a gracious intent for our good, so with expectation that we should improve them to his service? If God had allotted to us the calling of Rustics, or of Artificers, we had been impious in not diligently following it; but we are abominably ungrateful in neglecting this most incomparably excellent vocation.

Are we not extremely defective to ourselves, if indulging a wretched humour of laziness we will not enjoy those sweet pleasures, nor embrace those great profits to which God in mercy calleth us?

If *Solomon* said true, *He that getteth wisdom, loveth his own soul, he that keepeth understanding shall find good*; how little friends are we to our selves, how neglectful of our own welfare, by not using the means of getting wisdom?

The heart of him that hath understanding, seeketh knowledge, saith *Solomon*; what a fool then is he that shunneth it? who, though it be his way, and his special duty to seek it, yet neglecteth it; choosing rather to do nothing, or to do worse.

And do we not deserve great blame, displeasure and disgrace from mankind, if having such opportunities of qualifying our selves to do good, and serve the public, we by our idleness render our selves worthless and useless?

How, being slothful in our business, can we answer for our violating the wills, for abusing the goodness, for perverting the charity and bounty of our worthy Founders and Benefactors, who gave us the good things we enjoy, not to maintain us in idleness, but for supports and encouragements of our industry? how can we excuse our selves from dishonesty, and perfidious dealing, seeing that we are admitted to these enjoyments under condition, and upon confidence (confirmed by our free promises, and most solemn engagements) of using them according to their pious intent, that is in a diligent prosecution of our studies, in order to the service of God, and of the public?

Let every Scholar, when he mispendeth an hour, or sluggeth on his bed but imagine, that he heareth the voice of those glorious Kings, or Venerable Prelates, or worthy Gentlemen, complaining thus, and rating him; why, sluggard, dost thou against my will possess my estate? why dost thou presume to occupy the place due to an industrious person? why dost thou forget, or despise thy obligations to my kindness? thou art an usurper, a robber, or a purloiner of my goods, which I never intended for such as thee; I challenge thee of wrong to my self, and of sacrilege toward my God, to whose service I devoted those his gifts to me.

How reproachful will it be to us, if that expostulation may concern us, *Wherefore is there a price in the hand of a fool to get wisdom, seeing he hath no heart to it?*

If to be a dunce, or a bungler in any profession be shameful, how much more ignominious, and infamous to a Scholar to be such? from whom all men expect, that he should excel in intellectual abilities; and be able to help others by his instruction and advice.

Nothing surely would more grate on the heart of one, that hath a spark of ingenuity, of modesty, of generous good nature, than to be liable to such an imputation.

To avoid it therefore (together with all the guilt, and all the mischiefs attending on sloth) let each of us in God's name, carefully mind his business; And let the grace and blessing of God prosper you therein. *Amen.*

Robert South

SOUTH WAS born in Hackney in 1634. He was the son of a London merchant. He went to Westminster School and was there when Charles I was beheaded outside the Banqueting Hall a few hundred yards away. There is a story that he mentioned the King's name in the school's Latin prayers on that very day. It is certain that the scholars will have heard the great shout or groan of the crowd. In 1651 South went on to Christ Church, Oxford. He is said to have shown some Presbyterian leanings there but he certainly received episcopal ordination in 1658, when it could not be done openly. He travelled on the Continent.

His public career began with the Restoration, and he sided uncompromisingly, and some might say at times intemperately, with the victorious party. He became Public Orator at Oxford, chaplain to Clarendon and a prebendary of Westminster; on Clarendon's fall he became chaplain to the Duke of York. In 1670 he was made a canon of Christ Church and in 1676 went to Poland as chaplain to the ambassador. In 1678 he became rector of Islip and he was chaplain to Charles II. In 1689 he hesitated, then took the oath to William and Mary, but he is said to have declined a bishopric vacated by a Non-Juror. In the years immediately following he became involved—again in no very temperate spirit—in controversy with Sherlock and others about the nature of the Trinity—a subject which Swift later summed up, with trenchant orthodoxy, by saying that God commanded us 'to believe a Fact that we do not understand'. In Anne's reign, South, naturally enough, took part in the Sacheverell affair, but he ended with dignity, refusing in 1713 to become Bishop of Rochester on the grounds that 'such a chair would be too uneasy for an old infirm man to sit in'. He died in 1716.

South was a man of learning, and if he could get head over heels in controversy he could also stop to observe. In his mission to Poland he noted the beneficial effect of public baths, 'from the use of which, in all probability, it happens that the Polish children seldom break out in their head or face, and that not one of a thousand is distorted, crooked, or ill-shaped, as in other countries.' He had some fairly lucrative preferments, but he was generous and gave away a large part of the proceeds and his benefactions included provision for the education of the children of parishioners as well as church repairs out of his own pocket. He was often plain-spoken to the point of brutality, in the pulpit as elsewhere. He had a ready wit, and apparently found it hard to refrain from using it. He had all the talents required to make a churchman respected at the court of Charles II —an ambiguous testimonial, no doubt.

A Discourse against Long and Extempore Prayers: in Behalf of the Liturgy of the Church of England
Eccles. 5:2.
Be not rash with thy mouth, and let not thine heart be hasty to utter any thing before God: for God is in heaven, and thou upon earth: therefore let thy words be few.

OTHERS MIGHT have made other applications of this text against South himself. For South, the text pointed straight at the Puritans. The Prayer Book had become a centre of controversy immediately after the Restoration. During the troubles its use had been, not merely discouraged, but forbidden. There had been widespread persecution of the Anglican clergy and essential elements of church order, as understood through the centuries, had been eliminated, so far as public practice was concerned. The theological and the political quarrels were intertwined, and each contributed its peculiar bitterness to the other. It was inevitable that, after the Restoration, there should have been a sharp reaction. The Savoy Conference, of twelve bishops and twelve presbyterian divines, who met in 1661 under royal warrant to review the Prayer Book, did not reach a common mind and the outcome was a book which went none of the way to meet Puritan objections and, ultimately, the ejection of perhaps two thousand Presbyterian ministers. South was not the man to show the restraint which this situation required. He was apt to denounce dissenters as 'too great hypocrites to be martyrs' and among the many benefactions in his will he included penalty clauses for legatees who should give them any countenance.

The sermon which follows shows no very eirenic spirit, but it contains a good deal of solid argument in favour of a compendious and well-set-out liturgy. It is the second of two sermons South preached on this text. In the first, which is summarized at the beginning of this one, South had spoken bitterly against the emotionalism and declamation which characterized the worse sort of Puritan prayer. He had said that we could not 'word the great Creator . . . out of the steady purposes of his will, by all the vehemence and loudness of our petitions.' Warming to his subject, he had noted that in the psalms of David there was 'no mention at all of distortion of face, sanctified grimace, solemn wink, or foaming at the mouth'. But he had also argued seriously that 'whatsoever gives the soul scope and liberty to exercise . . . affection and devotion . . . does most effectually help and enlarge the spirit of prayer'; and that 'a set form leaves the soul wholly free' to conduct itself as the Spirit would. It is a point worth reflection, and which needed to be made against those who were given to identifying the operation of the Spirit with whatever came out of their mouths. Really the debate is about the function and use of words, and has applications beyond the liturgy.

The second sermon, here reproduced, develops the critique of verbal manifestations. In his praise of brevity and succinctness South is incontrovertibly on the right side of the argument, and incidentally close to his text. A 'few, close, home, and significant words' are best. A 'mutual communication of our thoughts' in such language is 'the next approach to intuition, and the nearest imitation of the converse of *blessed spirits made perfect*, that our condition in this world can possibly raise us to'. This part of the sermons contains some of the best fundamental literary criticism of the seventeenth century—and matter to which our wordy and windy age could well give attention. 'In God's laws, the words are few, the sense vast and infinite'; even 'in any art or science, the smallest and most compendious' books are the best. Or, in a summary Ezra Pound would have approved: 'In brevity of speech, a man does not so much speak words, as things'.

There is no doubt that South had thought long and deeply about his subject, and in something better than the partisan spirit which pushes so much of what he says askew. The latter part of the sermon—which also contains some stinging comparisons between the Puritans and the Pharisees—deals more specifically with the liturgy and there are some good remarks about the responses, which give the congregation an active part in the service and the use of which 'makes and denominates our liturgy truly and properly a book of common prayer.'

I FORMERLY began to discourse upon these words, and observed in them these three things.

1. That whosoever appears in the house of God, and particularly in the way of prayer, ought to reckon himself, in a more especial manner, placed in the sight and presence of God: And,

2. That the vast and infinite distance between God and him, ought to create in him all imaginable awe and reverence in such his addresses to God.

3. And *lastly*; That this reverence required of him, is to consist in a serious preparation of his thoughts, and a sober government of his expressions: Neither is his *mouth to be rash, nor his heart to be hasty in uttering any thing before God.*

These three things I showed were evidently contained in the words, and did as evidently contain the whole sense of them. But I gathered them all into this one proposition; namely,

That premeditation of thought, and brevity of expression, are the great ingredients of that reverence that is required to a pious, acceptable, and devout prayer.

The first of these, which is *premeditation of thought*, I then fully treated of, and dispatched; and shall now proceed to the other, which is a *pertinent brevity of expression; Therefore let thy words be few*.

Concerning which, we shall observe, first, in general, that to be able to express our minds briefly and fully too, is absolutely the greatest perfection and commendation that speech is capable of; such a mutual communication of our thoughts, being (as I may so speak) the next approach to *intuition*; and the nearest imitation of the converse of blessed *spirits made perfect*, that our condition in this world can possibly raise us to. Certainly the greatest and the wisest conceptions that ever issued from the mind of men, have been couched under, and delivered in a few, close, home, and significant words.

But to derive the credit of this way of speaking much higher, and from an example infinitely greater, than the greatest human wisdom, was it not authorized, and ennobled by God himself in his making of the world? Was not the work of all the six days transacted in so many words? There was no circumlocution, or amplification, in the case; which makes the rhetorician *Longinus*, in his book *of the loftiness of speech*, so much admire the height and grandeur of *Moses's* style in his first chapter of *Genesis*, [. . .] *The lawgiver of the* Jews (says he, meaning *Moses*) *was no ordinary man;* [. . .] because (says he) he set forth the divine power suitably to the majesty and greatness of it. But how did he this? Why, [. . .] For that (*says he*) in the very entrance of his laws, he gives us this short and present account of the whole creation: God said, *Let there be light, and there was light; Let there be an earth, a sea, and a firmament, and there was so*. So that all this high elogy and encomium given by this heathen of *Moses*, sprang only from the majestic brevity of this one expression; an expression so suited to the greatness of a Creator, and so expressive of his boundless, creative power, as a power infinitely above all control, or possibility of finding the least obstacle of delay, in achieving its mightiest and most stupendous works. Heaven, and earth, and all the host of both (as it were) dropped from his mouth; and nature itself was but the product of a word; a word not designed to express, but to constitute and give a being; and not so much the representation, as the cause of what it signified.

This was God's way of speaking in his first forming of the universe: And was it not so, in the next grand instance of his power, his governing of it too? For are not the great instruments of government, his laws, drawn up and digested into a few sentences? The whole body of them containing but ten commandments, and some of those commandments not so many words? Nay, and have we not these also brought into yet a narrower compass by him, who best understood them? *Thou shalt love the Lord thy God with all thy heart, and with all thy soul, and thy neighbour as thyself*. Precepts, nothing like the tedious, endless, confuted trash of human laws; laws so numerous, that they not only exceed men's practice, but also surpass their arithmetic; and so voluminous, that no mortal head, nor shoulders neither, must ever pretend themselves able to *bear* them. In God's laws the words are few, the sense vast and infinite. In human laws, you shall be sure to have words enough; but, for the most part, to discern the sense and reason of them, you had need read them with a microscope.

And thus having shown, how the Almighty utters himself, when he speaks, and that upon the greatest occasions; let us now descend from heaven to earth, from God to man, and show, that it is no presumption for us to conform our words, as well as our actions, to the supreme pattern, and, according to our poor measures, to imitate the wisdom that we adore. And for this, has it not been noted by the best observers, and the ablest judges, both of things and persons, that the wisdom of any people or nation has been most seen in the proverbs and short sayings commonly received amongst them? And what is a proverb, but the experience and observation of several ages, gathered and summed up into one expression? The scripture vouches *Solomon* for the *wisest of men*, and they are his *Proverbs* that prove him so. The seven wise men of *Greece*, so famous for their wisdom all the world over, acquired all that fame each of them, by a single sentence, consisting of two or three words. And γνῶθι σεαυτόν still lives and flourishes in the mouths of all, while many vast volumes are extinct, and sunk into dust and utter oblivion. And then for books, we shall generally find, that the most excellent, in any art or science, have been still the smallest, and most compendious: And this not without ground; for it is an argument that the author was a master of what he wrote; and had a clear notion, and a full comprehension of the subject before him. For the *reason* of things lies in a little compass, if the mind could at any time be so happy as to light upon it. Most of the writings and discourses in the world, are but illustration and rhetoric, which signifies as much as nothing to a mind eager in pursuit after the causes and philosophical truth of things. It is the work of fancy to *enlarge*, but of judgment to *shorten* and *contract*; and therefore this must needs be as far above the other, as judgment is a greater and a nobler faculty than fancy or imagination. All philosophy is reduced to a few principles, and those principles comprised in a few propositions. And as the whole structure of *speculation* rests upon three or four axioms, or maxims; so that of practice also bears upon a very small number of rules. And surely, there was never yet any *rule* or *maxim* that filled a volume, or took up a week's time to be got by heart. No; these are the *apices rerum*, the tops and sums, the very spirit and life of things extracted and abridged; just as all the lines drawn from the vastest circumference, do at length meet and unite in the smallest of things, a *point*; and it is but a very little piece of wood, with which a true artist will measure all the timber in the world. The truth is, there could be no such thing as art or science, could not the mind of man gather the general natures of things out of the numberless heap of particulars, and then bind them up into such short aphorisms or propositions; that so they may be made portable to the memory, and thereby become ready and at hand for the judgment to apply, and make use of, as there shall be occasion.

In fine, brevity and succinctness of speech, is that, which in philosophy or speculation we call *maxim*, and first principle; in the counsels and resolves of practical wisdom, and the deep mysteries of religion, *oracle*; and lastly, in matters of wit, and the finenesses of imagination, *epigram*. All of them severally, and in their kinds the greatest, and the noblest things that the mind of man can show the force and dexterity of its faculties in.

And now, if this be the highest excellency, and perfection of speech, in all other things, can we assign any true, solid reason, why it should not be so likewise in prayer? Nay, is there not rather the clearest reason imaginable, why it should be much more so? Since most of the forementioned things are but addresses to an human understanding, which may need as many words as may fill a volume, to make it understand the truth of one line. Whereas prayer is an address to that Eternal Mind, which (as we have shown before) such as rationally invocate, pretend not to inform. Nevertheless, since the nature of man is such, that while we are yet in the body, our reverence and worship of God must of necessity proceed in some analogy to the reverence, that we show to the grandees of this world, we will here see, what the judgment of all wise men is, concerning fewness of words, when we appear as suppliants before our earthly superiors; and we shall find, that they generally allow it to import these three things: 1. *Modesty*. 2. *Discretion*; And 3. Height of *respect to the person addressed to*. And first, for *Modesty*. Modesty is a kind of shame or bashfulness, proceeding from the sense a man has of his own defects, compared with the perfections of him whom he comes before. And that which is modesty towards men, is worship and devotion towards God. It is a virtue, that makes a man unwilling to be seen, and fearful to be heard; and yet, for that very cause, never fails to make him, both seen with favour, and heard with attention. It loves not many words, nor indeed needs them. For modesty addressing to any one of a generous worth and honour, is sure to have that man's honour for its advocate, and his generosity for its intercessor. And how then is it possible for such a virtue to run out into words? Loquacity storms the ear, but modesty takes the heart; that is troublesome, this gentle, but irresistible. Much speaking is always the effect of confidence; and confidence still presupposes, and springs from the persuasion that a man has of his own worth: Both of them, certainly, very unfit qualifications for a petitioner.

2. The second thing that naturally shows itself in paucity of words, is *discretion*; and particularly, that prime and eminent part of it, that consists in a care of offending: Which *Solomon*

assures us, that in much speaking, it is hardly possible for us to avoid: In *Prov. x. 19. In the multitude of words* (says he) *there wanteth not sin.* It requiring no ordinary skill for a man to make his tongue run by rule; and, at the same time, to give it both its lesson and its liberty too. For seldom or never is there much spoke, but something or other had better been not spoke; there being nothing that the mind of man is so apt to kindle, and take distaste at, as at words: And therefore, whensoever any one comes to prefer a suit to another, no doubt, the fewer of them the better; since, where so very little is said, it is sure to be either candidly *accepted*, or, which is next, easily *excused*: But, at the same time, to petition, and to provoke too, is certainly very preposterous.

3. The third thing, that *brevity of speech* commends itself by, in all petitionary addresses, is a peculiar respect to the person addressed to: For, whosoever petitions his superior, in such a manner, does, by his very so doing, confess him better able to understand, than he himself can be to express his own case. He owns him, as a patron, of a preventing judgment and goodness, and, upon that account, able, not only to answer, but also to anticipate his requests. For, according to the most natural interpretation of things, this is to ascribe to him a sagacity so quick and piercing, that it were presumption to inform; and a benignity so great, that it were needless to importune him. And can there be a greater and more winning deference to a superior, than to treat him under such a character? Or, can any thing be imagined so naturally fit and efficacious, both to enforce the petition, and to endear the petitioner? A short petition to a great man, is not only a suit to him for his favour, but also a panegyric upon his parts.

And thus I have given you the three commendatory qualifications of brevity of speech, in our applications to the great ones of the world. Concerning which, as I showed before, that it was impossible for us to form our addresses, even to God himself, but with some proportion and resemblance to those that we make to our fellow mortals, in a condition much above us; so it is certain, that whatsoever the general judgment and consent of mankind allows to be expressive and declarative of our honour to those, must (only with due allowance of the difference of the object) as really and properly declare and signify that honour and adoration that is due from us to the great God. And, consequently, what we have said for brevity of speech, with respect to the former, ought equally to conclude for it, with relation to him too.

But to argue more immediately and directly to the point before us: I shall now produce five arguments, enforcing brevity, and cashiering all prolixity of speech, with peculiar reference to our addresses to God.

1. And the first argument shall be taken from this consideration: *That there is no reason allegeable for the Use of length, or prolixity of speech, that is at all applicable to prayer.* For, whosoever uses multiplicity of words, or length of discourse, must of necessity do it for one of these three purposes; either to *inform*, or *persuade*; or lastly, to *weary* and *overcome* the person, whom he directs his discourse to. But the very first foundation of what I had to say upon this subject, was laid by me, in demonstrating, that prayer could not possibly prevail with God, any of these three ways. Forasmuch as being omniscient, he could not be informed; and, being void of passion, or affections, he could not be persuaded; and lastly, being omnipotent, and infinitely great, he could not, by any importunity, be wearied, or overcome. And, if so, what use then can there be of rhetoric, harangue, or multitude of words in prayer? For, if they should be designed for information, must it not be infinitely sottish and unreasonable, to go about to inform him, who can be ignorant of nothing? Or, to persuade him, whose unchangeable nature makes it impossible for him to be moved, or wrought upon? Or, lastly, by long and much speaking, to think to weary him out, whose infinite power, all the strength of men and angels, and the whole world put together, is not able to encounter, or stand before? So that the truth is, by loquacity and prolixity of prayer, a man does really and indeed (whether he thinks so or no) rob God of the honour of those three great attributes, and neither treats him as a person omniscient, or unchangeable, or omnipotent. For, on the other side, all the usefulness of long speech in human converse, is founded only upon the defects and imperfections of human nature. For he whose knowledge is at best but limited, and whose intellect, both in apprehending and judging, proceeds by a small diminutive light, cannot but receive an additional light, by the conceptions of another man, clearly and plainly expressed, and by such expression conveyed to his apprehension. And he again, whose nature subjects him to want and weakness, and consequently to hopes and fears, cannot but be moved this way, or that way, according as objects

suitable to those passions, shall be dexterously represented, and set before his imagination, by the arts of speaking; which is that that we call *persuasion*. And lastly, he whose soul and body receive their activity from, and perform all their functions by, the meditation of the spirits, which ebb and flow, consume, and are renewed again, cannot but find himself very uneasy upon any tedious, verbose application made to him: And that sometimes to such a degree, that through mere fatigue, and even against judgment and interest both, a man shall surrender himself as a conquered person, to the over-bearing vehemence of such solicitations: For when they ply him so fast, and pour in upon him so thick, they cannot but wear and waste the spirits, as unequal to so pertinacious a charge; and this is properly to weary a man. But now all weariness, we know, presupposes weakness; and consequently every long, importunate, wearisome petition is truly and properly a force upon him, that is pursued with it; it is a following blow after blow upon the mind and affections, and may, for the time, pass for real, though short persecution.

This is the state and condition of human nature; and prolixity or importunity of speech is still the great engine to attack it by, either in its *blind* or *weak* side: And I think I may venture to affirm, that it is seldom that any man is prevailed upon by words, but upon a true and philosophical estimate of the whole matter, he is either *deceived* or *wearied*, before he is so, and parts with the thing desired of him upon the very same terms, that either a child parts with a jewel for an apple, or a man parts with his sword, when it is forcibly wrested, or took from him. And that he who obtains what he has been rhetorically or importunately begging for, goes away really a conqueror, and triumphantly carrying off the spoils of his neighbour's understanding, or his will; baffling the former, or wearying the latter, into a grant of his restless petitions.

And now, if this be the case, when any one comes with a tedious, long-winded harangue to God, may not God properly answer him with those words in *Psal. 1.21. Surely thou thinkest I am altogether such an one as thyself?* And perhaps, upon a due and rational examination of all the follies and indecencies that men are apt to be guilty of in prayer, they will be all found resolvable into this one thing, as the true and sole cause of them; namely, *That men, when they pray, take God to be such an one as themselves*; and so treat him accordingly: The malignity and mischief of which gross mistake may reach farther than possibly at first they can well be aware of. For if it be idolatry to pray to God the Father, represented under the shape of a man, can it be at all better to pray to him as represented under the weakness of a man? Nay, if the misrepresentation of the object makes the idolatry, certainly by how much the worse, and more scandalous the misrepresentation is, by so much the grosser and more intolerable must be the idolatry. To confirm which, we may add this consideration, that Christ himself, even now in his glorified estate in heaven, wears the body, and consequently the shape, of a man, though he is far from any of his infirmities or imperfections: And therefore, no doubt, to represent God to ourselves under these latter, must needs be more absurd and irreligious, than to represent him under the former. But to one particular of the preceding discourse some may reply and object; that if God's omniscience, by rendering it impossible for him to be informed, be a sufficient reason against prolixity, or length of prayer; it will follow, that it is equally a reason against the using any words at all in prayer; since the proper use of words is to inform the person whom we speak to; and consequently, where information is impossible, words must needs be useless and superfluous.

To which I answer, First by concession, that if the *sole* use of words, or speech, were to *inform the person whom we speak to*, the consequence would be firm and good, and equally conclude against the use of any words at all in prayer. But therefore, in the second place, I deny information to be the sole and adequate use of words or speech, or indeed any use of them at all, when either the person spoken to needs not to be informed, and withal is known not to need it, as sometimes it falls out with men; or, when he is incapable of being informed, as it is always with God. But the proper use of words, whensoever we speak to God in prayer, is thereby to pay him *honour* and *obedience*. God having, by an express precept, enjoined us the use of words in prayer, commanding us in *Psal. l. 15.* and many other Scriptures, *to call upon him*: and in *Luke xi. 21. When we pray, to say, Our Father*, &c. But nowhere has he commanded us to do this with prolixity, or multiplicity of words. And though it must be confessed, that we may sometimes answer this command of calling upon *God*, and saying, *Our Father*, &c. by mental or inward prayer; yet since these words, in their first and most proper signification, import a vocal address, there is no doubt, but the direct design of the command is to enjoin this also, wheresoever there is ability and power to perform it. So that we see here the necessity of *vocal prayer*, founded upon the authority of a divine precept; whereas, for *long prolix prayer*, no such precept can be produced; and consequently, the divine omniscience may be a sufficient reason against multiplicity of words in prayer, and yet conclude nothing simply or absolutely against the bare use of them. Nevertheless, that we may not seem to allege bare command, unseconded by reason, (which yet, in the divine commands, it is impossible to do) there is this great reason for, and use of words in prayer, without the least pretence of informing the person whom we pray to; and that is, to *acknowledge and own those wants* before God, that we supplicate for a relief of. It being very proper and rational to own and acknowledge a thing even to him, who knew it before: Forasmuch as this is so far from offering to communicate, or make known to him the thing so acknowledged, that it rather presupposes in him an antecedent knowledge of it, and comes in only as a subsequent assent and subscription to the reality and truth of such a knowledge. For to *acknowledge* a thing in the first sense of the word, does by no means signify a design of notifying that thing to another, but is truly and properly a man's passing sentence upon himself, and his own condition: there being no reason in the world for a man to expect that God should relieve and supply those wants, that he himself will not own or take notice of; any more than for a man to hope for a pardon of those sins, that he cannot find in his heart to confess. And yet (I suppose) no man in his right senses does, or can imagine, that God is informed, or brought to the knowledge of those sins, by any such confession.

And so much for the clearing of this objection; and, in the whole, for the first argument produced by us, *for brevity, and against prolixity* of prayer; namely, *That all the reasons that can be assigned for prolixity of speech in our converse with men, cease, and become no reasons for it at all, when we are to speak or pray to God.*

2. The second argument for *paucity of words* in prayer, shall be taken from the *paucity* of *those things* that are necessary to be prayed for. And surely, where few things are necessary, few words should be sufficient; for where the *matter* is not commensurate to the words, all speaking is but tautology; that being truly and really tautology, where the same thing is repeated though under never so much variety of expression; as it is but the same man still, though he appears every day, or every hour, in a new and different suit of clothes.

The adequate subject of our prayers (I showed at first) comprehended in it *things of necessity*, and *things of charity*. As to the first of which, I know nothing absolutely necessary, but *grace* here, and *glory* hereafter. And for the other, we know what the apostle says, *1 Tim.vi.8. Having food and raiment, let us be therewith content.* Nature is satisfied with a little, and Grace with less. And now, if the matter of our prayers lies within so narrow a compass, why should the dress and outside of them spread and diffuse itself into so wide and disproportioned a largeness? By reason of which, our words will be forced to hang loose and light, without any matter to support them; much after the same rate, that it is said to be in transubstantiation; where *accidents* are left in the lurch by their proper *subject*, that gives them the slip, and so leaves those poor slender beings to uphold and shift for themselves.

In brevity of speech, a man does not so much speak words, as things; things in their precise and naked truth, and stripped of their rhetorical mask, and their fallacious gloss: And therefore, in *Athens* they circumscribed the pleadings of their orators by a strict law, cutting off prologues and epilogues, and commanding them to an immediate representation of the case, by an impartial and succinct declaration of mere matter of fact. And this was indeed, to speak things fit for a judge to hear, because it argued the pleader also a judge of what was fit for him to speak.

And now why should not this be both decency and devotion too, when we come to plead for our poor souls before the great Tribunal of heaven? It was the saying of *Solomon, A word to the wise*; and if so, certainly there can be no necessity of many words to Him, who is Wisdom itself. For, can any man think, that God delights to hear him make speeches, and to show his parts, (as the word is) or to jumble a multitude of misapplied Scripture-sentences together, interlarded with a frequent, nauseous repetition of *Ah Lord!* which some call *exercising their gifts*, but with a greater exercise of their hearers' patience? Nay, does not he present his Maker not only with a more decent, but also more free and liberal oblation, who tenders him much in a little, and brings him his whole heart and soul wrapped up in three or four words, than he who with full mouth, and loud lungs, sends up whole vollies of articulate breath to the throne of grace? For neither in the esteem of God, or man, ought multitude of words to pass for any more: In the present case, no doubt, God accounts and accepts of the former, as infinitely a more valuable offering than the latter. As that subject pays his prince a much nobler and more acceptable tribute, who tenders him a purse of gold, than he who brings him a whole cart-load of farthings; in which there is weight without worth, and number without account.

3. The third argument for brevity, or contractedness of speech in prayer, shall be taken from the very nature and condition of the person who prays; which makes it impossible for him to keep up the same fervour and attention in a long prayer, that he may in a short. For, as I first observed that the mind of man cannot with the same force and vigour attend two several objects at the same time; so neither can it with the same force and earnestness exert itself upon one and the same object for any long time. Great intention of mind spending the spirits too fast, to continue its first freshness and agility long. For while the soul is a retainer to the elements, and a sojourner in the body, it must be content to submit its own quickness and spirituality to the dullness of its vehicle, and to comply with the pace of its inferior companion. Just like a man shut up in a coach; who, while he is so, must be willing to go no faster than the motion of the coach will carry him. He who does all by the help of those subtle, refined parts of matter, called spirits, must not think to persevere at the same pitch of acting, while those principles of activity flag. No man begins and ends a long journey with the same pace.

But now, when prayer has lost its due fervour and attention, (which indeed are the very vitals of it) it is but the *carcass* of a prayer; and consequently, must needs be loathsome and offensive to God: nay, though the greatest part of it should be enlivened and carried on with an actual attention; yet, if that attention fails to enliven any one part of it, the whole is but a joining of the *living* and the *dead* together; for which conjunction, the *dead* is not at all the better, but the *living* very much the worse. It is not length, nor copiousness of language, that is devotion, any more than bulk and bigness is valour, or *flesh* the measure of the *spirit*. A short sentence may be oftentimes a large and a mighty prayer. Devotion so managed, being like water in a well, where you have fulness in a little compass; which surely is much nobler, than the same carried out into many petit, creeping rivulets, with *length* and *shallowness* together. Let him who prays, bestow all that strength, fervour and attention, upon shortness and significance, that would otherwise run out, and lose itself in length and luxuriancy of speech to no purpose. Let not his tongue out-strip his heart; nor presume to carry a message to the throne of grace, while that stays behind. Let him not think to support so hard and weighty a duty with a tired, languishing, and bejaded devotion: To avoid which, let a man contract his expression, where he cannot enlarge his affection; still remembering, that nothing can be more absurd in itself, not more unacceptable to God, than for one engaged in the great work of prayer, to hold on *speaking*, after he has left off *praying*; and to keep the *lips* at work, when the *spirit* can do no more.

4. The fourth argument for shortness, or conciseness of speech in prayer, shall be drawn from this, that it is the most natural and lively way of expressing the utmost agonies and outcries of the soul to God upon a quick, pungent sense, either of a pressing necessity, or an approaching calamity; which, we know, are generally the chief occasions of prayer, and the most effectual motives to bring men upon their knees, in a vigorous application of themselves to this great duty. A person ready to sink under his wants, has neither time, nor heart, to rhetoricate, or make flourishes. No man begins a long grace, when he is ready to starve: Such an one's prayers are like the relief he needs, quick and sudden, short and immediate: He is like a man in torture upon the rack; whose pains are too acute to let his words be many; and whose desires of deliverance too impatient to delay the thing he begs for, by the manner of his begging it.

It is a common saying; *If a man does not know how to pray, let him go to sea, and that will teach him*. And we have a notable instance of what kind of prayers men are taught in that school, even in the disciples themselves, when a storm arose, and the sea raged, and the ship was ready to be cast away, in the 8th of *Matthew*. In which case, we do not find that they fell presently to harangue it about seas and winds, and that dismal face of things that must needs appear all over the devouring element at such a time: All which, and the like, might, no doubt, have been very plentiful topics of eloquence to a man, who should have looked upon these things from the shore; or discoursed of wrecks and tempests safe and warm in his parlour. But these poor wretches, who were now entering (as they thought) into the very jaws of death, struggling with the last efforts of nature, upon the sense of a departing life; and consequently, could neither speak nor think any thing low or ordinary in such a condition, presently rallied up, and discharged the whole concern of their desponding souls in that short prayer, of but three words, though much fuller, and more forcible, than one of three thousand, in the 25th verse of the forementioned chapter; *Save us, Lord, or we perish*. Death makes short work when it comes, and will teach him, who would prevent it, to make shorter. For surely no man, who thinks himself aperishing, can be at leisure to be eloquent; or judge it either sense or devotion, to begin a long prayer, when, in all likelihood, he shall conclude his life before it.

5. The fifth and last argument that I shall produce for *brevity of speech*, or *fewness of words* in prayer, shall be taken from the examples which we find in Scripture, of such as have been remarkable for *brevity*, and of such as have been noted for *prolixity of speech*, in the discharge of this duty.

1. And first for *brevity*. To omit all those notable examples, which the *Old Testament* affords us of it; and to confine ourselves only to the *New*, in which we are undoubtedly most concerned. Was not this way of praying not only warranted, but sanctified, and set above all that the will of man could possibly except against it, by that infinitely exact form of prayer, prescribed by the greatest, the holiest, and the wisest man that ever lived, even Christ himself, the Son of God, and Saviour of the world? Was it not an instance both of the truest devotion, and the fullest and most comprehensive reason, that ever proceeded from the mouth of man? And yet withal, the shortest, and most succinct model, that ever grasped all the needs and occasions of mankind, both spiritual and temporal, into so small a compass? Doubtless, had our Saviour thought fit to amplify or be prolix, *He, in whom were hid all the treasures of wisdom*, could not want matter, nor he who was himself *the word*, want variety of the fittest to have expressed his mind by. But he chose rather to contract the whole concern of both worlds into a few lines, and to unite both heaven and earth in his prayer, as he had done before in his person. And indeed one was a kind of copy or representation of the other.

So then, we see here brevity in the *rule* or *pattern*, let us see it next in the *practice*, and after that, in the *success* of prayer. And, first, we have the practice, as well as the pattern of it, in our Saviour himself; and that, in the most signal passage of his whole life, even his preparation for his approaching death. In which dolorous scene, when his whole soul was nothing but sorrow, (that great moving spring of invention and elocution) and when nature was put to its last and utmost stretch, and so had no refuge or relief but in prayer; yet even then, all his horror, agony, and distress of spirit delivers itself but in two very short sentences, in *Matth. xxvi. 39. O my Father, if it be possible, let this cup pass from me; nevertheless, not as I will, but as thou wilt.* And again, the second time, with the like brevity, and the like words. *O my Father, if this cup may not pass from me, except I drink it, thy will be done.* And lastly, the third time also, he used the same short form again; and yet in all this, he was (as we may say, without a metaphor) even praying *for life*; so far as the great business he was then about, to wit, the redemption of the world, would suffer him to pray for it. All which prayers of our Saviour, and others of like brevity, are properly such as we call *Ejaculations*; an elegant similitude from a dart, or arrow, shot, or thrown out; and such an one (we know) of a yard long, will fly farther, and strike deeper, than one of twenty.

And then, in the last place, for the success of such brief prayers; I shall give you but three instances of this, but they shall be of persons praying under the pressure of as great miseries, as human nature could well be afflicted with. And the first shall be of the Leper, *Matth. viii. 2.* or, as St. *Luke* describes him, *a man full of leprosy, who came to our Saviour, and worshipped him*; and, as St. *Luke* again has it more particularly, *fell on his face before him*, (which is the lowest and most devout of all postures of worship) *saying, Lord, if thou wilt, thou canst make me clean.* This was all his prayer: And the answer to it was, That he was immediately cleansed. The next instance shall be of the poor *blind man*, in *Luke xviii. 28.* following our Saviour with this earnest prayer: *Jesus, thou Son of David, have mercy upon me.* His whole prayer was no more: For it is said in the next *verse*, that he went on, repeating it again and again: *Jesus, thou Son of David, have mercy upon me.* And the answer he received was, that his eyes were opened, and his sight restored.

The third and last instance shall be of the *Publican*, in the same chapter of St. *Luke*; praying under a lively sense of as great a leprosy, and blindness of soul, as the other two could have of body. In the 13th verse, *he smote upon his breast, saying, God be merciful to me a sinner.* He spoke no more; though 'tis in the 10th *verse*, that he went *solemnly and purposely up to the temple to pray*: The issue and success of which prayer was, *that he went home justified*, before one of those, whom all the *Jewish* church revered as absolutely the highest and most heroic examples of piety, and most beloved favourites of heaven, in the whole world. And now, if the force and virtue of these short prayers could rise so high, as *to cleanse a leper, to give sight to the blind, and to justify a Publican*; and, if the worth of a prayer may at all be measured by the success of it, I suppose, no prayers whatsoever can do more; and, I never yet heard or read of any *long prayer* that did so much. Which brings on the other part of this our fifth and last argument, which was to be drawn from the examples of such as have been noted in scripture for prolixity or length of prayer. And of this, there are only two mentioned; *The Heathens and the Pharisees*. The first, the grand instance of *idolatry*; the other, of *hypocrisy*: But Christ forbids us the imitation of both; *when ye pray*, says our Saviour in the VIth of *Matthew, be ye not like the Heathens*; But in what? Why, in this, *that they think they shall be heard for their much speaking*, in the 7th verse. It is not the multitude, that prevails in armies, and much less in words. And then for the *Pharisees*, whom our Saviour represents as the very vilest of men, and the greatest of cheats; we have them amusing the world with pretences of a more refined devotion, while their heart was that time in their neighbour's coffers. For does not our Saviour expressly tell us, in *Luke xx.* and the two last verses, that the great tools, the hooks or engines, by which they compassed their worst, their wickedest, and most rapacious designs, were *long prayers*? Prayers made only *for a show* or colour; and that, to the basest and most degenerate sort of villainy, even the robbing the spital, and *devouring the houses* of poor, helpless, forlorn widows. Their devotion served all along but as an instrument to their avarice, as a factor or under-agent to their extortion. A practice, which, duly seen into, and stripped of its hypocritical blinds, could not but look very odiously and ill-favouredly; and therefore, in come their *long robes*, and their *long prayers* together, and cover all. And the truth is, neither the length of one, nor of the other, is ever found so useful, as when there is something more than ordinary that would not be seen. This was the *gainful godliness* of the *Pharisees*; and, I believe upon good observation, you will hardly find any like the *Pharisees* for their long prayers, who are not also extremely like them for something else. And thus having given you five arguments for *brevity*, and against *prolixity* of prayer; let us now make this our *other great rule*, whereby to judge of the prayers of *our church*, and the prayers of those who *dissent* and *divide* from it. And,

First, For that excellent body of prayers contained in our liturgy, and both compiled and enjoined by public authority. Have we not here a great instance of brevity and fulness together, cast into several short, significant collects, each containing a distinct entire, and well-managed petition? the whole set of them being like a string of pearls, exceeding rich in conjunction; and therefore of no small price or value, even single, and by themselves. Nothing could have been composed with greater judgment; every prayer being so short, that it is impossible it should weary; and withal, so pertinent, that it is impossible it should cloy the devotion. And indeed, so admirably fitted are they all to the common concerns of a christian society, that when the rubric enjoins but the use of some of them, our worship is not imperfect; and when we use them all, there is none of them superfluous.

And the reason assigned by some learned men for the preference of many short prayers, before a continued long one, is unanswerable: namely, that by the former there is a more frequently repeated mention made of the name, and some great attribute of God as the encouraging ground of our praying to him; and withal, of the merits and mediation of Christ, as the only thing that can promise us success, in what we pray for; every distinct petition *beginning* with the *former*, and *ending* with the *latter*: By thus annexing of which to each particular thing that we ask for, we do manifestly confess and declare, that we cannot expect to obtain any one thing at the hands of God, but with a particular renewed respect to the merits of a Mediator; and withal, remind the congregation of the same, by making it their part to renew a distinct *Amen* to every distinct *Petition*.

Add to this the excellent contrivance of a great part of our Liturgy into alternate responses; by which means, the people are put to bear a considerable share in the whole service: which makes it almost impossible for them, to be only idle hearers, or, which is worse, mere lookers on: As they are very often, and may be always (if they can but keep their eyes open) at the long, tedious prayers of the *Nonconformists*. And this indeed is that which makes and denominates our Liturgy truly and properly a book of *Common-Prayer*. For, I think I may truly avouch (how strange soever it may seem at first) that there is no such thing as *Common*, or *Joint-prayer*, anywhere amongst the principal dissenters from the church of *England*: For, in the *Romish* communion, the priest says over the appointed prayers only to himself, and the rest of the people not hearing a word of what he says, repeat also their own particular prayers to themselves; and when they have done, go their way: Not all at once, as neither do they come at once, but scatteringly, one after another, according as they have finished their devotions. And then for the

Nonconformists; their prayers being all *extempore*, it is (as we have shown before) hardly possible for *any*, and utterly impossible for *all* to join in them. For, surely, people cannot join in a prayer before they understand it; nor can it be imagined, that all capacities should presently and immediately understand what they *hear*, when, possibly, the *holder-forth* himself understands not what he *says*. From all which we may venture to conclude, that that excellent thing, *Common-prayer*, which is the joint address of a whole congregation, with united voice as well as heart, sending up their devotions to Almighty God, is no-where to be found in these kingdoms, but in that best and nearest copy of primitive christian worship, the divine service, as it is performed according to the orders of our church.

As for those long prayers, so frequently used by some before their sermons, the constitution and canons of our church are not at all responsible for them; having provided us better things, and with great wisdom appointed a form of prayer, to be used by all before their sermons. But as for this way of praying, now generally in use, as it was first took up upon an humour of novelty and popularity, and by the same carried on, till it had passed into a custom, and so put the rule of the church first out of use, and then out of countenance also; so, if it be rightly considered, it will, in the very nature of the thing itself, be found a very senseless and absurd practice. For, can there be any sense or propriety in beginning a new, tedious prayer in the pulpit, just after the church has, for near an hour together, with great variety of offices, suitable to all the needs of the congregation, been praying for all that can possibly be fit for christians to pray for? Nothing certainly can be more irrational. For which cause, amongst many more, that old sober form of *bidding prayer*, which, both against law and reason, has been justled out of the church by this upstart, puritanical encroachment, ought, with great reason, to be restored by authority; and both the use and users of it, by a strict and solemn reinforcement of the canon upon all, without exception, be rescued from that unjust scorn of the factious and ignorant, which the tyranny of the contrary, usurping custom, will otherwise expose them to. For surely, it can neither be decency nor order for our clergy to *conform* to the fanatics, as many in their prayers before sermon now-a-days do.

And thus having accounted for the prayers of our church, according to the great rule prescribed in the *text, Let thy words be few*: Let us now, according to the same, consider also the way of praying, so much used, and applauded by such as have renounced the communion, and liturgy of our church; it is but reason, that they should bring us something better in the room of what they have so disdainfully cast off. But, on the contrary, are not all their prayers exactly after the *heathenish* and *pharisaical* copy? Always notable for those two things, length and tautology? Two whole hours for one prayer, at a fast, used to be reckoned but a moderate dose; and that, for the most part, fraught with such irreverent, blasphemous expressions, that, to repeat them, would profane the place I am speaking in; and indeed, they seldom *carried on the work of such a day* (as their phrase was) but they left the church in need of a new consecration. Add to this, the incoherence and confusion, the endless repetitions, and the insufferable nonsense, that never failed to hold out, even with their utmost prolixity; so that in all their *long fasts*, from first to last, from *seven* in the *morning*, to *seven* in the *evening*, (which was their measure) the pulpit was always the *emptiest* thing in the church: And I never knew such a *fast* kept by them, but their hearers had cause to begin a *thanksgiving*, as soon as they had done. And the truth is, when I consider the matter of their prayers; so full of ramble, and inconsequence, and in every respect, so very like the language of a dream; and compare it with their carriage of themselves in prayer, with their *eyes* for the most part shut, and their *arms* stretched out in a yawning posture, a man that should hear any of them pray, might, by very pardonable error, be induced to think, that he was all the time hearing one *talking in his sleep*: besides the strange virtue which their prayers had to procure sleep in others too. So that he who should be present at all their long cant, would show a greater ability in *watching*, than ever they could pretend to in *praying*, if he could forbear sleeping, having so strong a provocation to it, and so fair an excuse for it. In a word, such were their prayers, both for matter and expression, that, could any one truly and exactly write them out, it would be the shrewdest, and most effectual way of writing against them, that could possibly be thought of.

 I should not have thus troubled either you, or myself, by raking into the dirt and dunghill of these men's devotions, upon the account of any thing, either done or said by them in the late times of confusion; for as they have the *king's*, so I wish them *God's pardon also*, whom I am sure, they have offended much more, than they have both kings put together. But that which has provoked me thus to rip up, and expose to you their nauseous, and ridiculous way of addressing to God, even upon the most solemn occasions, is that intolerably rude and unprovoked insolence and scurrility, with which they are every day reproaching and scoffing at our liturgy, and the users of it, and thereby alienating the minds of the people from it, to such a degree, that many thousands are drawn by them into a fatal schism; a schism that, unrepented of, and continued in, will as infallibly ruin their souls, as theft, whoredom, murder, or any other of the most crying, damning sins whatsoever. But leaving this to the justice of the government, to which it belongs, to protect us in our spiritual, as well as in our temporal concerns, I shall only say this, that nothing can be more for the honour of our liturgy, than to find it despised only by those who have made themselves remarkable to the world for despising the *Lord's Prayer* as much.

In the mean time, for ourselves of the church of *England*, who, without pretending to any new lights, think it equally a duty and commendation to be *wise*, and to be *devout* only to *sobriety*, and who judge it no dishonour to God himself, to be worshipped according to law and rule: If the directions of *Solomon*, the precept and example of our Saviour; and lastly, the piety and experience of those excellent men and martyrs, who first composed, and afterwards owned our liturgy with their dearest blood, may be looked upon as safe and sufficient guides to us in our public worship of God; then, upon the joint authority of all these, we may pronounce our liturgy the greatest treasure of rational devotion in the christian world. And I know no prayer necessary, that is not in the liturgy, but one: which is this: *That God would vouchsafe to continue the liturgy itself in use, honour, and veneration in this church for ever.* And I doubt not, but all wise, sober, and good christians will, with equal judgment and affection, give it their *Amen*.

Now to God the Father, God the Son, and God the Holy Ghost, three Persons and one God, be rendered and ascribed, as is most due, all Praise, Might, Majesty and Dominion, both now and for evermore. Amen.

OBEDIENCE FOR CONSCIENCE-SAKE, THE DUTY OF GOOD SUBJECTS
Romans 13:5.
Wherefore ye must needs be subject, not only for wrath, but also for conscience sake.

THIS SERMON deals with the subject of obedience to the civil power. The subject played an important part—for obvious reasons—in the history of the first two centuries of post-Reformation Anglicanism. It is not, however, peculiar to Anglicanism and must recur wherever tension between Church and State is maintained. It became prominent for a while in France, in the latter part of the seventeenth century, and the Gallican Articles of 1682 affirmed that kings are not subject to the authority of the Church in temporal and civil matters and that the Pope could not dispense subjects from their allegiance. It was this latter point which lay at the root of the bitterness the subject aroused in England, on account of the papal bull against Elizabeth, which claimed to make precisely this dispensation and so to subvert the whole government of the country. South is certainly speaking for more of the English than his own party when he observes, in this sermon, that 'it is well that *cursed bulls* have short *horns*'.

None the less, the sermon which follows is full of the animus of the times, and continually evokes what his hearers had 'felt for twenty years' of Puritan politics. There are jeers at Calvin—'the great *Mufti* of *Geneva*'—whose opinion of kings is said to have been that it is 'better to spit in their faces than to obey them'. There is a mid-point between the treason of Puritans on the one hand and, on the other, the treason of the Papists, of which the service for the fifth of November was intended to keep people in mind. This is the classic stance of the Anglicanism of the period, put with gentleness and submission by such men as Ken and with common sense and asperity by Swift. With South it has a less pleasing face. This charitable man frequently talks like a bully. Here his fury carries him so far as to say that 'the magistrate is to take no notice of any man's erroneous conscience, but (if reason and religion will not set it right) to rectify and convince it with an axe or the gibbet.'

These characteristic excesses should not divert attention from the thread of the main argument, which is more respectable—and none the less worthy of consideration for being remote from current modes of thought. What is here taught is at the opposite pole from the doctrine of *l'homme revolté* enunciated by Camus —the man who says 'No' to oppression, whether of himself or others, and demands that a certain respect shall be shown to himself, as well as to the others. This popular twentieth-century doctrine goes back to the revolutionary platitudes of the eighteenth century, which of course had in them an element from Christian sources but which comported a great complacency about human nature and attempted to provide a sort of authority for egotism. The thirteenth chapter of Romans points in another direction, and there is this to be said for South's uncompromising exposition, that it at least makes the nature of the issue blindingly clear. As 'for the modern Roman saints', South says, in an allusion to the Fifth of November, 'it is their powder, not their faith, that has made such a report in the world.' But the Romans to whom Paul wrote were commanded to be subject to Nero, 'a mass of filth and impiety,' 'the disgrace of mankind'. So there is no countenance for not obeying a government of which you morally disapprove. 'Obedience to a magistrate is obedience to God at second hand . . . neither can a magistrate be so vile and unjust, but that still he is an officer by God's institution.' *The powers that be, are ordained of God.* It is a very hard doctrine, and it has often been used by people in authority to give an appearance of sanctity to their oppressions. But that is not the sense of it. Had Paul been writing to Nero he would have put the matter differently. But he was writing to the emperor's *subjects*, and telling them with what patience they should conduct themselves. South keeps his best argument to the end, where he reminds us that Christ, 'while he conversed upon earth, was subject to the civil power in his own person.'

THIS CHAPTER is the great and noted repository of the most absolute and binding precepts of allegiance, and seems so fitted to this argument, that it ought to be always preached upon, as long as there is either such a thing as obedience to be enjoined, or such a thing as rebellion to be condemned.

In the words that I have pitched upon, there are these two parts.

1. A duty enjoined, *ye must needs be subject.*
2. The ground or motive of that duty; *for conscience-sake.*

For the first of these; since men are apt to draw arguments for or against obedience from the qualifications of the persons concerned in it, we will consider here,

1. The persons, who are commanded to be subject.
2. The person, to whom they are commanded this subjection.

1. For the persons commanded to be subject, they were *believers*, the *faithful*, those who were the church of God in *Rome*, as we see in Chap. i. 7. *beloved of God, called to be Saints.* Neither were they Saints only, but Saints of the first rank and magnitude, heroes in the faith, verse 8. *your faith is spoken of throughout the whole world.* Their faith made *Rome* no less the metropolis of Christianity, than of the world. The *Roman* faith and fortitude equally spread their fame. And as the pagan *Romans* overcame the world by their fortitude, so did the christians by their faith.

But for the modern *Roman* Saints, it is their powder, not their faith, that has made such a *report* in the world; a race much different from their primitive ancestors, whose piety could not cancel their loyalty. No religion could sanctify treason; christian liberty was compatible with the strictest allegiance; they knew no such way as to put the sceptre into Christ's hand, by pulling it out from their prince's.

2. In the next place; the person, to whom they were commanded to be subject, was *Nero*; a person so prodigiously brutish, that whether we consider him as a man, or as a governor, we shall find him a *Nero*, that is, a monster, in both respects.

And first, if we consider his person; he was such a mass of filth and impiety, such an oglio of all ill qualities, that he stands the wonder and the disgrace of mankind. For, to pass over his monstrous obscenity, he poisoned *Britannicus* for having a better voice; he murdered his tutor *Seneca*; he kicked his wife big with child to death; he killed his mother, and ripped her up in sport, to see the place where he lay: so impious, that he would adore the statues of his Gods one day, and piss upon them another. But then, take him as an emperor, and he was the veriest tyrant and blood-sucker, the most unjust governor that ever the world saw: one, who had proceeded to that enormity, that the very army, the only prop of his tyranny, deserted him; and the senate sentenced him to be ignominiously drawn upon a hurdle, and whipped to death.

He was one, who had united in himself the most different and unsociable qualities, namely, to be *ridiculous*, and to be *terrible*; for what more ridiculous than a *fiddling emperor*, and more *terrible* than a *bloody tyrant*? In short, he was the plague of the world, the stain of majesty, and the very blush of nature. One, who seemed to be sent and prepared by providence, to give the world an experiment, *quid summa vitia in summa fortuna possint*; and by a new way of confirmation, to seal to the truth of Christianity, by his hatred of it.

And yet after all this, the believing *Romans* are commanded subjection even to this *Nero*, the best of saints to the worst of men: And indeed it was this, that gave a value to their obedience; for to be loyal to a just, gentle, and virtuous prince, is rather privilege than patience. But the reason of the whole matter is stated in these words, verse 1. *The powers that are, are ordained of God.* Obedience to the magistrate is obedience to God at the second hand; and as a man cannot be so wicked, so degenerate, but that still he is a man by *God's creation*; so neither can the magistrate be so vile, and unjust, but that still he is an officer by *God's institution.* And it is no small part of the divine prerogative, to be able to command *homage* to the worst of kings, as the majesty of a prince is never more apparent, than in its subjects' submission to an unworthy deputy or lieutenant. The baseness of the metal is warranted by the superscription, the office hallows the person; neither is there any reason, that the vileness of one should disannul the dignity of the other; forasmuch as he is *made wicked* by himself for the devil, but he is *stamped a magistrate* by God. We are therefore to overlook all impieties and defects, which cannot invalidate the function. Though *Nero* deserves worthily to be *abhorred*, yet still the *emperor is*, and ought to be sacred. And thus much for the duty, and the persons to whom it relates. *Ye must needs be subject.*

2. I come now to the second part, *viz.* the *ground or motive* upon which this duty is enforced; Ye must needs *be subject for conscience-sake.* A strange argument, I must confess, if we were to transcribe Christianity from the practice of modern Christians,

with whom it would proceed thus rather; ye must needs shake off all government, and rebel for *conscience-sake*. No such instrument to carry on a refined, and well-woven rebellion, as a *tender conscience*, and a sturdy heart. He who rebels conscientiously, rebels heartily; such an one carries his God in his scabbard, and his religion upon the point of his sword. He strikes every stroke for salvation, and wades deep in blood for eternity. But what now must be said of those impostors, who in the name of God, and with pretended commissions from heaven, have bewitched men into such a religious rage? Who have preached them out of the deadly sin of allegiance, into the angelical state of faction and rebellion? Whose saints were never listed but in the muster-roll for the field; and whose rubric is writ only with letters of blood. I believe, upon a due survey of history, it will be found, that the most considerable villainies, which were ever acted upon the stage of Christendom, have been authorized with the glistering pretences of conscience, and the introduction of a greater purity in religion. He who would act the *destroyer*, if he would do it effectually, should put on the *reformer*; and he who would be creditably, and successfully a villain, let him go whining, praying, and preaching to his work; let him knock his breast, and his hollow heart, and pretend to *lie in the dust before God*, before he can be able to lay others there.

But some may reply and argue, that conscience is to be obeyed, though erroneous; and therefore, if a saint (for with some all rebels are such) stands fully persuaded in his conscience, that his magistrate is an enemy to the Gospel, and the *kingdoms of Jesus Christ*, and so ought to be resisted; is not such an one engaged to act according to the dictates of his conscience? And since God would punish him for going against it, is it not high tyranny for the magistrate to punish him for complying with it?

To this I answer; that he who looks well into this argument, looks into the great *Arcanum*, and the *Sanctum Sanctorum* of Puritanism; which indeed is only *reformed Jesuitism*, as Jesuitism is nothing else but *Popish Puritanism*: And I could draw out such an exact parallel between them, both as to principles and practices, that it would quickly appear, that they are as truly brothers, as ever were *Romulus* and *Remus*; and that they sucked their principles from the same *wolf*.

But to encounter the main body of the argument, which, like the *Trojan* horse, carries both arms and armed men in the belly of it; I answer, that to act against conscience, erroneous, or not erroneous, is sinful; but then the error adds nothing to the excusableness of the action, when the same charge of sin lies upon the conscience for being erroneous. No man can err in matters of constant duty, which God has laid open to an easy and obvious discernment, but he errs with the highest malignity of wilfulness; And if any plea to the contrary be admitted, it will unhinge all society, and dissolve the bonds of all the governments in the world.

The magistrate is to take no notice of any man's erroneous conscience, but (if reason and religion will not set it right) to rectify or convince it with an axe, or the gibbet. *He*, who would without control disturb a government, because his erroneous conscience tells him he must, does all one, as if he should say, that it is lawful for a man to commit *murder*, provided that he, who does it, be *first drunk*. It were a sad thing, if the laws should be at a stand, and the weal-public suffer, because such and such persons are pleased *to be in an error*; (though by the way they are seldom or never seen to be so, but very beneficially to themselves.) He who brings down the law to the exceptions of any man's conscience, does really place the legislative power in that man's conscience; and by so doing, may at length bring down his own neck to the block. For certainly that subject is advanced to a strange degree of power, whose conscience has a prerogative to command the laws.

And I do not think ever to speak a greater truth than this, that the non-execution of the laws upon such hypocrites has been the fatal cause, which drew after it the execution of the supreme legislator himself [King Charles I]: and believe it, if a governor ever falls into the mercy of such persons, he will find that their *hands are by no means so tender, as their consciences* pretend to be. All indulgencies animate such persons, but mend them not: All reconcilements, and little puny arts of accommodation, are but as spiders' webs, which such hornets will quickly break through, and as truces to an old enemy to rally up his forces, and to fall on, when he sees his advantage; nothing will hold a sanctified, tender-conscienced rebel, but a prison, or a halter. And these are not angry words, but the oracular responses, and bitter truths of a long and bleeding experience; an experience, which began in a rebellion against an excellent Prince, proceeded to his imprisonment, and concluded in his murder.

But because conscience is a relative term, and so must refer to something, which it is to be conversant about; I shall show, that

men are commanded a *subjection to*, and dehorted from a *resistance of* the civil magistrate, by two things.
 1. The absolute unlawfulness; and
 2. The scandal of such a resistance.
 1. For the first of these, its *absolute unlawfulness*. Rebellion surely is a mortal sin, *mortal* to the rebel, and *mortal* to the prince rebelled against; it is the violation of government, which is the very soul and support of the universe, and the imitation of providence. Every lawful ruler holds the government by a certain deputation from God; and the commission, by which he holds it, is his word. This is the voice of Scripture, this is the voice of Reason. But yet we must not think to carry it so; for although in the Apostles' time this was divinity and truth, yea, and truth also stamped with necessity; yet we have been since taught, that Kings may be lawfully resisted, cast off, and deposed; and that by two sorts of men.
 1. The sons of *Rome*: And,
 2. Their true offspring, the sons of *Geneva*.
 1. For the first of these. It would be like the stirring of a great sink, which would be likelier to annoy, than to instruct the auditory, to draw out from thence all the pestilential doctrines and practices against the royalty and supremacy of princes.
 Gratian, in the decrees, expressly says, *imperator potest a papa deponi.* And *Boniface* VIII. in *lib. 1. Extrav. Com. titulo de majoritate, et obedientia*, has declared the subjection, or rather, the slavery of princes to the pope fully enough. 1. For first he tells us, that Kings and secular powers have the temporal sword, but to be used *ad nutum sacerdotis.* 2. He adds, 'Porro subesse Romano pontifici omni humanae creaturae, declaramus, dicimus, definimus, et pronuntiamus omnino esse de necessitate salutis.'
 And how far Princes are to be under him we have a farther account. 1. They ought to kiss his feet. 2. He may depose them. 3. No Prince may repeal his sentence, but he may repeal the sentences of all others. 4. He may absolve subjects from their allegiance. These, and some such other impious positions, they call *Dictatus Papae*; and were published and established by Pope *Gregory* VII. in the *Roman* synod, in the year one thousand seventy six, as *Baronius* tells us, *ad annum Christi millesimum septuagesimum sextum. Numero trices. primo et trices. secundo.*
 And that we may see, that he was not wanting to execute, as much as he had the face to assert; *Platina* tells us in his life, how he deposed *Henry* IV. emperor of *Germany*; and some of the

words of his bull are these. '*Henricum imperatoria administratione, regiaque dejicio: Et christianos omnes imperio subjectos juramento absolvo.*' The whole bull is extant in the bullery of *Laertius Cherubinus*, Tom. 1. p. 12. printed at *Rome* 1617. And then at last, with an equal affront to the majesty of Scripture, as well as to that of Princes, he puts his foot upon the Emperor's neck, quoting that passage in the Psalm, *super aspidem et basiliscum, thou shalt tread upon the asp and the basilisk*; a great encouragement surely for princes to turn papists. But to contain ourselves within our own country, where we are most concerned; the pope, we know, deposed King *Henry* VIII. and Queen *Elizabeth*, as far as the words, and the *bruta fulmina* of his bulls could depose them; absolving their subjects from their allegiance, and exposing their dominions to the invasion of any, who could invade them. The words of *Pius* V. in his bull against Queen *Elizabeth* are remarkable; which translated into *English*, run thus: 'Christ, who reigns on high, and to whom all power in heaven and earth is given, has committed the government of the one catholic and apostolic church only to *Peter*, and his successor the pope of *Rome*. And him has he placed prince over all nations and kingdoms, to pluck up, destroy, scatter, overturn, plant and build up; in order to the keeping of God's faithful people in the bond of charity, and in the unity of the spirit.'

And is not this a bold preface, able to blast the prerogative of all Kings at a breath? But it is well, that *cursed bulls* have short *horns*. Yet all this is but the voice of his *thunder*, the best is to come afterwards. Let us see how he proceeds.

'Wherefore, (says he) being upheld in the supreme throne of justice by Christ himself, who has placed us in it, we declare the aforesaid *Elizabeth* an heretic, and all who adhere to her, to have incurred an anathema, and to be actually divided and cut off from the unity of Christ's body. Moreover, we declare her to be deprived of all right to her kingdom, and of all dominion, dignity and privilege belonging thereto. Withal, that the subjects of that kingdom, and all others, who have any ways swore obedience to her are fully absolved from their oath, and from all debt of homage and allegiance to her; and accordingly by these presents we do absolve them. Furthermore, we charge and enjoin all her subjects, to yield no obedience to her person, laws, or commands. Given at *Rome* in the year 1575, in the fifth year of the pope's reign, and the thirteenth of Queen *Elizabeth's*.'

Is is possible now, that some *English* and *French* papists may dislike this doctrine of deposing Kings; but they owe this to their own good-natures, or some other principle, or indeed chiefly to this, that they live under such *Kings, as will not be deposed*. But that they owe it not to their religion, which (by little less than a contradiction in the terms) they miscall *Catholic*, is clear from hence: That by the very essential constitution of their faith, they are bound to believe, and to submit both their judgments, and practices, to all that is determined by a general council confirmed by the Pope. This being premised, we must know, that the fourth *Lateran council*, which they acknowledge *general*, and to have had in it above twelve hundred fathers (as they call them) in the third chapter *de haereticis*, thus determines: 'That all secular powers shall be compelled to take an oath to banish heretics out of their territories. *Moveantur, et, si necesse fuerit, compellantur potestates saeculares, cujuscunque sint officii, ut pro defensione fidei publice juramentum praestent, &c.*' But what now, if persons will not do this? If they refuse to be thus commanded like subjects, and to place their royal diadems upon their bald *pates*?

Why then the Fathers, or rather the Lords of the council thus proceed. 'If (say they) Princes refuse to purge their dominions from heresy; let this be signified to the Pope, that he may forthwith declare their subjects absolved from their allegiance, and expose their territories to be seized upon by Catholics.'

This is the canon of that *concilium Lateranum magnum*, (for so they term it) in which were above twelve hundred fathers, (so they tell us) a council by them acknowledged to be *general*, and confirmed by the Pope. Now I demand, is this council *infallible*, or is it not?

1. If not, then good night to their *Infallibility*, if the Pope and twelve hundred fathers, met together in a general council, be not infallible.

2. If it be *infallible*, (as they all do, and must say, unless they will deny a fundamental article of their faith) then they must all believe it, and by consequence acknowledge, that the Pope has power to excommunicate and depose Kings, and to give away their kingdoms, in case of heresy; and *what heresy* is, they themselves are to be judges? This we may be sure of, that all protestant Kings are heretics with them; and so the Pope may, when he will, and undoubtedly will, when he *can*, give away their kingdoms. I think it concerns Kings to consider this, and when they have a mind to submit to the Pope's tyranny, to subscribe

to the Pope's religion.

Thus much for the *Lateran* council; and to place the argument above all exception, this very council is expressly *confirmed* by that of *Trent*, in the 24th session of reformation, chap. 5. p. 412. also in the 25th session about reform. chap. 20. p. 624.

Now show me any thorough-paced *catholic*, who dares refuse to subscribe to the *council of Trent*; which being so, it is a matter of amazement to consider, that the men of this profession should be of such prodigious impudence, as to solicit any protestant Prince for protection, nay, indulgences to their persons, and religion; when by virtue of this religion they hold themselves bound, under pain of damnation, to believe those principles as articles of their faith, which naturally undermine, ruin, and eat out the very heart of all monarchy. But if any one should plead favour for them, it is pity but these *bulls and decrees*, and the *Scotch covenant*, were all drawn into one system, that so they might be *indulged* all together, and perhaps in time they may. You have seen here their principles, (i.e.) you have heard the *text*; and you need go no farther than this fifth of *November* for a comment.

I could farther add, that the popish religion, in the nature of it, is inconsistent with the just rights, and supremacy of princes: and that upon this invincible Reason, that it exempts all *the clergy from subjection to them*, so far, that (be their crimes what they will) Kings cannot punish them. For the proof of which, I shall bring that, which is *instar omnium*, and which I am sure they must stand to; *viz.* the decree of the council of *Trent*, which in the 24th session about reformation, chap. 5. p. 412. determines thus. '*Causae criminales majores contra episcopos ab ipso tantum summo pontifice Romano cognoscantur, et terminentur; minores vero in concilio tantum provinciali cognoscantur et terminentur.*' So that the King, for any thing that he has to do in these matters, may sit and blow his nails; for use them otherwise, he cannot. He may indeed be plotted against, have barrels of powder laid, and poniards prepared for him: But to punish the sacred actors of these villainies, that is reserved only to him, who gave the first command for the doing them.

These things, I say, I could prosecute much farther, but that I am equally engaged by the exigence of my subject, to speak something of their true seed, the sons of *Geneva*: who, though they seem to be contrary to those of *Rome*, and like *Sampson's* foxes, to look opposite ways; yet when they are to play the incendiaries, to fire kingdoms and governments, they can *turn tail* to one and the same *firebrand*.

In our account of these, we will begin with the father of the faithful; faithful, I mean, to their old antimonarchical doctrines and assertions; and that is the great *Mufti* of *Geneva*: Who in the *fourth book of his Institutions*, chap. 20. sec. 31. has the face to own such doctrine to the world as this; 'That it is not only not unlawful for the three estates to oppose their king in the exorbitances of his government, (of which they still are to be judges) but that they basely and perfidiously desert the trust committed to them by God, if they connive at him, and do not to their utmost oppose and restrain him.'

Let us see this wholesome doctrine and institution farther amplified in his commentaries upon *Daniel*. Chap. 2. verse 29. He roundly tells us, 'that those men are out of their wits, and quite void of sense and understanding, who desire to live under sovereign monarchies; for that it cannot be (says he) but order and policy must decay, where one man holds such an extent of government.'

Upon this good foundation he proceeds farther, chap. 6. verse 22. 'Princes (says he) when they oppose God,' (and oppose God, according to him, they do, when they refuse his new discipline) 'then, says he, *abdicant se potestate*, they deprive themselves of all power; and it is better in such cases, to spit in their faces, than to obey them.' Yet for all this, *Daniel*, who surely was as godly a man as Mr. *Calvin*, did not spit in *Nebuchadnezzar's* face.

But that we may know when princes oppose God, and so may bring his assertions together; he tells us farther, chap. 5. ver. 25. 'That kings forget that they are men, and of the same mould with others: they are, says he, styled *Dei gratia*; but to what sense or purpose, save only to show, that they acknowledge no superior upon earth? yet under colour of this, they will trample upon God with their feet; so that it is but an abuse, when they are so called.' It seems then, we must lay aside all appellations of honour, and hereafter say only, *Good-man such an one*, king of *England*, or *Laird such an one*, king of *Scotland*. But let us follow him a little farther; where in the same chapter we shall see him go on thus. 'See, says he, what the rage and madness of all kings is, with whom it is a common thing to exclude God from the government of the world. Again, chap. 6. ver. 25. *Darius* (says he) will condemn by his example all those, that profess themselves at this day, *catholic kings, christian kings*, and *defenders of the faith*; and yet do not only deface, and bury all true piety, and religion, but corrupt and deprave the whole worship of God.'

Could any thing be with greater virulence thrown at all the princes of Christendom, than this? and yet I believe there is never a *puritan* or *dissenter* in *England*, but would lick his spittle in every one of these assertions.

But let us now rally them together into one argument. When princes oppose God, we are not (in *Calvin's* judgment) *to obey them, but to spit in their faces*. But now, *to exclude God from his government of the world, and to corrupt his whole worship* (which he affirms all princes do) *is surely to oppose God*: and therefore, according to his doctrine, joined with his good manners, *we are not to obey them, but spit in their faces*. A doctrine fit only to come from him, who nested himself into the chief power of *Geneva* after the expulsion of the lawful prince.

In the last place, to speak one word of his epistles, which were published by *Beza*; one, who had been a long time licked by him into his own form; and so was likely to do him what advantage he could in their publication: he, who shall diligently read them, will find, that there was scarce any traitorous design on foot in Christendom, but there are some traces of correspondence with it extant in those epistles.

And so we dismiss him. *Beza* his disciple succeeds him both in place and doctrine; and to show, that he does so, he expressly owns, and commends the *French rebellion*, in his epistle before his *annotations*. And in the forty *articles of Berne*, published in the year 1574, and drawn up by *Beza*, in the fortieth article he affirms, 'that they were bound not to disarm, so long as their religion was persecuted by the king.'

If we would now see how this doctrine grew, being transplanted into *Scotland; Knox*, in his book to the nobility and people of *Scotland*, in the point of obedience to kings, instructs them thus: 'Neither *promise*, says he, nor *oath*, can oblige any man to obey, or give assistance unto tyrants against God.' And, what tyrants were in his sense, his practices against the queen regent sufficiently show.

In the next place, *Buchanan*, who was once prolocutor of the *Scotch* assembly, that is to say, something greater than their king, is copious upon this subject, in his history of *Scotland*, and in his book *de jure regni*, &c. In the former of which, at the 372d page, he wonders that there is not some public reward appointed for those private men, that should *kill tyrants*, as there is for those that *kill wolves*. And in his book *de jure regni*, he maintains an excellent dispute against such as defend kings. The royal advocates, says he, hold, *that kings must be obeyed, good or bad*. It is blasphemy to affirm that, says *Buchanan*. But God *placeth oftentimes evil kings*, say the royal advocates; so doth he often private men to kill them, says *Buchanan*. But in *1 Tim. we are commanded to pray for princes*, say they; so are we commanded to pray for *thieves*, says he; but yet may hang them up, when we catch them. But say the royal advocates, St. *Paul strictly commands obedience to all princes*: St. *Paul* wrote so, says *Buchanan*, in the infancy of the church, when they were not able to resist them; but if he had lived now, he would have wrote otherwise.

Now, if this be their prolocutor's doctrine, I leave it to any one to judge, whether every King has not cause to take up those words of *Jacob* to *Simeon* and *Levi*, with a little change; *O my soul, come not thou into their secret, and unto their general assembly, mine honour, be not thou united!*

But that we may come home to the very place of my text; I shall produce one more of them, and that is *Pareus*; a *German* divine, but fully cast into the *Geneva* mould. He in his comment upon *Romans* xiii. full fraught with a pestilent discourse against the sovereignty of kings, assigns several cases in which their subjects may lawfully take up arms against them, p. 1338. As 1. 'If their prince blasphemes God, or causes others to do so. 2. If he does them some great injury: his words are, *si fiat ipsis atrox injuria*. 3. If they cannot otherwise enjoy their lives, estates, and consciences.' Now with all these large conditions, still join this, that themselves are to be judges in all these cases against their prince; and then, if they have but a mind to rebel, they may blame themselves, if they are to seek for a lawful cause. This made King *James* award this worthy piece to the *fire* and the *hangman*. A prince, who though bred up under Puritans, yet hated their opinions heartily, because he understood them throughly.

And now last of all, as it is the nature of dregs, and the worst part of things, to descend to the bottom, it were easy to bring up the rear with our *English Genevizers*, and to show how these doctrines of disloyalty to princes have thriven amongst them; were it not impertinent to think, that you could be farther instructed by hearing that for an hour, that you have felt for twenty years. And here by the way, it is a glorious justification of the church of *England*, still to have had the same enemies with the monarchy of *England*. For an account of their tenets, I shall not send you to their papers, to their sermons, though some of the greatest blots to christianity, next to their authors; but I shall send you to *the field, to the high courts of justice*, where they stand writ to eternity in the massacre of thousands, in the blood and banishment of princes; actions, that much outdo the business of this present anniversary; but to be buried in silence, because not to be reprehended with safety.

However, as for Puritanism, since it had so long deceived the world with a demure face, I have been often prone to think, that it was in some respect a favour of providence, to let it have its late full scope, and range, to convince, and undeceive Christendom, and by an immortal experiment to demonstrate, whither those principles tend, and what a savage monster, *Puritanism*, armed with power, would show itself to the world.

So that if any christian prince should hereafter forget the *English* Rebellion, and himself, so far as to be deceived with those stale, threadbare baffled pretences of *Conscience*, and *Reformation*, he would fall in a great measure unpitied, as a martyr to his senseless fondness, and a sacrifice to his own credulity.

And for those amongst us, they are of that incorrigible, impregnable malice, that forgetting all their treasons, they have made the *King's oblivion* the chief subject of their own; and rewarding all his unparalleled mercies with continual murmurs, libels, plots and conspiracies, seem only to be pardoned into fresh treasons, and *indemnified* into new rebellions.

We have seen here the adversaries, which this great duty of allegiance to kings has on both sides: Which that we may enforce against all arts of evasion, which the *Papist* and *Puritan*, the mortal, sworn *covenanted* enemies of all magistracy, but especially of monarchy can invent; it will be expedient briefly to discuss this question:

Whether, and how far, human laws bind the conscience?

To the determination of which, if we would proceed clearly, and rationally, we must first state, what it is to *bind the conscience. To bind the conscience therefore, is so to oblige a man to the performance of a thing, that the non-performance of it, brings him under the guilt of sin, and the liableness to punishment before God.*

Now to proceed: Some are of opinion, that human laws oblige only to the penalty annexed to the violation of them; and that the conscience contracts the guilt of no sin before God; a man's person being only subject to the outward penalties, which the civil magistrate shall inflict for the expiation of his offence.

But the confutation of this opinion, I need fetch no farther than from the text. For I demand of the most subtle Expositor, and acute Logician in the world, what sense he will make here of the words [*for conscience-sake*;] if by Conscience is not meant *Conscience of sin*, but only of liableness to punishment before the magistrate.

For then the sense of the words will be this: *You must needs be subject not only for wrath*, that is, for fear of punishment; *but also for conscience-sake*, that is, for fear of punishment too; since according to them, the term [for conscience-sake] referred to the laws of the civil magistrate, can signify no more. But this is so broad a depravation of the rules of speaking, that it banishes all sense and reason from the whole scheme and construction of the words.

To the whole matter therefore I answer by a distinction.

1. That a law may bind the Conscience, either *immediately*, by virtue of its own power, conveyed to it, by its immediate legislator. Or,

2. *Mediately*, in the strength of a superior law, owning and enforcing the obligation of the inferior.

This distinction premised: I affirm that the laws of man neither do, nor can thus immediately bind the conscience; that is, by themselves, or by any obliging power transfused into them from the human legislator. That this is so, I demonstrate upon these reasons.

1. No power can oblige any farther, than it can take cognizance of the offence, and inflict penalties, in case the person obliged does not answer the obligation, but offends against it. This proposition stands firm upon this eternal truth; that nothing can be an obligation, that is absurd and irrational. But it is absurd for any power to give laws, and obligations to that, of which it can take no account, nor possibly know, whether it keep or transgresses those laws, and which, upon its transgression of them, it cannot punish.

But what man alive, what judge or justice, what *Minos*, or *Radamanthus*, can carry his inspection into the *Conscience*? What evidence, what witness, or rack, can extort a discovery of that, which the conscience is resolved to conceal, and keep within itself? Nay, admit that it were possible to force it to such confessions against itself; yet what penalty could human force, and the short reach of the secular arm, inflict upon a spiritual, immaterial substance? which defies all our engines of torment, and arts of cruelty; which laughs at the hostilities and weak invasions of all the elements. Conscience is neither scorched with the fire, nor pricked with the sword; it feels nothing under a deity, nothing but the stings and insinuations of an angry, sin-revenging Omnipotence.

2. A second reason is this: That if human laws, considered in themselves, immediately bind the Conscience, then human laws, as such, carry in them as great an obligation as the divine. The consequence is most clear; for the divine law can do no more than bind the Conscience; the *nature* of man not being capable of coming under greater obligation. But now a law can have no more force or power in it, than what it receives from the legislator; and since the obliging force of it follows the proportion of his power and prerogative; to affirm that any sanction of man has the same binding force, and sacred validity, that the laws of God have, amounts to a blasphemous equalling of him, who is a worm, and a pitiful nothing, to him, who is God blessed for ever.

Let these arguments suffice to demonstrate, that human laws cannot of *themselves*, and by any power *naturally inherent* in them, immediately bind the conscience. But then in the next place, I add, that it is as certain, that every human law enjoining nothing sinful, or wicked, really binds the conscience, by virtue of a superior obligation superadded to it, from the injunction and express mandate of the divine law, which commands subjection to the laws and ordinances of the civil magistrate; whether of the king as supreme, or of such as be his viceregents and deputed officers.

And thus to assert, that human laws have the same obligation with divine, is neither absurd, nor blasphemous; forasmuch as this is not affirmed to be by any prerogative immanent in themselves, but derivative, and borrowed from the divine. As it is not either treason, or impropriety to affirm, that the word of the constable obliges as much as the word of the King, when the King commands that his constable's word, in such or such matters, should be as much obeyed as his own.

Having thus therefore, by a due and impartial distribution, assigned to God the prerogative of God, and to *Caesar* the prerogative that is *Caesar's*; and withal, pitched the obligation of human laws upon so firm, and so unshakeable a basis; we shall pass from the first ground, upon which obedience to the civil magistrate is enforced, namely, *Conscience of the unlawfulness of resisting it*; and proceed to the

2. With which I shall conclude. And that is, *Conscience of the scandal* of such a resistance; which surely is an argument to such, whose principles are not scandalous. How tender does St. *Paul*, in all his epistles show himself of the repute of Christianity; and what stress does he still lay upon this one consideration? *1 Thess. iv. 12. I beseech you, that ye walk honestly towards them that are without.* And in *2 Cor. vi. 3. Giving no offence in any thing, that the ministry be not blamed.* And surely, could we strip rebellion of the sin, yet this would be argument enough against it, that it gives the enemies of Christianity *cause to blaspheme*, and with some show of reason decry and reject that excellent profession.

How impossible had it been for the christian religion to have made such a spread in the world, at least ever to have gained any countenance from the civil power, had it owned such anti-magistratical assertions, either by its own avowed principles, or by the practices of its primitive professors?

And very probable it is, that at this very day the most potent enemy it has in the world, which is the *Mahometan*, takes up his detestation of it in a great measure, from his observance of those many *rebellions, wars, tumults* and *confusions*, that have so much, and so particularly infested *Christendom*.

For may he not naturally argue; Can that religion be true, or divine, that does not enforce obedience to the magistrate? Or can that do so, whose loudest professors are so rebellious? Is it not rational to imagine, that the religion men profess, will have a suitable influence upon their practice? Are not actions the genuine off-spring of principles? I wish that answer would satisfy the world, that *must* satisfy us, because we have no better; that *Christians* live below *Christianity*, and by their *lives* contradict their *profession*.

In the mean time, let those incendiaries, those spiritual *Abaddons*, whose doctrine, like a scab, or leprosy, has overspread the face of Christianity; and whose tenets are red with the blood of Princes; let such, I say, consider, what account they will give to God for that scandal and prejudice, that they have brought upon so pure, and noble a religion, that can have no other blemish upon it in the world, but that such persons as they profess it.

If they had but any true ingenuity, (a principle much lower

than that of grace) surely it would tie up their consciences from those infamous exorbitancies, that have given such deep gashes, such incurable wounds to their religion. For shall Christ have bled *once for* our sins, and shall christian religion *bleed* always by our practices? I could now beseech such by the mercies of God, and the bowels of Christ, did I think this would move those, who have torn in pieces the body of Christ, that they would bind up the broken reputation of Christianity, by showing henceforth, that subjection is part of their religion: That they would reflect upon the desolations they have made, with one eye, and upon their great *exemplar* with the other; remembering him, who, while he conversed upon earth, was subject to the civil power in his own *person*, and commanded subjection to it by his *precepts*. So that what was said of Christ in respect of the *law of Moses,* may be equally said of him in reference to the *laws of the magistrate, that he came not to destroy but to fulfil.*

Edward Stillingfleet

STILLINGFLEET WAS born in Cranborne, Dorset, in 1635 and educated at St John's College, Cambridge, where he was elected to a fellowship immediately on his graduation at the age of eighteen. No doubt he was a brilliant student; it may be concluded also that his views were not offensive to Presbyterians. He received ordination, however, at the hands of Brownrig, the deprived Bishop of Exeter. Brownrig was a man with whom Stillingfleet must have felt at home. A Cambridge man himself, he was a Calvinist who did not like Laudian ways but said he liked the Church of England 'better and better as he grew older'; and it is recorded that 'persons of all denominations' were present at his funeral. In 1659—when he was only twenty-four—Stillingfleet produced a book called *The Irenicum*, in which he advocated a union between episcopalians and Presbyterians.

In 1655 Pepys 'heard the famous young Stillingfleet', whom he had known at Cambridge; he reports that 'he did make the most plain, honest, good, grave sermon, in the most unconcerned and easy yet substantial manner'. It is the impression one gets from Stillingfleet's works. He was a man of great ability, and had great learning but, even more notably, active practical sense. He preached in an outspoken manner at Court, but maintained good relations there as well as with the dissenters. In 1678 he became Dean of St Paul's. He was not prominent during James II's reign, but 1689 saw him Bishop of Worcester, a member of the Commission which considered the revision of the Prayer Book and the possibility of comprehension. Nothing came of the Commission's proposals. In his later years Stillingfleet engaged in controversy with Locke. He died in 1699.

Stillingfleet was a man to whom practical objectives were important, yet—as many men of affairs are—he was of an abstracting turn of mind. He was a close reasoner, and apparently believed that by reasoning he could persuade. At the end of his book on *Idolatry Practised in the Church of Rome* (1671) there are a few pages in which 'The Faith of Protestants' is 'Reduced to Principles'. It is a characteristic production. Such work points forward to an eighteenth-century rationalism of which Stillingfleet would not have approved, for he was himself very much a man of the seventeenth century and a convinced, if at times Latitudinarian, churchman.

[PREACHED AT WHITEHALL]
Luke 7:35.
But wisdom is justified of all her children.

'BELIEVE ME no farther', Stillingfleet says in the address to the reader at the beginning of the volume in which this sermon was published in 1669, 'than thou seest reason for what I say.' He is more than willing to throw Christianity open to the reason of his times—and nothing is more subject to fashion than the notion of what passes for a reasonable argument. Theology is in a sense an attempt to meet the objections of fashion. Stillingfleet saw as the 'great concernment' in his age 'the vindication of *Christianity* in general' against two sorts of people: atheists—he had been a reader of Hobbes—and those—the emergent deists—'who acknowledge a *God* and *Providence*, but have very mean thoughts of the *Christian Religion*.' The sermon that follows was particularly directed to the latter.

No doubt one of the things which impressed Pepys, who had a busy life at the Navy Office—and came to Whitehall Chapel from the Harp and Bull, where he had been chatting up the maid —was Stillingfleet's sense, not only of the current intellectualisms but of the world of elbowing self-interests in which he lived. There was nothing 'fugitive and cloistered' about Stillingfleet. He was always aware—to use words from another of his sermons —of 'those, who never think the breaches of the world wide enough, till there be a door large enough for their own interests to go in at by them; that would rather see the world burning, than one peg taken out of their Chariot-wheels.' The sermon which follows points to some of the sorts of self-interest which kept people from acknowledging Christ when he was on earth. The congregation would make their own applications to the world around them or—more rarely, for the very reasons Stillingfleet gives—to themselves.

But for the fact that 'interest and prejudice' had 'a far more absolute power and dominion over them, than they had over the rest of the people', the Jewish Sanhedrin 'might have been some of the first converts to Christianity.' Instead they reproached and defamed Jesus, using arguments well chosen to flatter the hopes and fears of their listeners. To those who were zealous for 'the present peace and prosperity of the Nation' under Roman rule, he was represented as dangerously seditious. To those who were bent on getting rid of the Roman yoke, it was represented that 'a person so mean and inconsiderable as our Saviour' would be unequal to the task. His company was 'none of the best'; Luke 7 tells the story of the woman who washed Jesus's feet with her tears, while the Pharisee concluded that Jesus could not be a prophet, since if he had been he would have known what sort of woman she was, and not allowed her to touch him.

Stillingfleet is less concerned with those 'who make a mere jest and scoff at Religion' than with serious, decent people, 'who are of a degree above the other, though far enough short of any true and solid wisdom.' These are the ordinary trained minds, 'intelligent people', as we should say. They 'seem to make a slender offer at reason in what they say' and see through Christianity, though their 'cavils and exceptions' are no more than could be urged against their own opinions. 'Every advantage which another hath got above them, and every cross accident which befalls themselves' is an argument against God. 'Thus either God shall not govern the World at all, or if he do, it must be upon such terms as they please and approve of.' Unpalatable words in a world in which so much is made of opinion. But 'God is wise, and we are not.' Mankind is quarrelling in the dark, and the precepts of Christianity are 'very suitable to the nature of Mankind'. It is a religion which could satisfy 'the expectation of the *Jews*, the reason of the *Greeks*, or the wisdom of the *Romans*'. This does not amount to a proof of Christianity; it is a plea for the removal of prejudice, and a modest claim that this religion is at least as deserving of serious consideration as any of the other notions intelligent people recommend to mankind.

OF ALL the Circumstances of our Blessed Saviour's appearance and preaching in the World, there is none which to our first view and apprehension of things, seems more strange and unaccountable, than that those persons who were then thought of all others to be most conversant in the Law and the Prophets, should be the most obstinate opposers of him. For since he came to fulfil all the Prophecies which had gone before concerning him, and was himself the great Prophet foretold by all the rest, none might in human probability have been judged more likely to have received and honoured him, than those to whom the judgment of those things did peculiarly belong; and who were as much concerned in the truth of them as any else could be. Thus indeed it might have been reasonably expected; and doubtless it had been so, if interest and prejudice had not had a far more absolute power and dominion over them, than they had over the rest of the people. If Miracles, and Prophecies, if Reason and Religion; nay, if the interest of another World could have prevailed over the interest of this among them; the *Jewish Sanhedrin* might have been some of the first Converts to Christianity, the *Scribes* and *Pharisees* had been all Proselytes to Christ, and the Temple at *Jerusalem* had been the first Christian Church. But to let us see with what a jealous eye Power and Interest looks on every thing that seems to offer at any disturbance of it, how much greater sway partiality and prejudice hath upon the minds of Men than true Reason and Religion; and how hard a matter it is to convince those who have no mind to be convinced; we find none more furious in their opposition to the person of Christ, none more obstinate in their infidelity as to this Doctrine, than those who were at that time in the greatest reputation among them for their authority, wisdom, and knowledge. These are they, whom our Saviour, as often as he meets with, either checks for their ignorance, or rebukes for their pride, or denounces woes against for their malice and hypocrisy: These are they who instead of believing in Christ persecute him; instead of following him seek to destroy him: and that they might the better compass it, they reproach and defame him, as if he had been really as bad as themselves. And although the people might not presently believe what they said concerning him, yet they might at least be kept in suspense by it, they endeavour to fasten the blackest calumnies upon him? and suit them with all imaginable arts to the tempers of those they had to deal with.

If any appeared zealous for the present peace and prosperity of the Nation; and for paying the duty and obedience they owed to the *Roman* Power, which then governed them: to them he is represented as a factious and seditious person, as an enemy to *Caesar*, as one that intended to set up a Kingdom of his own, though to the ruin of his Country: That it was nothing but ambition and vain-glory, which made him gather Disciples, and preach to multitudes; that none could foretell what the dangerous consequences of such new Doctrines might be, if not timely suppressed, and the Author of them severely punished. Thus to the prudent and cautious, reason of State is pretended as the ground of their enmity to Christ. But to those who are impatient of the *Roman* yoke, and watched for any opportunity to cast it off; they suggest the mighty improbabilities of ever obtaining any deliverance by a person so mean and inconsiderable as our Saviour appeared among them: and that surely God who delivered their Forefathers of old from a bondage not greater than theirs, by a mighty hand and out-stretched arm, did never intend the redemption of his people by one of obscure Parentage, mean Education, and of no interest in the world. To the great men, they need no more than bid them, behold the train of his followers, who being generally poor, the more numerous they were, the more mouths they might see open, and ready to devour the Estates of those who were above them. The Priests and Levites they bid consider what would become of them all, if the Law of *Moses* was abrogated, by which their interest was upheld? for if the Temple fell, it was impossible for them to stand. But the grand difficulty was among the people, who began to be possessed with so high an opinion of him by the greatness of his Miracles, and excellency of his Doctrine, and the innocency of his Conversation, that unless they could insinuate into their minds some effectual prejudices against these, all their other attempts were like to be vain and unsuccessful. If therefore they meet with any who were surprised by his Miracles, as well as ravished by his Doctrine; when they saw him raise the dead, restore sight to the blind, cure the deaf and the lame, and cast out Devils out of possessed persons, they tell them presently that these were the common arts of Impostors, and the practice of those who go about to deceive the people; that such things were easily done by the power of Magic, and assistance of the evil Spirits. If any were admirers of the Pharisaical rigours and austerities (as the people generally were) when Men's Religion was measured by the sourness of their countenances, the length of their Prayers, and the distance they kept from other persons; these they bid especially beware of our Saviour's Doctrine; for he condemned all zeal and devotion, all mortification and strictness of life, under the pretence of Pharisaical hypocrisy; that he sunk all Religion into short Prayers and dull Morality; that his conversation was not among the persons of any reputation for piety, but among Publicans and Sinners; that nothing extraordinary appeared in his Life; that his actions were like other men's, and his company none of the best, and his behaviour among them with too great a freedom for a person who pretended to so high a degree of holiness.

Thus we see the most perfect innocency could not escape the venom of malicious tongues; but the less it entered, the more they were enraged, and made up what wanted in the truth of their calumnies, by their diligence in spreading them. As though their mouths indeed had been open Sepulchres by the noisome vapours which came out of them; and we may well think no less a poison than that of Asps could be under their lips, which so secretly and yet so mischievously conveyed itself into the hearts of the people. The only advantage which malice hath against the greatest Virtue, is, that the greater it is, the less it takes notice of all the petty arts which are used against it; and will not bring its own innocency so much into suspicion as to make any long Apologies for itself. For, to a noble and generous spirit, assaulted rather by noise and clamour, than any solid reason or force of argument, neglect and disdain are the most proper weapons of defence; for where malice is only impertinent and troublesome, a punctual answer seems next to a confession. But although innocency needs no defence as to itself, yet it is necessary for all the advantages it hath of doing good to mankind, that it appear to be what it really is; which cannot be done, unless its reputation be cleared from the malicious aspersions which are cast upon it. And from hence it was that our blessed Saviour, though he thought it not worth the while to use the same diligence in the vindication of himself, which his enemies did in the defamation of him; yet when he saw it necessary in order to the reception of his Doctrine among the more ingenious and tractable part of his auditors, he sometimes by the quickness of his replies, sometimes by the suddenness and sharpness of his questions, and sometimes by the plain force of argument and reason baffles his adversaries, so that though they were resolved not to be convinced, they thought it best for the time to be quiet. This was to let them see how easy it was for him to throw off their reproaches as fast as their malice could invent them; and that it was as impossible for them by such weak attempts to obscure the reputation of his innocency, as for the spots which Astronomers discern near the body of the Sun, ever to eclipse the light of it. So that all those thinner mists which envy and detraction raised at his first appearance, and those grosser vapours which arose from their open enmity when he came to a greater height, did but add a brighter lustre to his glory, when it was seen that notwithstanding all the machinations of his enemies, his innocency brake forth like the light, which shineth more and more to the perfect day.

But it pleased God, for the trial of men's minds so to order the matters of our Religion, that as they are never so clear, but men of obstinate and perverse spirits will find something to cavil at; so they were never so dark and obscure in the most difficult circumstances of them, but men of unprejudiced and ingenuous minds might find enough to satisfy themselves about them. Which is the main scope of our Saviour in the words of the Text, (and shall be of our present discourse upon them) *but wisdom is justified of all her Children.* Where without any further Explication, by *Wisdom* we understand the method which God useth in order to the salvation of mankind; by the *Children of Wisdom*, all those who were willing to attain the end by the means which God affordeth, and by *justifying* not only the bare approving it, but the declaring of that approbation to the World by a just vindication of it from the cavils and exceptions of men. Although the words are capable of various senses, yet this is the most natural, and agreeable to the scope of what goes before. For there our Saviour speaks of the different ways wherein *John Baptist* and himself appeared among the *Jews*, in order to the same end, v. 32. For *John Baptist came neither eating bread nor drinking wine, and ye say, he hath a Devil.* A very severe Devil surely, and one of the strictest order among them, that was so far from being cast out by fasting and prayer, that these were his continual employment! But what could we have sooner thought than that those persons who made the Devil the author of so much mortification and severity of life, should presently have entertained Religion in a more free and pleasing humour? but this would not take neither, for *the Son of Man comes eating and drinking*; i.e. was remarkable for none of those rigours and austerities which they condemned in *John*, and applauded in the *Pharisees*;

and then presently they censure him, *as a gluttonous man, and a Wine-bibber, a friend of Publicans and Sinners, v.* 34 i. e. the utmost excess that any course of life was capable of they presently apply to those who had no other design in all their actions, than to recommend true piety and goodness to them. So impossible it was by any means which the wisdom of Heaven thought fit to use, to persuade them into any good opinion of the persons who brought the glad tidings of Salvation to them: and therefore our Saviour, when he sees how refractory and perverse they were, in interpreting everything to the worse, and censuring the ways which infinite Wisdom thought fittest to reclaim them by, he tells them that it was nothing but malice and obstinacy which was the cause of it; but if they were men of teachable spirits (who by an usual Hebraism are called the Children of Wisdom) they would see reason enough to admire, approve and justify all the methods of divine Providence for the good of Mankind. *For Wisdom is justified of all her Children.*

That which I mainly design to speak to from hence is, *That although the wisest Contrivances of Heaven for the good of Mankind are liable to the unjust cavils and exceptions of unreasonable Men, yet there is enough to satisfy any teachable and ingenuous Minds concerning the wisdom of them.* Before I come more particularly to examine those which concern our present subject, *viz.* the life and appearance of our Lord and Saviour, it will take very much off from the force of them, if we consider, that thus it hath always been, and supposing human nature to be as it is, it is scarce conceivable that it should be otherwise. Not that it is necessary or reasonable it should be so at all, any more than it is necessary that Men should act foolishly or inconsiderately; but as long as we must never expect to see all Men either wise or pious, either to have a true judgment of things, or a love of Religion; so long we shall always find there will be some, who will be quarrelling with Religion when they have no mind to practise it. I speak not now of those who make a mere jest and scoff at Religion (of which our Age hath so many Instances) but a sort of Men who are of a degree above the other, though far enough short of any true and solid wisdom; who yet are the more to be considered, because they seem to make a slender offer at reason in what they say. Some pretend they are not only unsatisfied with the particular ways of instituted Religion, any further than they are subservient to their present interest (which is the only God they worship) but to make all sure, the foundations even of Natural Religion itself cannot escape their cavils and exceptions. They have found out an *Index Expurgatorius* for those impressions of a Deity which are in the hearts of Men; and use their utmost arts to obscure, since they cannot extinguish, those lively characters of the power, wisdom and goodness of God, which are every where to be seen in the large volume of the Creation. Religion is no more to them but an unaccountable fear; and the very notion of a spiritual substance (even of that without which we could never know what a contradiction meant) is said to imply one. But if for quietness' sake, and it may be to content their own minds as well as the World, they are willing to admit of a Deity, (which is a mighty concession from those who have so much cause to be afraid of him) then to ease their minds of such troublesome companions as their fears are, they seek by all means to dispossess him of his Government of the World, by denying his Providence, and care of human affairs. They are contented he should be called an excellent Being, that should do nothing, and therefore signify nothing in the World; or rather, that he might be styled an Almighty *Sardanapalus*, that is so fond of ease and pleasure, that the least thought of business would quite spoil his happiness. Or if the activity of their own spirits may make them think that such an excellent Being may sometimes draw the Curtains and look abroad into the World, then every advantage which another hath got above them, and every cross accident which befalls themselves (which by the power of self-flattery most Men have learned to call the Prosperity of the wicked, and the Sufferings of good Men) serve them for mighty charges against the justice of Divine Providence. Thus either God shall not govern the World at all, or if he do, it must be upon such terms as they please and approve of, or else they will erect an High Court of Justice upon him, and condemn the Sovereign of the World, because he could not please his discontented Subjects. And as if he were indeed arraigned at such a bar, every weak and peevish exception shall be cried up for evidence; when the fullest and clearest vindications of him shall be scorned and contemned. But this doth not in the least argue the obnoxiousness of him who is so accused but the great injustice of those who dare pass sentence; where it is neither in their power to understand the reason of his actions, nor if it were, to call him in question for his proceedings with Men. But so great is the pride and arrogance of human Nature, that it loves to be condemning what it cannot comprehend; and there needs to be no greater reason given concerning the many disputes in the world about Divine Providence, than that God is wise, and we are not but would fain seem to be so. While Men are in the dark they will be always quarrelling; and those who contend the most, do it that they might seem to others to see, when they know themselves they do not. Nay, there is nothing so plain and evident, but the reason of some Men is more apt to be imposed upon in it, than their senses are; as it appeared in him who could not otherwise confute the Philosopher's argument against motion, but by moving before him. So that we see the most certain things in the world are liable to the cavils of Men who employ their wits to do it; and certainly those ought not to stagger Men's faith in matters of the highest nature and consequence, which would not at all move them in other things.

But at last it is acknowledged by the Men who love to be called the Men of wit in this Age of ours, that there is a God and Providence, a future state, and the differences of good and evil, but the Christian Religion they will see no further reason to embrace than as it is the Religion of the State they live in. But if we demand what mighty reasons they are able to bring forth against a Religion so holy and innocent in its design, so agreeable to the Nature of God and Man, so well contrived for the advantages of this and another life, so fully attested to come from God by the Miracles wrought in confirmation of it, by the death of the Son of God, and of such multitudes of Martyrs, so certainly conveyed to us, by the unquestionable Tradition of all Ages since the first delivery of it; the utmost they can pretend against it is, that it is built upon such an appearance of the Son of God which was too mean and contemptible, that the Doctrine of it is inconsistent with the Civil Interests of Men, and the design ineffectual for the Reformation of the World. For the removal therefore of these cavils against our Religion, I shall show,

1. That there were no circumstances in our Saviour's appearance or course of life, which were unbecoming the Son of God, and the design he came upon.

2. That the Doctrine delivered by him is so far from being contrary to the Civil Interests of the World, that it tends highly to the preservation of them.

3. That the design he came upon was very agreeable to the Infinite Wisdom of God, and most effectual for the reformation of Mankind.

For clearing the first of these, I shall consider, (1.) The Manner of our Saviour's appearance. (2.) The Course of his Life; and what it was which his enemies did most object against him.

1. The manner of our Saviour's Appearance; which hath been always the great offence to the admirers of the pomp and greatness of this World. For when they heard of the Son of God coming down from Heaven, and making his Progress into this lower world, they could imagine nothing less, than that an innumerable company of Angels must have been dispatched before, to have prepared a place for his reception; that all the Sovereigns and Princes of the World must have been summoned to give their attendance and pay their homage to him: that their Sceptres must have been immediately laid at his feet and all the Kingdoms of the earth been united into one universal Monarchy under the Empire of the Son of God: That the Heavens should bow down at his presence to show their obeisance to him, the Earth tremble and shake for fear at the near approaches of his Majesty; that all the Clouds should clap together in one universal Thunder, to welcome his appearance, and tell the Inhabitants of the World what cause they had to fear him whom the Powers of the Heavens obey: that the Sea should run out of its wonted course with amazement and horror; and if it were possible, hide itself in the hollow places of the earth: that the Mountains should shrink in their heads, to fill up the vast places of the deep; so that all that should be fulfilled in a literal sense, which was foretold of the coming of the *Messias, (a) That every Valley should be filled, and every Mountain and Hill brought low; the crooked made straight, and the rough ways smooth, and all flesh see the salvation of God.* Yea, that the Sun for a time should be darkened, and the Moon withdraw her light, to let the Nations of the Earth understand that a Glory infinitely greater than theirs did now appear to the World. In a word, they could not imagine the Son of God could be born without the pangs and throes of the whole Creation; that it was as impossible for him to appear, as for the Sun in the Firmament to disappear, without the notice of the whole World. But when instead of all his pomp and grandeur he comes *incognito* into the World, instead of giving notice of his appearance to the Potentates of the Earth, he is only discovered to a few silly Shepherds and three Wise men of the East; instead of choosing either *Rome* or *Jerusalem* for the place of his Nativity, he is born at *Bethlehem*, a mean and obscure Village; instead of the glorious and magnificent Palaces of the East or West, which were at that time so famous; he is brought forth in a

Stable, where the Manger was his Cradle, and his Mother the only attendant about him: who was herself none of the great persons of the Court, nor of any fame in the Country; but was only rich in her Genealogy, and honourable in her Pedigree. And according to the obscurity of his Birth was his Education too: his Youth was not spent in the Imperial Court at *Rome*, nor in the Schools of the great Rabbis at *Jerusalem*: but at *Nazareth*, a place of mean esteem among the *Jews*, where he was remarkable for nothing so much as the Virtues proper to his Age, Modesty, Humility and Obedience. All which he exercises to so high a degree, that his greatest kindred and acquaintance were mightily surprised when at 30 years of age, he began to discover himself by the Miracles which he wrought, and the Authority which he spake with. And although the rays of his Divinity began to break forth through the Clouds he had hitherto disguised himself in, yet he persisted still in the same course of humility and self-denial; taking care of others to the neglect of himself; feeding others by a Miracle, and fasting himself, to one: showing his power in working miraculous Cures, and his humility in concealing them: Conversing with the meanest of the people, and choosing such for his Apostles, who brought nothing to recommend them but innocency and simplicity. Who by their heats and ignorance were continual exercises of his patience in bearing with them, and of his care and tenderness in instructing them. And after a life thus led with such unparalleled humility, when he could add nothing more to it by his actions, he doth it by his sufferings; and completes the sad Tragedy of his Life by a most shameful and ignominious Death. This is the short and true account of all those things which the admirers of the greatness of this world think mean and contemptible in our Saviour's appearance here on earth. But we are now to consider whether so great humility were not more agreeable with the design of his coming into the World, than all that pomp and state would have been which the Son of God might have more easily commanded than we can imagine. He came not upon so mean an errand, as to dazzle the eyes of Mankind with the brightness of his Glory, to amaze them by the terribleness of his Majesty, much less to make a show of the riches and gallantry of the World to them: But he came upon far more noble and excellent designs, to bring life and immortality to light, to give men the highest assurance of an eternal happiness and misery in the World to come, and the most certain directions for obtaining the one, and avoiding the other:

and in order to that, nothing was judged more necessary by him; than to bring the vanities of this World out of that credit and reputation they had gained among foolish men. Which he could never have done, if he had declaimed never so much against the vanity of worldly greatness, riches and honours, if in the meantime himself had lived in the greatest splendour and bravery. For the enjoining then the contempt of this world to his Disciples in hopes of a better, would have looked like the commendation of the excellency of fasting at a full meal, and of the conveniencies of poverty by one who makes the greatest haste to be rich. That he might not therefore seem to offer so great a contradiction to his Doctrine by his own example, he makes choice of a life so remote from all suspicion of designs upon this world, that *though the foxes had holes, and the birds of the air had nests, yet the Son of Man*, who was the Lord and Heir of all things, *had not whereon to lay his head*. And as he showed by his life how little he valued the great things of the World, so he discovered by his death how little he feared the evil things of it: all which he did with a purpose and intention to rectify the great mistakes of Men as to these things: That they might no longer venture an eternal happiness for the splendid and glorious vanities of this present life; nor expose themselves to the utmost miseries of another world, to avoid the frowns of this. From hence proceeded that generous contempt of the World, which not only our Saviour himself, but all his true Disciples of the first Ages of Christianity were so remarkable for; to let others see they had greater things in their eye than any here, the hopes of which they would not part with for all that this world thinks great or desirable. So that considering the great danger most Men are in, by too passionate a love of these things, and that universal and infinite kindness which our Saviour had to the Souls of Men; there was nothing he could discover it more in as to his appearance in the world, than by putting such an affront upon the greatness and honour of it, as he did by so open a neglect of it in his life, and despising it in his death and sufferings. And who now upon any pretence of reason dare entertain the meaner apprehensions of our Blessed Saviour because he appeared without the pomp and greatness of the world, when the reason of his doing so was, that by his own humility and self-denial he might show us the way to an eternal happiness? Which he well knew how very hard it would be for Men to attain to, who measure things not according to their inward worth and excellency, but the splendour and appearance which they make to the world: who think nothing great but what makes them gazed upon; nothing desirable but what makes them flattered. But if they could be once persuaded how incomparably valuable the glories of the life to come are above all the gaieties and shows of this; they would think no condition mean or contemptible, which led to so great an end; none happy or honourable which must so soon end in the grave, or be changed to eternal misery. And that we might entertain such thoughts as these are, not as the melancholy effects of discontent and disappointments, but as the serious result of our most deliberate enquiry into the value of things, was the design of our Saviour in the humility of his appearance, and of that excellent Doctrine which he recommended to the World by it. Were I to argue the case with Philosophers, I might then at large show from the free acknowledgements of the best and most experienced of them, that nothing becomes so much one who designs to recommend Virtue to the World, as a real and hearty contempt of all the pomp of it, and that the meanest condition proceeding from such a principle is truly and in itself more honourable, than living in the greatest splendour imaginable. Were I to deal with the *Jews*, I might then prove, that as the Prophecies concerning the *Messias* speak of great and wonderful effects of his coming, so that they should be accomplished in a way of suffering and humility. But since I speak to Christians, and therefore to those who were persuaded of the great kindness and love of our Saviour in coming into the World, to reform it, and that by convincing men of the truth and excellency of a future state, no more need to be said to vindicate the appearance of him from that meanness and contempt, which the pride and ambition of vain Men is apt to cast upon it.

2. But not only our Saviour's manner of Appearance, but the manner of his Conversation gave great offence to his enemies, *viz.* That it was too free and familiar among persons who had the meanest reputation, *the Publicans and Sinners*; and in the mean time declaimed against the strictest observers of the greatest rigours and austerities of life. And this no doubt was one great cause of the mortal hatred of the *Pharisees* against him, though least pretended, that even thereby they might make good that charge of hypocrisy which our Saviour so often draws up against them. And no wonder, if such severe rebukes did highly provoke them, since they found this so gainful and withall so easy a trade among the people, when with a demure look and

a sour countenance they could cheat and defraud their Brethren; and under a specious show of devotion could break their fasts by devouring Widows' houses, and end their long Prayers to God with acts of the highest injustice to their Neighbours. As though all that while, they had been only begging leave of God to do all the mischief they could to their Brethren. It is true, such as these were, our Saviour upon all occasions speaks against with the greatest sharpness, as being the most dangerous enemies to true Religion: and that which made men, whose passion was too strong for their reason, abhor the very name of Religion, when such baseness was practised under the profession of it. When they saw Men offer to compound with Heaven for all their injustice and oppression, with not a twentieth part of what God challenges as his due; they either thought Religion to be a mere device of Men, or that these men's hypocrisy ought to be discovered to the World. And therefore our Blessed Saviour, who came with a design to retrieve a true spirit of Religion among Men, finds it first of all necessary to unmask those notorious hypocrites, that their deformities being discovered, their ways as well as their persons might be the better understood and avoided. And when he saw by the mighty opinion they had of themselves, and their uncharitableness towards all others, how little good was to be done upon them, he seldom vouchsafes them his presence; but rather converses with those who being more openly wicked were more easily convinced of their wickedness, and persuaded to reform. For which end alone it was that he so freely conversed with them, to let them see there were none so bad, but his kindness was so great to them, that he was willing to do them all the good he could: And therefore this could be no more a just reproach to Christ, that he kept company sometimes with these, than it is to a Surgeon to visit Hospitals, or to a Physician to converse with the Sick.

2. But when they saw that his Greatness did appear in another way, by the authority of his Doctrine, and the power of his Miracles, then these wise and subtle Men apprehend a further reach and design in all his actions: *viz*. That his low condition was a piece of Popularity, and a mere disguise to ensnare the people, the better to make them in love with his Doctrine, and so by degrees to season them with Principles of Rebellion and Disobedience: Hence came all the clamours of his being *an Enemy to Caesar*, and calling himself *the King of the Jews*, and of his design to erect a Kingdom of his own, all which they interpret

in the most malicious though most unreasonable sense. For nothing is so politic as malice and ill-will, for that finds designs in everything; and the more contrary they are to all the Protestations of the persons concerned, the deeper that suggests presently they are laid, and that there is the more cause to be afraid of them. Thus it was in our Blessed Saviour's case; it was not the greatest care used by him to show his obedience to the Authority he lived under, it was not his most solemn disavowing having anything to do with their civil Interests, not the severe checks he gave his own Disciples for any ambitious thoughts among them, not the recommending the doctrine of Obedience to them, nor the rebuke he gave one of his most forward Disciples for offering to draw his sword in the rescue of himself, could abate the fury and rage of his enemies, but at last they condemn the greatest Teacher of the duty of Obedience as a Traitor, and the most unparalleled example of innocency as a Malefactor. But though there could be nothing objected against the life and actions of our Blessed Saviour, as tending to sedition and disturbance of the Civil Peace, yet that, these Men (who were inspired by malice, and prophesied according to their own interest) would say, was because he was taken away in time, before his designs could be ripe for action, but if his doctrine tended that way, it was enough to justify their proceedings against him. So then, it was not what he did, but what he might have done: not Treason but Convenience which made them take away the life of the most innocent Person: but if there had been any taint in his doctrine that way, there had been reason enough in such an Age of faction and sedition to have used the utmost care to prevent the spreading it. But so far is this from the least ground of probability, that it is not possible to imagine a Religion which aims less at the present particular interests of the embracers of it, and more at the public interests of Princes than Christianity doth, as it was both preached and practised by our Saviour and his Apostles.

And here we have cause to lament the unhappy fate of Religion when it falls under the censure of such who think themselves the Masters of all the little arts whereby this world is governed. If it teaches the duty of Subjects, and the authority of Princes, if it requires obedience to Laws, and makes men's happiness or misery in another life in any measure to depend upon it; then Religion is suspected to be a mere trick of State, and an invention to keep the world in awe, whereby Men might the better be moulded into Societies, and preserved in them. But if it appear to enforce anything indispensably on the Consciences of Men, though human Laws require the contrary; if they must not forswear their Religion, and deny him whom they hope to be saved by, when the Magistrate calls them to it, then such half-witted Men think that Religion is nothing but a pretence to Rebellion, and Conscience only an obstinate plea for Disobedience. But this is to take it for granted that there is no such thing as Religion in the World; for if there be, there must be some inviolable Rights of Divine Sovereignty acknowledged, which must not vary according to the diversity of the Edicts and Laws of Men. But supposing the profession and practice of the Christian Religion to be allowed inviolable, there was never any Religion, nay, never any inventions of the greatest Politicians, which might compare with that for the preservation of civil *Societies*. For this in plain and express words tells all the owners of it, that they must live in subjection and obedience; *(a) not only for wrath, but for Conscience sake; that they who do resist receive unto themselves damnation, and that because whosoever resisteth the Power, resisteth the Ordinance of God*. Than which it is impossible to conceive arguments of greater force to keep men in obedience to Authority; for he that only obeys because it is his interest to do so, will have the same reason to disobey when there is an apprehension that may make more for his advantage. But when the reason of obedience is derived from the concernments of another life, no hopes of interest in this world can be thought to balance the loss which may come by such a breach of duty in that to come. So that no persons do so dangerously undermine the foundations of civil Government, as those who magnify that to the contempt of Religion; none so effectually secure them as those *who give to God the things that are God's*, and by doing so, are obliged *to give to Caesar the things that are Caesar's*. This was the doctrine of Christianity as it was delivered by the first author of it; and the practice was agreeable, as long as Christianity preserved its primitive honour in the world. For, so far were men then from making their zeal for Religion a pretence to Rebellion, that though Christianity were directly contrary to the Religions then in vogue in the world, yet they knew of no other way of promoting it, but by patience, humility, meekness, prayers for their persecutors, and tears when they saw them obstinate. So far were they then from fomenting suspicions and jealousies concerning the Princes and Governors they lived under, that though they were generally known to be some of the worst of men as well as of Princes, yet they charge all Christians in the strictest manner, as they loved their Religion and the honour of it, as they valued their souls and the salvation of them, that they should be subject to them. So far were they then from giving the least encouragement to the usurpations of the rights of Princes under the pretence of any power given to a Head of the Church: that there is no way for any to think they meant it, unless we suppose the Apostles such mighty Politicians, that it is because they say nothing at all of it; but on the contrary, *bid every soul be subject to the higher powers*; though an Apostle, Evangelist, Prophet, whatever he be, as the Fathers interpret it. Yea, so constant and uniform was the doctrine and practice of Obedience in all the first and purest ages of the Christian Church, that no one instance can be produced of any usurpation of the rights of Princes under the pretence of any title from Christ, or any disobedience to their authority, under the pretence of promoting Christianity, through all those times wherein Christianity the most flourished, or the Christians were the most persecuted. And happy had it been for us in these last ages of the World, if we had been Christians on the same terms which they were in the Primitive times; then there had been no such scandals raised by the degeneracy of men upon the most excellent and peaceable Religion in the World, as though that were unquiet and troublesome, because so many have been so who have made show of it. But let their pretences be never so great to Infallibility on one side, and to the Spirit on the other, so far as men encourage faction and disobedience, so far they have not the Spirit of Christ and Christianity, and therefore are none of his. For he showed his great wisdom in contriving such a method of saving men's souls in another World, as tended most to the preservation of the peace and quietness of this; and though this wisdom may be evil spoken of by men of restless and unpeaceable minds, yet it will be still justified by all who have heartily embraced the Wisdom which is from above, who are pure and peaceable as that Wisdom is, and such, and only such are the Children of it.

3. I come to show, That the design of Christ's appearance was very agreeable to the infinite Wisdom of God; and that the means were very suitable and effectual for carrying on of that design for the reformation of Mankind.

1. That the design itself was very agreeable to the infinite Wisdom of God. What could we imagine more becoming the Wisdom

of God, than to contrive a way for the recovery of lapsed and degenerate Mankind: who more fit to employ upon such a message as this, than the Son of God? for his coming gives the greatest assurance to the minds of men, that God was serious in the management of this design, than which nothing could be of greater importance in order to the success of it. And how was it possible he should give a greater testimony of himself, and withal of the purpose he came about, than he did when he was in the world? The accomplishment of Prophecies, and power of Miracles showed who he was; the nature of his Doctrine, the manner of his Conversation, the greatness of his Sufferings, showed what his design was in appearing among men: for they were all managed with a peculiar respect to the convincing mankind, that God was upon terms of mercy with them, and had therefore sent his Son into the world, that he might not only obtain the pardon of sin for those who repent, but eternal life for all them that obey him. And what is there now we can imagine so great and desirable as this, for God to manifest his wisdom in? It is true, we see a great discovery of it in the works of Nature, and might do in the methods of Divine Providence if partiality and interest did not blind our eyes; but both these, though great in themselves, yet fall short of the contrivance of bringing to an eternal happiness man who had fallen from his Maker, and was perishing in his own folly. Yet this is that which men in the pride and vanity of their own imaginations either think not worth considering, or consider as little as if they thought so; and in the meantime think themselves very wise too. The *Jews* had the wisdom of their Traditions which they gloried in, and despised the Son of God himself when he came to alter them. The *Greeks* had the wisdom of their Philosophy which they so passionately admired, that whatever did not agree with that, though infinitely more certain and useful, was on that account rejected by them. The *Romans*, after the conquest of so great a part of the World, were grown all such Politicians and Statesmen, that few of them could have leisure to think of another world, who were so busy in the management of this. And some of all these sorts do yet remain in the World, which makes so many so little think of, or admire this infinite discovery of divine Wisdom: nay, there are some who can mix all these together, joining a *Jewish* obstinacy, with the pride and self-opinion of the *Greeks*, to a *Roman* unconcernedness about the matters of another life. And yet upon a true and just enquiry never any Religion could be found, which could more fully satisfy the expectation of the *Jews*, the reason of the *Greeks*, or the wisdom of the *Romans*, than that which was made known by Christ, *who was the Wisdom of God, and the power of God*. Here the *Jew* might find his *Messias* come, and the Promises fulfilled which related to him; here the *Greek* might find his long and vainly looked for certainty of a life to come, and the way which leads to it; here the *Roman* might see a Religion serviceable to another world and this together. Here are Precepts more holy, Promises more certain, Rewards more desirable than ever the Wit or Invention of Men could have attained to. Here are Institutions far more pious, useful and serviceable to mankind, than the most admired Laws of the famous Legislators of *Greece* or *Rome*. Here are no popular designs carried on, no vices indulged for the public interest, which *Solon, Lycurgus* and *Plato* are charged with. Here is no making Religion a mere trick of State, and a thing only useful for governing the people, which *Numa* and the great men at *Rome* are liable to the suspicion of. Here is no wrapping up Religion in strange figures and mysterious nonsense, which the *Egyptians* were so much given to. Here is no inhumanity and cruelty in the Sacrifices offered, no looseness and profaneness allowed in the most solemn mysteries, no worshipping of such for Gods who had not been fit to live if they had been Men, which were all things so commonly practised in the Idolatries of the Heathens. But the nature of the Worship is such as the minds of those who come to it ought to be, and as becomes that God whom we profess to serve, pure and holy, grave and serious, solemn and devout, without the mixtures of superstition, vanity or ostentation. The precepts of our Religion are plain and easy to be known, very suitable to the nature of Mankind, and highly tending to the advantage of those who practise them, both in this and a better life. The arguments to persuade men are the most weighty and powerful, and of as great importance, as the love of God, the death of his Son, the hopes of happiness, and the fears of eternal misery, can be to men. And wherein is the contrivance of our Religion defective, when the end is so desirable, the means so effectual for the obtaining of it?

2. Which is the next thing to be considered. There are two things which in this degenerate state of man are necessary in order to the recovery of his happiness: and those are Repentance for sins past, and sincere Obedience for the future: now both these the Gospel gives men the greatest encouragements to, and

therefore is the most likely to effect the design it was intended for.

1. For Repentance for sins past. What more powerful motives can there be to persuade men to repent, than for God to let men know that he is willing to pardon their sins upon the sincerity of their Repentance, but without that, there remains nothing but a fearful expectation of judgment, and fiery indignation? that their sins are their follies, and therefore to repent is to grow wise: that he requires no more from men, but what every considerative man knows is fitting to be done whenever he reflects upon his actions: that there can be no greater ingratitude or disingenuity towards the Son of God than to stand at defiance with God when he hath shed his blood to reconcile God and Man to each other: that every step of his humiliation, every part of the Tragedy of his life, every wound at his death, every groan and sigh which he uttered upon the Cross, were designed by him as the most prevailing Rhetoric, to persuade men to forsake their sins, and be happy: that there cannot be a more unaccountable folly, than by impenitency to lose the hopes of a certain and eternal happiness for the sake of those pleasures which every wise Man is ashamed to think of: that to continue in sin with the hopes to repent, is to stab a man's self with the hopes of a cure: that the sooner men do it, the sooner they will find their minds at ease, and that the pleasures they enjoy in forsaking their sins, are far more noble and manly than ever they had in committing them: but if none of these arguments will prevail with them, perish they must, and that unavoidably, insupportably, and irrecoverably: And if such arguments as these will not prevail with men to leave their sins, it is impossible that any should.

2. For Holiness of Life: For Christ did not come into the World, and die for us, merely that we should repent of what is past, *(a) by denying ungodliness and worldly lusts, but that we should live soberly, righteously and godly in this present world*. And what he doth expect, he hath given the greatest encouragements to perform: by the clearness of his precepts, the excellency of his own example, the promise of his Grace, and the proposition of eternal rewards and punishments, whereby he takes off all the objections men are apt to make against obedience to the Commands of Christ: the pretence of ignorance, because his Laws are so clear; the pretence of impossibility by his own example; the pretence of infirmity by the assistance of his Grace; the pretence of the unnecessariness of so great care of our actions by making eternal rewards and punishments to depend upon it.

Let us then reflect upon the whole design of the Gospel, and see how admirably it is suited to the end it was intended for, to the condition of those whose good was designed by it, and to the whole honour of the great contriver and manager of it. And let not us by our impenitency and the unholiness of our lives, dishonour God and our Saviour, reproach our Religion, and condemn that by our lives which we justify by our words. For when we have said all we can, the best and most effectual vindication of Christian Religion is to live according to it: But oh then how unhappy are we that live in such an Age wherein it were hard to know that men were Christians, unless we are bound to believe their words against the tenor and course of their actions! What is become of the purity, the innocency, the candour, the peaceableness, the sincerity and devotion of the Primitive Christians! What is become of their zeal for the honour of Christ and Christian Religion! If it were the design of men, to make our Religion a dishonour and reproach to the *Jews, Mohametans*, and *Heathens*, could they do it by more effectual means than they have done? Who is there that looks into the present state of the Christian World, could ever think that the Christian Religion was so incomparably beyond all others in the world? Is the now *Christian Rome* so much beyond what it was while it was *Heathen*? Nay, was it not then remarkable in its first times for justice, sincerity, contempt of riches, and a kind of generous honesty, and who does not (though of the same Religion, if he hath any ingenuity left) lament the want of all those things there now? Will not the sobriety of the very *Turks* upbraid our excesses and debaucheries? and the obstinacy of the *Jews* in defence and practice of their Religion, condemn our coldness and indifferency in ours? If we have then any tenderness for the honour of our Religion, or any kindness for our own Souls, let us not only have the Name, but let us lead the lives of Christians; let us make amends for all the reproaches which our Religion hath suffered by the faction and disobedience of some, by the Oaths and Blasphemies, the impieties and profaneness of others, by the too great negligence and carelessness of all, that if it be possible, Christianity may appear in its true glory, which will then only be, when those *who name the Name of Christ depart from iniquity, and live in all manner of holy conversation and godliness.*

THOMAS KEN

KEN WAS born at Berkhamstead in Hertfordshire in 1637, the youngest son of an attorney. He was educated at Winchester and New College, Oxford, where he graduated in 1661. In 1663 he became rector of Little Easton, in Essex, and two years later went back to Winchester, where he undertook to look after a small neglected parish on the outskirts of the city. From 1672 he taught at the college, and it was about this time that he composed his *Manual of Prayers for the Use of the Winchester Scholars*. In 1675 he travelled as far as Rome. In 1679 he was appointed chaplain to Princess Mary at the Hague, and seems to have got on less well with William. He afterwards became chaplain to Charles II, who took in good part his refusal to allow Nell Gwynn to lodge in his house in Winchester. Ken apparently thought he should not countenance the King's irregularities and the King thought this was a perfectly proper line for a clergyman to take. The following year Ken was made bishop of Bath and Wells. He attended at the death-bed of Charles II, giving him an absolution to which the King perhaps paid little attention, and he was outwitted by a Roman priest at the last moment.

The most important public events in Ken's life were in connection with the changes of 1688-9. He was one of the seven bishops who protested against James II's order that his Declaration of Indulgence should be read in all churches. The matter of the declaration was no more than everyone now takes for granted; there was to be full liberty of worship and an end to discrimination on grounds of religion. The bishops' protest led to their arrest. They were provided with good lawyers. An initial argument on a purely technical point about their standing as peers led to their being incarcerated in the Tower of London. To those who did not understand the issues this must have looked like the first of those acts of popish oppression which they were expecting from James, while the more knowledgeable of his opponents must have been delighted at the misunderstanding. When the main case came on the bishops themselves had only a passive role to play. The case was entirely managed by their lawyers. First came a long argument as to whether the bishops were properly before the court; then as to whether the petition and the signatures were in the handwriting of the accused. All this niggling looks odd in relation to the position of the bishops as political heroes. The lawyers were forced in the end to the substance of the argument, which had been made in the protest itself, and was the constitutional issue as to whether the King could dispense with laws passed in due form by Parliament. The charge was one of issuing a seditious libel, and the jury returned a verdict of 'Not guilty'. By the time he heard the verdict James II was already in camp with his troops at Hounslow, and soon he was out of the country and William and Mary were on their way over from Holland.

For Ken this was only the beginning of the end. When William was in the saddle he required an oath of allegiance. Ken with four other bishops and about four hundred of the clergy felt that they could not take it. It was a matter of conscience. They had sworn allegiance to James. There were two sides to the question, and Ken recognized this. It could be argued that there was a duty of obedience to the *de facto* government. When Ken made his decision he wrote to the Non-Juror Dodwell: 'Only in one thing I cannot go as far as you seem to do, in condemning those who are of another persuasion, because I think there are more degrees of excusability in what they have done than perhaps you will admit.' Ken and the other Non-Jurors were deprived and ejected. For many of the clergy and their families this meant extreme hardship. Ken retired to the protection of Lord Weymouth's mansion at Longleat, with no more than seven hundred pounds from the sale of his effects in Wells. He continued to take an interest in the affairs of his fellow Non-Jurors, but opposed the consecration of further Non-Juring bishops when others sought to continue the succession—and the schism—in that way.

Ken was a man of great generosity and charm, ascetic and assiduous in his devotions and morally fastidious. He can hardly be said to have been intellectually outstanding among the churchmen of his day. His prose works are not important, most of his verse is weak and self-indulgent, quite different in kind from the splendid Morning, Evening and Midnight Hymns for which he is remembered and which he used regularly in his own devotions. He took care of his diocese, while he had it, and was always actively charitable. He worked day and night for the relief of the hundreds of prisoners in Bridgwater, Taunton and Wells after the battle of Sedgemoor. After he was deprived he had, of course, no public function. There were twenty years of religious retreat at Longleat. He died in 1711.

At the Funeral of the Right Honourable the Lady Margaret Mainard
Proverbs 11:16.
A gracious woman retaineth honour.

ONLY THREE of Ken's sermons are extant. That given here was preached at Little Easton in 1682. Ken was forty-five and it was nearly twenty years since he had been rector there. The Lady Mainard who is the subject of the sermon had at that time been a girl of about twenty or twenty-one, six years his junior, newly married to Lord Mainard as his second wife and with step-children to look after. The Mainards occupied the big house at Little Easton.

There is little doubt that Ken developed at the least a serious affection for Lady Mainard. One may even speculate that his scruples on this score had something to do with his going off to Winchester, where he had no preferment. However that may be, Lady Mainard must have been a perfect parishioner, during those early years, for a rigorous and sensitive young priest. What sort of woman she was is set out by Ken in the funeral sermon, and he was not the man for flattering inventions on such, or indeed on any, occasion. In the dedication of the sermon to Lord Mainard—for it was printed by the latter's orders—Ken says that but for the 'many unexceptionable witnesses' he might indeed have been thought 'guilty of most gross flattery'. The 'incomparable lady now in heaven' was spoken of throughout in 'the words of truth'. The language is not such as would be used in our day, but there is no room to doubt its sincerity.

The contemporary reader of this sermon will perhaps be scandalized by Ken's discrimination between the sexes. Perhaps, he says, 'women are made of a temper more soft and frail, are more endangered by snares and temptations, less able to control their passions, and more inclinable to extremes of good or bad than men.' In them 'Goodness is a tenderer thing, more hazardous and brittle'. These were the commonplaces of the time. There is, however, more than a touch of personal and pastoral experience in his further assertion: 'I know not how to call it, but there is a meltingness of Disposition, and an affectionateness of Devotion, an easy Sensibility, an industrious Alacrity, a languishing Ardour, in Piety, peculiar to the Sex, which naturally renders them, Subjects more pliable, to the Divine grace, than Men commonly are.' 'Beauty is often incident to stark fools.' Lady Mainard, if her portrait does not lie, had beauty, and Ken cannot have been insensitive to it. But 'her understanding was admirable, and she daily improved it by reading, in which she employed most of her time' and 'she was a perfect despiser, of all those vanities, and divertisements, which most of her sex, do usually admire'. She was constant in prayers and fasting, and 'never failed, on all opportunities to approach the holy altar, came with a spiritual hunger and thirst to that heavenly feast, and communicated with a lively, with a crucifying, but yet endearing remembrance, of her crucified Saviour.' There can be no doubt that Ken's early and close acquaintance with this young woman served, at the least, to confirm the pattern of piety which became his own.

THE WORLD was never yet so bad, but the good Man, though his life was a continued Satire to the Age he lived in, did always either find, or extort, a Veneration from it. So true is it of both Sexes, which *Solomon* here affirms of Woman only, that *gracious Persons*, they who are in the *Grace* and favour of God, and are strengthened by his *gracious assistances*, they who by the *covenant of Grace*, are enrolled in his service, and in whose hearts, there is a conspiration, of *all the Graces of his holy Spirit*; all which particulars, are included in the word *Grace*, and do all concur, to make up a *gracious Soul*; Such persons, I say, as these, shall from the generality of Men, gain an inward esteem, and a great Opinion, and for the most part, an outward, and a suitable respect, or as the Wise man words it, shall *retain honour*.

I must confess, that there are many instances, even in our own perverse generation, wherein Virtue has rather been *contemned* and *ridiculed* than *Honoured*, but I will mention no other than the most signal of all, God Incarnate, whose example, though it was as perfect, and unblameable, as the fulness of the God-head, could render it; yet his most divine Person, was so far from being *honoured*, by many of the *Jews*, that he lay under the utmost imputations of Slander and Blasphemy, which words could express; and as glorious as all his Miracles were, they were ascribed to no other, than *Beelzebub*, the Prince of the very Devils.

But though it be true, that our blessed Lord, in regard to his state of Humiliation, seemed to have no form, no comeliness in him; yet all his Conversation, had so many irradiations of Divinity in it, which did abundantly evince his heavenly Extraction; and it is no wonder he should suffer such contradictions of sinners, it being usual for an Heroic virtue, which is singly to encounter whole Legions, to contend with inveterate Errors, or reigning Vices, to reprove, and reform the World, as our Saviour was, to be loaded, with most diabolical reproaches. But Goodness has an inseparable splendour, which can never suffer, a total eclipse, and when it is most reviled, and persecuted, it then shines brightest out of Cloud. So that all who are not wilfully blind, who will but make use of their eyes to see, must acknowledge the force of its rays.

This did the very *Jews* themselves, as many as had any relics of common ingenuity left: The Multitude owned our Saviour for a great Prophet, wondered at his gracious words, confessed he had done all things well, insomuch, that they would have exalted him to the throne, and have made him their King; *Pilate* could find no fault in him at all; and the *Centurion*, a Heathen, even when he saw him hanging on the Cross, as a Malefactor, cried out, *Certainly this was a Righteous man*. So that a *gracious Person*, under the most extreme degree of Infamy and Slander, shall yet *retain honour*, shall from all that are in their right minds, have at least an inward Veneration.

If this be verified of a public Virtue, there can be less doubt of it in a private one, which not being on such a stage, as may provoke and affront the angry World, by openly contradicting, or upbraiding, or chastising it, passes along with a less assaulted, and less envied reputation, and more undisturbedly *retains honour* than the former.

There is, I know, an *honour* which is due to all men, as they are God's workmanship, and have some lines of his Image in them, but especially to Kings, and to Magistrates, whom it is our duty to honour, whether they *be gracious Persons* or no; this we are to render to the *Froward, and Pagan*, as well as to *gentle and believing Masters*; to Princes that are *Infidels and Persecutors*, as well as to *Christian and nursing Fathers*. But then this *honour* is not paid them out of respect to any real Goodness in them, but only to their Authority, as they are God's ordinance, as we depend on their Protection, and as our Obedience is enforced, by Law and Penalties; But the *honour* we give to a *gracious Person*, is purely in reference to his moral excellencies, which are legible in the whole conduct of his life: The former is merely civil, the latter may in some sort, be styled Religious: Empire is honoured as it resembles God's power, abstracted from his Holiness, and therefore it is compatible with an ungracious Person, it is confined only to this World, and reaches no farther: But *Graciousness is honoured* as a participation of the divine Nature, appropriate to no other than Saints, and which has its prospect only on Heaven: The former is like Thunder and Lightning, and works on our Fear; the latter is like the appearance of a good Angel, arrayed in Beams, awful, but kind, which do not afflict, but cheer the sight, and raise in us a mixed passion, of Love and Veneration together; and in this sense it is, that the *gracious Person*, for the venerable goodness that is visible in him, *shall retain honour*.

To attempt any laborious Proof, of so clear a Truth as this, were needless; do but consult the universal practice of Mankind, and read it there. What Rules do the Philosophers prescribe to render our lives most satisfactory to ourselves, and most commendable to others? with what Colours do the Orators paint those persons they intend to Celebrate? what Images do the Poets form when they design an Hero, are they any other than the Rules, and Colours, and Images of moral Goodness? Do not Hypocrites, to court the esteem of the Vulgar, personate the Saint, and Politicians, to make the People honour them, pretend to Religion? and why do they both put on this disguise, but because they know, that Wickedness bare-faced, is in the eyes of all men most detestable, and that the names of Saint, and of Religion, are creditable in the World? Show me that profligate Wretch, who in his cool thoughts, or on his Death-bed, does not decline all his loose Companions, and seeks out for men truly good, and conscientious, to whom he may entrust his Estate, his Children, and all that is dearest to him, even his own Soul too, for which he then begs their ghostly counsel? What man is there so wicked, who on his death-bed does not wish that he may *die the death of the Righteous*, and that *his latter end may be like his*? Look into the Histories and customs of Ages past, see how greedily coveted, how dearly purchased, and how highly valued, the Statues, and all the little remains of Good Men have been: The Heathens, to express their great esteem of Goodness, built Temples to Virtue and Honour, and joined these Temples together, and made the former the only passage into the latter, they thought Praise to Good men as just a Tribute, as Sacrifice to their Gods; and one of the Wisest of them, wonderfully pleased himself, in fancying how lovely and venerable, how divine and transporting an Idea he should see, could he but look into the breast of a Good man. We have then the practice and the judgment of the whole World, to confirm this truth, that Virtue has always had a great and a general esteem, *that the gracious Person retains honour.*

On the contrary, is there not a natural shame, a sense of turpitude, or a confusion of face in vicious and unclean actions? why else are men afraid to commit them, before the most inconsiderable Spectator, and choose darkness for a thick Mantle to cover them? why else do they blush to own them, wish a thousand times they had never been done, and reflect on them with dissatisfaction, and horror? why else do their own Consciences, lash and upbraid them? whereas if we will but take the pains, to make up an Induction of all Christian graces, we shall easily see, that there is none, whose friendship is more ambitiously sought, none with whom men would sooner change Persons, none who are accounted of more substantial worth, or more generally revered, or more influential to the good of Mankind, or sooner wanted in the World, or who make a nobler figure in Story, than the Devout, the Humble, the Just, the Meek, the Temperate, the Charitable; or to express all in one word, the *gracious Person*, who therefore shall always *retain honour*.

I need not reckon up the numerous places of Holy Scripture, where Goodness and Honour are linked together; how *the Wise are said to inherit glory; the humble and meek to be exalted;* how we are commanded *to keep our Vessels in sanctification and honour*, and how God has promised to *honour those who honour him*: I need not mention the primitive Dyptics, or how the Church Catholic, has celebrated the Festivals, and honoured the memories of the Saints, and of the Martyrs; I need not suggest that obvious Conclusion, That if gracious Persons can draw even wicked Men, to a reverential love of their Virtue, much more will they engage the friendship, of all that are Holy, and not only of holy Men, but of holy Angels too, who being all ministering Spirits, deputed by God to attend them, the more heavenly, they see any committed to their charge does grow, the more respectful attendance, in all probability they give him.

And there is the highest reason in the World, why there should be so honourable a loveliness, in a *gracious Person*, if we consider, the likeness he bears to that great God, whom we Adore. For as there are on all men, innate impressions of God's Existence, so there are also of his Attributes, and none ever yet in earnest, believed there was a God, but he also believed that God was a Being, Infinite in all Perfections, in Wisdom and Power, Justice and Mercy, Purity and Holiness, Veracity and Beneficence, and as these excite our Love, and our Adoration to God, so wherever we see any, though but imperfect resemblances, of his imitable perfections, in the Saints here on earth, wherever we see men in any measure Holy and Pure, Just and Merciful, Faithful and Beneficent, we there see the image of God himself, and cannot but pay them a suitable *honour*: Thus as Goodness and Adorableness are co-eternal in God, so are Sanctity and Venerableness coeval, in *gracious Persons*.

Nor are we only by *Grace* made like to God, but he is also pleased actually to dwell in us, and to consecrate our Souls to be his Temples; and as God commanded the *Jews* to reverence his Sanctuary, the place of his residence among them, where he sat between the Cherubims, and a glorious Light that shined on the Propitiatory, was the Symbol of his Presence: So when in gracious Souls, we discover all the fruits of the Spirit, a kind of glory brightening their Conversation, and a sacred Amiableness breathed on them from Heaven, we are sure that God inhabits there, and cannot but reverence his Temples.

Such Honour have all God's Saints from even wicked men, from all holy persons, and from the good Angels, and infinitely above all these, from God himself, who honours them with his Image, after which they are renewed, and with his Presence, of which they are possessed; Such Honour, I say, have all his Saints even in this life, which if we did but seriously Contemplate, would stir us up to a generous emulation, would encourage us to implore the Divine Grace, that we may bewail all our past sins, cleanse ourselves from all filthiness, both of Flesh, and of Spirit, which produce nothing in the end, but Shame, and Horror, and daily grow more conformable to his Likeness, which is the only way, to assert the dignity of our Nature, and to *retain honour*.

But when once our Souls, shall be divorced from our bodies, when the name of the wicked shall rot, and stink, sooner than his carcase, leaving no memorials behind, unless it be, of his sin, his infamy, his madness, or his folly; Precious then in the sight of the Lord, shall be the death of his Saints, blessed shall be their memories. They shall be had in everlasting remembrance, and their good Names, being Registered in the book of Life, shall flourish to Immortality.

All this while, I have not done Justice to my Subject, by affirming only in general, that Goodness is honourable, I must therefore be more particular, and enquire, why *Solomon* does here instance, in the Woman, rather than in the Man, *A gracious Woman retains honour*.

And the reason seems to me, to be either this, that as Vice is more odious, and more detested, so on the other hand, Virtue is more attractive, and looks more lovely, in Women, than it usually does in Men, insomuch that the *gracious Woman*, shall be sure to purchase, and to *retain honour*.

Or it is, because Men have more advantages, of aspiring to *honour*, in all public stations, of the Church, the Court, the Camp, the Bar, and the City, than Women have, and the only way for a Woman to gain honour, is an exemplary Holiness; This makes *her Children, rise up and call her blessed, her Husband and her own works, to praise her in the gate*, the sole glory then of that Sex, is to be good, for 'tis a *gracious Woman* only, who *retains honour*.

Or it is, because Women are made of a temper, more soft and frail, are more endangered by snares, and temptations, less able to control their passions, and more inclinable to extremes of good, or bad, than Men, and generally speaking, Goodness is a tenderer thing, more hazardous, and brittle in the former, than in the latter, and consequently a firm, and steady Virtue, is more to be valued in the weaker Sex, than in the stronger; So that a *gracious Woman*, is most worthy to receive, and to *retain honour*.

Or it is, because Women in all Ages, have given, many Heroic examples of Sanctity, besides those recorded in the *Old Testament*, many of them are named, with great honour in the *New*. For their Assiduity and Zeal, in following our Saviour, and their Charity, in ministering to him of their substance, they accompanied him to Mount *Calvary*, lamented his Sufferings, waited on the Cross, attended the Sepulchre, prepared Spices, and Ointments, and regardless, either of the Insolence of the rude Soldiers, or of the Malice of the *Jews*, with a love that cast out all fear, they came on the first day of the Week, before the morning light, to Embalm him; and God was pleased to honour these holy Women accordingly, for they first saw the Angel, who told them the joyful news that he was risen, and as if an Angel, had not been a Messenger honourable enough, *Jesus* himself first appeared to the Women, the Women first saw, and adored him; and it was these very gracious Women, whom our Lord sent to his Disciples, that Women might be the first Publishers of his Resurrection, as Angels had been of his Nativity; Our Saviour himself, has erected an everlasting Monument in the Gospel, for the penitent Woman that anointed him, and God Incarnate honoured the Sex to the highest degree imaginable, in being born of a Woman, in becoming the Son of a Virgin Mother, whom all Generations shall call Blessed; and I know not how to call it, but there is a meltingness of Disposition, an affectionateness of Devotion, an easy Sensibility, an industrious Alacrity, a languishing Ardour, in Piety, peculiar to the Sex, which naturally renders them, Subjects more pliable, to the Divine Grace, than Men commonly are; So that *Solomon*, had reason to bestow the Epithet *Gracious*, particularly on them, and to say, that a *gracious Woman retains honour*.

I am well aware, that if we consult the sensual, and debauched rank of Men, 'tis not the Gracious, or the Chaste Woman they esteem, but only the Fair, or the Lascivious; Esteem, did I say! Men may court an idle, or a wanton Beauty, for their Lust, but they can only esteem, a *Gracious;* and a Chaste one, and when all is done, she only deserves the name of Beautiful: As for the Lascivious, and the Prostitute, against whom *Solomon* so often, and so pathetically, warns the Young man, She is so utterly impure, that I will not so much as name her, in the same discourse with a gracious Woman; I will then, make the Comparison, between mere outward Beauty only, and *Grace*, and you will soon perceive the difference.

For Beauty, if it be Natural, is from a Woman's birth, 'tis her chance, and not her merit; if it be Artificial, it makes her no other, than a painted Sepulchre, Gaudy without, and that has nothing but Rottenness, and Stench within: But Grace, is the free gift of God, and our own free choice, in a happy conjunction, 'tis no other than a God-like loveliness, impressed on our Spirit.

Beauty is often incident to stark Fools, and to the Profane, and Irreligious; But *Grace* is peculiar to holy Persons, who like *the King's Daughter, are all glorious within.*

Beauty is prone to admire itself, and to swell with Pride; *Grace* instills a just sense of our own vileness, and teaches Humility: That is apt to invite Temptation; This is a Preservative against it: The former spends her morning hours, at her glass; The latter at her Prayers: That most delights herself, in new fashions, and fine clothes, *in plaiting the hair, and wearing of Gold*; This puts *on the ornament of a meek and quiet spirit, which is in the sight of God, of great price.*

Beauty has been often, to the best, and wisest of Men, witness *Solomon* himself, destructive, and fatal, for which reason holy *Job made a Covenant with his eyes*; and our Saviour commands us, *not to look on a Woman, to lust after her*, and the fairer she is, the greater is the danger; But *Grace*, secures our Innocence, awes men into Sobriety, looks them into Chastity, and the more intense it grows, its influence, is the more sovereign, and efficacious.

Beauty, gratifies only our outward sense, 'tis a mixture of Colour, and Figure, and Feature, and Parts, all in a due Proportion, and Symmetry; or indeed, 'tis a well shaped Frame of dust and ashes, beloved by fond Men only, who like the most stupid of Idolaters, worship the bare Statue, without regard to the Deity there enshrined: But *Grace*, is a confluence of all Attractives, which approves itself to our own most deliberate judgments, and is beloved by God: Do but imagine you were in the Spouse's Garden, where, when the South-wind blows, the several Spices, and Gums, the Spikenard and the Cinnamon, the Frankincense and the Myrrh, send forth their various smells, which meeting together, and mixing in the Air, make a compounded Odour; Such a composition, of all Virtues, such an universal and uniform Agreeableness, is there in a *gracious Soul*, which in a manner, whether we will or no, engages our affections.

Beauty is vain, and Favour is deceitful, says the Wise man, it soon evaporates, and cheats our expectation, in a little time it decays, by cares, or Child-bearing, or Sickness, or a thousand other accidents; Men no sooner begin to crop the Flower, but it fades, and sinks, and dies, or it is often soured, with such inward dispositions, which render it afflicting, and insupportable; But *Grace*, creates to our minds an entire satisfaction, has a goodness intrinsic, and eternal, grows more amiable, the more it is enjoyed, so that the *Woman that feareth the Lord, she shall be praised, she shall* for ever, *retain honour*.

As a jewel of Gold in a Swine's snout, which is hung there on purpose to be defiled, to be rolled in filth, and mire, and is one of the most notorious, and ugly incongruities, in the World; Such a kind of absurdity, if you will believe *Solomon, is a fair Woman without discretion*; her beauty 'tis true, is a Jewel, but a Jewel extremely ill-placed, and serves for no other purpose, but to make her folly more conspicuous, to expose her the more to impurity, and to a swinish sensuality; But *Grace makes a Woman a Crown to her Husband, the glory of the Man, and advances her price above Rubies*; So that a gracious Woman, is a Jewel of a value inestimable, she has worth, and ornament, and lustre, and beauty, and honour, all combined together. Most deservedly then, did wise *Solomon*, give the preference to Grace, and did assure us, that a *strong Man*, is not more powerful to get, and when gotten, *to retain his riches*, than a *gracious Woman* to acquire *honour*, and *to retain* it, when acquired.

It is now time, to do all the right I am able, to the noble Lady deceased, who was a woman, so remarkably *Gracious, and retained an Honour*, so entire, and unblemished, that all the measures I have hitherto laid down, either of Grace, or of Honour, are but a faint Copy, drawn after her, she was all the while before my thought, her holy example is the original, and though I will not say, that among the many daughters, who have done virtuously, she absolutely excels them all, yet I am sure, she deserves to be esteemed, one of the highest order.

But alas! we have nothing now left, except this poor relic of

Clay, which in a few minutes must be restored to its native earth, and for ever hid from our eyes, the *gracious Soul* that informed it, is flowed back again to God, from whom it first streamed, and his most blessed will be done, who is compassionate and adorable, in all his chastisements; yet as we are flesh and blood, we cannot but feel the stroke, which even his Fatherly hand has given us. It is the Curse of the wicked, to die unlamented, unless it be, that they are sometimes carried to the Grave, with the mercenary tears, of those who make mourning a trade; But the death of the Righteous, being a loss irrecoverable, and a real calamity, to us who survive, must needs fill us, with sad resentments, when we consider, of how great a blessing we are deprived.

Our Saviour himself, has countenanced a moderate grief for our friends, in weeping over, his own dead friend *Lazarus*; So that if we shed our tears, over the Grave of this *gracious and honourable* Lady, 'tis but to be just to her ashes, to ease our own sorrowful Spirits, and to testify to the World, how dear a sense we have of her worth. For had she had nothing but her Quality, to have recommended her, we might have performed her Funeral Ceremonies, with a bare outward Solemnity, but without any more concern, than a common object of Mortality gives us; But she was a *Woman* so truly *gracious*, that we could not but most affectionately *honour* her, and cannot but have a grief, that bears some proportion to our loss.

For 'tis our loss only we can bewail, we grieve for ourselves, not for her; She has a joyful deliverance from temptation and infirmity, from sin and misery, and from all the evil to come, she is now past all the storms, and dangers of this troubled life, and is safely arrived, at her everlasting Haven; she is now fully possessed, of all that she desired, which was, to be dissolved, and to be with Christ, and we cannot lament, her being happy. When we weep for common Christians, we are not to be sorry, as men without hope, but when we have so many, so uninterrupted, and so undeniable demonstrations, of the sanctity of a Person, as we have of this *gracious Woman*, we have no reason at all to grieve on her account, since we have not only a bare hope, but an assurance rather, that she is now in glory.

But why did I call her death a loss? 'tis rather our gain, we were all travelling the same way, as Pilgrims, towards our heavenly Country, she has only got the start of us, and is gone before, and is happy first; and I am persuaded that we still enjoy her prayers for us above; However, I am sure, that we enjoy her good works here below, which now appear more illustrious, and without that veil, her modesty, and her humility cast over them; we still enjoy her example, which being now set, in its true light, and at its proper distance, and delivered from that cloud of flesh, which did obscure and lessen it, looks the more gracious, and the more honourable; and if we follow the track, she trod, we shall ere long, enjoy her society in Heaven.

Let us then alter our Note, and rather *honour*, than bewail her, she was a *gracious Woman*, and *honour* is her due; Her good Name, like a precious Ointment poured forth, has perfumed the whole Sphere, in which she moved. To paint her fully to the life, I dare not undertake, she had a *graciousness* in all her Conversation, that cannot be expressed, and should I endeavour to do it, I must run over, all the whole Catalogue of Evangelical Graces, which do all concentre in her Character; I must tell you, how inflamed she was with heavenly love, how well guided a Zeal, she had for God's glory, how particular a reverence she paid, to all things, and to all persons, that were dedicated to His Service, how God was always in her thoughts, how great a tenderness she had, to offend her heavenly Father, how great a delight to please him; But you must be content, with some rude strokes only, for such particulars would be endless; All my fear is, that I shall speak too little, but I am sure, I can hardly speak too much.

Say, All you who have been Eye-witnesses of her Life, did you from her very Cradle, ever know her any other, than a *gracious Woman*? As to myself, I have had the honour to know her, near twenty years; and to be admitted, to her most intimate thoughts, and I cannot but think, upon the utmost of my observation, that she always preserved her Baptismal Innocence, that she never committed any one mortal Sin, which put her out of the state of Grace; Insomuch, that after all the frequent, and severe examinations, she made of her own Conscience, her Confessions were made up, of no other than sins of Infirmity, and yet even for them, she had as deep an Humiliation, and as Penitential a Sorrow, as high a sense of the Divine forgiveness, and as much, as if she had had *Much to be forgiven*: So that after a life of above Forty Years, Nine of which were spent in the Court, bating her involuntary failings, which are unavoidable, and for which, allowances are made, in the Covenant of Grace, she *kept herself unspotted from the World*, and if it may be affirmed of any, I dare venture to affirm it of this, *gracious Woman*, that by the peculiar favour of Heaven, she passed from the Font, unsullied to her Grave.

    Her understanding was admirable, and she daily improved it, by reading, in which she employed most of her time, and the Books she chose, were only serious, or devout, and her memory was faithful, to retain what she read: She took not up her Religion on an implicit faith, or from education only, but from a well-studied choice, directed by God's holy Spirit, whose guidance she daily invoked, and when once she had made that choice, she was immoveable as a rock, and so well satisfied in the Catholic faith, professed in the Church of *England*, that I make no doubt, but that she always lived, not only with the strictness of a Primitive Saint, but with the resolution also, of a Martyr: It was strange to hear, how strongly she would argue, how clearly she understood, the force of a Consequence, and how ready at all times she was, *to give a reason of the hope that was in her, with meekness, and fear*; Her Letters which were found in her Cabinet, not to be delivered till after her death, and very many others, in the hands of her Relations, sufficiently show, how good, and how great she was, In them this humble Saint, before she was aware, has herself made an exact impression, of her own *Graciousness*; They are penned in so proper and unaffected a Style, and animated throughout with so divine a Spirit, with such ardours of Devotion, and Charity, as might have become a *Proba*, a *Monica*, or the most eminent of her Sex, Insomuch, that her very absence, was the more supportable to her friends, in regard she compensated the want of her presence, by writing, and sent them a blessing, by every return.

    I cannot tell, what one help she neglected, to secure her perseverance, and to heighten her graces, *that she might shine more and more, to a perfect day*; Her Oratory was the place, where she principally resided, and where she was most at home, and her chief employment, was Prayer, and Praise; Out of several Authors, she for her own use, transcribed many excellent Forms, the very choice of which does argue, a most experienced Piety, she had Devotions suited, to all the primitive hours of Prayer, which she used, as far as her bodily Infirmities, and necessary Avocations would permit, and with *David, Praised God seven times a day*, or supplied the want of those solemn hours, by a kind of perpetuity of Ejaculations, which she had ready, to answer all occasions, and to fill up all vacant intervals, and if she happened to wake in the Night, of proper Prayers even for midnight, she was never unprovided. Thus did this gracious Soul, having been enkindled by fire from Heaven, in her Baptism, lived a continual Sacrifice, and kept the fire always burning, always in ascension, always aspiring towards Heaven from whence it fell. Besides her own private Prayers, she Morning, and Evening offered up to God the public Offices, and when she was not able, to go to the house of Prayer, she had it read to her, in her Chamber.

To Prayers she added Fasting, till her weakness had made it impossible to her constitution, and yet even then, on days of Abstinence, she made amends for the Omission, by other supplemental Mortifications. Her Devotions she enlarged, on the Fasts and Festivals of the Church, but especially on the Lord's days, dividing the hours, between the Church and her Closet.

She never failed, on all opportunities, to approach the holy Altar, came with a Spiritual hunger, and thirst to that heavenly Feast, and Communicated with a lively, with a Crucifying, but yet endearing Remembrance, of her Crucified *Saviour*.

The Sermons she heard, when she came home she recollected, and wrote down out of her memory, abstracts of them all, which are in a great number, among her Papers, that she might be, *not only, a hearer of the Word, but a doer also*.

The Holy Scripture she attentively read, and on what she read, she did devoutly meditate, and did by Meditation, appropriate to herself, it was her Soul's daily Bread, it was *her delight, and her Counsellor*, and, like the most blessed Virgin Mother, *she kept all things she read, and pondered them in her heart.*

Who is there can say, they ever saw her idle? no, she had always affairs to transact with Heaven, she was all her life long *numbering her days, and applying her heart to wisdom*, or, to describe her with her own Pen, she was *making it her business, to fit herself for her change, knowing, the moment of it to be uncertain, and having no assurance, that her warning would be great*; Oh happy Soul, that was thus wise, in a timely consideration of that, which of all things in the World, is of greatest importance to us, to be considered, namely our Latter end!

You may easily conclude, that a Saint, who was always thus conversant with her Grave, and had heaven always in her view, must have little or no value for things below, as indeed she had not, she did not only conquer the World, but she triumphed over it, had a noble contempt of Secular greatness, lived several years in the very Court, with the abstraction of a Recluse, and was so far from being *solicitous for Riches, for her self, or her Children*, that, to use her own words, she looked on them, *as dangerous* things, *which did only clog, and press down our souls to this earth*, and judged *a Competency, to be certainly the best.*

All the temporal blessings, the divine Goodness, was pleased to vouchsafe her, she received, with an overflowing thankfulness, yet her affections were so disengaged, her temperance, and moderation so habitual, that she did rather use, than enjoy them, and was always ready to restore them, to the same gracious hand that gave them, but no one can express her thoughts, so pathetically as her own self; O, says that blessed Saint, *since God gives us all, let us not be sorrowful, though we are to part with all, the Kingdom of Heaven, is a prize, that is worth striving for, though it costs us dear: Alas! what is there in this World, that links our hearts so close to it!* and elsewhere she affirms, that *All blessings are given on this condition, that either they must be taken from us, or we from them, if then*, we lose anything, which *we esteem a blessing, we are to give God the glory, and to resign it freely.*

She was a perfect despiser, of all those vanities, and divertisements, which most of her sex, do usually admire; her chief, and, in a manner, sole recreation was to do good, and to oblige, and if we will be advised, by one so wise to Salvation, *We are to seek for comfort, and joy, from God's ordinances, and the converse of pious Christians, and not to take the usual course of the World, to drive away Melancholy, by exposing ourselves to temptations;* and this was really her practice, insomuch that next to the Service of the Temple, which she daily frequented, There was no entertainment in the whole World, so pleasing to her, as the discourse of heavenly things, and those she spake of, with such a Spiritual relish, that at first hearing, you might perceive she was in earnest, that she really *tasted the Lord was good*, and felt all she spake.

Amidst all her pains, and her sicknesses, which were sharp, and many, who ever saw her show, any one symptom of Impatience? So far was she from it, that she laments, when she reflects, *how apt we are to abuse prosperity*, Demands, *where our conformity is to the great Captain of our Salvation, if we have no sufferings;* Professes, *that God by suffering our Conditions to be Uneasy, by that gentle way, invites us to higher satisfactions, than are to be met with here*, and with a prostrate spirit, *acknowledges, that God was most righteous in all that had befallen her, and that there had been so much mercy mixed with his chastising, that she had been but too happy.* Thus humble, thus content, thus thankful, was this *gracious Woman*, amidst her very afflictions. Her Soul always rested on God's Paternal mercy, and on all his exceeding great, and precious promises, as on a sure and steadfast Anchor, which she knew would secure her, in the most tempestuous Calamities; To his blessed will, she hourly offered up her own, and knew it was as much her duty, to suffer his fatherly inflictions, as to obey his commands. Her Charity, made her sympathize, with all in Misery, and besides her private Alms, wherein her left hand, was not conscious to her right, she was a common Patroness to the Poor, and Needy, and a common Physician to her sick Neighbours, and would often with her own hands, dress their most loathsome sores, and sometimes keep them in her Family, and would give them both Diet, and Lodging till they were cured, and then clothe them, and send them home, to give God thanks for their recovery, and if they died, her Charity accompanied them sometimes to the very grave, and she took care even of their burial. She would by no means endure, *that by the care of plentifully providing for her Children, the wants, and necessities of any poor Christian, should be overlooked*, and desired it might be *remembered that, Alms and the Poor's prayers, will bring a greater blessing, to them, than Thousands a year.* Look abroad now in the World, and see, how rarely you shall meet, with a Charity, like that of this *gracious Woman*, who next to her own flesh and blood, was tender of the Poor, and thought an Alms as much, due to them, as Portions to her Children.

To corporal Alms, as often as she saw occasion, she joined spiritual, and she had a singular talent, in dispensing that alms to Souls, she had a masculine Reason to persuade, a steady Wisdom to advise, a perspicuity both of thought, and language to instruct, a mildness that endeared a reproof, and could comfort the afflicted, from her own manifold experience of the Divine Goodness, and with so condoling a tenderness, that she seemed to translate their anguish, on her self.

And happy was it for others, that her Charity was so comprehensive, for she often met with objects so deplorable, that were to be relieved in all these capacities, so that she was fain to become, their Benefactress, their Physician, and their Divine altogether, or if need were, she bid them *show themselves to the Priest*, or else took care, to send the Priest to them; Thus was it visibly her constant endeavour, to be in all respects *merciful, as her Father in Heaven is merciful.*

She could bear long, and most easily forgive, and no one ever injured her, but she would heap coals of fire on his head, to melt him into a charitable temper, and would often repay the injury, with a kindness so surprising, that if the injurious person were not wholly obdurate, and brutish, must needs affect him. But if anyone did her, the least good office, none could be more grateful, she would if possible, return it a hundred-fold, if she could not in kind, she would at least do it, in her prayers to God, that out of his inexhaustible goodness, he would reward him.

Her Soul seemed to possess, a continued serenity, at peace with herself, at peace with God, and at peace with all the World, her study was to give all their due, and she was exactly sincere, and faithful to all her obligations, she kept her heart always with all diligence, was watchful against all temptations, and naturally considerate in all her actions, her disposition was peaceful, and inoffensive, she looked always pleased, rather than cheerful, her converse was even, and serious, but yet easy and affable; her Interpretations, of what others did, or said, were always candid, and charitable, you should never see her indecently angry, or out of humour, never hear her give an ill character, or pass a hard censure, or speak an idle word, but *she opened her mouth in wisdom, and in her tongue, was the law of kindness.*

If you look on her, in her several Relations, in her Childhood, her Father, the Right Honourable, the Earl of *Dyzart*, being banished for his Loyalty, she was under the breeding, of the Excellent Lady her Mother, to whom she was in all respects, so dutiful a Child, that she protested, her Daughter had never, in any one instance, offended her; By that time, the young Lady was about Eleven or twelve years old, God was pleased to take her good Mother to himself, and from that time to her Marriage, this *gracious Woman* lived with a discretion so much above her years, with so conspicuous a Virtue, and so constant a Wariness, that she always *retained honour*, such an *honour*, as never had the least Mote in it. And to her *honour* be it spoken, that in an Age, when the generality of the Nation, *were like Children, tossed to and fro, with every wind of Doctrine*, she still continued steadfast in the Communion of the Church of *England*, and when the Priests and Service of God, were driven into Corners, she daily resorted, though with great difficulty, to the public Prayers, and was remarkably Charitable to all the suffering Royalists, whom she visited, and relieved, and fed, and clothed, and condoled, with a zeal, like that which the Ancient Christians showed, to the Primitive Martyrs.

The silenced, and plundered, and persecuted Clergy, she

thought worthy, of double honour, did vow a certain Sum yearly, out of her Income, which she laid aside, only to succour them. The Congregations, where she then usually communicated, were those, of the reverend and Pious, Dr. *Thruscross*, and Dr. *Mossom*, both now in Heaven, and that of the then Mr. *Gunning*, the now most worthy Bishop of *Ely*, for whom she ever after had a peculiar Veneration.

But I must by no means pass by, the Right Reverend Father in God, Bishop *Duppa*, then of *Salisbury*, afterwards of *Winchester*, but now with God, who was then put out of all, and an Exemplary Confessor, for the King, and the Church; This holy Man, when she resided in the Country, lived in the Neighbourhood, and she often visited him, and he seemed to be designed on purpose, by God's most gracious direction, to be her spiritual Guide, to confirm her in all her holy Resolutions, to satisfy all those Scruples, to becalm all those Fears, and regulate all those Fervours which are incident to an early, and tender Piety, and God's goodness rendered him so successful, that she retained, the happy influence of his ghostly Advice, to her dying day.

Before the Age of twenty, she was married, to the Right Honourable, *William* Lord *Mainard*, to whom in her Letters, she often gives, the most affectionate thanks imaginable, for *his unvaluable, and unparalleled kindness towards her*, as she herself terms it, and most fervently prays, that *The Lord Jesus Christ would be his exceeding great reward, and his portion for ever*; But I forbear to offer violence to the modesty of the Survivor, and will content myself, to say only in general, that when she was a Wife, she still retained her accustomed devotion, which she practised when a Virgin, and her greatest concern, was *for the things of the Lord, how she might please the Lord, how in a Marriage honourable, and a Bed undefiled, she might be holy both in body, and in spirit, and attend upon the Lord, without distraction*. And since, as *Solomon* affirms, *a prudent Wife is from the Lord*, she was certainly the immediate gift of God, and sent by propitious Heaven, for a good Angel, as well as for a Wife.

As a Mother she was unspeakably tender, and careful, of the two Children, with which God had blessed her; but her zeal for their eternal welfare, was predominant, and she made it her dying request, that in their education, their piety should be principally regarded, or to speak her own words, *that the chief care should be, to make them pious Christians, which would be the best provision, that could be made for them*.

In reference to her Son, it was her express desire, that he should be good, rather than either rich, or great, *that he should be bred in the strictest principles of Sobriety, Piety, and Charity, of Temperance and Innocency of life, that could be, that he should never be indulged in the least sin, that he should never be that, which these corrupt days call a Wit, or a fine Gentile man, but an honest, and sincere Christian, she desired he might be.*

She professed, *there was nothing hard to be parted with, but her Lord, and her dear Children*, but though her passion for them, was as intense, as can well be imagined, yet for the sake of her God, whom she loved infinitely better, she was willing to part with them also, had long foreseen the parting, and prepared for it, and *humbly begged of her heavenly Father, to take them, into his protection*; she took care of their Souls, even after her death, in the Letters she left behind her, and comforted herself, with an entire acquiescence, in the good pleasure of her beloved, with hopes, that she should still, pray for them in Heaven, and that she should ere long, meet them there; and this consideration of meeting above, put her into a transport, which makes her, in one of her Letters, cry out, *O how joyful shall we be, to meet at* Christ's *right hand, if we may be admitted, into that Elect number!*

In her Family, she always united *Martha, and Mary* together, took a due care of all her domestic Affairs, and managed them with a wise frugality, and a constant deference, to God's merciful Providence, and without either covetous fears, or a restless anxiety; but withal; *she sat at the feet of* Jesus, *and heard his word, and of the two*, was still most intent *on the better part.*

She studiously endeavoured, by private, and particular, and warm applications, to make all that attended her, more God's Servants, than her own, and treated them, with a meekness, and indulgence, and condescension, like one, who was always mindful, *that she herself also, had a Master in Heaven.*

Her near Relations, and all that were blessed with her friendship, had a daily share in her intercessions, all their concerns, all their afflictions were really her own; her chief kindness was for their Souls, and she loved them with a charity, like that which the Blessed show to one another in Heaven, in their reciprocal complacence at each other's happiness, and mutual incitements to devotion.

In respect of the Public, which she often laid sadly to heart, *her eyes ran down in secret*, for all our National Provocations, and she had a particular Office, on fasting Days, for that purpose; which shows how importunate she was, at the Throne of Grace, to avert God's Judgments, and to implore his Blessing on the Land.

And now, after all these great truths, which I have said of this Excellent Lady, one Grace I must add, greater than all I have hitherto mentioned, and it is her Humility; she was so little given to talk, and had that art to conceal her goodness, that it did not appear at first sight, but after some time, her virtue would break out, whether she would or no; she seemed to be wholly ignorant of her own Graces, and had as mean an opinion of herself, as if she had had no Excellence at all, like *Moses*, her *Face shined, and she did not know it*; others she esteemed so much better, had that abasing sense of her own Infirmities, and that profound awe of the Divine Majesty, that though she was great in God's eyes, she was always little in her own.

After the *Whitsun-week* was over, she removed from *Whitehall*, to *Eastonlodge* in *Essex*, not out of any hopes of recovery, but only that she might have, some little present relief from the Air, or that she might die in a place which she loved, in which God had made her, an instrument of so great good to the Country, and which was near her Grave; and you may easily imagine, that after a life so holy, the death of *this gracious Woman*, must needs be signally happy; and so it was, not but that during her pains, she had often doubts, and fears that afflicted her, with which in her health she was unmolested, and which did manifestly arise from her Distemper, and did cease as that intermitted; but the day before she died God was pleased to vouchsafe her, some clearer manifestations of His mercy, which in the tenderness of His compassion, he sent her, as preparatives of her last conflict, and as earnests of Heaven, whither he intended, the day following to translate her.

How she behaved herself in her sickness, I cannot better express, than by saying, that she *prayed continually*; and when the Prayers of the Church were read by her, or when the hour of her own private Prayer came, though she was not able to stand, or to help herself, she would yet be placed on her Knees; and when her Knees were no longer able to support her, she would be put, into the humblest posture, she could possibly endure, not being satisfied, unless she gave God his entire oblation, and *glorified him in her body, as well as in her spirit, which were both God's own* by purchase here, and were both to be united in bliss hereafter.

On *Whit-Sunday*, she received her *viaticum*, the most holy Body, and Blood of her Saviour, and had received it again, had not her death surprised us, yet in the strength of that immortal food, she was enabled to go out her journey, and seemed to have had a new transfusion of Grace from it, insomuch, that though her Limbs were all convulsed, her Pains great, and without intermission, her strength quite exhausted, and her Head disturbed, with a perpetual drowsiness, yet above, and beyond all seeming possibility, she would use force to herself, to keep herself waking, to offer to God her customary Sacrifice to the full, to recollect her thoughts, and to lodge them in Heaven, where her Heart, and her Treasure was, as if she had already taken possession of her mansion there, or as if she was teaching her Soul, to act independently from the Body, and practising beforehand the state of separation, into which having received absolution, she in a short time, happily launched; for all the bands of Union being untied, her Soul was set at liberty, and on the wings of Angels, took a direct, and vigorous flight, to its native Country, Heaven from whence it first flew down.

There then we must leave her, in the bosom of her heavenly Bridegroom, where, how radiant her Crown is, how ecstatic her Joy, how high exalted she is in degrees of glory, is impossible to be described, for *neither eye hath seen, nor ear heard, nor has it entered into the heart of man, to be conceived, the good things, which God hath prepared for those that love him*, of all which she is now partaker.

We have nothing then to do, but to congratulate *this Gracious Woman*, her eternal and unchangeable honour, and as she always and in all things, gave God the Glory here, so that his praise was continually in her mouth, for all the multitude of his Mercies, and of his loving-Kindnesses towards her, and is now praising him in Heaven; Let us also offer up a Sacrifice of Praise, for her great example, her light has long shined before us, and we have seen her good works, Let us therefore glorify the father of Lights, at whose beams, her Soul was first lighted.

Blessed then for ever, be the infinite goodness of God, who was so liberal of his Graces, to this humble Saint, who made her so lively a picture, of his own perfections, *so gracious, and so honourable*; blessed be his mercy, for indulging her to us so long, for taking her in his good time to himself, and for that happiness she has now in Heaven; To God be the glory of all that *honour*, her *graciousness* did here acquire, for to him only it is due; let therefore his most holy name, have all the praise.

To our Thanksgiving let us add our Prayers also, that God would vouchsafe us all his holy Spirit, so to assist, and sanctify, and guide us, that every one of our Souls, may be *gracious* like hers, that our life may be like hers, our latter end like hers, and our portion in Heaven like hers, which God of his infinite mercy grant for the sake of his most beloved Son, To whom with the Father, and the blessed Spirit, be all honour and glory, adoration, and obedience, now and for ever. *Amen*.

John Tillotson

TILLOTSON WAS born in 1630 at Sowerby in Yorkshire. He was the son of a clothier of good family, a man of Calvinist and Puritan views. Tillotson went to the grammar school at Colne and then, in 1647, to Clare College, Cambridge. The part of Clare where he and his friends lived is said to have been called 'Roundheads' Corner' and no doubt he held views acceptable to the time for he became a fellow of the college in 1651. He was acquainted with Cudworth, Henry More and the other Cambridge Platonists, but he was of a more practical turn of mind than they. On leaving the university, he became tutor in the family of Edmund Prideaux, who was Cromwell's Attorney-General, and almost exactly at the moment of the Restoration sought episcopal ordination. He became a preacher at Lincoln's Inn and married in 1663; his bride's reluctance is said to have been over-ruled by her father with the words: 'You shall have him, Betty, for he is the best polemical divine in England.' Through his father-in-law's influence he became a regular preacher at St Lawrence Jewry, where he made a great reputation, so that all the best people and all the most ambitious young clergymen went to hear him. In 1672 he became Dean of Canterbury, in which capacity he managed to meet and be of service to Prince William of Orange, who had just married the Princess Mary and was carrying her off to Holland. In 1688 he helped the Seven Bishops draw up the document explaining why they could not read James's Declaration of Indulgence. When Sancroft refused to take the oath to William and Mary, and was deposed, Tillotson was appointed Archbishop of Canterbury. William III said he was the best friend he ever had.

Tillotson was one of those ordinary able men, common enough in the world of affairs, who owe their eminence to the utter suitability of their opinions to the political requirements of the times. He was probably not particularly devious and he was always hostile to popery, even during the reign of James II when it might have paid to talk differently; though James, of course, was anxious to keep on good terms with the less orthodox Protestants. With his Presbyterian past, his tepid common sense and his tendency to drift with the growing rationalism of the age, Tillotson was the perfect ecclesiastical figurehead after 1689.

As a churchman he counts for very little. His mind was

without originality and his expositions of doctrine are notably shallow. He achieved the distinction of a favourable mention in Collins's *Discourse of Free-Thinking*—a work which Swift characterized as '*a brief compleat Body of* Atheology'. Swift summarized Collins's tribute as follows:

> But *Arch Bishop Tillotson* is the person whom all *English Free Thinkers* owe as their Head; and his Virtue is indisputable for this manifest Reason, that Dr. *Hicks*, a Priest, calls him an Atheist; says, he caused several to turn Atheists, and to ridicule the Priesthood and Religion. These must be allowed to be noble effects of *Free Thinking*. This great Prelate assures us, that all the Duties of the Christian Religion, with respect to God, are no other but what natural Light prompts Men to, except the two Sacraments, and praying to God in the name and Mediation of Christ: As a Priest and a Prelate he was obliged to say something of Christianity; but pray observe, Sir, how he brings himself off. He justly observes that even these things are of less Moment than natural Duties; and because Mothers nursing their Children is a natural Duty, it is of more moment than the two Sacraments, or than praying to God in the name and by the Mediation of Christ. The *Free Thinking* Archbishop would not allow a Miracle sufficient to give Credit to a Prophet who taught anything contrary to our natural Notions: By which it is plain, he rejected at once all the Mysteries of Christianity.

It is Collins, rather than Tillotson, who is being held up to ridicule. On the other hand, no one could miss the undercurrents of irony directed at the great Whig mediocrity who had stepped into a better man's shoes. For Sancroft, Swift had had as a young man something very like a cult.

THE ADVANTAGES OF RELIGION TO PARTICULAR PERSONS
Psalm 19: 11.
—*And in keeping of them there is great reward.*

TILLOTSON SET the pattern for what, throughout the eighteenth century, reasonable parsons would want to preach and reasonable and respectable congregations would want to listen to. By comparison Barrow, and even Stillingfleet—precursors of the eighteenth century though they in a sense were—are of the past. The sermon in the new style was on the whole shorter than the old; it made three good points and sent people home to their dinner. Above all it said nothing that would strike sensible people as out of the way; and one might say that the respectable public at this time were becoming dangerously sensible, to the point of imagining that what decent people think must be right. Decent people, in the eighteenth century, on the whole meant Whigs—people who were getting on in the world and the time was coming when to get on in any spectacular way you had to be a Whig. Tillotson has the tone of the new epoch perfectly. In another sermon—not given here—the text 'Righteousness exalteth a Nation' (Proverbs 14:34) becomes in Tillotson's rendering: 'Religion and Virtue are the great causes of Public happiness and prosperity.' He proceeds to demonstrate that religion 'is the greatest Friend to our temporal interests'. It is but a step from that to Mandeville, who demonstrated in *The Fable of the Bees* (1714) that private vices are public benefits.

The sermon which follows is complementary to that on 'Righteousness exalteth a Nation'. It does not deal with public welfare but shows that 'Religion and obedience to the Laws of God, do likewise conduce to the happiness of particular persons, both in respect of this world, and the other.' The argument in relation to the other world is in a manner tautological; the interest centres on what is said about the advantage of religion in this one. Tillotson makes them out to be so considerable, and so obvious to any reasonable person, that it is hardly to be wondered at if reasonable persons concluded that they would have those advantages, or as much of them as they cared for, without the fatigue of theology. 'Religion tends to the ease and pleasure, the peace and tranquillity of our minds.' 'Religion does likewise tend to the happiness of the outward man'; it virtually assured the success of worldly undertakings—though there was fortunately provision for making up in the next world for the odd case of failure in this. Moreover, if wealth did not come everybody's way, the 'shortest way to be rich' was to be content with what one had, and religion pointed the way to contentment. Besides, what a lot it could do for a man's reputation! And it was good for the whole family, for it taught a man to make provision 'both for their comfortable subsistence here in this world, and their salvation in the next'. Machiavelli, one may feel, saw more clearly into the complacency of good people.

IN THIS *Psalm David* celebrates the glory of God from the consideration of the greatness of his Works, and the perfection of his Laws. From the greatness of his Works, *verse 1. The heavens declare the glory of God, and the firmament showeth his handiwork*, &c. From the perfection of his Laws, *verse 7. The Law of the Lord is perfect, converting the soul*, &c. And among many other excellencies of the Divine Laws, he mentions in the last place the benefits and advantages which come from the observance of them, *verse 11. and in keeping of them there is great reward.*

I have already shown how much Religion tends to the public welfare of mankind; to the support of Government, and to the peace and happiness of human Societies. My work at this time shall be to show that Religion and obedience to the Laws of God do likewise conduce to the happiness of particular persons, both in respect of this world and the other. For though there be but little express mention made in the *Old Testament* of the immortality of the Soul and the rewards of another life, yet all Religion does suppose these principles, and is built upon them.

I. And *First*, I shall endeavour to show how Religion conduceth to the happiness of this life; and that both in respect of the inward and outward man.

First, As to the mind; to be pious and religious brings a double advantage to the mind of man. 1. It tends to the improvement of our understandings. 2. It brings peace and pleasure to our minds.

1. It tends to the improvement of our understandings. I do not mean only that it instructs us in the knowledge of divine and spiritual things, and makes us to understand the great interest of our souls and the concernments of eternity better, but that in general it does raise and enlarge the minds of men and make them more capable of true knowledge. And in this sense I understand the following Texts; *The commandment of the Lord is pure, enlightening the eyes; The fear of the Lord is the beginning of wisdom, a good understanding have all they that keep his commandments; Thou through thy commandments hast made me wiser than mine enemies*, which plainly refers to political prudence; *I have more understanding than all my teachers, for thy Testimonies are my meditation, I understand more than the ancients, because I keep thy precepts; Through thy precepts I get understanding; The entrance of thy word giveth light, it giveth understanding to the simple.*

Now Religion doth improve the understandings of men by

subduing their lusts, and moderating their passions. The lusts and passions of men do sully and darken their minds, even by a natural influence. Intemperance and sensuality and fleshly lusts do debase men's minds, and clog their spirits, make them gross and foul, listless and unactive; they sink us down into sense, and glue us to these low and inferior things like *birdlime*; they hamper and entangle our souls, and hinder their flight upwards; they indispose and unfit our minds for the most noble and intellectual considerations. So likewise the exorbitant passions of wrath and malice, envy and revenge, do darken and distort the understandings of men, do tincture the mind with false colours and fill it with prejudice and undue apprehensions of things.

There is no man that is intemperate, or lustful, or passionate, but besides the guilt he contracts which is continually fretting and disquieting his mind, besides the inconveniences he brings upon himself as to his health, he does likewise stain and obscure the brightness of his Soul and the clearness of his discerning faculty. Such persons have not that free use of their reason that they might have; their understandings are not bright enough, nor their spirits pure and fine enough for the exercise of the highest and noblest acts of reason. What clearness is to the eye that purity is to our mind and understanding, and as the clearness of the bodily eye doth dispose it for a quicker sight of material objects, so doth the purity of our minds, that is, freedom from lust and passion, dispose us for the clearest and most perfect acts of reason and understanding.

Now Religion doth purify our minds and refine our spirits by quenching the fire of lust and suppressing the fumes and vapours of it, and by scattering the clouds and mists of passion. And the more any man's soul is cleansed from the filth and dregs of sensual lusts the more nimble and expedite it will be in its operations. The more any man conquers his passions, the more calm and sedate his spirit is, and the greater equality he maintains in his temper, his apprehensions of things will be the more clear and unprejudiced, and his judgment more firm and steady. And this is the meaning of that saying of *Solomon*, *He that is slow to wrath is of great understanding, but he that is hasty of spirit exalteth folly. Ira furor brevis est*—Anger is a short fit of madness, and he that is passionate and furious deprives himself of his reason, spoils his understanding, and helps to make himself a fool: whereas he that conquers his passions and keeps them under, doth thereby preserve and improve his understanding.

Freedom from irregular passions doth not only signify that a man is wise, but really contributes to the making of him such.

2. Religion tends to the ease and pleasure, the peace and tranquillity of our minds; wherein happiness chiefly consists and which all the wisdom and Philosophy of the world did always aim at, as the utmost felicity of this life. And that this is the natural fruit of a religious and virtuous course of life, the Scripture declares to us in these Texts; *Light is sown for the righteous, and gladness for the upright in heart; Great peace have all they that love thy Law, and nothing shall offend them; Her ways are ways of pleasantness, and all her paths are peace; The fruit of righteousness is peace, and the effect of righteousness quietness and assurance for ever*; The plain sense of which Texts is, that pleasure and peace do naturally result from a holy and good life. When a man hath once engaged himself in a Religious course, and is habituated to piety and holiness, all the exercises of Religion and devotion, all acts of goodness and virtue are delightful to him. To honour and worship God, to pray to him and to praise him, to study his will, to meditate upon him and to love him, all these bring great pleasure and peace along with them. What greater contentment and satisfaction can there be to the mind of man, when it is once purified and refined from the dregs of sensual pleasures and delights, and raised to its true height and pitch, than to contemplate and admire the infinite excellencies and perfections of God, to adore his greatness and to love his goodness? How can the thoughts of God be troublesome to any one who lives soberly and righteously and godly in the world? No man that loves goodness and righteousness hath any reason to be afraid of God, or to be disquieted with the thoughts of him. There is nothing in God that is terrible to a good man, but all the apprehensions which we naturally have of him speak comfort and promise happiness to such a one. The consideration of his attributes is so far from being a trouble to him that it is his recreation and delight. It is for wicked men to dread God and to endeavour to banish the thoughts of him out of their minds; but a holy and virtuous man may have quiet and undisturbed thoughts even of the justice of God, because the terror of it doth not concern him.

Now Religion doth contribute to the peace and quiet of our minds these two ways. *First*, By allaying those passions which are apt to ruffle and discompose our spirits. Malice and hatred, wrath and revenge are very fretting and vexatious and apt to make our minds sore and uneasy, but he that can moderate these affections will find a strange ease and pleasure in his own spirit. *Secondly*, by freeing us from the anxieties of guilt, and the fears of divine wrath and displeasure; than which nothing is more stinging and tormenting and renders the life of man more miserable and unquiet. And what a spring of peace and joy must it needs be to apprehend upon good grounds that God is reconciled to us and become our friend; that all our sins are perfectly forgiven and shall never more be remembered against us! What unexpressible comfort does overflow the pious and devout soul from the remembrance of a holy and well-spent life and a conscience of its own innocency and integrity! And nothing but the practice of Religion and Virtue can give this ease and satisfaction to the mind of man. For there is a certain kind of temper and disposition which is necessary to the pleasure and quiet of our minds, and consequently to our happiness: and that is holiness and goodness, which as it is the perfection so is it likewise the happiness of the Divine nature: And on the contrary, the chief part of the misery of wicked men, and of those accursed spirits the Devils is this, that they are of a disposition contrary to God; they are envious and malicious and cruel, and of such a temper as is naturally a torment and disquiet to itself. And here the foundation of Hell is laid, in the evil disposition of men's minds; and till this be cured, which can only be done by Religion, it is as impossible for a man to be happy, that is, pleased and contented within himself, as it is for a sick man to be at ease. Because such a man hath that within him which torments him, and he cannot be at ease till that be removed. The man's spirit is out of order and off the hinges, and till that be put into its right frame he will be perpetually disquieted and can find no rest within himself. The *Prophet* very fitly describes to us the unquiet condition of wicked men, *The wicked is like the troubled sea when it cannot rest, whose waters cast up mire and dirt; there is no peace (saith my God) to the wicked.* So long as sin and corruption abound in our hearts they will be restlessly working, like wine which will be in a perpetual motion and agitation till it have purged itself of its dregs and foulness.

Secondly, Religion does likewise tend to the happiness of the outward man. Now the blessings of this kind are such as either respect our *health*, or *estate*, or *reputation*, or relations; and in respect of all these Religion is highly advantageous to us.

1. As to our health, a Religious and virtuous life doth eminently

conduce to that, and to long life as a consequent of it. And in this sense I understand these following Texts; *My Son forget not my Law, but let thy heart keep my Commandments; for length of days, and long life, shall they add to thee*; and [Proverbs] v. 7, and 8. *Fear the Lord and depart from evil, it shall be health to thy navel, and marrow to thy bones*; and v. 16. among the temporal advantages of wisdom or Religion this is mentioned as the first and principal, *length of days is in her right hand*; and v.18. *she is a tree of life to them that lay hold upon her*; and again, *Whoso findeth me, findeth life, but he that sinneth against me wrongeth his own soul*; (that is, injurious to his own life) *all they that hate me love death*; all which is undoubtedly true in a spiritual sense, but is certainly meant by *Solomon* in the natural sense. And these promises, of the blessings of health and long life to good men are not only declaratory of the good pleasure and intention of God towards them, but likewise of the natural tendency of the thing. For Religion doth oblige men to the practice of those virtues which do in their own nature conduce to the preservation of our health, and the lengthening of our days; such as temperance and chastity and moderation of our passions. And the contrary vices to these do apparently tend to the impairing of men's health and the shortening of their days. How many have wasted and consumed their bodies by lust, and brought grievous pains and mortal diseases upon themselves! See how the wise man describes the sad consequences of this sin, *He goes as an Ox to the slaughter, till a dart strike through his Liver; as a Bird hasteneth to the snare, and knoweth not that it is for his life*; and [Proverbs] v. 25, 26, 27. *Let not thy heart decline to her ways, go not astray in her paths; for she hath cast down many wounded; yea many strong men have been slain by her; her house is the way to Hell* (that is to the grave) *going down to the chambers of death*. How many have been ruined by intemperance and excess, and most unnaturally have perverted those blessings which God hath given for the support of nature to the overthrow and destruction of it? How often hath men's malice and envy and discontent against others terminated in a cruel revenge upon themselves? How many by the wild fury and extravagancy of their own passions, have put their bodies into a combustion, and fired their spirits; and by stirring up their rage and choler against others have armed that fierce humour against themselves?

2. As to our estates, Religion is likewise a mighty advantage

to men in that respect. Not only in regard of God's more especial providence and peculiar blessing which usually attends good men in their undertakings and crowns them with good success, but also from the nature of the thing. And this, I doubt not, is the meaning of those expressions of the *Wise man* concerning the temporal benefits and advantages of wisdom or Religion; *In her left hand are riches and honour; They that love me shall inherit substance, and I will fill their treasures*; and this Religion principally does, by charging men with truth and fidelity and justice in their dealings, which are a sure way of thriving and will hold out when all fraudulent arts and devices will fail. And this also *Solomon* observes to us; *He that walketh uprightly walketh surely, but he that perverteth his way shall be known*; his indirect dealing will be discovered one time or other, and then loses his reputation, and his interest sinks. Falsehood and deceit only serve a present turn, and the consequence of them is pernicious; but truth and fidelity are a lasting advantage; *The righteous hath an everlasting foundation; The lip of truth is established for ever, but a lying tongue is but for a moment*. And Religion does likewise engage men to diligence and industry in their Callings, and how much this conduces to the advancement of men's fortunes daily experience teaches, and the *Wise man* hath told us, *The diligent hand makes rich*; and again, *Seest thou a man diligent in business, he shall stand before Princes, he shall not stand before mean persons*.

And where men by reason of the difficult circumstances of their condition cannot arrive to any eminency of estate, yet Religion makes a compensation for this by teaching men to be contented with that moderate and competent fortune which God hath given them. For the shortest way to be rich is not by enlarging our estates, but by contracting our desires. What *Seneca* says of Philosophy, is much more true of Religion, *praestat opes sapientia, quas cuicunque fecit supervacuas dedit*, it makes all those rich to whom it makes riches superfluous, and they are so to those who are taught by Religion to be contented with such a portion of them as God's Providence hath thought fit to allot to them.

3. As to our reputation. There is nothing gives a man a more firm and established reputation among wise and serious persons (whose judgment is only valuable) than a prudent and substantial Piety. This doth many times command reverence and esteem from the worser sort of men, and such as are no great

friends to Religion; and sometimes the force of truth will extort an acknowledgement of its excellency, even from its greatest enemies. I know very well that good men may, and often do, blemish the reputation of their piety by over-acting some things in Religion; by an indiscreet zeal about things wherein Religion is not concerned, by an ungrateful austerity and sourness which Religion doth not require; by little affectations, and an imprudent ostentation of devotion; but a substantial and solid, a discreet and unaffected piety, which makes no great noise and show, but expresses itself in a constant and serious devotion, and is accompanied with the fruits of goodness and kindness and righteousness towards men, will not only give a man a credit and value among the sober and the virtuous, but even among the vicious and more degenerate sort of men. Upon this account it is that the Apostle adviseth Christians, if they would recommend themselves to the esteem of God and men, earnestly to mind the weighty and substantial parts of Religion; *Let not then your good be evil spoken of; for the Kingdom of God is not meats and drinks, but righteousness and peace, and joy in the Holy Ghost; for he that in these things serveth Christ is acceptable to God, and approved of men.*

It is true indeed, there are some persons of so profligate a temper, and of such an inveterate enmity to all goodness, as to scorn and reproach even Religion and Virtue itself. But the reproach of such persons does not really wound a man's reputation. For why should any man be troubled at the contumelies of those whose judgment deserves not to be valued, who despise goodness and good men out of malice and ignorance? If these reproaches which they cast upon them were the censures of wise and sober men, a man's reputation might be concerned in them; but they are the rash words of inconsiderate and injudicious men, the extravagant speeches of those who are unexperienced in the things they speak against; and therefore no wise man will be troubled at them, or think either Religion or himself disparaged by them.

4. As to our Relations. Religion also conduceth to the happiness of these, as it derives a large and extensive blessing upon all that belongs to us; the goodness of God being so diffusive as to scatter his blessings *round about the habitations of the just*, and *to show mercy unto thousands of them that love him and keep his Commandments*. So *David* tells us, *Blessed is the man that feareth the Lord, and delighteth greatly in his Commandments. His seed shall be mighty upon earth: the generation of the upright*

shall be blessed. *Wealth and riches are in his house, and his righteousness endureth for ever.* And so *Solomon; A good man leaveth an inheritance to his Children's Children*; and again, *In the fear of the Lord is strong confidence, and his Children shall have a place of refuge*. But the wicked derives a curse upon all that is related to him, he is said *to trouble his own house*; and again, *The wicked are overthrown and are not, but the house of the righteous shall stand.*

But setting aside the consideration of God's Providence, Religion doth likewise in its own nature tend to the welfare of those who are related to us; because it lays the strictest obligations upon men to take care of their Families and Relations, and to make the best provision both for their comfortable subsistence here in this world and their salvation in the next. And those who neglect those duties, the Scripture is so far from esteeming them Christians that it accounts them worse than Heathens and Infidels, *He that provideth not for his own, especially those of his own house, is worse than an Infidel, and hath denied the faith.* This I know is spoken in respect of temporal provision, but it holds *a fortiori* as to the care of their souls.

Besides, it is many times seen that the posterity of holy and good men, especially of such as have evidenced their piety towards God by bounty and charity to men, have met with unusual kindness and respect from others, and have by a strange and secret disposition of Divine providence been unexpectedly cared and provided for; and that, as they have all the reason in the world to believe, upon the account and for the sake of the piety and charity of their Parents. This *David* tells us from his own particular observation; *I have been young, and now am old, yet have I not seen the righteous forsaken, nor his seed begging bread.* And that by the *righteous* is here meant the *good and merciful man* appears from the description of him in the next words, *He is ever merciful and lendeth, and his seed is blessed.* And on the contrary, the posterity of the wicked do many times inherit the fruit of their fathers' sins and vices; and that not only by a just judgment of God, but from the natural course and consequence of things. And in this sense that expression in *Job* is often verified, that *God lays up the iniquity of wicked men for their Children.* And doth not experience testify that the intemperate and unjust do many times transmit their bodily infirmities and diseases to their Children, and entail a secret curse upon their estates, which does either insensibly waste and consume it, or eat out the heart and comfort of it? Thus you see how Religion in all respects conduces to the happiness of this life.

II. Religion and Virtue do likewise most certainly and directly tend to the eternal happiness and salvation of men in the other world. And this is incomparably the greatest advantage that redounds to men by being Religious, in comparison of which all temporal considerations *are less than nothing and vanity*. The worldly advantages that Religion brings to men in this present life are a sensible recommendation of Religion even to the lowest and meanest spirits: But to those who are raised above sense and aspire after immortality, who believe the perpetual duration of their souls and the resurrection of their bodies; to those who are throughly convinced of the inconsiderableness of this short dying life and of all the concernments of it, in comparison of that eternal state which remains for us in another life; to these, I say, the consideration of a future happiness of those unspeakable and everlasting rewards which shall then be given to holiness and virtue, is certainly the most powerful motive and the most likely to prevail upon them. For those who are persuaded that they shall continue for ever cannot choose but aspire after a happiness commensurate to their duration, nor can anything that is conscious to itself of its own immortality be satisfied and contented with anything less than the hopes of an endless felicity. And this hope Religion alone gives men, and the Christian Religion only can settle men in a firm and unshaken assurance of it. But because all men who have entertained any Religion have consented to these principles, of the *immortality of the soul* and the *recompenses of another world*, and have always promised to themselves some rewards of piety and virtue after this life; and because I did more particularly design from this *Text* to speak of the temporal benefits and advantages which redound to men from Religion, therefore I shall content myself to show very briefly how a religious and virtuous life doth conduce to our future happiness. And that upon these two accounts; from the promise of God, and from the nature of the thing.

1. From the promise of God. *Godliness* (saith the Apostle) *hath the promise of the life that is to come*. God hath all along in the Scripture suspended the promise of eternal life upon this condition. He hath peremptorily declared that without obedience and holiness of life no man shall ever see the Lord. And this very thing, that it is the constitution and appointment of

God, might be argument enough to us (if there were no other) to convince us of the necessity of obeying the Laws of God in order to our happiness, and to persuade us thereunto. For eternal life is the gift of God, and he may do what he will with his own. He is master of his own favours and may dispense them upon what terms and conditions he pleases. But it is no hard condition that he hath imposed upon us. If Religion brought no advantages to us in this world, yet the happiness of heaven is so great as will abundantly recompense all our pains and endeavours; there is temptation enough in the reward to engage any man in the work. Had God thought fit to have imposed the most grievous and difficult things upon us, ought we not to have submitted to them and to have undertaken them with cheerfulness upon such great and glorious encouragements? As *Naaman's* servants said to him in another case, *Had he bid thee do some great thing wouldest thou not have done it?* So if God had said that without poverty and actual martyrdom *no man shall see the Lord*, would not any man that believes heaven and hell and understands what these words signify and what it is to escape extreme and eternal misery, and to enjoy unspeakable and endless glory, have been willing to accept these conditions? *How much more, when he hath only said, Wash and be clean*; and *Let every man that hath this hope in Him, purify himself as he is pure?* But God hath not dealt thus with us, nor is the imposing of this condition of eternal life a mere arbitrary constitution, therefore I shall endeavour to show,

2dly, That a Religious and Holy life doth from the very nature and reason of the thing conduce to our future happiness, by way of necessary disposition and preparation of us for it. We cannot be otherwise happy but by our conformity to God, without this we cannot possibly love him nor find any pleasure or happiness in communion with him. For we cannot love a nature contrary to our own, nor delight to converse with it. Therefore Religion, in order to the fitting of us for the happiness of the next life, does design to mortify our lusts and passions, and to restrain us from the inordinate love of the gross and sensual delights of this world; to call off our minds from these inferior things, and to raise them to higher and more spiritual objects, that we may be disposed for the happiness of the other world, and taught not to relish the delights of it; whereas should we set our hearts only upon these things, and be able to taste no pleasure in anything but what is sensual and earthly, we must needs be extremely miserable when we come into the other world, because we should meet with nothing to entertain ourselves withal, no employment suitable to our disposition, no pleasure that would agree with our depraved appetites and vicious inclinations. All that Heaven and Happiness signifies is unsuitable to a wicked man, and therefore could be no felicity to him. But this I shall have occasion to speak more fully to in my last Discourse.

From all that hath been said, the reasonableness of Religion clearly appears which tends so directly to the happiness of men, and is upon all accounts calculated for our benefit. Let but all things be truly considered and cast up and it will be found that there is no advantage to any man from an irreligious and vicious course of life. I challenge any one to instance in any real benefit that ever came to him this way. Let the sinner declare what he hath found by experience. Hath lewdness and intemperance been more for his health than if he had lived chastely and soberly? Hath falsehood and injustice proved at the long run more for the advancement and security of his estate than truth and honesty would have done? Hath any vice that he hath lived in made him more true friends, and gained him a better reputation in the world than the practice of holiness and virtue would have done? Hath he found *that* peace and satisfaction of mind in an evil course, and *that* quiet enjoyment of himself, and comfortable assurance of God's favour, and good hopes of his future condition, which a religious and virtuous life would have given him? Nay on the contrary, have not some of his vices weakened his body and broken his health, have not others dissipated his estate, and reduced him to want? What notorious vice is there that doth not blemish a man's reputation, and make him either hated or despised, and that not only by the wise and the virtuous but even by the generality of men? But was ever any wicked man free from the stings of a guilty conscience and the torment of a restless and uneasy mind, from the secret dread of Divine displeasure, and of the vengeance of another world? Let the sinner freely speak the very inward sense of his soul in this matter, and spare not; and I doubt not, if he will deal clearly and impartially, but that he will acknowledge all this to be true, and is able to confirm it from his own sad experience. For this is the natural fruit of sin and the present revenge which it takes upon sinners, besides that fearful punishment which shall be inflicted on them in another life.

What reason then can any man pretend against Religion, when it is so apparently for the benefit not only of human society but of every particular person; when there is no real interest of this world but may ordinarily be as effectually promoted and pursued to as great advantage, nay usually to far greater, by a man that *lives soberly and righteously and godly in the world,* than by any one that leads the contrary course of life? Let no man then say, with those profane persons whom the *Prophet* speaks of, *It is in vain to serve the Lord, and what profit is it that we have kept his Commandments?* God has not been so hard a master to us that we have reason thus to complain of him. He hath given us no Laws but what are for our good, nay so gracious hath he been to us as to link together our duty and our interest, and to make those very things the instances of our obedience which are the natural means and causes of our happiness. The Devil was so far in the right, when he charged *Job* that he did not *serve God for nought.* 'Tis he himself that is the hard master and makes men serve him for nought, who rewards his drudges and slaves with nothing but shame and sorrow and misery. But God requires no man's service upon hard and unreasonable terms. The greatest part of our work is a present reward to itself, and for whatever else we do or suffer for him, he offers us abundant consideration. And if men did but truly and wisely love themselves they would upon this very ground if there were no other, become Religious. For when all is done there is no man can serve his own interest better than by serving God. Religion conduceth both to our present and future happiness, and when the Gospel chargeth us with piety towards God, and justice and charity towards men, and temperance and chastity in reference to our selves, the true interpretation of these Laws is this, God requires of men in order to their eternal happiness that they should do those things which tend to their temporal welfare, that is, in plainer words, he promises to make us happy for ever upon condition that we will but do that which is best for our selves in this world. To conclude, Religion is founded in the interest of men rightly apprehended. So that if *the God of this world* and the lusts of men did not *blind their eyes,* so as to render them unfit to discern their true interest, it would be impossible, so long as men love themselves and desire their own happiness to keep them from being religious; for they could not but conclude that to be their interest, and being so convinced they would resolve to pursue it and stick to it.

WILLIAM SHERLOCK

SHERLOCK WAS born in Southwark and educated at Eton and Peterhouse, Cambridge. He was ordained, and some years later became rector of St George's, Botolph Lane, in the city. In 1674 he published a work attacking Puritan spirituality, and in 1684 a book on the duty of passive obedience. This view he maintained throughout James II's reign, combining it with strong attacks against popery. His passivity did not extend so far as complying with James's command to read the Declaration for Liberty of Conscience. At the Revolution of 1689 he was at first inclined to side with the Non-Jurors, as might have been expected from his declared views. In 1690, however, he took the oath. It is reported to have been said as he walked through the city: 'There goes Dr Sherlock, with his reason for taking the oath.' The reason was Mrs Sherlock. In 1691 there was a new book, *The Case of Resistance*, in which Sherlock took the view, reasonable enough in itself, that the Anglican Church has always recognized *de facto* government. In 1691 Sherlock was rewarded by being made Dean of St Paul's in succession to Tillotson, who was succeeding the Non-Juror Sancroft as Archbishop of Canterbury. In the nineties Sherlock gave much time and energy to a 'vindication' of the doctrine of the Trinity which took him so far that he was accused of saying that there were three Gods instead of one. He later modified his position. During his last years he was rector of Therfield, Hertfordshire and continued to write vigorously against dissenters. He died in 1707.

It is hard to avoid the impression that Sherlock was a rather silly man. He was almost certainly a rather weak one. South, whose tongue was admittedly none of the kindest, said: 'There is hardly any one subject he has wrote upon (that of Popery only excepted) but he has wrote for and against it too.' One has the impression that he couldn't stop writing and couldn't stop talking. He certainly did not impress his contemporaries as a man of any great solidity. His sermons show a marked facility of language and, as to content, a little meaning goes a long way.

The Charity of Lending without Usury
Luke 6:35.
But love your enemies, and do good, and lend, hoping for nothing again; and your reward shall be great, and ye shall be the children of the Highest: for he is kind unto the unthankful and to the evil.

THIS SERMON was preached before the Lord Mayor, at St Bridget's church, on Tuesday in Easter week, 1692. The subject was one of which the audience no doubt had a certain knowledge. It must have saved a great deal of embarrassment in both preacher and congregation that in his examination of the text Sherlock did not find anything to take exception to in the ordinary business of the city. Merely lending money on interest was not in itself usury, Sherlock explains, though some thought so. 'We all know, That Trade, to which we owe all the Riches and Greatness of our Nation, and so many excellent Charities too, cannot be maintained without it.' Sherlock had a gift for saying quite sensible things that do not quite carry conviction. Here it is not what he says which gives us pause, but the fact that it is too precisely what his audience would want him to say. The exposition which follows avoids getting near to the motives of merchants and money-lenders, but the conclusion that what really matters is offences against charity, is unexceptionable.

The interest of the sermon lies less in the doctrinal exposition, such as it is, than in the project which Sherlock recommends to the city in the latter part of it. He there makes a proposal for the setting up of charitable bank, which would be provided with funds by rich men who could afford to lend money for nothing, or for something below the current rate. There was no merit in rich men simply lending to one another. The poor had to be helped. However full of difficulties the proposal must have seemed to the Lord Mayor and the merchants, it shows a certain grasp of the relationship between credit and activity, and of the benefits which freer credit might bring. Sherlock was perhaps a little carried away by his enthusiasm, as he often was. 'It would enlarge your Hospitals, clear your Streets of Beggars, the great reproach of this City; maintain those who can't work, and employ those who can; put poor Children to Apprentice, provide Stocks for Ingenious and Industrious Young Men, who want them; redeem Prisoners.' All these were certainly matters to which the attention of a city congregation could properly be directed.

OUR CONFORMITY to the Death and Resurrection of our Saviour, consists in dying to sin, and walking in newness of life, which St. *Paul* tells us is represented by the External Ceremony of Baptism; the baptised Person being buried with Christ in Baptism, and rising out of his watery grave a new born Christian, *6. Rom. 3,4. For in that he died, he died unto sin once; but in that he liveth, he liveth unto God: Likewise reckon ye also yourselves to be dead indeed unto sin, but alive unto God, through Jesus Christ our Lord, 9,10.* And the principal Exercise of this Divine Life, which is our conformity to the Resurrection of Christ, is a Divine Conversation. *If ye then be risen with Christ, seek those things which are above, where Christ sitteth at the right hand of God: Set your affections on things above, not on things on the earth, 3. Col. 1,2.* And *to set our affections on things above*, does not only signify to think sometimes of Heaven, and to desire to go to Heaven when we die, which very worldly-minded men may do; but to lay up for ourselves Treasures in Heaven, which are durable and eternal, in opposition to those perishing Treasures on Earth, which are subject to Thieves, to Moths and Rust. *6 Matth. 19,20,21. To make to ourselves friends of the mammon of unrighteousness, that when we fail, they may receive us into everlasting habitations, 16. Luke 9.* Now ye all know what this means: *viz.* To purge our minds from the love of Riches, and from all covetous Desires; to improve our Estates in Acts of Piety and Charity, for the Service of God, and to supply the wants of the poor and miserable: to return our Money into the other World, where it will increase into Eternal Life and Glory: for this is truly to have our Conversation in Heaven, to live above this World, to sit loose from all the Enjoyments of it; to live to God, and another World, to improve everything we enjoy here, to secure and advance our future Happiness: when men are Charitable upon these Principles and these Designs, they must live a very heavenly Life; *For where our Treasure is, there our hearts will be also.*

This our Ancestors, who appointed this Annual Solemnity, seem to have been very sensible of, That there is no particular Grace or Virtue, the exercise of which is a more visible demonstration of a Divine and purified Mind, which is risen with Christ, and lives to God, as Christ doth, than the Grace of Charity; and therefore that there was no time more proper to exercise Charity, and to exhort Christians to Charity, and to show Charity in all its Pomp, and humble Bravery, than the Feast of the Resurrection;

wherein we commemorate the Love of our Lord in dying for us, and his triumph over Death, and in full assurance of a blessed Immortality, of which the Resurrection of our Saviour was an ocular Demonstration, send our Hearts and our Eyes after him to Heaven, and contemplate that Glory to which he is advanced, and to which he has promised to advance us.

This then is my proper work at this time, to exhort you to Charity; proper both to the nature of this Holy Feast, and to the original Institution of this Solemnity; and it may reasonably be hoped, that the Annual Returns of it, wherein all the Arguments to Charity are so earnestly pressed on you, should keep this Divine Fire always burning and glowing in your Breasts. You have so often heard all the Arguments to Charity, that it is impossible you should forget them; and there is one that is worth all the rest, which no Christian can forget, who remembers that there is a Heaven and a Hell, and which no Christian can resist, without despising his Soul, and Eternal Life and Death; and that is, That Heaven is the Reward of Charity; that Hell is the Punishment of Uncharitableness; which is so plainly and expressly taught, and so frequently repeated by our Saviour, that it is as certain and unavoidable, as that there is a Heaven and a Hell; and if Heaven be not a sufficient Encouragement to Charity, nor Hell sufficient to deter us from Uncharitableness, it is to no purpose to use any other Arguments, which can never persuade, if these can't; or if they could, would neither carry us to Heaven, nor keep us out of Hell; for to be charitable only for temporal reasons, is to give our goods to feed the poor, without a true Divine Charity; which St. *Paul* tells us, will profit nothing, *1 Cor. 13*. For such a Charity as does not raise us above this world, can neither carry us to Heaven, nor keep us out of Hell. And therefore instead of drawing together all the Arguments for Charity which you have so often heard, and showing them in a new dress, my design at present is to recommend to you a very excellent, but a very neglected part of Charity, which our Saviour presses on us in my Text, *viz.* The Charity of Lending, *Do good, and lend, hoping for nothing again.*

In speaking to which Words, I shall 1. Show you what this Duty is. 2. What an excellent Charity it is to lend. And how this may be improved to the most excellent purposes.

1. What this Duty is, or what our Saviour means by *lending, hoping for nothing again*. And it can signify but two things; and I see no reason to think, but that our Saviour might mean both.

1. To Lend, without hoping for any increase; or to lend freely, without Usury. 2. To lend, where the very Principal may be in danger, when we have little reason to hope that we shall ever see our own again.

1. To lend freely, without Usury; for our Saviour commands this, as an Act of Charity, *Do good, and lend*: And though to lend, even upon Usury, may in many cases prove a great kindness to the Borrower, yet Charity is not the motive of the Lender, it is not Charity, but Traffic and Merchandise of Money: and though the *Jews* were expressly forbid to lend their Brethren upon Usury, yet our Saviour intimates there was something like this, and equivalent to it, which spoiled the Charity of lending, even without Usury; that they would not lend to the poor; who though they should repay them what they borrowed, yet were never likely to be in a condition to lend to them again; but they would lend to the Rich, from whom they expected the like returns of kindness; as you may see in the Verses before my Text; *33, 34. And if ye do good to them that do good to you, what thank have ye? for sinners also do even the same. And if ye lend to them, of whom ye hope to receive,* (not only your own, but the like kindness of lending to you when your occasions require it), *what thank have ye? for sinners also lend to sinners, to receive as much again*; equal returns of kindness; which if it be not Usury of Money, is Usury of Kindnesses, but is not Charity; like inviting our Rich Friends and Neighbours to a Feast, who can invite us again; which though it be no fault, is no Charity, for that consists in entertaining the poor, who can make us no return, *14. Luke 12, 13, 14.* And thus our Saviour exhorts us here, but *do you do good, and lend, hoping for nothing again*; neither for Usury, nor for such returns and exchanges of kindness.

It was for the sake of this Duty, that Usury was so strictly forbidden by the *Jewish* Law, that men might the more freely lend their Money to those who wanted, when they had no present use for it themselves; and had no way to increase it; and as far as the Reason and Charity of this Law extends, so far it still obliges, and so far Usury is still forbid to Christians.

This is not well considered by those who so universally condemn all Usury; and because the right understanding of this will be of great use to settle some men's minds, and to explain and enforce this duty of Lending, which I now recommend to you, it cannot be thought a digression from my present Design, to give you the true, but short state of this matter.

It is confessed on all hands, That Usury is forbid by the Law of *Moses*; but the great mistake is concerning the Nature of Usury, or what that is which the Law forbids and condemns by the name of Usury.

Some think that all Increase of Money, when men lend a Sum of Money to receive the Principal again with Interest, is the Usury which the Law forbids; and therefore that this is absolutely unlawful in all cases, and in all degrees; though we all know, That Trade, to which we owe all the Riches and Greatness of our Nation, and so many excellent Charities too, cannot be maintained without it: That some men, who now live comfortably in the world, maintain their Families with Credit and Reputation, and do many acts of Charity themselves, could not Trade at all; others could not drive such flourishing and spreading Trades without borrowed Money, nor borrow without Interest: That many Widows and Orphans are maintained by Interest, who must in a few years be Beggars, had they no other way to live, but to spend the Principal. This is so contrary to the sense and reason of Mankind, and to all the rules of Justice and Charity, and so impracticable in the present state of the world, that while it is possible to put any other sense upon the Law, I would never think of this. And the comfort is, that the Law expounds itself otherwise, and gives no colour for such an interpretation as this,That all Increase of Money is forbid by it.

For 1. The Law itself allowed the *Jews* to take Usury of Strangers of other Countries, though not of their Brethren, or natural *Jews*, 23. *Deut.* 20. *Unto a stranger thou mayest lend upon usury, but unto thy brother thou shalt not lend upon usury*. And therefore God did not absolutely forbid the *Jews* to increase their Money, for they might lend to strangers upon Usury; which proves, that this was not an universal Law to them, much less is it so to all mankind. And that proves that there is no moral and intrinsic evil in Usury; for if all Usury had in its own nature been unlawful, God could not have allowed the *Jews* to take Usury of strangers; for he cannot allow the least moral evil. The truth is, I never could yet see the least shadow of an Argument to prove, that Usury is evil in its nature, unless that Money can't beget Money, be thought an Argument; but that is as good an Argument against buying Corn or Wine, or anything else with Money; for it is unnatural for Money to beget Corn or Wine: But if the barren nature of Money, that it cannot naturally propagate itself, be a reason against Usury of Money, this is no reason against Usury of Corn, which is equally forbid: for it is natural for Corn to propagate its kind, and multiply itself; and yet the Usury of all Victuals is as much forbid, as the Usury of Money, *23. Deut. 19.* Now if Usury be not morally evil, it can be unlawful to none, but those to whom God has forbid it; and there being no prohibition of it in the New Testament, which is the Law of the Christian Church, it cannot be unlawful to Christians, whatever it was to the *Jews*.

2. And yet the *Jews* themselves were not expressly forbid, however they might understand it, to lend their Money upon Usury, to all their own Brethren, but only to the Poor: So that had any Rich *Jew* come to borrow Money of them, for any thing that appears by the Law, they might have lent Money to him upon Usury. This Observation will clear this whole matter; and therefore I shall turn you to all the Texts of the Law, which forbid Usury, and the reading of them will convince you, That Usury was forbid only in favour of the Poor.

The first Text is, *22. Exod. 25. If thou lend money to any of my people that is poor by thee, thou shalt not be to him as an Usurer, neither shalt thou lay upon him Usury*: Where no Usury is forbid, not only lending to the Poor upon Usury: Thus *25. Lev. 35, 36, 37. And if thy brother be waxen poor, and fallen to decay with thee, then thou shalt relieve him. Take thou no usury of him nor increase, but fear God, that thy brother may live well with thee: Thou shalt not give him thy money upon usury, nor lend him thy victuals for increase.* It is true, in the Repetition of this Law, *23. Deut. 19, 20.* it is only said, *Thou shalt not lend upon usury to thy brother, usury of money, usury of victuals, usury of any thing that is lent upon usury. Unto a stranger thou mayest lend upon usury, but unto thy brother thou shalt not lend upon usury, that the Lord thy God may bless thee in all that thou settest thine hand unto, in the land whither thou goest to possess.* This seems to forbid lending upon Usury to any *Jew*, whether Rich or Poor: but this being only a repetition of those Laws in *Exodus* and *Leviticus*, in all reason must be expounded by them; and though the Poor are not expressed, the Circumstances of the place prove, that they only are meant; for though Rich Men may sometimes have occasion to borrow Money, yet none but the Poor, who have no Money to buy, can ever have occasion to borrow Victuals upon Usury; and the difference the Law makes between a Brother and a Stranger shows, that it is intended as an Act of Charity, which they owe to their Brethren, though not to strangers. For which Reason also they were forbid to make any of their Brethren Bondmen, though they might buy the Children of the Heathen and Strangers for Bondmen and Bondmaids, *25. Levit. 39,* &c. and the Blessing God promises shows, that it is the Reward of Charity.

In other places, where Usury is mentioned, some Circumstance or other determines it to the Poor. This was the case, when *Nehemiah* reproved the Nobles and the Rulers for exacting Usury, *5. Nehem*. When the Prophet *Isaiah* threatens great Desolations against the Land, he thus describes it, *And it shall be as with the people, so with the priest—as with the lender, so with the borrower, as with the taker of usury, so with the giver of usury to him, 24. Isa. 2.* That is, the Lender and the Usurer shall be reduced to the same Distress and Poverty, as those suffer who borrow upon Usury; which shows, that none but Poor Men used to borrow upon Usury in those days. Thus when the Prophet *Jeremiah* complains, *Woe is me, my Mother, that thou hast born me a man of strife, and a man of contention to the whole earth: I have neither lent on usury, nor men have lent to me on usury, yet every one of them doth curse me, 15. Jer. 10.* it plainly intimates, that Usury is such an Oppression of the Poor, as both deserves and very often procures Curses. And therefore the Prophet *Ezekiel* joins Usury with the Oppression of the Poor, and other Acts of Violence, *18. Ezek. 7, 8, 10, 11, 16, 17. He who hath oppressed the poor and needy, hath spoiled by violence, hath not restored the pledge, hath given forth upon usury, and hath taken Increase, he shall die. But he that hath neither oppressed the poor, nor hath withholden the pledge, neither hath spoiled by violence, but hath given his bread to the hungry, and clothed the naked with a garment, that hath taken off his hand from the poor, that hath not received usury nor increase, he shall live.* Which makes it very plain, what is meant by Usury, when to take Usury, is joined with Violence and Oppression of the Poor; and to lend without Usury is reckoned among Acts of great Charity and Goodness.

There is but one place more, as I remember, that mentions Usury, *15. Psalm 5.* and there putting forth Money to Usury is joined with taking a Reward against the Innocent, which shows, that it was an Act of Violence and Oppression. For indeed among the *Jews*, who were no Merchants, nor maintained any Foreign Trade with other Nations, no men had occasion to borrow Money, much less Victuals, but to supply their present wants, and to take advantage of the Necessities of the Poor, to increase their own Fortunes by increasing their Poverty, was against all the Laws of Goodness and Charity; and therefore this Usury, which was the only Usury known in those days, is strictly forbid, as all other Acts of Oppression are. All other kinds of Usury are introduced by Trade and Commerce; and though it is against Charity to lend upon Usury to men, who borrow to supply their wants, yet if men borrow to increase their Trade and Fortunes, there is Justice and Equity in it, that the Lender shall make some Increase of his Money, as well as the Borrower. This is not properly Usury, but Traffic and Commerce; and I know no reason, why Men may not Trade with Money, as well as with other Commodities.

And this I take to be the true reason, why the *Jews* were permitted to take Usury of Strangers, but not of their Brethren, because their Heathen Neighbours were Merchants, as is plain of *Tyre* and *Sidon, 23. Isa.* They improved their Money by Trade, and therefore it was fit they should pay Interest for it; especially if they were to lend upon Usury only to such Strangers as came among them for Trade, but did not dwell and sojourn with them; which seems probable from *25. Levit. 35.* where the Stranger that sojourns with them seems to be entituled to the like Charity as a Brother. *If thy Brother be waxen poor, and fallen to decay, thou shalt relieve him, yea, though he be a stranger, or a sojourner, that he may live with thee, take thou no usury of him, nor Increase.* For a *Stranger* never signifies a Proselyte of Justice, who by Circumcision was incorporated into the Body of *Israel,* made a Brother, and entituled to the Privileges of a Natural *Jew,* but only a Proselyte of the Gate, who renounced Idolatry, but did not undertake the Observation of the Law of *Moses*; and yet they were not to take Usury of these Strangers if they were poor, no more than of their Brother, according to that Law, *22. Exod. 21. Thou shalt not vex a stranger, nor oppress him, for ye were strangers in the land of Egypt.*

The Answer our Saviour gives to the Servant who hid his Talent in the Napkin, seems to justify this Account, unless we can suppose, that his Lord would have been pleased with unjust and wicked Gain. *25. Matth. 27. Thou oughtest to have put my money to the Exchangers, and then at my coming I should have received mine own with usury.* So that though it was unlawful to lend Money upon Usury to the Poor, it was not so to the Exchangers, who traded in Money. And our Saviour's driving the Money

Changers out of the Temple, no more proves that he disallowed that Profession, than that he disallowed selling Oxen, and Sheep, and Doves for Sacrifice, for he drove them out also; the Fault was not in the Merchandise no more of Money, than of Sheep, or Oxen, or Doves, but they made *his Father's house, a house of Merchandise,* 2. *John* 14, 15, &c.

It is certain the ancient Fathers, who were professed Enemies to Usury, opposed it under this Notion; for their great Arguments against Usury, are levelled against Uncharitableness and Oppression of the Poor, as appears from *Gregor. Nyssen, St. Ambrose, St. Basil,* and others; and yet it is no wonder, should we meet with some Passages in them against Usury considered as Trading and Merchandise of Money: For it is well known, that they were not much greater Friends to Trade and Merchandise, than they were to Usury, which they thought unbecoming a Christian, as ministering only to Covetousness and Luxury. And yet I suppose, the greatest Enemies at this day to Usury, will not carry the Quarrel so far, as to condemn Merchandise. And yet under this Notion of Covetousness and sordid Gain (which is equally applicable to all Trade) Usury is forbid the Clergy by the Seventeenth Canon of the First Council of *Nice*; but no Council ever forbade it to the Laiety, or threatened Church-Censures against them for it, which they would certainly have done, had they thought it evil in itself.

This may satisfy us in what Sense Usury is forbid, both by the Law of *Moses* and the ancient Writers of the Christian Church, *viz.* as contrary to Charity; when we lend upon Usury, where Charity requires us to lend freely: When we take Increase of the Poor, who borrow to supply their Wants, and sink them still more irrecoverably into Poverty by such Exactions: This always was, and always will be hateful to God, and to all Good Men, and yet such detestable Usurers there are among us, who grow rich upon the Ruins and Spoils of the Poor, and drink the Tears of Widows and Orphans; but when to lend without Usury is no Charity, and to take Usury is no Oppression, there Usury itself is no Crime.

And hence we learn (which is the great thing I aimed at) that Usury was forbid only for the sake of Lending, which proves, that to lend freely to the Poor, is a great and necessary Act of Charity: Though a Man never took a Penny for Usury in his Life, yet if he neither gives, nor lends to the Poor, he is guilty of all that Uncharitableness, for which Usury is condemned; nay in most Cases, even these worst sort of Usurers are the more charitable Men: For excepting some very hard Cases, it is greater Charity to lend even to the Poor for Usury, than not to lend at all.

For this Reason the Emperor *Leo* was forced by a New Constitution to permit Usury, which his Father out of a pious Zeal had wholly forbid, because he found, that when Men were forbid to take any Usury, they would not lend at all, which was a greater Hardship to the Poor, than Usury itself.

Merely not to take Usury is no Virtue, but to lend to the Poor without Usury is. To lock up our Money in our Chests to rust and canker, and to do no good with it, is what St. *James* so severely threatens rich Men for, *Go now ye rich men, weep and howl for your miseries, which shall come upon you; your riches are corrupted, and your garments are moth-eaten; your gold and your silver is cankered, and the rust of them shall be a witness against you*, a Witness of your Covetousness and Uncharitableness, that you have done no good with it, but hoarded it up to rust and canker for want of use. *5. James 1, 2, 3*.

This Controversy then may be stated and decided in a few words. Usury is a very great Sin, that is, to lend our Money upon Usury to those who borrow for Necessity and Want, and to exact such Payments with Rigour and Severity, to strip such miserable People of that little that remains, to imprison their Persons, and make them end their lives in a Gaol. To lock up our Money, and do no good with it, is to hide our Talent in a Napkin; for Money is improvable, and must be improved, either for Charity or Increase, to be a new and perpetual Spring of Charity. To declaim against Usury, and not to exhort men to lend to the Poor without Usury, is to mistake or overlook the true End and Design of the Law, and to betray uncharitable Men to a greater Evil than Usury itself; but if men lend freely to the Poor in such Proportions as Charity requires, they may very innocently and virtuously, without transgressing this Law against Usury, lend their Money for Increase to the Rich.

2. But our Saviour seems to mean something more by *lending, hoping for nothing again*, not only to lend freely without Usury, but to lend, where the Principal may be in Danger, when we cannot reasonably promise ourselves to receive our own again: no man can deny, but this is great Charity; but then this must be conducted by the measures and proportions of giving: what Charity will oblige us to give, it will as reasonably oblige us to lend; but where the Return is very hazardous, it can oblige us to

lend, no more than what it would become us to give, and yet in such Cases, lending may be a greater Charity than giving, which is the Second thing proposed, which I can speak but briefly to.

2. The Excellency and Advantages of this Charity of Lending, and how it may be improved to be the best Purpose.

Now if we compare Giving and Lending together, Lending has much the Advantage of Giving, as to the true End and Purposes of Charity.

To lend is a greater Obligation to Industry, than to give; and there cannot be a greater Kindness done to the Poor, next to keeping them from starving, than to teach them Industry. I need not tell you, that there are many Poor, who will never work, while they can meet with charitable People to give; nay, who choose to be sick, to be lame, to be blind, to move Charity, rather than work to supply their Wants; but when Men have nothing to live on, but the improvement of lent Money, which they know they must repay when it is called for, this must make them industrious; for it both encourages their Industry, and keeps the Rod over them; especially were this made a standing Rule to give nothing to those who are able, but will not work, who have a Stock lent them to trade with, and neglect to improve it.

Thus what we give does but one single Act of Charity, for we can give it but once; but what we lend may circulate, as the Blood does in our Veins, and communicate Warmth and Spirits to more parts of the Body than one: that is, what we lend, may be lent again, and do a great many successive Charities, as great, or greater than that one single Charity had been, if we had given it: And that certainly is one of the greatest and noblest Charities which is most diffusive.

But yet to make this Charity of Lending the more effectual, it must be confessed, that a Public Bank of Charity raised out of such free Loans, will have many Advantages above any Private Acts of this Nature; and I can by no means think this either impracticable or difficult.

I doubt not but most of this Honourable Assembly could contrive very Advantageous ways of doing this, were Men but Charitably disposed. For suppose you should make your Hospitals, or your Companies, such Public Banks, or if it could be more Public, still the more Useful, and the more secure, where charitable People may safely deposit their Money without Use, or those who cannot spare the whole Interest, may abate some part of it; and where the running Cash may be lodged, which Men expect no Interest for; this might easily rise to a very vast Sum, which with wise Improvement would make a sure and lasting Fund of Charity.

And could anything in the World be more easy than this, which no man could feel? What would it be to a Rich Man, who has many thousands employed in Trade, or secured at Interest; or if he knows when he has enough, has no need to increase it, to drop some thousands into such a free Bank, to sanctify and prosper his Trade, and other ways of Gain, and to secure a Blessing to his Posterity? How many others are there, who could spare a hundred, or it may be some hundred pounds out of their Stock, and not feel the want of Interest, or at least, if they could not spare the whole Interest, might spare the half, or third part of it? How many are there, who have some hundreds by them useless, which they would not, and could not with any reason grudge to lay up in a safe Bank? How many are there, who would easily be persuaded to lend, were there such a safe Bank to receive it, who are very unwilling to give? And were there such a Bank of Charity once settled, there would be very little need of giving.

For I know not any kind of Charity, but might be provided for in this way, were men but free and liberal in lending. It would enlarge your Hospitals, clear your Streets of Beggars, the great Reproach of this City; maintain those who can't work, and employ those who can; put poor Children to Apprentice, provide Stocks for Ingenious and Industrious Young Men, who want them; redeem Prisoners, and, which Justice and Honour requires of you, as far as possibly you can, may in some measure provide a Fund for your Orphans.

This would advance the Glory of this great City, it would perpetuate and consecrate the Memory of such worthy Persons, as would begin and promote such a lasting and extensive Charity; the Children which are unborn, would rise up and call them blessed; it would draw a great share of the Charitable Money of the Nation into your hands, which would quicken Trade, and increase your Riches; and above all, it would procure all the great Rewards which are promised to Charity, both in this World, and in the next.

But whatever becomes of this Proposal, you must always remember, that it is great Charity to lend as well as to give: This is what our Saviour expects from us, this is what he Commands, *To do good, and lend, hoping for nothing again*; and if out of a greedy desire of gain, we will lend nothing freely to the Relief and Encouragement of the Industrious Poor, this will make all our other Usury and Increase, which is Lawful and Innocent in itself, when it neither Oppresses the Poor, nor stops our Charity, to become sin.

Joseph Bingham

BINGHAM WAS born in 1668 in Wakefield, Yorkshire, of which his father was 'a respectable inhabitant', though what other occupation he had, is not known. The boy went to school in the town and then to University College, Oxford. He graduated in 1688 and shortly afterwards became a fellow and then a tutor of the college. Everything points to his learning having been extraordinary, even at this stage. According to his great-grandson, who wrote his life and produced an edition of his works in the 1840s, he had 'employed the greater portion of his time in studying the writings of the Fathers, making himself intimately acquainted with their opinions and doctrines, and fully able both to explain, and to defend, their interpretation of the difficult or disputed passages of Scripture.' A formidable young man, and of the most dangerous kind, for he could not readily be corrected by his seniors.

By 1695 he had outstayed his welcome in Oxford, and was presented to the rectory of Headborne-Worthy near Winchester, a living worth about a hundred pounds a year. This was the scene of his labours for the rest of his life. Those labours were extraordinary. 'The duties of his profession', says his great-grandson, 'he punctually discharged, not only with great ability, but with devout and fervent zeal, directed by pious and conscious rectitude.' Every other moment, one might think, must have been given up to his studies. Yet he married, after about six years at Headborne-Worthy, and as if inadvertently became, 'in the course of a few years', the father of 'ten children, two sons and eight daughters'. This must have stretched the hundred pounds, and made the rectory rather less peaceful than a fellow's rooms. There is evidence that Bingham was extremely hard up for books; he had no resource but the cathedral library at Winchester. It was not until 1712 that he had any addition to his living.

Meanwhile, in 1708, he had produced the first volume of his great work, *The Antiquities of the Christian Church*, a systematic compendium of information about the organization, rites, discipline and calendar of the Church in the first four or five centuries, which after two hundred and fifty years has not been superseded. The last of the ten original volumes appeared in 1722, and a few months afterwards Bingham was dead, it is said of old age, although he was only fifty-five.

Bingham is an engaging character, a scholar of great intellectual endowments, kind and affectionate, mild and charitable. When, in 1720, his books had brought him at least a little money which he put aside to maintain his family in case he should die, he lost it all in the South Sea Bubble. He met this trouble with complete equanimity or—a cynic might say—left his wife to worry about it, and did not let it interrupt his studies for a single day. He disliked pompous monuments, in an age which was certainly too fond of them, and had a plain tomb. A pity, perhaps, for his old schoolmaster in Wakefield wrote a splendid Latin inscription, which ended by saying that Bingham, who deserved a patriarchate, had no preferment but to Headborne-Worthy and Havant.

ON THE TRINITY
1 John 5:7.
There are Three that bear record in Heaven, the Father, the Word, and the Holy Ghost: and these Three are One.

THIS SERMON was the occasion of Bingham resigning his fellowship and leaving Oxford. The circumstances were as follows. There was in the 1690s some sharp controversy about the nature of the Trinity. It arose immediately from Sherlock's *Vindication of the Doctrines of the Trinity and of the Incarnation*, but in a more general way may be said to have been the technical accompaniment of the reaction against a rising deism. The book naturally received attention at Oxford, and in 1695 had been the subject of what the twenty-seven-year-old Bingham regarded as unsatisfactory treatment by a senior member of the University, from the pulpit of St Mary's. When his turn came to preach, Bingham thought he would put his betters to rights, in the most scholarly way, so that no one in those learned circles could possibly object. He preached a sermon which merely explained what the Fathers had said on the subject. This effrontery brought on him the formal censure of 'the ruling members of the University', who charged him with having asserted doctrines which were 'false, impious, and heretical, contrary and dissonant to those of the Catholic Church'. All the hounds were turned on him and within a month he had to resign his fellowship and withdraw from the University. These events have somehow attracted less attention than the simple act of college discipline exercised on the undergraduate Shelley.

The sermon is somewhat abstruse and technical, but the

exposition is clear and masterly. As *The Antiquities of the Christian Church* was to show, in an almost overwhelming manner, Bingham was not the man to be fuddled by his learning. His style has been characterized as 'strong, energetic and convincing', and that fits it. The passionate elucidation of doctrine suggests a mind akin to that of an earlier generation of divines, but Bingham brings to his work the lucidity of the eighteenth century.

THOUGH THERE be no article in our creed more necessary to be known and understood, because none more necessary to be believed, than the doctrine of the Trinity: yet perhaps there is no one thing in the whole body of Divinity, we are generally less ashamed to own ourselves ignorant of, than this most necessary article of religion. Most men are so possessed with a sense of its darkness and obscurity, that they avoid all enquiries of this nature, as utterly despairing of ever attaining any tolerable notion of it. But I wish, this do not rather reflect upon the honour of our religion, as if it obliged us to believe something, which no one will pretend to give a rational account of: if so, the Oracles of God are as dark and unintelligible as the Oracles of Apollo; and we must verify that ancient calumny, so often objected by the Heathens to the Primitive Christians, but as oft with scorn again by them rejected: [. . .] as Origen give it in the words of Celsus, 'Never enquire, but believe, and your faith will save you.' Certainly faith presupposes a competent degree of knowledge, and knowledge a competent idea of the object to be known: else a man may be saved by a faith of words, without sense, and a confident belief of he knows not what. [This I presume shows us the necessity of having some tolerable knowledge of the doctrine of the Trinity, though we can never attain to a full comprehension of it.]

And yet after all, it must be confessed, that this article, according to some authors' explication of it, is one of the most obscure, unintelligible, not to say inconsistent things in the world, and were this obscurity justly chargeable upon the doctrine itself, it were perhaps a very just and rational prejudice against it: it were enough at least to make us despair of ever giving either ourselves or others any tolerable satisfaction concerning it. But if this obscurity be wholly owing to a sect of men, whose business was to invent novelties, and make new additions to old doctrines, for General Councils afterwards to improve into Articles of Faith: I say, if the Schoolmen, and their admirers since, who only drain their fountains, have spoken some things unintelligibly of this doctrine, and utterly inconsistent with themselves, we are not obliged to believe or follow them in all their usurpations: we may safely leave them where they have left Antiquity, and seek for a clearer notion from better expositors: and these certainly were the Fathers, who wrote since the Council of Nice against the heresy of Arius.

It is manifest to any one, who will but be at the pains to

compare the doctrine of the Fathers and the Schoolmen together, that the latter have made a very great deviation in this particular from the former, and have advanced several propositions quite contradictory to the Fathers, whence it is no wonder, that, mixing truth with error, they have spoken inconsistently with themselves and unintelligibly to their readers.

Some of their deviations will manifestly appear from what will be hereafter said: at present I shall only mention one relating to the notion of Three Persons, which I design to make the main subject of the following discourse. It is agreed both by Fathers and Schoolmen, that the notion of person is an *individual substance of a rational or intelligent nature, rationalis naturae individua substantia*; according to the definition given by Boethius, who speaks the sense of the Fathers and is not rejected by the Schoolmen. It is agreed further, at least in expression, that there are Three such Persons in the Godhead, really distinct from one another: thus far they are agreed. [And one might reasonably now expect to hear, that, according to this notion and discourse, they should both agree further in asserting three individual substances in the Unity of the Godhead. This is certainly the natural consequence of allowing three persons, whereof every one is an individual substance.] But herein they differ.

The Fathers, speaking consistently with themselves, and agreeably to their definition of the term Person, say that in the same sense that there are three persons, and every one of those an individual substance, in that sense there are three distinct substances too, that is, Three Minds or Spirits in the Unity of the Godhead. Yet in another sense they safely say, without a contradiction, that there is but one undivided substance in the Godhead, viz. by virtue of a community of nature, and inseparable union; as well as three individual substances by virtue of their real distinction. And this is no absurdity nor inconceivable thing: for three substances may be actually united into one, and yet remain distinct without confusion. Three angels or spirits, suppose they were united into one being (and that is no impossible supposition) would still be three distinct substances; though in another sense they might rationally be likewise said to be one individual substance [by virtue of that common angelic nature of which they all partake] or one undivided being by virtue of their actual union. In like manner, the Fathers tell us, Three Infinite and Eternal Beings, still remaining distinct without confusion, are in a more exquisite manner One: because their union is absolutely natural, necessary and eternal; they are as necessarily three as one, and as necessarily one [by union] as three [by distinction, without separation or division]. And this notion of Unity in Trinity, given us by Antiquity, is, I conceive, a very rational and intelligible account of the Unity of the Divine Nature in a Trinity of Persons: for by this we need neither confound the persons nor divide the substance.

But on the other hand, the Schoolmen, though they allow a person to be an individual substance, and say that there are three such persons in the Godhead, yet they commonly deny three individual substances, in any sense: and assert that the Divine Nature is absolutely a single substance utterly exclusive of three; as the nature of a single Angel is a simply individual substance: which is a manifest deviation from the doctrine of the Fathers, and is in effect to say, that three persons are but one person; which without a great deal of subtlety and nice unintelligible distinctions, will hardly be freed from a contradiction.

Others there are, who have still refined upon the Schoolmen's notion and more corrupted the genuine sense of Antiquity, by introducing new and foreign senses of the term person, which were never heard of in the Catholic Church before. So that the very words are now become a matter of dispute and controversy, and almost as much a mystery as the very mystery they were designed to unfold.

In order therefore to contribute something towards the clearing this controversy, I shall propose these four things to be the subject of this and another discourse.

1. To consider the notions which some modern authors have given of the term person, and show how unfit it is in their sense to explain the distinction which both Scripture and Antiquity put betwixt Father, Son and Holy Ghost.

2. To show that the Fathers did believe the Three Persons to be three distinct individual substances in one sense, as well as one substance in another.

3. That this notion is most agreeable to the sense of Scripture.

4. That it is very consistent with any notion the Fathers had of the Unity of the Godhead.

And this I conceive will be a just exposition and intelligible account of the Apostle's words, 'There are three, &c.' but at present I can only dispatch the two first.

And here I purposely omit all disputes concerning the original and authority of this text, as no way relating to the business in hand: since no one, with whom we are at present concerned, can pretend to raise any scruple about it. And the learned Dr. Hammond will give any man sufficient satisfaction concerning it; who shews that it was anciently read in the copies used by Cyprian and Tertullian, which was long before Arianism was ever set on foot in the world or dreamed of: and that the first corruptors of the text were the Arians themselves, as he proves from the testimonies of St. Ambrose and St. Jerome, who charge them with the erasing of it.

I omit likewise all direct proofs of the Divinity of the Son and of the Holy Ghost, as a thing presupposed by all good Catholics, and no ways necessary to be insisted on in an enquiry of this nature, which takes it for granted that they are truly divine, and upon that supposition proceeds to enquire, whether according to the representation made us in Scripture and Antiquity it can be rationally conceived and understood, that there are Three who are truly distinct from one another and yet truly One without a contradiction; that the thing is possible and conceivable, is what I hope clearly to evince.

But first we are to consider the notions which some modern authors give of the term person, and shew how unfit it is in their sense to explain the distinction of the Trinity.

Some Protestant authors, no doubt in their zeal for Christianity, thinking to confute their Socinian adversaries and force them to own three Persons in the Godhead, have forsaken the ancient ecclesiastical notion of the term person, and taken up with the antiquated and foreign sense of it; that I mean so much contended for by Laurentius Valla, in the sixth book of his Elegancies 34th Chapter, as the only true Latin notion of it: in which acceptation it signifies, not a substance but only a mode, an office, an habitude or quality; in which sense one and the same man (to go no further for an instance) may sustain no less than an hundred or a thousand persons: i.e. as many persons as there are different relations, circumstances or capacities, under which he may either act or be conceived.

Now it is true, this is one very proper and ancient signification of the word person in the Latin tongue, and may very well be allowed in criticism; but it is to be feared, it will not so well answer the end of religion, nor give us that true distinction which the Scripture seems to put betwixt Father, Son, and Holy Ghost. For according to this hypothesis, the Father alone may sustain three persons and the Son as many, and the Holy Ghost as many: and so instead of a Trinity we shall have an endless number of persons multiplied *in infinitum*. It is easy to conceive one single person to be three persons in this sense, which if we allow, it is as easy to tell what heresies have gained their point. This opens a way to those ancient heresies so often condemned by the Primitive Church under the name of Praxeas, Noetus Samosetenus and Sabellius: and this is not to confute the Socinian, but really to yield up the cause to him, who will not scruple here to join issue with us, and profess it in his creed, that he believes three persons in the Godhead, if we will once give it under our hands, that by person we mean no more than this. [This, if I mistake not, is however the very thing, which Sabellius of old contended for, and made the first article of his creed: i.e. taking person to signify an individual or particular substance, so there was but one single person in the Godhead; but τρία πρόσωπα, and *tres personae,* let Sabellius have the interpretation of them himself to make them signify only office or mode or quality, in this sense they were his own terms; and he could safely allow three persons or more in one single substance without any detriment to his own hypothesis.] And this I think is sufficient reason to discard this notion of the word person from the doctrine of the Trinity: because if closely followed and maintained, it must bring us at last to those very heresies, which we most studiously design to avoid.

Another disallowable notion, taken from some of the Schoolmen and not much unlike the former, is, that the Three Persons are only one single substance under three modes of subsisting: i.e. That the same single individual Divine substance is in the Father as *quid ingenitum*, in the Son as *quid genitum*, in the Holy Ghost as *quid procedens*. These men take the substance in the strictest sense of that word, as it signifies a single substance utterly exclusive of three in any sense.

But then this hypothesis is only words, that leave us more in the dark than we were before, and labours under very great absurdities: for to say that one single substance, in their sense of substance, subsists in three persons by three modes of subsisting, is what no man clearly understands. Besides that it makes the persons only three modes [at least two of them as distinct from the first must needs be mere modes], and not *tres res subsistentes*; to deny which is Sabellianism, because it confounds the persons into one. And further it will reduce us to this difficulty, and oblige us to say, that the same single substance, or person, is both *genitum* and *ingenitum*, both Father and Son, which cannot be freed from a contradiction.

I know indeed this hypothesis is usually fathered upon the author of the Expositio Fidei, under the name of Justin Martyr: for the critics are agreed that that treatise is none of his. That author says, that the three persons in the Trinity do not differ in nature, but only by three different τρόποι ὑπάρξεως, *or different modes of subsisting*; hence some very illogically concluded, that person and τρόπος ὑπάρξεως were synonymous terms; as if three persons were merely three abstracts and not three things, as well as three modes of subsisting, whereas that author gives no countenance to such a wide conclusion. For his notion is quite different, but, as he explains it, very rational and intelligible. For he tells us, in the explication of it, that Adam and those that came of him (suppose Eve and Seth) do not differ in nature, but only by a different τρόπος ὑπάρξεως, by having that common nature three different ways.

Adam, suppose, had his existence from God alone by immediate creation out of dust; and that was his τρόπος ὑπάρξεως: Eve had the same nature, but by a different mode of existing, and that was by being created out of the rib of man: and Seth had the very same nature, but by a different way from them both, viz. by being begotten, not created immediately by God as they were. This, though I have somewhat enlarged and paraphrased the words, is that author's notion of τρόπος ὑπάρξεως, common to him with many others; whence a man might as well conclude, that Adam and Eve and Seth were three mere modes of the same single substance, as that the three Persons in the Trinity are only three modes of subsisting; for he says the same of both. It is plain therefore that author meant, by nature, common nature, of which several individual substances might partake; and by persons, three such substances partaking of that common nature; and by [. . .] the different ways that three such beings might partake of one common nature: so that in his sense he might rationally say, the three Divine Persons (meaning three divine individual substances) did not differ in nature, but only by [. . .] partaking of that one common nature three different ways: the Father's τρόπος being ἀγεννησία, or existing from none: the Son's γέννησις, as receiving his Being from the Father, and the Holy Ghost's ἐκπόρευσις as receiving Being from both. This is a rational and intelligible account of three persons in one nature, and agreeable to the sense of all the primitive Fathers; who took not nature for a single individual substance, but for a common nature or substance, that might be contained without division in many particular individuals, so that they, who fix this notion, of three persons being merely three modes of subsisting without three substances that distinctly subsist, upon this author, do manifest injury both to him and all antiquity; as I come now more particularly to prove, by proceeding in the

2nd place to shew, that the Fathers by three persons always understand three distinct individual substances really distinct from one another, though at the same time they believe them to be one substance in another sense, as shall be shewn in its proper place.

But because this doctrine is very liable to be mistaken, I must here briefly premise two things, in order to state and settle a little more clearly the true notion of unity and distinction.

1st. I desire it may be observed, that by three distinct substances the Fathers do not mean three of a different nature, but only three numerical substances agreeing in one common nature, which unity of nature is sufficient to denominate any three substances one nature, though not one individual being: for three men or three Angels are, in their sense, but one nature, yet not one undivided being, because separated and divided from each other. Therefore it must be observed further,

2ndly. That by three distinct substances they mean not three actually divided or separated from each other; but three, who by virtue of their infinity must be conceived most inseparably and eternally united into one, yet with distinction and without confusion.

Thus in short the Fathers reconciled their notion of a Trinity with the Unity of the Godhead, making the three persons what we call specifically one by an unity of nature, and numerically one by an undivided union: so that according to their notion something more is required than a bare specific unity to make three persons one being [as well as three;] and that is actual union without confusion: which is the closest unity three persons are capable of without being confounded into one.

Some other notions of unity will be considered, and those more fully explained in their proper place; but thus much was necessary to be premised at present in order to prevent the heavy charge of Tritheism, which some have so liberally, but most unjustly, bestowed upon this hypothesis; thereby arraigning all antiquity at once and condemning the most genuine sense of all the best and primitive Fathers.

The proposition now to be shewn I could make good with great variety of arguments: but they will not come within the compass of a sermon, therefore I shall content myself barely to hint a few, and to insist upon one which I think will be an infallible argument against the Schoolmen.

Arg. 1. Now then first, the very definition, which the ancients give of *persona* and *hypostasis* does fully evince the thesis, for if one person be defined *rationalis naturae individua substantia*, then three persons must be *rationalis naturae tres individuae substantiae*; unless the Schoolmen can teach us to distinguish between the definition and the thing defined. [It is true the schools retain this very definition, as well as the term *persona* itself; but every man sees, it is utterly inconsistent with their hypothesis of an absolutely single substance, and therefore whilst the Fathers speak sense and reason, in allowing the three Persons to be three Substances in one sense as well as one Substance only in another, the Schoolmen, who deny them to be three real Substances in any sense, are justly charged with a contradiction.]

Arg. 2. The Fathers expressly say, that there are three Substances in the Trinity, taking them for individual Substances agreeing in one common nature: and they tell us further, that to say there is but one absolutely single Substance in that sense, is heresy, and particularly the heresy of Sabellius. [There is nothing more certain than that the Greeks by hypostasis always mean substance and not mere modes or qualities: sometimes it signifies substance or nature in general, the same with the known senses of οὐσία and *essentia*; but more commonly it is used by them for a particular substance or individual: and yet in this sense, it is well known they always said there were three hypostases against Sabellius, i.e. three distinct individual substances of the same common nature. In compliance with whom, the Latins, using the word *substantia* in the same sense, say against the same heretic that there are three Substances in the Trinity. St. Hilary in particular asserts that they are *per substantiam tria*; and that there is, *propria unius cujusque substantia*,] and upon this account they rejected the words μονοούσιος and ταυτοούσιος, and even ὁμοούσιος itself, whenever it was abused to signify a particular substance.

Arg. 3. They expressly tell us, that when they say the three Divine Persons are of one nature and one substance, they then take substance in a larger sense, for nature and essence in general which never subsists but in particulars: so that by the three Persons being ὁμοούσιοι, they only mean that they are not ἑτεροούσιοι, of a *different nature from one another.* Thus they often explain themselves, when they distinguish betwixt οὐσία and hypothesis, as betwixt a general and particular substance.

And all this is pretty fairly owned by Estius himself, who tells us, that when the Arians demanded of the Orthodox what the three persons were, they would not then say they were *tres Res*, or *tres Entes*, or *tria Entia*, for fear of seeming to own with them that there were three distinct essences of a different nature and unequal to one another, but that at other times they made no scruple to assert that they were *tres Res* and *tria Entia*. Now what are *tres Res* and *tria Entia*, but three individual substances, unless they be mere modes and accidents? If substances, then immaterial, if immaterial, then rational and intelligent Beings, if rational and intelligent, then three Minds or Spirits; unless there be any other intelligent substances besides minds or spirits. This deduction is clear and rational, and agreeable to the sense of all antiquity; who in their discourses of the Trinity always distinguish betwixt general and particular substance; as carefully as philosophers do betwixt *substantia prima et secunda:* this is so fully demonstrated by Petavius, in his 4th Book De Trinitate, cap. 7. that though his authorities could not prevail upon him to forsake the hypothesis of the schools, [perhaps for reasons best known to himself,] yet they cannot but convince any impartial reader.

Arg. 4. The Fathers often tell us, that the three Persons are united into one Being without confusion, which is a very inconceivable thing upon the hypothesis of one single substance, mind or spirit; for whatever things are properly united must be substances really distinct from one another: for there is one proper union of one single substance with itself. Yet the Ancients looked upon this to be so proper an union, that they made use of it as a known instance to prove that the two natures in Christ, his Divinity and humanity, soul and body, were united without confusion: which would have been a very impertinent instance, had they believed the three persons to be only one single substance. Nay, it would have proved the quite contrary to what they designed, and the heretics might have retorted it upon them and have said, that as the three Persons in the Trinity were but one single Substance, so the two natures in Christ were but one single nature after union.

But I pass over these and the like arguments to insist upon one, which I conceive is an invincible argument (at least *ad hominem*) against the Schoolmen. The Fathers constantly assert, that the substance of the Son is begotten of the substance of the Father: but now the Schoolmen themselves tell us, that the consequence of this assertion is, that the Father and Son are two distinct substances, numerically distinct from one another, whence we may form this regular syllogism.

Arg. 5. They who assert that the substance or being of the Son is begotten of the substance of the Father do thereby assert that the Persons in the Trinity are three distinct individual substances.

But the generality of the Fathers do assert that the substance of the Son is begotten of the substance of the Father; therefore they believed the three Persons to be three individual substances in the sense so often explained.

The first proposition of this syllogism is allowed us by Bellarmin, Estius, and generally all the Schoolmen, who are agreed in this, that the consequence of, *Essentia in Divinis generat essentiam*, must be, that there are distinct individual essences or substances in the Trinity. Estius's words are these, '*Si essentia essentiam gigneret, fatendum esset in Deo esse plures numero essentias.*' And Bellarmin to the same purpose, '*Si essentia gignit et gignitur; ergo duae sunt essentiae; nec enim intelligi potest unum et idem a seipso produci; i.e. If essence begets or is begotten, then there must be two numerical essences; else this great absurdity will follow, that one and the same thing must be produced by itself.*' [I do not now stand to take notice, that this great absurdity does certainly fall upon the Schoolmen by denying the distinct substances of the persons, whilst they allow that the person of the Son is begotten of the person of the Father, but not his essence of his essence; which distinction of a person from his own proper peculiar essence is an airy notion, that might sufficiently be exposed; but I only observe what is to our present purpose, viz. that it is confessed by all the schools, that substance generating substance does imply numerically distinct substances.] And here Calvin likewise falls in with the schools; for in his Admonitio ad Fratres Polonos Contra Blandratam, amongst his Theological Tracts he makes use of the same principle to prove his own heterodox notion of the Son's being [. . .] *God of himself*, and not of the

Father: 'if,' says he, 'the Father has his essence from himself, and the Son his essence from the Father, and the Holy Ghost from both, then there are three essences:' he means three individual substances or essences only numerically distinct from one another; which he, as well as the Schoolmen, thinks absurd, but however they all agree in this, that it is the natural consequence of asserting that the Divine substance of the Son is begotten of the substance of the Father.

Therefore if the second proposition of the syllogism can be made good, that the Fathers do generally assert, that the essence of the Son is begotten of the essence of the Father, it will infallibly follow, at least upon the Schoolmen's principles, that they likewise believed the three persons to be three individual substances or essences numerically distinct from one another, notwithstanding their belief of the indivisible unity of the Godhead. Now that they have asserted this in plain terms, may be fully evidenced from their own words: a few of which I shall therefore beg leave to produce.

Gregory Nazianzen, the famous Bishop of Constantinople, was never suspected for favouring Arianism, or Tritheism, or any other heresy: and yet he expressly asserts, that the Father is the author and cause of the Deity that is in the Son and in the Holy Ghost: his words are, ' Ἀρχὴ καὶ αἴτιος τῆς Θεότητος τῆς ἐν υἱῷ καὶ πνεύματι Θεωρουμενης ;' where by the Deity of the Son and the Holy Ghost, he cannot without great violence be understood to mean any thing else but the peculiar numerical substances of the Son and Holy Ghost, as distinct from that of the Father, which was the eternal cause of them both. So that the Schoolmen themselves being judges, Gregory Nazianzen must be one of those who assert three numerical substances in the Trinity, agreeing in one common nature.

Next to Nazianzen I shall produce the testimony of another patriarch, the famous Cyril of Alexandria. He, in his first dialogue De Trinitate calls the Son, [. . .] *the fruit or natural offspring of the Father's ineffable nature.* [Here it is plain he evidently distinguishes betwixt the particular nature of the Father and the nature common to the whole Trinity: and asserts that the Son is the offspring of the Father's nature; but not of the nature of the whole Trinity; for then he must have been the cause of Himself and the Son of Himself, which would be absurd and contradictious.]

The same he asserts more plainly in his excellent book against the Arians, called his Thesaurus; where amongst many other things he has this remarkable expression, [. . .] '*we must both know the nature that begets and the nature that is begotten of that,*' which is the direct contradictory to that assertion of the schools, *Essentia non generat essentiam nec gignitur.* Hence therefore I likewise conclude, that Cyril of Alexandria was one of those, who allow three particular substances in the Trinity united in one common nature.

To these I shall add a Latin Father or two, and first, Hilary Bishop of Poitiers, the famous Gallican defender of the Catholic faith against the Arian heresy. [There is nothing more common with him, than to speak of *natura generans* and *natura genita*, meaning the particular natures or substances of the Father and the Son, as they are numerically distinguished from one another. Thus in his Book de Synodis, against the Arians, he lays down this assertion, '*Subsistens Filius per naturam in se genitam consistit, the Son subsists by the nature that is begotten in him.*' What is this less than to say that the particular substance of the Son is begotten, and that the particular substance of the Father begat the particular substance of the Son? which implies two distinct individual substances, and is utterly irreconcilable with the opinion of the Schoolmen. To the same purpose he says again, '*Omnis nativitas, quaecunque est, in naturam suam ex natura gignente consistit, every thing that is begotten, whatsoever it be, has its nature from the nature that begets it*: which does certainly suppose that one single nature or substance begets another, though the Schoolmen's hypothesis will not allow it. But further]

He, particularly speaking of the Son of God, says, '*Ex natura generante naturam sumpsit genita natura, the nature of the Son begotten had that essence from the nature of the Father of which he was begotten*: which whoever will pretend to reconcile with the opinion of the Schools may believe anything in the world, and need never stand at any sort of contradictions.

I could demonstrate this to have been the constant judgment of St. Hilary from many other passages both out of this and others of his writings: but these are so clear and evident, that it would be impertinent to add any more to prove this to have been the opinion of so famed an author.

I proceed to other writers of the same century, but for brevity's sake I shall only name two more.

The first is Fulgentius, who, in his Book de Fide ad Petrum, speaking of the Son, says, 'we must believe Him so to be the true God, as not to doubt but that his Divinity was begotten of the nature of the Father.' His words are, *'Sic Deum verum credo, ut Divinitatem ejus de natura Patris natam esse non dubites.'* Now what the Divinity of the Son of God (that was begotten) is, but his own proper peculiar substance, as distinct from that of the Father, which is unbegotten, I think will not be very easily explained or understood. [Men may tell us that by nature and Divinity begotten is only meant person; so far they are right, if by person they mean an individual substance proper and peculiar to such a person; that is the thing here contended for, that person, and the individual substance of that person are only two synonymous names for one and the same thing, whence it must follow, that if there be two or three persons, there must be as many individual substances peculiar to those persons, or else some of the persons must want that which should constitute itself: but if by person they only mean mode, and so make both the Divinity of the Son a mode and that which was begotten a mode too, without any substance or essence begotten with it; here I must beg leave to dissent and think the Fathers were of another opinion. If any man's faith be so strong, as to believe that the Divinity begotten is a mode, and not a substance begotten too; or if his head be so acute and subtle as to distinguish that from Sabellianism, he may enjoy his opinion for me; I shall never pretend to go about to convince him to the contrary. Others, I hope, who are not wedded to an opinion, will judge of the doctine of the Fathers with more candour and a Christian liberty.]

The other testimony and the last I shall produce, is out of the author of the second homily In Diversos Scripturae Locos, under the name of Origen (printed amongst his works though it is none of his, but a Latin Author's, who wrote against the Arian heresy.) That author expressly asserts, that the proper substance of the Son is begotten of the proper substance of the Father; *Cor Patris est sua propria substantia, de qua genita est Filii propria substantia.* Here it is plain [he speaks of two distinct substances, the one begotten the other unbegotten, yet] he does not mean that they were two substances of a different nature, or that there was upon this account any inequality betwixt them; but only that they are two distinct numerical substances; whereof the one is the natural and eternal cause of the other: as he brings in our Saviour Himself, asserting there in the words immediately following, *'Ejus substantia est causa Meae substantiae.'* This I can safely say is agreeable to the sense of all antiquity.

One amongst the Schoolmen themselves, and no inconsiderable author, is of the same opinion. I mean Richardus de St. Victore, in his sixth book de Trinitate, cap. 22. where he lays down this assertion: *'Absque dubio substantia Filii est genita, substantia Patris ingenita: nec ingenita susbtantia est genita, nec genita ingenita.'* And there he severely reflects upon some of his brethren for innovating in this particular, and forsaking the Catholic doctrine of all the Primitive Fathers, and further boldly challenges them to produce but any one single passage of any one author before their own time, that ever denied that the substance of the Son was begotten of the substance of the Father. *'Afferant,'* says he, *'si possunt, autoritatem, non dicam plures, sed saltem unam, quae neget substantiam gignere substantiam.'*

This was a bold challenge, but no one of the Schoolmen was ever so bold as to give it a satisfactory answer, and it is no wonder they should not: since perhaps, until Peter Lombard, the Father of the Schoolmen, first innovated in this particular, and was defended in it by the Council of Lateran, (that very Council which established transubstantiation and many other heterodox points in religion) I say, perhaps till that time no one author can be produced that ever denied, that the substance of the Son was begotten of the substance of the Father. [The Ancients indeed often tell us, that the divine nature or substance in general, absolutely considered without regard to its subsisting in this or that particular Person, is neither begotten nor unbegotten: for then all the Persons must be either begotten, which, besides other absurdities attending it, would destroy the Trinity of Father, Son, and Holy Ghost; or else they must be all unbegotten, and that would introduce Tritheism, or *Tria Ingenita*, which is three Gods: for this reason I say, the Fathers always peremptorily deny, that the Divine nature in general is either wholly unbegotten or wholly begotten: but their doctrine is, that it is capable of both. Upon which account it is that the proper substance of the Father is unbegotten, because He is the Father and never the Son; the proper substance of the Son is begotten, and cannot be said to be unbegotten; for then He would not be a Son: and the proper substance of the Holy Ghost neither strictly unbegotten as the Father is, nor begotten as the Son is, but in a way (as unknown to us as the generation of the Son) peculiar to Himself, proceeding from Both. And according to this explication

I do assert, and challenge any one whomsoever to disprove it, that the Fathers in general do maintain that the Divine substance of the Son is begotten of the substance of the Father: and consequently, according to the Schoolmen's own concession, they must believe Them to be two single or numerical substances really distinct (but not divided or separated) from each other.]

At present, if any one questions whether I have fairly represented the difference betwixt the Fathers and Schoolmen in this particular, or requires greater satisfaction upon the point, he may please to consult a very competent judge in this case, who perhaps will fully answer all his scruples. I mean the learned Dr. Bull, in his most incomparable and immortal work, his Defensio Fidei Nicaenae against the Arians, in the 4th section of which book, cap. 1. he undertakes to prove both against Calvin, Petavius and all the Schoolmen, that the Divinity, nature and essence, and the *totum esse* of the Son of God was always believed by antiquity to be the natural and eternal Offspring of the Father's nature. [And indeed the very reason of the thing itself will tell a man, that it is absurd to talk, as the Schoolmen do, of a person's being begotten, but not his essence or substance begotten with him: for that makes the formal notion of the person of the Son to be a mere τρόπος ὑπάρξεως, which with all the subtlety in the world will never be freed from Sabellianism.]

So that this argument [to sum up the minutes of it] both in itself and *ad hominem*, has almost the strength of a demonstration, for if what the Schoolmen say, be true, that wherever there is *substantia genita et ingenita* there must be two distinct numerical substances; then it will infallibly follow, that the Fathers, by asserting that the substance of the Son was begotten of the substance of the Father, do thereby assert, that They are two distinct numerical substances, and consequently that they believed the three Persons in the Trinity to be three distinct individual substances, not only notionally, or modelly, but really distinct from one another, which was the proposition to be shown.

When I can see this argument fairly answered by any of the Schoolmen, I shall then begin to have a more favourable opinion of them: but till that be done, I must beg leave to think, that they have in this particular, as well as in many others, manifestly prevaricated and deviated from the doctrine of the Fathers.

The Fathers could rationally say, that the substance of the Father was unbegotten and yet the substance of the Son begotten:

because this was agreeable to their hypothesis, who believed them to be two distinct numerical substances agreeing in one common nature. But the Schoolmen, who had advanced the hypothesis of one absolutely single substance utterly exclusive of three [substances in any sense] could not say so without a contradiction. And therefore as they had forsaken the Fathers, first in saying there was but one single substance in the Godhead, taking substance in another sense than the Fathers did; so they were forced to forsake them a second time and say that that substance did neither beget nor was begotten, for fear of involving themselves in a manifest contradiction. For to say, that the same single substance is both begotten and unbegotten, is in the opinion of the Schoolmen themselves, as well as all mankind, a downright contradiction. And then upon that supposition we have an infallible proof, that unless the Ancients spoke most apparent absurdities and contradictions, since they have spoken of a substance begotten, and a substance unbegotten, and a substance proceeding, they could not mean one single substance utterly exclusive of three, but three individual substances agreeing in one common nature. [The consequence of all which is, that the Fathers had a clear notion about the doctrine of the Trinity fairly reconcileable to our reason; whilst the Schoolmen inventing new notions and fixing them upon some old terms (still retained but grossly mistaken,) have involved themselves in inextricable difficulties and contradictions.]

Having thus shown in the second place, in what sense the Ancients did believe the Father, Son and Holy Ghost to be three, I should now proceed to show their notion agreeable to Scripture and consistent with any notion they had of the unity of the Godhead. But the time not allowing, I shall only obviate again the charge of Tritheism, by showing briefly what was their notion of Tritheism, and in what sense they did not believe them to be three, and so conclude.

Now Tritheism or three Gods in the sense of Antiquity, for what I have been able to observe, always implies one of these five things. 1st. Either three Beings of a different nature and unequal to one another; which was the heresy of Arius, who made *Deus maximus, minor, et minimus*: or else 2dly, three Beings actually separated or divided from each other: for all actual separation is utterly inconsistent with union; which yet is absolutely necessary to the Unity of the Godhead: therefore three Beings actually divided or separated from each other, as three men or three Angels are, though they were of the same nature, yet could not be said to be one undivided Being, much less one God: 3dly, when three Beings are supposed to be, as it were three parts of one whole, having Divine perfections amongst them, but none of them or not all of them possessed of all: this was the Polytheism of some of the Gentiles, who [as Nazianzen in one of his orations observes] divided the government of the world into a Triarchy, assigning Jupiter, Neptune, and Pluto their distinct limits of nature as well as jurisdiction: 4thly, when three infinite Beings are supposed to exist equally absolute and independent of each other, without any natural order or subordination to One First, as the first fountain and original of the Deity: this is the heresy of Autotheanism, commonly charged upon Calvin, whether justly or unjustly I shall not now undertake to determine; but only say that three ἄναρχοι or αὐτοθεοί, as the Fathers word it, *i. e.* three co-ordinate Beings, whereof one is not the necessary and eternal cause of the other two, are in the sense of Antiquity three Gods: 5thly and lastly, when three Beings, for want of such a subordination to One First are supposed to be three different Creators or three different Providences clashing and interfering with one another; which was the heresy of the Marcionites and Manichees and other such like heretics, who set up contrary principles, a good and a bad one, thwarting and opposing one another.

These five things the Fathers commonly charge with Polytheism: but none of them are applicable to their notion of the Trinity. For though the three Persons in their sense be three distinct numerical substances yet they are neither, 1st, three Beings of a different nature as Arius meant, nor 2dly, three Beings actually divided or separated from each other, as three men or three Angels are, but most inseparably and eternally (yet without confusion) united into One; which union of substances is so necessary in infinite Beings, that we cannot possibly conceive them otherwise than as actually and eternally united into One: nor, 3dly, are they three parts of one whole, sharing Divine perfections amongst them, but every one is equally possessed of all: [and this naturally follows from their being equal in nature, and so falls in with the first sort of Unity] nor, 4thly, are they three Beings that have Divine nature independently, every one from himself: but the Father alone has his Being from Himself, the Son from the Father, and the Holy Ghost from Both: for though they all have a Divine nature, that is a necessary existence (for necessary existence is the properest notion we can frame of a Divine nature) yet they have that necessary existence three different ways: the Father necessarily exists, but of Himself alone; the Son necessarily exists but from the Father: the Holy Ghost necessarily exists too, but from the Father and the Son. So that the Son and the Holy Ghost are not properly without original though necessarily existing from all eternity; but are as necessary and eternal emanations of a necessary and eternal Cause, which cannot but produce two such Beings of the same nature with Himself; by a natural and eternal necessity of acting: and this way of existing is what distinguishes the Son and the Holy Ghost both from the Father and the creatures, and at once preserves the Unity of the Godhead. Fifthly and lastly, by virtue of this original and natural subordination of the Son and Holy Ghost to the Father, they are not three opposite principles or three Providences clashing and interfering with one another, but one harmonious Providence and one undivided principle of all other things: for it is impossible to conceive three infinite Beings under the economy of Father, Son and Holy Ghost, without conceiving Them at the same time united in an eternal harmony and concord.

[So that in effect he that says but these two things, 1st, That the Son and Holy Ghost are equal to the Father in infinity of nature and all Divine perfections, and, 2dly, that They have this equality, not unoriginate from themselves, but necessarily and eternally from the Father, so as to make the Father alone the only principle and fountain of the Deity, such an one, if he does not contradict himself, believes all that the Ancients thought necessary to establish the Unity of the Deity: for 1st, he who says They are all infinite and equal in nature, says virtually and by consequence that they are neither parts nor divided from each other: for these would be absurd conceptions of infinite Beings to suppose them either parts or separated from one another: then again, 2dly, he who says They are subordinate in their existence, says likewise that They are of one will and operation; since it would be absurd to conceive the Son and Holy Ghost of a different will or operation from the Father, to whom they are subordinate, and from whom they derive their nature and power of acting: and to one of these heads every thing the Fathers have said of the Unity of the Trinity may very fairly be reduced.]

So that upon the whole, they who believe three infinite Beings [i. e. persons or individual substances] numerically distinct from one another, but under these several limitations [i. e. neither of a different nature, nor divided from one another, nor united as parts that make up a whole, nor collateral and co-ordinate, nor of a different will and operation, but on the contrary one by unity of nature, one by mutual [. . .] immeation or perfect union and conjunction, one by unity of principle or subordination, and one by unity of will and action,] they cannot in the sense of Antiquity be justly charged with Tritheism nor be said to believe any more than one God.

And this, I conceive, is an intelligible account of a Trinity of Persons in the Unity of the Godhead; and shows us how we may believe, without a contradiction on the one hand or fear of heresy on the other, that 'there are Three, who bear record in heaven, the Father, the Son, and the Holy Ghost and yet that these Three are One.'

And thus much may be sufficient to be hinted at present concerning the Primitive notion of Divine Unity; the fuller explication and proof whereof I shall reserve for some other opportunity.

FRANCIS ATTERBURY

ATTERBURY WAS the second son of the rector of Milton Keynes, where he was born in 1662. He was educated by his father at home, then under Dr Busby at Westminster. In 1680 he went to Christ Church, Oxford. He seems to have been brilliant and engaging, with the weaknesses with which those qualifications usually comport. His early works included a Latin translation of Dryden's *Absalom and Achitophel* and an essay in defence of the Church of England against Romanist innuendo, and he later became involved in the controversy with Bentley which is the subject of Swift's *Battle of the Books*. A taste for controversy was among his weaknesses. He was ordained in 1687, and was soon well known as a preacher, a success to which his social charm must have contributed as well as his manner of delivery. In 1691 he became lecturer at St Brides and chaplain to William and Mary; on Mary's death in 1694 he was the only one of the royal chaplains who was retained. Apparently he was already a favourite with Anne and he became her chaplain in ordinary on her accession to the throne. Other preferments were not lacking; he became Archdeacon of Totnes in 1701, Dean of Carlisle in 1704, Dean of Christ Church in 1711/12 and in 1713 Bishop of Rochester. No wonder Swift, who knew him well and was on good terms with him, characterized him lightly in the *Journal to Stella* as 'one that understands his own interests', and in his correspondence showed some sensitivity about his own less sparkling course and 'the deanery they thought fit to throw me into'. But if Atterbury had the art of pleasing he also had a more serious talent for friendship, and not only Swift himself but Bolingbroke, Pope, Arbuthnot, Gay, Prior and South were among his friends. Moreover he allowed himself to be swept along steadily by the causes to which he was attached and served them with more enthusiasm than prudence.

It was his determination, as well as his ability and charm, which made him the spokesman of the Lower House of Convocation against bishops of the Upper House. Behind the long and sometimes obscure procedural wrangles was a division with its roots deep in the history of the seventeenth century. Atterbury was the spokesman of those who were more royalist than the King and more episcopalian than the bishops. The bench of bishops had been filled up, after 1689, with Whigs and Latitudinarians and the tension of this situation was felt in the quarrels of Convocation. Atterbury was sympathetic—to put it no more strongly—with the Jacobite cause, and there is a story that in 1715 he offered to lead the way to a Proclamation in his lawn sleeves. His dealings or his reputation, or both, led in the early twenties to his arrest, imprisonment in the Tower and finally, in 1723, to his being deprived of all his ecclesiastical offices and banished from the country for ever. He served the Pretender for a short time in Paris but this seems not to have been a satisfactory situation and his last years were spent in the south of France. There is extant a letter to Pope in which he briefly describes the last hours he spent with his daughter, who came out to see him and died twenty hours after their meeting in Toulouse.

ON THE MARTYRDOM OF KING CHARLES I
Luke 23: 28.
Daughters of Jerusalem, weep not for me, but weep for yourselves and your Children.

FROM 1662 until 1859 there was annexed to the Book of Common Prayer an order of service for use on 30 January, the anniversary of the death of Charles I. It was not the only service of its kind. There was an order of service for the Gunpowder Treason, or Papists' Conspiracy, on 5 November, which was introduced in 1606. There was also one for Oakapple Day, 29 May, commemorating the Restoration; and William III managed to intrude something about his own happy arrival. These services were something less than entirely eirenic. It was probably not until the nineteenth century that any considerable body of opinion objected to the notion that 5 November commemorated 'the happy deliverance of the King, and the three Estates of the Realm, from the most Traitorous and bloody intended Massacre by Gun-powder'—even though almost everybody had long before ceased to bother about the matter. But 'the Martyrdom of King CHARLES the first', as that service was entitled, was a conception which stuck in many throats from the beginning; if it had not been, the King would not have met with the end he did. By the early years of George I's reign, which is the probable date of the composition of the following sermon, attitudes to 30 January were deeply and sharply implicated with current politics. It would be wrong to attribute to those times the virtual indifference to regicide which is common enough in the nineteenth and twentieth centuries, but the day meant one thing to High Church Tories and another—or nothing —to Whigs and Latitudinarians. It was in any case not only the King's death that was commemorated, for the Church had been persecuted when the King's cause had been lost, and the issue went deep in the Anglican mind. The appeal of Atterbury's sermon is a religious one, but we are in that almost always painful and disputed area in which political passions and religious convictions cannot be separated, and in which the clarity of both insights therefore becomes questionable.

It happened that the lesson for the day on which Charles I went to the scaffold contained St Luke's account of the Passion. This lesson was accordingly read to the King on that day in 1649 and was included in the form of service designed to commemorate it. It is from this chapter that Atterbury takes his text. It is dangerous ground, as Atterbury himself saw, though without withdrawing from it on that account. He hopes he will not incur the imputation 'of drawing unseemly Parallels' but he must have known that this was a risk he ran. Moreover he goes on, already lurching into the field of politics, to express the hope that he will not give offence to any, 'but those, who are Offended with the *Anniversary* itself, and with our solemn and devout *Manner* of observing it.' It must be remembered, however, that Atterbury was not speaking on behalf of a powerful and complacent oligarchy but of a defeated and hounded opposition. 'Those who are Offended with the *Anniversary* itself' were the triumphant Whigs, who had all the places in their gift and gave them to their followers as surely as the Tories would have given them to theirs if they had been in power. And this defeated Toryism, which was also Samuel Johnson's—he defined a Tory as 'one who adheres to the ancient constitution of the state, and the apostolical hierarchy of the church of England'—never raised its head again, for the party that went by that name was never allowed to take power again until it had absorbed Whig indifferentism and a taste for city interests to the point of becoming something which was not in the old meaning Tory at all.

It can indeed be charged against the Toryism Atterbury was defending that it was an impractical and losing doctrine. In Atterbury it was also a little over-heated and sometimes silly; that was a matter of temperament. But personal considerations—and the flavour of Jacobitism—apart, it was much the same as Swift's, and Swift was a hard-headed man as well as a soft-hearted one.

If it was impractical, it was certainly not without principles which could reasonably appeal to an honest man; and if it was in its nature a losing doctrine, that gave it only a greater affinity with the cause of the defeated Charles I, who was certainly at his most attractive when it was evident that he had lost. A dangerous, suicidal admiration, it might be said, for a politician, but not without meaning to those whose doctrine directs them to consider a kingdom which is not of this world. Whatever one's view of the political analysis—and no one now would be likely to take the stance of a cleric born just after the Restoration—one has to see the possibility of a Christian element in Charles I's final resignation to read this sermon with understanding or even with patience. 'Many Kings there have been', Atterbury says, 'as happy as all worldly Felicity could make them.' It was not one of these he was talking about. Instead, 'the Royal Virtues, which we this Day celebrate, shone brightest in *Affliction*, and when all external Marks of Royal State and Dignity were wanting to recommend them.'

Another point in Atterbury's sermon which seems very remote to a mind of the twentieth century is 'That Nations, *as* Nations, are liable to Guilt, and consequently to Punishment.' There is something of this in Kipling, though the more popular picture of him is of a writer sold to the glories of imperialism. Atterbury makes his point in a manner which may seem odd, but perhaps only because theological considerations have faded so far from the public mind. The punishments on nations, he says, 'must be inflicted in this Life, in which alone those Nations and Communities subsist, and cannot be extended to another World, where all Kingdoms and People are to be swallowed up in the Kingdom of the Lamb, and to become *one Fold under one Shepherd*.' One can go beyond the limits of Atterbury's politics, or find them distasteful even at this distance in time, yet see that he is preaching a *sermon*, and not merely making a political exhortation.

THIS IS a *Day of Trouble, of Rebuke, and Blasphemy*; distinguished in the Annals of our Nation, and the Calendar of our Church, by the sad Sufferings of an excellent Prince, who fell a Sacrifice to the Rage of his Rebellious Subjects; and, by his Fall, derived Infamy, Misery, and Guilt, on them, and their sinful Posterity.

We are met here, to acknowledge our Sin, to express our public Detestation of it, and to deprecate the Vengeance which hath pursued, and doth still, I fear, pursue us on the Account of it. In order to raise and improve these good Thoughts and Dispositions, I have pitched on the Words spoken by our Blessed Saviour in his sad Procession towards *Calvary*, as the Ground of our present Meditations,—*Daughters of* Jerusalem, &c.

Since Providence so ordered it, that one of the Lessons for that Day, whereon the Royal Martyr suffered, and which was read to him just before his ascending the Scaffold, should contain an Account of the Passion of our Lord; and the same Lesson is still by Authority appointed to be read in these annual Assemblies; I may be allowed, I hope, from the History of that Passion, written by St. *Luke*, to take the Words you have heard, and apply them to the Subject I am now about to handle, without incurring the Imputation of drawing unseemly Parallels, and without giving Offence to any, but those, who are Offended with the *Anniversary* itself, and with our solemn and devout *Manner* of observing it.

As *Jesus* went to his Crucifixion, St. *Luke* tells us, that *there followed him a great Company of People, and of Women, which also bewailed and lamented him. But Jesus, turning unto them, said, Daughters of* Jerusalem, *Weep not for me, but weep for yourselves, and for your Children: For, behold, the Days are coming, in the which they shall say, Blessed are the Barren, and the Wombs that never bare, and the Paps that never gave suck!* His present Sufferings, and approaching Death, withheld him not from reflecting with Concern on the Calamities, which were ready to overtake others, on his Account. And because the Women who followed him to *Calvary*, out of a Tenderness of Nature peculiar to their Sex, indulged themselves in the loudest Expressions of Grief; therefore to *These* he particularly addresses the Admonition of the Text; directs them to turn their well-meant Compassion from *him* upon *themselves*, to reserve all their Tears for a Time, now at hand, when the whole Nation of the *Jews* would be called to a strict Account for spilling his

Blood, and be made an astonishing Instance of Divine Vengeance.

The good Prince, whose unhappy Fate we commemorate, did in *this*, as well as *other* respects, follow the Steps of *the great Captain of his Salvation, who was made perfect through Sufferings*: For the last Moments of his Life, which his Murderers allowed him, were employed in awakening a drowsy Nation into a Sense of its Guilt, and a Dread of its impending Punishment. Secure of his own Innocence and Happiness, he seemed to have conquered all Concern for himself; and, like a true Father of his People, was chiefly solicitous for the Peace and Welfare of his People: His dying Words breathed nothing but Pity and Tenderness towards his Subjects, who were to survive his Fall, and to feel the sad Effects of it. And, therefore, to *those*, who with weeping Eyes then beheld that bloody Scene, and to us, who with like Grief now look on, at a Distance, may we suppose the Royal Sufferer (consistently with the Character he then maintained) to say,—*Weep not for me; but weep for yourselves, and for your Children.*

This, I am sure, is an Instruction, which the Day itself seems naturally to afford us, and which I shall, therefore, pursue in both its Branches; showing you,

I. *First,* That we misplace our Grief, if we employ it in bewailing and lamenting our Martyred Sovereign,

And,

II. *Secondly,* That the true End of these annual Humiliations is, *to weep for ourselves, and for our Children*; to deplore the Guilt which our Forefathers contracted by this inhuman Deed, and which, we have Reason to fear, is not even yet fully Expiated.

I. In the early Ages of the Church the Custom was annually to observe those Days on which the *Martyrs* were *Crowned* (such was the Language of that Time) not with dejected Looks, or any outward Expressions of Sorrow; but with the Solemnities usual on *Birth-Days* (and such also they were styled) even with all possible Instances of devout Exultation and Joy. Upon these Occasions, pious *Christians* flocked to the Places, where those faithful Servants of *Christ* slept, or had sealed the Truth of their Testimony with their Blood: *There* they held their sacred Assemblies (as they afterwards built their Churches;) *There* they made their *Eucharistic* Oblations, and celebrated their Feasts of Love; gave Thanks to God for the exemplary Virtues and Graces, which adorned the Lives and Deaths of those holy Persons, and excited themselves into like degrees of

Christian Zeal and Fervour.

Their Behaviour in these Cases should be the Rule of *ours*, and teach us to observe this Anniversary in such a Manner, as may render it most honourable to the Dead, and most useful to the Living. To that end, it will become us, not vainly to indulge our Grief, or our Resentments, in behalf of our much injured Prince; not fruitlessly to spend our Time in lamenting his Misfortunes; but rather to employ it in magnifying the Grace of God, which enabled him so constantly to endure them, and so heartily to forgive the Authors of them; which armed him with such a wondrous Degree of Meekness and Patience; inspired him with such *Christian* Magnanimity and Courage, as made him shine with a greater Lustre in the Depth of his Sufferings, than he did in his most flourishing Circumstances; and put off his Crown after a more glorious Manner, than he first wore it on the Day of his Coronation.

Indeed, the Mind of Man, filled with vain Ideas of worldly Pomp and Greatness, is apt to admire those Princes most, who are most fortunate, and have filled the World with the Fame of their successful Achievements. But to those, who weigh things in the Balance of right Reason, and true Religion, it will, I am persuaded, appear, that the Character of this excellent King, even while he was in his lowest and most afflicted State, had something in it, more truly Great and Noble, than all the Triumphs of Conquerors: Something, that raised him as far above the most prosperous Princes, as they themselves seem raised above the rest of Mankind.

Many Kings there have been, as happy as all worldly Felicity could make them; and some of these have distinguished themselves as much by their Virtues, as their Happiness. But the Possessors of those Virtues, being seated on a *Throne*, displayed them from thence with all manner of Advantage; their good Actions appeared in the best Light, by reason of the high Orb, in which they moved, while performing them: Whereas, the Royal Virtues, which we this Day celebrate, shone brightest in *Affliction*, and when all external Marks of Royal State and Dignity were wanting to recommend them. Others, perhaps, may have been as Just, as Beneficent, as Merciful, in the Exercise of their Royal Power, as this good King was: But none surely did ever maintain such a majestic Evenness and Serenity of Mind, when despoiled of that Power; when stripped of everything but a good Cause, and a good Conscience; when destitute of all Hopes of

Succour from his Friends, or of Mercy from his Enemies: *Then*, even *then*, did he possess his Soul in Peace, and patiently expect the Event, without the least outward-Sign of Dejection or Discomposure. He remembered himself to be a King, when all the World beside seemed to have forgotten it; when his Inferiors treated him with Insolence, and his Equals with Indifference; when he was brought before that infamous Tribunal, where his own Subjects sat as his Judges; and even when he came to die by their Sentence.—In *all* these sad Circumstances, on *all* these trying Occasions, he spake, he did nothing, which misbecame the high Character he bore, and will always bear, of a great King, and one of the best of *Christians*. And this Mixture of unaffected Greatness and Goodness, in the Extremity of Misery, was, I say, his peculiar and distinguishing Excellence: Other Royal Qualities, that adorn Prosperity, he shared in common with others of his Rank: But in the decent and kingly Exercise of these Passive Graces, he had, among the List of Princes, no Superior, no Equal, no Rival.

Indeed, the last Scene of his Sufferings was very dismal; and such, from which mere Human Nature, unsupported by extraordinary Degrees of Grace, must needs have shrunk back a little Affrighted, and seemed desirous of Declining. But those Succours were not wanting to him; for he went even through this last Trial, unshaken; and submitted his Royal Head to the Stroke of the Executioner, with as much Tranquillity and Meekness, as he had borne lesser Barbarities. The Passage through this *Red Sea* was bloody, but short; a divine Hand strengthened him in it, and conducted him through it; and he soon reached the Shore of Bliss and Immortality.

He is now at Rest in those Mansions, where *Tears are wiped from all Eyes, where there is neither Death, nor Pain, nor Crying*, and from whence *Sorrow and Sighs do flee away*. Wherefore, *Let us not mourn, refusing to be comforted*; but let us rather (as those early *Christians* did on the like Occasions) *rejoice with exceeding Joy*: Rendering to God our Thanks, that he hath been pleased in these last and most degenerate Times, to afford us such an illustrious Pattern of Virtue and Goodness, as even the purest Ages of *Christianity* would have looked up to with Reverence; that, by this Means, he hath given to loose and profane Men an Instance of the great Power of those Religious Principles, which *did*, and which only *could* support the Mind of this pious Prince, under all the Indignities and Miseries that befell him.

What an Honour is it to that Church at whose Breast he first sucked these Principles, to have been instrumental in sowing the first Seeds, from whence such excellent Fruits afterwards sprang! How ought she to boast and triumph in this Thought, That a Prince, who excelled as much in the Knowledge, as in the Practice of Religion, should be so firm and unmoveable an Assertor of her Doctrine, and Discipline, and Worship! Which he *therefore* valued highly, *because* he understood them thoroughly: That he should go on to maintain *Her* Cause, even long after he despaired of maintaining his *Own*, or of being able to retrieve his lost Crown and Dignity! and that, after he had thus defended her *Faith*, during his *Life*, he should recommend it still more at his *Death*, by dying *in* it, and *for* it.

But the more Excellent the Character of this Prince was, the more barbarous and brutal was the Rage by which he fell: Every Consideration which heightens his matchless Virtues, and endears his Memory to us, serves also to enhance the Wickedness of those sons of *Belial*, who were the Instruments of his Ruin, and embrued their Hands in his Blood. And, therefore, though we have no Occasion to *weep for him*, yet have we great Reason to *weep for ourselves, and for our Children*; for the Guilt which the Nation contracted, and the Infamy it underwent, by Reason of that inhuman Deed, and for the other fatal Consequences, which *then did*, and which (as we have just Reason to fear) *may still* attend it. And this is the *second* Point, upon which I proposed to enlarge:

II. That Nations, *as* Nations, are liable to Guilt, and consequently to Punishment; that such Punishments must be inflicted in this Life, in which alone those Nations and Communities subsist, and cannot be extended to another World, where all Kingdoms and People are to be swallowed up in the Kingdom of the Lamb, and to become *one Fold under one Shepherd*; and that the Punishments inflicted by God on Nations in this Life, may be altogether or in part deferred by God, for some time, till the Iniquity of those Nations is full, and the Sinners grown ripe for Vengeance: These are all Points sufficiently evident from Reason and Scripture, and the History of the World; they need no solemn Proof, because they admit of no great Doubt. Little indeed is said on this Head in the Books of the *New* Testament, which were all written for the Use of private scattered Christians, ere as yet any one entire Nation was converted, or any of the great Rulers of the World had submitted their Sceptres to the Sceptre of *Christ*: And, therefore, the Precepts there contained relate chiefly, if not solely, to the Conduct of particular Persons, and are silent as to the Methods of God's dealing with public Bodies and Societies of Men. And there was the less Occasion for any Instructions of this kind in the *New* Testament, because they had been given so frequently and fully in the *Old*, the Prophetic Parts of which do everywhere inculcate these Doctrines, as the Matters of Fact, recorded in the Historical Books, illustrate and confirm them. And from thence therefore, all our Observations must be drawn, concerning the Influence which a People's Sins have upon their Sufferings, and concerning the Measures of that Political Justice, by which God governs the World. And in truth, it was proper that the Directions of this kind should be given under the Institution of *Moses*; the *Letter* of which extended no farther than to the Concerns of *this* Life: Whereas the Duties, the Promises, and Threatenings of the *Gospel* do all look beyond the Grave, and are designed to regulate our Behaviour in *this* World, as it relates, and leads to *another*.

The Doctrine then of God's Visiting Nations, *as* such, for Sins committed by them in that Capacity, being supposed, let us briefly apply it to the present Case, and see how far we ourselves are concerned in it.

That the Sin of this Day was *National*, is not to be denied; the Nation itself confesseth it, by appointing and observing these public and stated Humiliations. It was under the Colour of a *National Authority*, that the *Rebellion* was first raised, and all along carried on, and at last consummated by the Erection of that infamous *High Court of Justice*; which gave the finishing Stroke to the successful Villanies of that Time, by taking away the Life of our Sovereign. Indeed, the greatest Part of the Nation abhorred that barbarous Act; (and had their Power been equal to their Inclination, would have prevented it:) But many of them had contributed to it too much, and too long before; and, having joined in all the *Steps* that led to the Murder of the King, could not at last, by expressing their Detestation of the *Crime*, excuse themselves entirely from the *Guilt* of it.

It was the *Nation* therefore, that *sinned*; and sinned with a high Hand, and with all the inflaming Circumstances of Guilt and Aggravation. They made their way to the Completion of this Wickedness, through the most solemn *Engagements*, through all the Ties of *Reason*, and the Reluctances of *Conscience*: The *Laws* of God and Man were but as *Withies* upon the Arms of *these Sampsons*, which they broke at Pleasure; and, when they had once overleaped the Mounds and Fences of Justice, were resolved to think every Step lawful, which was necessary to justify those they had already taken. Many Years they continued steadfastly pursuing these unrighteous Measures; *they held fast Deceit, and refused to return*; and after heaping Transgression upon Transgression, did, at last, through the Blood of many of their *Fellow-Subjects* arrive at that of their *Sovereign*, and in the calmest and most deliberate Manner perpetrate the black Design they had for some time meditated.

The *common* Methods, made use of by *rebellious Subjects* in the *Destruction of Princes*, did not please them; *Poison*, or a private *Assassination* was too *hasty* and *clandestine* a way: They were resolved to have the Proceeding more *Public*, and *Slow*, and *Solemn*; to carry it on by the *Forms of Law*, and with the *mock* Show and Pageantry of *Justice*, (a Way which crowned Heads had not hitherto been treated in,) and since the *Crime* itself was *old*, and had been often repeated, to recommend it at least by the *Newness of the Invention*: In which respect, it must be confessed, that they *outstripped* all their *Rivals* in this Sort of Wickedness, even the bloodiest of their *King-killing Neighbours*. Indeed *new Inventions* for slaughtering Kings, and overturning States, are the *peculiar Reproach of this Nation*; of which we have *two* eminent Proofs upon Record, not to be paralleled in other Histories, the *Gun-Powder-Treason*, and *that of this Day; One* of them contrived by *Papists*, the *Other* by wild *Sectaries* and *Enthusiasts; neither* of them (God be thanked) by the Members of *the Church of* England.

And, *Shall I not visit for such Things, saith the Lord? shall not my Soul be avenged of such a Nation as this?* Shall a People sin in this remarkable Manner; and shall not that Sin be as remarkably punished? *It was* immediately, and in some Measure punished by the fatal and necessary Consequences of it, by the sad Disorders and Confusions that attended it. For *had* Zimri *Peace who slew his Master*? Did the Partners in this black Crime quietly reap the expected Fruits of it? No! they did not, they were soon displaced from the high Seat of Authority which they had usurped; and gave Way to other Usurpers, and to various Forms of Government which prevailed in their Turns. The feverish Nation rolled from one Posture, one Expedient to another; and found Rest in none. It then soon appeared, how great the Loss was of their admirable Prince, and of their ancient Constitution which perished with him. The People, who had miscalled his mild and gentle Reign, Oppression and Tyranny, found themselves now *ruled with a Rod of Iron, and broken in Pieces like a Potter's Vessel.* They had *complained* of Arbitrary Power *without Cause,* and now *smarted* under it *without Remedy.* To secure their *Liberty* and *Laws,* they had made this *Change;* which left both of them at the Mercy of *standing Armies.* Thus *did their own Wickedness correct them, and their backslidings did reprove them!* They had pulled down a regular Primitive Church; and immediately Churches, Sects, and Religions without Number sprang up in the room of it; instead of the honest English *Plainness* and *Simplicity,* a demure and sly *Hypocrisy* prevailed; instead of sober and well-weighed *Devotions,* all the Freaks and Rants of *Enthusiasm. Every* Way of worshipping God, *but* the true One was publicly *allowed; all Men* were admitted to the Exercise of the *Sacred Function, but those* who were most *lawfully called* to it, and best *qualified* for it. A loud and causeless *Complaint* of Impositions on the *Consciences* of Men, in Things pertaining to God, had helped to ruin the *Church*; and now, every *little* Society pretending to that *venerable* Name, did the very *thing* they had complained of; imposed the Platform of their Doctrine, Discipline, and Worship, as Divine; and were for rooting out all that opposed, or did not comply with it. In the meantime, they, who preserved themselves free from this sort of Infection, were in as much Danger of swerving to a contrary Extreme, and of making Inferences to the Prejudice of Religion itself, which they saw perverted and prostituted to the worst Designs. Even *good* Men, at the Sight of these prosperous *Hypocrites,* were ready to cry out, in the Words of complaining *Jeremiah.—Righteous art thou, O Lord, when I plead with thee; yet let me talk with thee of thy Judgments: Wherefore doth the Way of the Wicked prosper? why are all they happy that deal very treacherously? Thou hast planted them, yea, they have taken Root, they grow, they bring forth Fruit; thou art near in their Mouth, and far* (very far) *from their Reins! Then,* when these hypocritical Pretenders to Godliness abounded, did an opposite Spirit of open Levity and Profaneness begin to gain Ground upon a serious and religious People: *Then* were those *Seeds* of Infidelity first sown among us, which have since sprung up, and increased into a mighty *Harvest.* Our endless *Divisions* were a Scandal to the truly Pious, the Boast of *Rome,* and the Sport of *Atheists*: We were *made a Reproach to our Neighbours, a Scorn and a Derision to them that were round about us; a Byword among the Heathen, a Shaking of the Head among the People: We lay down in our Shame, and our Confusion covered us.* No Words can express the various Sorts of Misery, under which this Nation then groaned *by reason of the Multitude of Oppressions* and Oppressors. *New Lords had Dominion over us*; the very *Refuse and Outcast of the People*; the Head became the Tail, and the Tail the Head; *the Child behaved himself proud against the Ancient, and the Base against the Honourable.* From Violence and Bloodshed this new Model of Government had arisen; and the same Methods were requisite to cement and uphold it. Plunder and Rapine completed the Devastations which War had begun: Armed Force decided Right, or executed the Sentence of those who had no manner of Right to decide it: They were altogether *like Wolves, ravening the Prey to shed Blood, and to destroy Souls to get dishonest Gain. As the Voice of a Woman in Travail, as the Anguish of her that bringeth forth her first Child; such was then the Voice of the Daughter of Sion, that bewailed herself, that spread forth her Hands, saying; Woe is me now! for my Soul is weary because of Murderers!*

At last this Storm ceased, the Clouds dispersed, and the Sun shone out again in his Strength; the Royal Family returned, and with it our old Constitution in Church and State; the Regicides suffered, and *the Land* seemed to be *cleansed of the Royal Blood, that was shed therein, by the Blood of those that shed it.* Thus, for a while, we vainly imagined; but sad Experience soon undeceived us. Not many Years passed, before God did again empty, as it were, at once, all the Vials of his Wrath upon us: The Sword raged abroad; Fire, and Pestilence at home: And when this goodly City was laid in Ashes, and Desolation and Emptiness reigned in her Streets, doubtless pious Persons did often reflect, how much her misemployed Wealth, and misguided Zeal had formerly contributed to the Miseries and Confusions under which we laboured: And even they, whom a few Years' Plenty and Prosperity had lulled into a Forgetfulness of their Guilt, began then to lay their Hands upon their Hearts, and with *Joseph's* Brethren, to say: *Verily, we are guilty concerning our Prince; therefore is this Destruction come upon us!*

There was still a more terrible Judgment behind, which we were threatened with, and in some measure felt: Though the Providence of God did not suffer it thoroughly to lay hold of us: I mean, the Advances made by Popery in a late Reign towards establishing itself among us. And this also was the Fruit of our former Iniquities; for to speak a plain Truth, which plain as it is has been lately treated with Scorn and Derision by shameless Writers, the Attempt of introducing a *Foreign Religion* was but too natural a Consequence of our forcing the *Royal Family* to take shelter in *Foreign Countries*; where they might be allured by the tempting Appearances of a splendid Worship and a regular Hierarchy, and by glorious but empty Pretences to Universality and Infallibility; especially at a Time, when the good *Frame* of our Ecclesiastical Polity here at *home* was shattered and dissolved, and the *Honour of our* Zion *was laid low in the Dust*. Still therefore our Punishment was from ourselves; nor was God *a hard Master* in inflicting it; for we *reaped* only *what we had sowed, and gathered what we had strawed*; and the *first* Subversion of our Constitution involved us in all the Confusions and Miseries, in which we long *afterwards* laboured. But *that* Storm also blew over, and Times of *Liberty* succeeded, wherein we promised ourselves the settled Enjoyment of all manner of Advantages and Blessings. Can we say, that those Hopes were not in great Measure defeated by the Spirit of Irreligion and Libertinism, which then, and ever since that Time notoriously prevailed; by those intestine Factions and Discords by which we have been torn, and that foreign War, under the Weight of which we for more than twenty Years groaned? Till the vast Expense of Blood and Treasure, which it occasioned, made us ready to cry out in the pathetic Words of the Prophet, *O thou Sword of the Lord, how long will it be ere thou be quiet! put thyself up in thy Scabbard; rest, and be still!*

And when that Sword rested in its Scabbard, was not the Manner of Sheathing it as unwelcome to us, as even the Havoc it had occasioned, when naked and drawn! Was not the good Queen (now with God) the Subject of malicious, but groundless Reproaches on that very Account? Did we not murmur at the Blessing, and bring ourselves, at last, with great Difficulty to relish and approve it?

But may we not now at length hope, that all is well with us, and that the ill Consequences of spilling the Royal Blood of this Day are ceased, the Anger of God appeased, and our National Guilt utterly pardoned? How can that be, until the Nation itself hath manifestly repented? And the Repentance of a Nation for any Sin is best testified by its general Abhorrence of the Principles and Practices that caused it. And are we able in this manner to purge ourselves of this Day's Transgression? Do we, indeed, give evident Proofs, that we heartily and universally detest it? If that be really our Case, *what meaneth then this Bleating of the Sheep in our Ears, and this Lowing of the Oxen which we hear?* How comes it to pass, that these Anniversary Humiliations are so openly spoken against, ill-treated and derided? Why has the horrid *Guilt* of the Day been *lessened* in Public Discourses, and represented with all manner of Alleviations and *Softenings?* As if it were unpopular and imprudent, to paint such a Villainy to the Life, or to speak of it in suitable Terms of Ignominy and Reproach! Why have the *Doctrines*, which *paved* the Way to this bloody Deed been freely revived, embraced, and cherished? And *those*, for which the Sufferers in the Royal Cause underwent all manner of Persecutions, been discountenanced and exploded? Why has the Spirit of *Liberty* been indulged to an outrageous Degree of *Licentiousness?* The Reverence due to Thrones shaken by mean and insolent Pens? And Contempt poured on the sacred Character of Princes, *as though they had not been anointed with Oil?* Why have Lectures, in such sacred Places as these, been more than once read to the People, not only with Permission, but Applause, instructing them how *near* they might approach towards the *Sin* of Rebellion, without *actually* incurring the Guilt of it? And why have impious Wretches by their *Mock-Feasts* ridiculed our *Solemn Fasts*, without being punished or (which is yet a worse Sign) even without being detected in order to Punishment? Certainly, these are no good *Proofs* of our Abhorring the Sin of the Day; and why then should we flatter ourselves with the Thought, that God hath left off to abhor, and will no longer continue to chastise us for the sake of it? *Truly*, (to use our Saviour's Words) *ye bear witness, that ye allow the Deeds of your Fathers; for they indeed killed the Prophets; and ye build their Sepulchres;* that is, Ye pay some outward Respect to their Ashes, some ceremonious Regard to their Memories; but without renouncing the Principles and abominating the Practices, that led to the spilling that *Righteous Blood*, which, therefore, we have Reason to fear, may be *required even of this Generation*. When, and in what manner, God will require it, he alone knows. But if we consider the Height of all sorts of Wickedness, to which we are now arrived; the open Contempt of Religion, and Scorn of sacred Persons and Things that reigns among us; the intestine Discords, by which we are torn at home; the Dangers which have threatened us from abroad, and (however we may say, *Peace, Peace,* to ourselves) still do threaten us, we have just Cause to apprehend, that the complete Measure of our Iniquity is almost filled up, and that the Day of our Visitation is not far off.

But do not thou, *O Lord, to whom Vengeance belongeth*, do not thou deal with us according to our Deserts; *be not displeased at us for ever, neither stretch out thy Wrath from one Generation to another!* Command thy *destroying Angel, when he goeth through the City* (as the Prophet *Ezekiel* speaks) *to set a Mark upon the Forehead of all those that sigh and that cry for the Abomination which hath been done in the midst thereof*; and either to spare the whole for their sakes; or, at least, not to smite *the Righteous* together *with the Wicked.* Make us deeply sensible of this, and all other our great Enormities, and of thy wondrous Lenity and Forbearance: *Teach us, even yet in this our Day* (if it be possible) *the things that belong to our Peace, ere they be hid from our Eyes.* Teach us, by a Reflection on *past* Calamities, to prevent *new* ones, and to avoid those Rocks and Shelves on which our Forefathers were shipwrecked.

Which God of his infinite Mercy grant, through the Merits of that *Blood, which speaketh better Things than the Blood of* Abel!

To him, Father, Son, and Holy Ghost, be ascribed, as is most due, all Honour, Adoration and Thanks, now, and for evermore. Amen.

A Discourse Occasioned by the Death of the Right Honourable the Lady Cutts

Eccles. 7:2.
It is better to go to the House of Mourning, than to go to the House of Feasting: for that is the End of all Men; and the Living will lay it to Heart.

THIS SERMON was preached in 1718. The subject was a girl of eighteen—'eighteen Years, and as many Days' old when she died. She was a great lady, and one must try not to hold that against her. Her virtues, as Atterbury describes them, were in play in a milieu which no longer exists, but if one can exercise imagination enough to make some allowance for this, and for what is by our standards the somewhat formal rhetoric of some parts of the discourse, one can hardly fail to be struck by the genuineness of the impression. The seventeenth century had been fond of writing 'characters', of a rather abstract kind; the best and most illuminating book of this kind is Fuller's *Holy State*. There is a touch of this tradition about Atterbury's sermon, though in place of the homeliness of Fuller there is something which is akin to the display of the eighteenth-century church monument.

The text is a rather shocking one or, at first sight, an uncomfortable one for a funeral sermon, and it is evident from the induction that Atterbury thought it would seem so to his congregation. He goes on to quote further from Ecclesiastes: 'The Day of one's Death is better than the Day of one's Birth.' So much is done now to sweep death out of our sight that we hardly know how squeamish we have become. Atterbury gives no quarter on this subject, not because, like Donne, he was a man who could dwell on the corruption of death, but simply because he felt dogmatically bound not to blink the matter. 'As Death to a good Man is more advantageous than Life; so to a wise Man the Contemplation of the First is more desirable than all the Enjoyments of the Latter.' Behind the charming portrait which this sermon gives of one who was evidently a very gracious young woman is Atterbury's conviction, which contrasts somewhat with the easiness and success of his earlier life, that, as he said in another sermon, on *The Christian State, a State of Suffering*, 'the most difficult Part of our Duty is to suffer well'.

THE FIRST Step towards Happiness is, to correct our false Opinions concerning it, by learning to esteem everything, not according to that Rate and Value, which the World, or our own mistaken Imaginations may have placed upon it, but according to that which in itself, and in the Accounts of right Reason and Religion, it really bears.

The Preacher therefore hath, in this Chapter, laid together a Set of Religious Paradoxes; which, however they may startle and shock us a little, upon the first hearing, yet, when closely examined, will appear to be clear unquestionable Truths, by which the whole Course of our Lives ought to be steered and governed.

In the first Verse of this Chapter (the Verse before the Text) he tells us, that a *Good Name is better than precious Ointment, and the Day of one's Death than the Day of one's Birth. A Good Name is better than precious Ointment;* i. e. rich Oils, and sweet Odours (in the Use of which the People of the *East* much delighted) are not half so grateful, or valuable, as a good Reputation, well founded: This is more truly fragrant, more diffusive of its Influence, more durable: It gives a Man greater Comfort and Refreshment, while he is Living; and preserves him, when Dead, better than the most precious Embalmings.

And again, *The Day of one's Death is better than the Day of one's Birth;* i. e. the *Day of the Death* of such an one, as possesses and deserves a *Good Name;* of such an one, as hath lived well, and died well, is preferable by far to the *Day of his Birth:* For it gives him Admittance into a State of perfect Rest and Tranquillity, of undisturbed Joy and Happiness; whereas the Day of his Birth was only an Inlet into a troublesome World, and the Beginning of Sorrows.

And then it follows, very naturally, in the Words of the Text, that *It is better* also *to go to the House of Mourning, than to go to the House of Feasting.* As Death to a good Man is more advantageous than Life; so to a wise Man the Contemplation of the First is more desirable than all the Enjoyments of the Latter: He had much rather be present at the sad Solemnities of a Funeral, than partake of those Festival Rejoicings, which are usual in all Nations, but especially among the *Jews,* at the Birth of a Child.

Hard Doctrine this, to the Men of Liberty and Pleasure! who have said to themselves, *Come on, let us enjoy the things that are present, let us fill ourselves with costly Wine and Ointments, and let no Flower of the Spring pass by us; let us crown ourselves with Rosebuds before they be withered*. Hard Doctrine, I say, it is to such Men as these; and which will run the Hazard of not being entertained by them. The Wise Man therefore hath condescended to prove, as well as assert it, and to back the severe Rule he hath laid down, with very convincing Reasons: *For that*, saith he, *is the End of all Men, and the Living will lay it to heart*. As if he had said, This Dark and Melancholy State it will one Day certainly come to Our share to try; and what must some time or other be undergone, ought to be considered beforehand: this is *the End of all Men*; and all Men therefore should have their Eye and their Thoughts upon it. And then farther—We are most of us so immersed in the Pleasures, and so taken up with the Follies of Life, that we need all Methods of reducing our straggling Thoughts and Desires, and of giving ourselves a serious Frame and Composure of Mind: and of all Methods, this of repairing to the House of Mourning, is best adapted to that Good End, and will soonest and most effectually bring it about; *The living will lay it to heart*.

I have largely explained the Connection and Meaning of the Words, which have been pitched upon to employ Your Thoughts on this mournful Occasion. The next thing should be, to excite You to a Compliance with the Direction there given, by the particular Arguments suggested in the Text, and by several other powerful and moving Considerations: to prove to You, the Folly and Emptiness of a Life led all in Mirth and Jollity, and Pleasure; the Wisdom and Reasonableness of shifting the Scene sometimes, of turning the gloomy side of Things towards ourselves, of exchanging *the House of Feasting* for *the House of Mourning*, and of making a discreet and decent Use of those sad Opportunities of Reflection, which God, mercifully severe, is pleased to put into our Hands.

But I am prevented in this part of my Discourse, by the Pious Design of this present Assembly; You are already doing that which I should recommend to You from the Text; paying the Tribute of Your Tears to the Memory of One whose Worth you knew, and whose Loss You sensibly feel; and bewailing Her, under the different Characters She bore of a Wife, a Daughter, a Relation, a Mistress, a Friend.

All, therefore, I have to do, on this Occasion, is, to fall in with Your Pious Grief, already raised, and to bear a part in it, by dwelling together with You a while on the Character of that *Incomparable Lady*, whose Death we lament; by uniting, as well as I am able, the scattered Parts of it, and recalling to Your Thoughts at once the several Excellencies and Perfections of which it was composed: which made her beloved and reverenced by You while Living, and will make her Memory ever Dear and Desirable to You, now she is Dead; and which raised her above the greatest Part of her Sex, much more than any Outward Marks of Rank and Distinction.

It is now, after her Disease, a fit time to speak of her in those Terms of Respect which she deserved: for in her Lifetime she would not suffer it, and took some Pains to avoid it; hiding as many of her Virtues as she could from Public Observation, and so behaving herself in the Practice of those she could not hide, as showed, she had no mind to be told of them: discountenancing, as far as lay in her Power, that odious and designing Flattery, which, through the wicked Fashion of an Insincere World, is now thought to be a kind of Customary Debt due to her Sex, and almost a necessary Part of good Breeding.

But though the Living can seldom be praised with Decency, yet the Dead certainly often may; especially such of the Dead, as had a very unusual Degree of Indifference and Unconcernedness for what was said to their Advantage, while they were Living.

There is a public Homage due to Desert, if we take a proper Season of paying it; and the Ministers of the Gospel, who are entrusted with so many Methods of promoting Piety in the World, are, among the rest, entrusted with This, of *giving Honour where Honour is due*; and of truly representing to the Minds of Men such shining Patterns of Virtue, as are most likely to engage their Attention, and provoke their Imitation: It is our immediate and particular Employment to praise God; and it doth, no doubt, in some measure also belong to us, to praise those that are Like him.

And now how shall I enter upon this fruitful Argument? What Particular of her comprehensive Character shall I first choose to insist on? Let us determine ourselves to begin there where she always began, at her Devotions. In These she was very Punctual and Regular: Morning and Evening came not up more constantly in their Course, than her stated Hours of Private Prayer; which she observed not formally, as a Task, but returned to them always with Desire, Delight, and Eagerness. She would on no Occasion dispense with herself from paying this Duty: no Business, no common Accident of Life could divert her from it: She esteemed it her great Honour and Happiness, to attend upon God;

and she resolved to find Leisure for That, for whatever else she might want it.

How she behaved herself in these Secret Transactions, between God and her own Soul, is known to Him alone whom She worshipped: But, if we may guess at her Privacies by what was seen of her in Public, we may be sure, that she was full of Humility, Devotion, and Fervency; for so she remarkably was always, during the time of Divine Service. Her Behaviour was then very devout and solemn, and yet the most decent, easy, and unaffected, that could be; there was nothing in it either negligent and loose, or extravagant and strained: it was throughout such, as declared itself not to be the work of the Passions, but to flow from the Understanding, and from a clear Knowledge of the true Grounds and Principles of that her reasonable Service.

This Knowledge she attained by early Instructions, by much Reading, and Meditation, (to which she appeared from her Childhood to be addicted) and, give me leave to add, by a very diligent and exact attendance on the Lessons of Piety which were uttered from the Pulpit, which no one practised better, because no one delighted in, listened to, or considered more. For, at these Performances, she was all Attention, all Ear; she kept her Heart fixed and intent on its holy Work, by keeping her Eye from wandering.

It was her Misfortune indeed, that the Exemplariness of her Behaviour called off the Eyes of several to observe it; but more Her, and Their Misfortune, that, when they had seen it, and satisfied their Curiosity, they did not go on also to imitate it. She often expressed her Dissatisfaction at the Indecency of Carriage which universally prevails in our Churches; and wondered that They should be most careless of their Behaviour towards God, who are most scrupulously nice in exacting and paying all the little Decencies that are in Use among Men.

When the Bread of Life was distributed, she was sure to be there, a devout and never-failing Communicant; and the Strictness of her Attention, and the Reverence of her Behaviour were, if it were possible, raised and improved on those Occasions: The lively Image of a crucified Saviour, then exhibited, could not but make very moving Impressions on a Mind that abounded with so much pious Warmth and Tenderness.

Books she took Pleasure in, and made good Use of; chiefly Books of Divinity, and Devotion; which she studied, and relished above all others. History too had very often a Share in her

Reflections; and sometimes she looked into Pieces of pure Diversion and Amusement; whenever she found them written in such a Way, as to be innocently entertaining. I need not tell You, to how narrow a Choice she was, by this means, confined.

But of all Books, the Book of God was That, in which she was most delighted and employed; and which was never, for any considerable time, out of her Hands. No doubt, she knew, and felt the great Use and sweet Influence of it, in calming her Mind, and regulating her Desires, and lifting up her Thoughts towards Heaven, in feeding and spreading that Holy Flame, which the Love of God had kindled in her Heart, and which she took care, by this means, to keep perpetually burning.

When she met with any thing there, or in any other pious Book, which would be of remarkable Use to her in the Conduct of her Life and Affairs, she trusted not her Memory with it; not even that excellent Memory, which she safely trusted with Things of lesser Moment; but immediately committed it to Writing. Many Observations of this kind she hath left, drawn from good Authors, but chiefly from those Sacred Pages; in collecting which, whether her Judgment, or her Piety had the largest Share, it is not easy to say.

The Passages of Holy Writ which she took notice of, were indeed commonly such, as related either to the Concerns of her Spiritual Estate, or to Matters of Prudence: but it appears also that she spent some time in meditating on those Places where the Sublimest Points of Christian Doctrine are contained, and in possessing herself with a deep Sense of the wonderful Love of God towards us, manifested in the mysterious Work of our Redemption; for she had something more than what, in the Language of this loose Age, is called, *a Lady's Religion*. She endeavoured to understand the great Articles of Faith, as well as to practise the good Rules of Life, contained in the Gospel; and she sensibly found, that the best way to excite herself to the Practice of the one, was to endeavour to understand the other.

And in this Book of God she was more particularly conversant on God's Day; a Day ever held sacred by her, and which therefore, always in her Family wore a Face of Devotion suitable to the Dignity of it. It was truly a Day of Rest to all under her Roof: her Servants were then dismissed from a good part of their Attendance upon her, that they might be at Liberty to attend on their great Lord and Master, whom both She, and They, were equally bound to obey. There was such a Silence and

Solemnity at that time, observed by all about her, as might have become the *House of Mourning*; and yet so much Ease and Serenity visible in their Looks (at least in her Looks there was) as showed, that They, who were in the *House of Feasting*, were not better satisfied. Thus did she prepare and dispose herself for the Enjoyment of that perfect Rest, the Celebration of that endless Sabbath, which she is now entered upon; thus did she practise beforehand upon Earth, the Duties, the Devotions, the Customs, and Manners of Heaven.

To secure her Proficiency in Virtue, she kept an exact Journal of her Life; in which was contained the History of all her Spiritual Affairs, and of the several Turns that happened in her Soul: A true, naked, impartial History! and yet, (which seldom happens in true ones) such an one, where the Person described is not charged with many Blemishes and Failings. Alas for Us, that the Thread of it was no longer continued!

In this Glass she every day dressed her Mind, to this faithful Monitor she repaired for Advice and Direction; compared the past with the present, judged of what would be, by what had been, observed nicely the several successive Degrees of Holiness she got, and of Human Infirmity she shook off; and traced every single Step she took onward in her Way towards Heaven.

One would have imagined, that so much Exactness and Severity in private should have affected a little her public Actions and Discourses, and have slid insensibly into her Carriage; and yet nothing could be more free, simple, and natural. She had the Reality, without the Outside and Show of Strictness: all her Rules, all her Performances sat so well and graceful upon her, that they appeared to be as much her Pleasure as her Duty; She was, in the midst of them, perfectly easy to herself, and a Delight to all that were about her: ever Cheerful in her Behaviour, but withal ever Calm and Even; her Satisfaction, like a deep untroubled Stream, ran on, without any of that Violence, or Noise, which sometimes the shallowest Pleasures do most abound in.

However, Cheerful and Agreeable as she was, yet she never carried her good Humour so far, as to smile at a Profane, and Ill-natured, or an Unmannerly Jest; on the contrary, in her highest Mirth, it made her remarkably Grave and Serious. She had an extraordinary Nicety of Temper as to all the least Approaches to Faults of that kind, and showed a very quick and sensible Concern at anything which she thought it did not become either Her to hear, or others to say.

True Piety, which consists chiefly in an Humility and Submission of Mind towards God, is attended always with Humility and Goodness towards his Creatures; and so it was in this *Excellent Lady*. Never was there a more deep, and unfeigned, and artless Lowliness of Mind seen in her Rank and Station: As far as she was placed above the most of the World, she conversed as it were upon the Level with all of them; and yet, when she stooped the lowest towards them, she took care even at that time to preserve the Respect that was due to her from them. She had so much true Merit, that she was not afraid of being looked into, and therefore durst be familiar: And the Effect of that Familiarity was, that, by being better known, she was more loved and valued. Not only No one of her Inferiors ever came uneasy from her, (as hath been said of some Great Ones;) but no one ever went uneasy to her; so assured were all beforehand of her Sweetness of Temper, and obliging Reception! When she opened her Lips, Gracious Words always proceeded from thence, and *in her Tongue was the Law of Kindness*. Her Reservedness, and Love of Privacy, might possibly be misinterpreted sometimes for an Overvalue of herself, by those who did not know her; but the least Degree of Acquaintance made all those Suspicions vanish. For, though her Perfections both of Body and Mind were very extraordinary, yet she was the only Person that seemed, without any Endeavour to seem, insensible of them. She was, 'tis true, in as much Danger of being Vain, as great Beauty, and a good Natural Wit could make her: But she had such an Overbalance of Discretion, that she was never in Pain to have the one seen, or the other heard. Indeed, This was particular to her, and a very distinguishing Part of her Character, that she never studied Appearances, nor made any Advances towards the Opinion of the World; being contented to *be* whatever was Good or Deserving, without endeavouring in the least to be *thought* so: and this, not out of any affected Disregard to Public Esteem, but merely from a Modesty and Easiness of Nature, which made her give way to others, who were more willing to be observed. And yet she had also her Hours of Openness and Freedom, when her Soul eased itself to Familiars and Friends; and then *out of the good Treasure of her Heart* what *good things* did she *bring forth*? And with what Delight was she listened to by those who had the Happiness to converse with her? So that a Doubt it is, whether she were most to be admired for what she did, or for what she did not say. It was wonderful that One, who, when she pleased, could discourse so fitly and so freely, should yet choose to be silent on many Occasions; and it was surprizing that She, who was such a Lover of Silence, should, whenever she spake, charm all that heard her.

We may be sure, that, whilst she thus commanded her Tongue, she kept as strict and watchful a Guard upon her Passions; those especially of the Rough and Troublesome kind, with which she was scarce ever seen to be disquieted. She knew not what the Disorders of Anger were, even on Occasions that might seem to justify, if not to require it: As much as she hated Vice, she chose rather to look it out of Countenance, than to be severe against it; and to win the bad over to the Side of Virtue by her Example, than by her Rebukes.

Her sweet Deportment toward Those who were with her, could be outdone by nothing but her Tenderness in relation to the Absent; whom she was sure to think, and speak as well of as was possible: And when their Character was plainly such, as could have no good Colours put upon it, yet she would show her Dislike of it no otherwise than by saying nothing of them. Neither her Good Nature, nor her Religion, neither her Civility, nor her Prudence, would suffer her to censure any one: She thought she had enough to do at home, in that way, without looking much abroad; and therefore turned the Edge of all her Reflections upon herself. Indeed she spared others as much as if she had been afraid of them, and herself as little, as if she had had many Faults that wanted mending: And yet, 'twas because she could, after the severest Scrutiny, find no great Harm in herself, that she could scarce be brought to suspect any in others.

Her Conversation might, for this Reason, seem to want somewhat of that Salt and Smartness, which the ill-natured Part of the World are so fond of; a Want, that she could easily have supplied, would her Principles have given her leave: but her settled Opinion was, that the Good Name of any one was too nice and serious a thing to be played with; and that it was a foolish kind of Mirth, which, in order to divert some, hurt others. She could never bring herself to think, that the only thing which gave Life and Spirit to Discourse, was, to have Somebody's Faults the Subject of it; or, that the Pleasure of a Visit lay, in giving up the Company to one another's Sport and Malice, by turns. And if these are the chief Marks of Wit and Good-breeding, it must be confessed that she had neither.

With all this Goodness, Gentleness, and Meekness of Nature,

she had at the same time a Degree of Spirit and Firmness, unusual in her Sex; and was particularly observed to have a wonderful Presence of Mind in any Accident of Danger: for Innocence and Courage are nearly allied, and even in the softest Tempers, where the one of these is in Perfection, there will and must be a good Degree of the other.

Shall I say anything of that innate Modesty of Temper, and spotless Purity of Heart, which shone throughout her whole Life and Conversation? A Quality so strictly required of her Sex, that it may be thought not so properly commendable in any of them to have it, as infamous to want it. However, in the most common and ordinary Graces, there are uncommon Heights and Degrees; and it was the particular Happiness of this *Lady* Remarkably to excel in every Virtue that belonged to her; even in those, in which Christians of the lowest Attainments do in some degree Excel.

Shall I add, that this Love of Purity was the Cause, why she banished herself from those Public Diversions of the Town, at which it was scarce possible to be present, without hearing somewhat that wounded chaste Ears; and for which, she thought, no Amends could be made to Virtue by any degree of Wit, or Humour, with which, perhaps, they might otherwise abound? These Good Qualities, she knew, served only to recommend the Poison, and make it palatable; and, therefore, she thought it a piece of Service to other People, (who might perhaps be influenced by her Example) to stand off, though she herself were secured from the Infection. This, questionless, was One Reason of her allowing herself in those dangerous Entertainments so sparingly; but it was but One of Many: She had really neither Relish nor Leisure for them; nor for a thousand other things, which the World miscalls Pleasures. Not that she wanted naturally a Taste for anything of this kind; for her Apprehension was fine, and her Wit very good, and very ready at Command, whenever she pleased to exercise it: but she had turned her Thoughts so much towards Things of Use and Importance, that Matters of mere Pleasure grew flat and indifferent to her; She was so taken up with the Care of improving her Understanding, and bettering her Life, in the Discharge of the Offices necessary to her Rank, in the Duties of her Closet, and the Concerns of her Family, that, she found, at the Foot of the Account, but little Time (and had less Mind) to give in to those vain Amusements.

She did not think it (as, I fear, it is too often thought) the peculiar Happiness and Privilege of the Great, to have nothing to do; but took care to fill every Vacant Minute of her Life with some useful or innocent Employment. The several Hours of the Day had their peculiar Business allotted to them, (whether it were Conversation, or Work, Reading, or Domestic Affairs) each of which came up orderly in its turn; and was, as the Wise Man speaks, (to be sure, under Her Management it was) *beautiful in its Season*.

And this Regularity of Hers, was free and natural, without Formality or Constraint; it was neither troublesome to Her, nor to those that were near her: when, therefore, any Accident intervened, it was interrupted at that time with as much Ease as it was at other times practised: for among all her discretionary Rules, the chief was, to seem to have none; and to make those she had laid down to herself give way always to Circumstances and Occasions.

She wrought with her own Hands often, when she could more profitably, and pleasingly have employed her time in Meditation, or Books: but she was willing to set an Example to those, who could not; and she took care, therefore, that her Example should be well followed by all that were under her immediate Influence: for she knew well, that the Description of a Good Wife and a Perfect Woman in the Proverbs, (a Description which she much delighted in, and often read) was spent chiefly in commending that Diligence by which *She looketh well to the Ways of her Household, and eateth not the Bread of Idleness*: And she knew likewise also, that the Person, whose Words these are said to be, was no less a Woman than the Mother of King *Lemuel*.

Diligence and Frugality are Sisters; and She, therefore, who was so well acquainted with the one, was not likely to be a Stranger to the other. She was strictly careful of her Expenses; and yet knew how to be Generous and to abound, when the Occasion required it. But of all Ways of good Management, she liked That the worst which shuts our Hands to the Poor: towards whom she always showed herself very Compassionate and Charitable. Of the other Delights, with which an high Fortune furnished her, she was almost insensible; but on This account she valued it, that it gave her an Opportunity of pursuing the several Pleasures of Beneficence, and of tasting all the Sweets of Well-doing. *She delivered the Poor that cried, and the Fatherless, and Him that had none to help him: The Blessing of him that was ready to perish came upon her, and She caused the Widow's Heart to sing*. Very easy, sure, will this make her Audit at the great Day of Account; That Charity will, doubtless, be allowed to screen her few Infirmities and Faults, which is of Efficacy sufficient to *cover the Multitude of Sins*.

In the Exercise of this, and of all other Virtues, She was wonderfully secret; endeavouring to come up, as near as she could, to the Rule of *not letting her right Hand know what her left Hand did*. And this Secrecy of hers she managed so well, that some of the most remarkable Instances of her Goodness were not known, till after her Death; no, not by Him, who was Partaker of all her Joys and Sorrows.

Retirement and Privacy she always loved, and therefore chose it, when, after the Death of a near Relation, who had the Care of Educating Her, she was at liberty to have lived otherwise. From that Time to her Marriage, which was more than Three Years, she hid herself in the Country; having an early and settled Aversion to the Noise and Inconveniences of a Town life; and too little an Opinion of herself, to think, that it was so much the Interest of Virtue and Religion, as it really was, that she should be known and distinguished.

When, afterwards, she went to Court, (as it was necessary for Her sometimes to do) she did it with an Air, which plainly showed, that she went to pay her Duty there, and not to delight herself in the Pomp and Glitter of that Place. Had she gone thither soon enough to see that *Good and Glorious Queen*, who was the Ornament of It, and of her Sex, she had been taken, we may presume, into her Intimacy: for their Minds were nearly allied, and their Characters, and Manners, and Ways of Life not unlike; allowing for the Difference of Stations.

I need not, I cannot well say more of her: and if, therefore, I have fallen short of her Character, (as I am sensible I have, in many Parts of it, which are here mentioned, and in others, which are still left untouched) I desire, those particular Defects may be supplied from this General Account; that she did not a little resemble *Her*, who was the Pattern of all that is Good and Amiable in Womankind.

Whether she had this excellent Pattern in her Eye, I am not able to say, when, soon after her Marriage, she declared to several Friends her Thoughts, that Every Woman of Quality was as much more Obliged, as she was more Enabled than other Women, to do Good in the World; and that the shortest and surest

Way of doing this was, to endeavour, by all means, to be as good a Christian, and as good a Wife, and as good a Friend, as was possible.

She endeavoured to be all this, and she fell not far short of it: for she excelled in all the Characters that belonged to her, and was in a great measure equal to all the Obligations that she lay under: She was devout, without Superstition; strict, without Ill-humour; good-natured, without Weakness; cheerful, without Levity; regular, without Affectation. She was to her Husband, the best of Wives, the most agreeable of Companions, and most faithful of Friends; to her Servants, the best of Mistresses; to her Relations, extremely respectful; to her Inferiors, very obliging: and by all that knew her, either nearly, or at a Distance, She was reckoned, and confessed to be one of the best of Women.

And yet all this Goodness, and all this Excellence, was bounded within the Compass of eighteen Years, and as many Days: for no longer was she allowed to live among us. She was snatched out of the World as soon almost as she had made her Appearance in it; like a Jewel of high Price, just shown a little, and then put up again; and We were deprived of her by that time We had learned to value her. But Circles may be complete, though small; the Perfection of Life doth not consist in the Length of it: if it did, Our Saviour to be sure would not have died so soon after thirty.

Short as her Life was, She had time enough to adorn the several States of Virginity and Marriage; and to experience the Sadness of a kind of Widowhood too: for such she accounted it, when her Lord was long absent from her; mourned as much, and refused as much to be comforted, till his Return.

As her Life was short, so her Death was sudden; She was called away in haste, and without any warning. One day she drooped, and the next she died; nor was there the Distance of many Hours between her being very easy in this World, and very happy in another.

However, though she was seized thus suddenly by Death, yet was she not surprised; for She was ever in Preparation for it; *her Loins girt,* (as the Scripture speaks) *and her Lamp ready trimmed, and burning*: The Moment also that She was taken ill, she was just risen from her Knees, and had made an end of her Morning Devotions. And to such an One a sudden Death could be no Misfortune. We pray, indeed, against it, because few, very few, are fit for it; and the Church is to proportion her Forms to the Generality of Christians: But where a Good Soul is in perfect

Readiness, there the sooner the fatal Stroke is struck, the better; all Delays in this Case, are uncomfortable to the Dying, as well as to those Friends who survive them.

In truth, she could not be called away more hastily, than she was willing to go. She had been used so much to have *her Conversation in Heaven*, and her Soul had been so often upon the wing thither, that it readily left its Earthly Station upon the least Notice from Above; and took the very first Opportunity of quitting her Body, without lingering or expecting a second Summons. She stayed no longer, after she was called, than to assure her Lord of her entire Resignation to the Divine Will; and of her having no manner of Uneasiness upon her Mind; and to take her Leave of him, with all the Expressions of Tenderness. When this was over, she had nothing more to do with her Senses; she sunk immediately under her Illness, and, after a short unquiet Slumber, slept in Peace.

Thus lived, and thus died this Excellent Lady, whose Character I have so far represented, as my Time, and the Measure of such Discourses as these would suffer me; and endeavoured to renew a faint Image of her several Virtues and Perfections upon your Minds. I have done it in a confused manner, and without the nice Divisions of Art; for Grief is not Methodical: It is enough, if I have been able to set before you some Resemblance of her, though I should not have done it after the best and liveliest manner: When the Life is gone, a Picture drawn even by an unskillful Hand, hath its Use and Value; and those who loved what it doth (however unequally) represent, will be touched at the sight of it.

You all are so, I question not, touched, by what hath been said, in various Manners, and in different Degrees, as Your Relation to her was nearer, or remoter; as you knew more, or less of her. But you do not mourn alone; many *Living* there are, that do now, and many more there are, who shall hereafter, when her Character hath spread itself, *lay it to heart*. The World hath had a Loss, as well as You; True Virtue and Piety have suffered in her Fall; and all, therefore, that have any Regard for These, shall bear a Part with You in your Sorrows.

The *True Servants of God shall lay it to heart*, who from their Souls desire the Increase of Religion and Goodness, and know the Power and Influence of so sweet, so winning, so perfect a Pattern as was set by Her; who promised Themselves a mighty Countenance, and the World strange Advantages, from her exemplary Sanctity and Goodness.

They that *minister in holy Things will lay it to heart*, to whom she repaired, with so much Constancy and Seriousness, to hear the Divine Oracles explained by them, and to *enquire the Law at their Mouths*. They will consider, what an Helper and Furtherer of their pious Labours they have lost; and how much more lifeless and ineffectual their Discourses are now likely to be, than they were heretofore, when she encouraged those Exercises by her Presence, and taught others to attend, by the strict Attention she herself paid to what was said in them. In whatever Congregation she appeared, she secretly raised and improved the Devotions of the Place; every Day of her Life preached up Goodness, as effectually as the most rational and moving Sermon.

The *Enquirers into the Methods and Mysteries of Divine Providence will lay it to heart*. Why, will they say, when God hath most Work to do in the World, is one of the best and most faithful Instruments of his Glory called out of it? Why is she snatched away from us, at a Time when we could least have spared her? when Iniquity and Irreligion run high, and Piety is in danger of growing out of Fashion, and out of Countenance? Why, in such a Juncture, is this *Good Lady* taken? And why are so many of her Sex, so unlike her, left? Is it in Mercy to her, or in Judgment to Us? Is it because She was too good to live here, or because We were too wicked to deserve her Company? *Righteous art Thou, O Lord, when we plead with Thee: yet let Us talk with Thee of thy Judgments!*

Her *Domestics will lay it to heart*, whom she shone upon always with a singular Goodness; who were near Witnesses of her most retired Graces and Virtues and had the best Opportunities of forming themselves upon her admirable Model: and who will now (alas!) be destitute of her Example and Encouragement; of her sweet Advice, and gentle Reproofs; and will be left to live upon that Stock of Virtue, which hath been happily laid in by them, that Measure of Goodness which They have already derived, from attending and observing Her.

Finally, the *Poor will lay it to heart*, whose Bowels she refreshed, and whose Wants she relieved; and was ever their sure Refuge and Support, their Kind and Merciful Patroness and Friend.

But, above all, her *Relations will lay it to heart*; Those, to whom she was most nearly joined by Blood, or Love; and who had a more particular Interest in all her Virtues: They will lay their Hands on their Breasts, *in the Day of Adversity*, and *consider*; how have we offended, that we are thus grievously punished? and which of Our Miscarriages is it, that this heavy Infliction is intended to reform?

This is the wisest and best Use that can be made of such Solemnities as these; not, by the means of them, to excite our truly pious and Christian Grief to an immoderate and unchristian Degree, nor *to sorrow as Men without hope*; but to take Occasion from thence, to search and enquire into ourselves; to learn the Meaning of these Divine Admonitions; and, after we have interpreted them truly, to resolve upon obeying them.

The Deceased Person, whose Loss we deplore, is Happy without Question: Happy will the Living be also, if they thus wisely, thus effectually *lay it to heart! It is better*, doubtless, *to go into the House of Mourning, than into the House of Feasting*; but upon this Condition, that we come better out of the one, than out of the other: That we leave our Vanities and our Vices behind us; that we lay aside our Affections towards this World, and our Indifference towards another; that we put on holy and hearty Resolutions of being even Now, what we shall wish we had been, Hereafter, when the fatal Hour approaches; and of *living the Life* of this *Righteous* Person, that we may *die her Death* too; and be remembered and lamented, as she is, by those who survive us.

Let us assure ourselves, that the best way of doing Honour to her Memory will be, by making her Character still live in Our Lives and Actions; that the truest instance of our Love and Esteem of Her is, to endeavour to be Like Her: for Thus, we shall even add some farther Degrees of Happiness and Honour to the vast Reward which she is already entitled to; and shall make the Crown of Glory, she is to wear, bright as it will be, yet brighter, in the Day of General Retribution: Till when, (it may be piously supposed) the Saints departed are not admitted to the *Fulness of Joy*, that, in the mean time, the Influence of their good Examples and good Deeds spreading far and wide, That too, when their Accounts are made up, may be taken into them; and the Fitness and Proportionableness of their exceeding great Recompense, then bestowed, may be manifested in the Sight of Angels and Men.

Wherefore, *lift up the Hands that hang down, and the feeble Knees!* Think not so much and so long on the incomparable Character of the Deceased, as to forget the true Use You are to make of this afflicting Accident; and to neglect those good Improvements under it, which the Wise and Kind Inflicter expects at Your Hands. You have paid Your last Respects to Her, be not now wanting to Yourselves; but *Gird up the Loins of Your Mind*, and be Ye comforted!

The Consideration of what She was, which Afflicts You, should much rather Cheer and Revive You: Had She not been so good a Woman, You would with more reason have bewailed her. But, why should You continue to mourn for One, who is entered upon a state of unspeakable Joy? Why should you be dejected at Her Advancement?

She is gone to the place, where all Tears are wiped from her Eyes; where there is no more Death, nor Sorrow, nor Crying; She is gone, and her Works have followed, and will follow her, to her great and Endless Advantage. God grant that, when We also follow her, we may do it with as little Surprise, and as much Cheerfulness!

Thomas Wilson

WILSON WAS born at Burton, in Cheshire, and went to school in Chester, then to Trinity College, Dublin, where he studied medicine. He was ordained deacon in 1686, and served as curate to his uncle in a Lancashire parish. In 1689 he became a priest, and three years afterwards chaplain to the Earl of Derby. It was through this connection that he was offered the see of Sodor and Man, which had been vacant for four years and was rather down-at-heel. He accepted, and was installed in St German's Cathedral, Peel, in 1698. Both the cathedral and the bishop's residence were in a ruinous condition, and the income was not more than three hundred pounds a year. Wilson 'had a practical turn', as his first biographer said. He farmed energetically and with success, planted orchards and woodlands, and ran a mill, besides for some years being the only doctor on the island and providing a free service to the poor. His economic preoccupations, which were strictly subordinate to his work as a bishop and certainly not undertaken for personal gain, enabled him to extend his care for his diocese in several directions. No doubt he infected others with his energy. Not only were the cathedral and Bishop's Court repaired at great expense and almost entirely out of his own funds; other churches were built and the grammar schools and parish schools of the island were improved.

Perhaps unfortunately, it was Wilson's administration of Church discipline that made most noise in the world, and he has been held up as a model of apostolical simplicity in this matter. In fact, he was the inheritor of a practically medieval system and continued it in a manner which would have been possible only in that out-of-the-way corner of the world. Warnings, penances and excommunications were the ordinary stock-in-trade, for offences ranging from fornication to playing with a dog in church. Wilson left the old 'spiritual statutes' of the island largely untouched and introduced Ecclesiastical Constitutions of his own in 1704. Whether one views these activities with the mawkish admiration of Keble, or regards them with more reserve, there is no doubt that Wilson was absolutely fearless in his administration. It was his mitigation of the fines in the ecclesiastical courts which first raised the hackles of the civil authorities, who were anxious about losing revenue. In 1721 he ordered the Governor's wife to ask forgiveness for slanderous statements, as a sort of mitigated penance; this naturally did not improve his standing among the 'best people'. There was a first-class provincial row. He suspended his archdeacon, who not only sided with the lady but approved the *Independent Whig* which Wilson had censured. The old-world customs of the island extended beyond ecclesiastical censures, and Wilson and his vicars-general found themselves confined in a dungeon. His later years in the diocese were less eventful.

Wilson was a man of energy and simplicity, and his devotion to his function and his diocese was irreproachable. Three times he declined an English bishopric, saying on the last occasion: 'I will not leave my wife in my old age because she is poor.' Nor should he be thought of as itching to manage the conduct of others. 'Generally speaking,' he wrote in his private notebook, 'men have more need of a confessor than of a director.' His most striking characteristic was a far-reaching seriousness. It was no doubt this which so attracted Matthew Arnold. There are a number of references to Wilson in Arnold's notebooks, and he wrote about Wilson's *Maxims* at some length in the preface to *Culture and Anarchy*. Less deep and powerful than the *Meditations* of Marcus Aurelius, Arnold said, they were a work of the same kind, with 'something peculiarly sincere and first-hand about them'. He admired their balance but, perhaps above all, 'that downright honesty and plain good sense which our English race has applied so powerfully to the divine impossibilities of religion'. Dangerous qualities, and a dangerous recommendation, but they probably sum up well the character of this man about whom there was so little nonsense.

THE LORD'S SUPPER THE MEDICINE OF THE SOUL
Mark 6: 56.
As many as touched Him were made whole.

WILSON'S SERIOUSNESS did not abandon him in the pulpit; no one is further from mere eloquence. His discourses are at once practical and uncompromising—an uncomfortable combination. His sermon on *The True Christian Method of Educating Children* could hardly be reproduced as an article in *The Times Educational Supplement*. 'The fear of God, and the knowledge of ourselves', were to be the basis of education. Once children had been 'suffered to grow wild', once their souls had been 'polluted, their senses depraved', it would be 'the hardest thing in the world to persuade them even to hear what we have to say on the part of religion'; and the first aim of schools should be 'to make children Christians in deed as well as in name'. In his sermon on *The Duty of Self-Denial*, the old are told that they should not 'put the thoughts of death far from them', or imagine that they are at liberty 'to make the remainder of their lives as easy and as pleasant as possibly they can'; and the rich are reminded that they are 'but too apt to take it for granted, that they have a right to please themselves in spending their incomes'. There is little in his exhortations that is 'grateful to flesh and blood', so that he often sounds harsh—and let no one imagine that the words did not sound harsh to listeners in the eighteenth century. Yet the root of Wilson's attitude was not Puritanism, and there is none of the egotism that goes with a claim to righteousness. The fear of God, and the love of God, were for him movements of the mind, rather than theological conceptions. He is straightforward rather than subtle.

The following sermon illustrates the nature at once of his personal religion and of his pastoral concern. 'My own reason, my own power, would no more help me, or keep me from ruining myself, than these would keep a new-born child from perishing, if it were left to itself.' He looks towards Christ, in the Holy Communion. 'The bread that nourisheth to eternal life' is 'everywhere to be met with, as Jesus Christ himself was when he was on earth. Wherever Christians live, whether in villages, or cities, or towns, or country, they may have this blessed cure of their disorders, if it is not their own fault.' Wilson the bishop is still the physician, offering now not something to ease this or that ailment but a 'sovereign medicine'.

THE WHOLE verse is as followeth:—'Whithersoever Jesus entered, into villages, or cities, or country, they laid the sick in the streets, and besought him that they might touch, if it were but the border of his garment; and AS MANY AS TOUCHED HIM WERE MADE WHOLE.'

What a blessed opportunity had these people of being healed of all their diseases!—How happy did they think themselves in having Jesus Christ present amongst them!—How good and kind was he, to go from one place to another, that everybody who had a desire to be healed, and who had faith in his power, *might be made whole!*

We cannot but esteem this a mighty blessing, and wish it were our own case. Why now, my Christian brethren, it *is* our own case, and to much greater purposes. And we should certainly be convinced of it, if we were but as sensible of our spiritual disorders, as these people were of the diseases of their bodies; and we should, with as much zeal and faith in his power and readiness to help us, apply to him now he is in heaven, as earnestly as these people did when he was on earth and amongst them.

All that we want is, *to feel our disorders*, and to see the danger we are in without his help; for then we should, with thankful hearts, accept of the sovereign medicine which he has prescribed for the cure of all our maladies.

Well then, how may we become sensible of our disorders and danger?

Let every one, who desires to know this, look into his own heart, and ask himself some such questions as these:—

Do I love with all my heart the God who made me, who preserves and gives me all that I want, or enjoy, or hope for?

Do I fear to offend him, who, for my own good, has given me rules to live by, and has assured me, that if I do not observe those rules, I shall lose his favour, and deprive myself of greater happiness than all this world can give me?

The true answer *must* be this:—I find myself prone to evil continually; of myself I am not able to resist the temptations to sin that I meet with; I do many things which my own conscience tells me *I ought not to do*, and I omit very many duties which I owe to God my Maker, to my neighbour, and to myself; I cannot but be sensible that I do not love God as I ought to do; I have not had that regard to his commands, that so great a Majesty demands of me; I have received infinite mercies and favours from his goodness, and have never thanked him for them; I have, times without number, broken his commands, without fearing what must follow; I have little minded what his own Son has made known to us, that a day is coming when God will judge the world in righteousness, according to our behaviour in this life; and that they that have done good shall go into life and happiness everlasting, and they that have done evil, and have not timely repented, shall go into everlasting fire.

This I have heard a thousand times, without being awakened, or bettered by it; I cannot but see that every day brings me nearer to death; that death is the end of my trial in this life, and that after that there is no repentance.

Jesus Christ in his holy gospel assures us that, the moment we die, our souls are carried to places of happiness or misery, according as our lives have been spent here, there to remain till the judgment of the great day.

Now, who is there that hears and understands this, who does not know that every syllable of this is true? For these are not the sayings of men, but THE WORDS OF GOD, the God of Truth, who cannot deceive his creatures, but would have all men to repent, and to come to the knowledge of the truth, and of their own interest.

And can any man hear these truths, and apply them to himself, without seeing that this is his own case,—without seeing the danger he is in without some help besides his own,—and without laying hold of that help that is offered him by a merciful Saviour and Physician of our souls?

Do but look back to the text, and the history set before you for your consideration and pattern.

All that found themselves sick and in danger, made no delay, lest they should lose so good an opportunity of being healed of their infirmities.

Wherever Jesus Christ came, they saw his power and his mercy to help poor miserable people; and they besought him to heal them; and he did so most willingly. They saw plainly that without his help they must suffer or die; and they *besought him*, they begged of him, to heal them of their diseases:—And *as many as did so, were made whole*.

Now, my Christian brethren, what have I set this history before you for, but to persuade you to follow the example of these diseased people? Not one soul of us will dare to say, 'Nothing ails me, I am in no danger.' *If we say that we have no sin, we deceive ourselves, and the truth is not in us*, saith St. John; and so saith every man's own conscience, who will but look inwards.

And what saith the Spirit of Truth in the gospel?—*No wicked person can enter into the kingdom of heaven,*—can inherit eternal life,—but shall be sent into outer darkness, *where there shall be weeping, and wailing, and gnashing of teeth.*

Now can any sinner, can any man who knows any thing of himself, be easy under the belief and thoughts of this, until he knows whether there be any help for him or not?

Here therefore is seen the blessing of Christianity, which offers, which has provided, a remedy for all our disorders, and for all our fears. *The blood of Jesus Christ cleanseth us from all sin*, saith the Holy Spirit by St. John; and our Lord Christ himself says, *Verily, all sins shall be forgiven unto men*; that is, unto those who are weary and heavy laden with the burden of their sins, who confess and forsake their sins, and, through faith in his blood, beseech him to help, and to heal them; and this with that sincere desire and earnestness, that these sick people desired to touch, if it were but the border of his garment, and were thereby made whole.

This will lead us to consider, how Jesus Christ has appointed us to apply to him for his help, and the cure of our disorders. For though he is gone into heaven, yet he is still ready and has promised to heal all the diseases of our souls, when we apply to him out of a true sense of our sad condition without his help and mercy.

Jesus Christ, while he was on earth, had told his disciples and followers, That he was *the bread of life*, the life-giving bread, *which came down from heaven, which if any man should eat, he should live for ever.*—That *this bread is his flesh, which he would give for the life of the world.*—He adds, *Verily, verily, I say unto you, Except ye eat the flesh of the Son of Man, and drink his blood, ye have no life in you. Whoso eateth my flesh, and drinketh my blood, hath eternal life; and I will raise him up at the last day.*

These were then indeed strange sayings to his followers. Some said, How can this man give us his flesh to eat? Others were offended, and departed from him. But when his time came, that he was to die, and to become a sacrifice for the sins of the world, he explained himself to his apostles, when he appointed that ordinance or sacrament, which is called THE LORD'S SUPPER. For then he took bread, and having blessed it, he gave it to his disciples, and said, *This is my body, which is given for you.* And of the wine he said, *This is my blood, which is shed for you, and for many:*—EAT THE ONE, AND DRINK THE OTHER, IN REMEMBRANCE OF ME.

Then they understood, that when before he had spoken of eating his flesh and drinking his blood, as necessary to eternal life, he did not mean it in such a manner as they then understood it, but in a spiritual manner, as he now explained it; namely, that Christ is our life, the food of our souls, in this sacrament. As common bread is the food of our bodies, so this is the support of our spiritual life.

He therefore ordained this sacrament to be for ever observed by all Christians, not only as a testimony of his great love, in laying down his life for his poor creatures; but as a way by which he would communicate to them all the blessings he had by his death obtained for them; *the pardon of their sins in this world, and eternal life after death.*

Happy therefore will all those be, who, after the example of these sick and diseased people, being sensible of their infirmities and danger, do go to him for help, and take all opportunities of going by faith to the physician of their souls; he having blessed this very ordinance, for our help and comfort, with a power of healing all our spiritual diseases.

We see, that the very border of his garment, by his blessing, had the virtue to heal all those, that through faith in him touched it, of all their bodily infirmities. And shall we doubt the blessed effects of this holy ordinance to every worthy communicant, to procure for him the favour of God,—the pardon of his sins,—the assistance of God's Holy Spirit,—and eternal life and happiness after death?

God forbid we should any of us doubt this! God can affix and join his blessings and helps to whatever he pleaseth. By his appointment, the common waters of Jordan healed Naaman the Syrian. By his appointment, a brazen serpent healed all those that were bitten, only by looking upon it with faith in God's commandment. By the very shadow of St. Peter, many, we are assured, were healed of their diseases. And here, *as many as touched our Saviour's garment were made whole.*

And it is thus that the two sacraments become means of salvation to all such as with faith receive them. The *water* in BAPTISM, with the blessing and grace of God, has power in it to cleanse us from our sins. And the *bread* in the LORD'S SUPPER, being set apart and blessed, becomes the bread that nourisheth to eternal life.

Why then does any Christian neglect this sovereign medicine? It is everywhere to be met with, as Jesus Christ himself was when he was on earth. Wherever Christians live, whether in villages, or cities, or towns, or country, they may have this blessed cure of their disorders, if it is not their own fault.

Our Lord himself gives us the true reason why people are not sensible of this mercy which is offered them: *They that be whole*, that do not feel their disorders and danger, *will not be persuaded that they need a physician, but they that are sick*. These, and these only, will be glad of, and look out for help.

For my own part, I am not ashamed to confess, that were it not for the blood of Christ, offered us in this holy ordinance,— were it not through faith in his blood,—I should never dare to apply to the great God for the pardon of my sins,—for the assistance of his grace to keep me from ruining myself for ever. My own reason, my own power, would no more help me, or keep me from ruining myself, than these would keep a new-born child from perishing, if it were left to itself.

And this I am sure is the case of every man living, of every soul that hears me. We have every one of us the seed of every evil, of every sin we ever heard of, lodged in our corrupt nature, ready to spring out upon every suitable temptation, if not hindered by the grace or providence of God.

When we hear that such a man has robbed or murdered his neighbour, we wonder at it. Why; not one of us but would have done the same, had we been left wholly to ourselves and to the temptation of the devil, and had the same occasion offered us; and God had not interposed his grace or his providence to hinder us.

We easily see, and are very ready to censure, other people's faults. Such a man, we cry, is *covetous*; such a man is *unjust*; such a man is *litigious*; such a man is a *drunkard*; such a man is an *adulterer*; such a man is a *common swearer*: though all these must know that God has forbidden every one of these sins, upon pain of damnation.

You do not consider why these people have fallen into these damnable sins, and why you yourself have not perhaps done so; but it is fit you should know why you have not; for, be assured of it, let a man be never so *learned*, never so *wise* in his own opinion, never so *cautious*, never so *resolved* against any or all of these sins; yet if he shall provoke God to leave him to himself; if he shall despise those means which God has appointed to keep us under his especial favour and protection; there is not one of these sins but he is liable to fall into. And this is the reason why the Spirit of God has given us all, even the best of us, this caution:—*Let him that thinketh he standeth, take heed lest he fall.*

Will any one of us, after this, if this be true, (as we are sure it is) will any man say, I hope I am in no such danger; I have no such ailments to be cured of; I hope I shall be governed by reason; my own sense of what is good and evil will keep me from such unworthy, from such destructive and shameful vices. God help him that thinks so! Indeed, God must help you, or your danger is greater, your maladies and disorders are more deadly, than you are aware of.

And were it not for the wonderful love of our blessed Redeemer, in laying down his life as a sacrifice for our sins, and restoring us to the favour of an offended God; if he had not appointed these means of grace, by which we can plead before God, that his own Son has redeemed us from the power of the devil, if it be not our own fault; if *he* had not obtained for us the assistance of an all-powerful Spirit, to direct and assist us, not one soul of us would be saved.

And now, if after what has been said, and I hope believed, (for we dare not say anything but what Christ has commanded us to say and speak) if, after what you have heard, you are not sensible that your disorders are many, and great, and of very dangerous consequences if not cured, there is no help for it, you must perish.

This is not what our merciful God and Saviour designed, when he appointed this holy sacrament to be observed by all that hope for salvation through his merits. He laid down his life, to convince all mankind that their souls were in danger without his grace and help. He appointed this service, that they might not forget their danger; and that they might have a cure for their diseases, and their fears. Whoever will not accept of this remedy, there is no hope left for him:—This being the only remedy for our sins, which are the diseases of our souls; the only medicine to obtain our pardon and the grace of God, to mend the corruption of our nature, to increase and to confirm our faith, without which it will be impossible to please God, or to be made whole.

In short; this is the only medicine to supply the graces we want, the bread by which the life and health of our souls is to be preserved. It is as much the support of our souls, as common bread is the food and support of our bodies. These, and many more, are the blessings which every Christian may expect, who goes worthily to the Lord's table.

But who, some will say, can be sure that he shall be a worthy communicant? Let a man sincerely purpose and strive to amend what he knows to be amiss in himself;—let him sincerely purpose and strive to lead a Christian life for the time to come;—let him firmly believe, that, for the sake of what Jesus Christ hath done and suffered for us, *we have peace with God* upon our repentance;—let him, with a thankful heart, remember the great goodness of God in giving his only Son for his sinful and otherwise lost creatures;—and let him remember the sufferings of Christ, in order to redeem mankind from the slavery of sin and Satan; and lastly, let him be as ready to forgive others as God has been to forgive him, and as he hopes for that mercy from God: Every such person may humbly hope to be a meet partaker of these holy mysteries, and may return home healed of all his maladies.

In short; let me observe to you, that Jesus Christ, *the great physician*, comes to our doors, as he did to these people.

All they that were distressed, and wanted his help, most readily and thankfully applied to him. There was no need to exhort and press them to go to him for a cure. They were convinced, that there was an healing power in him to cure them. Their faith in him cured them of all their diseases:—And the same faith in his power, and the same sense of our disorders, and earnest desire to be relieved, will as certainly obtain the help we wish for, *the cure of all our disorders.*

And may the Lord pity and awaken all such, if there be any such, as are so senseless, and blind, as not to see and feel, that they want his help every day of their lives! When once they are sensible of this, they will not need to be told how often they should go to him for relief. The oftener they go, the better it will be for them, if they go with a sincere desire to be made better.

And be assured of it, Christians, it is with this spiritual food, as it is with the food of our bodies:—A man may fast so long as quite to lose his appetite, and thereby endanger his life; even so, by abstaining from the Lord's supper, he may forget the wants he labours under; he may forget the want and blessing of a Redeemer, of the Physician of his soul, till he is past cure without a miracle, which he will have no reason to expect.

And now, may all we, who, through the grace of God, desire

and purpose to partake of this blessed medicine of our souls, be ever prepared to 'receive it worthily', whenever it is offered to us, by resolving, through God's help and grace, never to live in any known sin; never to act against our conscience; never to neglect the known duties of our calling; but to live in the fear of God, and to pray daily for his pardon and grace to do our duty; and that he may increase and confirm our faith, for his mercy's sake in Jesus Christ, our only Physician and Redeemer.

To whom, with the Father and the Holy Spirit, be all glory and thanksgiving, now and for ever. *Amen.*

Jonathan Swift

SWIFT WAS born in Dublin in 1667; He 'happened, indeed, by a perfect accident,' as he says, to be born in Ireland, but he came of an old Yorkshire family and did not regard himself an Irishman. His father, one of several brothers who had gone to Ireland to make a living, died before the boy was born, and his mother soon went back to England. Swift owed his education to an uncle. He was sent to school in Kilkenny, then to Trinity College, Dublin, where he seems to have been more noted for his independence than for his academic attainments. He became secretary, at Moor Park in Surrey, to Sir William Temple, with whom there were family connections. Temple was a Whig ex-statesman and *littérateur*, who was perhaps pleased with Swift until he found the young man was abler than himself. Temple certainly contributed greatly, both wittingly and unwittingly, to Swift's education, and it was to him that Swift owed his introduction into the great world. Swift showed as much independence as gratitude. In 1694 he left Temple and was ordained, but not before he had been offered a civil appointment which gave him, as he says, 'an opportunity of living without being driven into the Church for a maintenance'. He was not over-pleased with his living at Kilroot, and soon returned to Moor Park, but went over to Ireland again in 1699 as chaplain to the Earl of Berkeley and soon after became vicar of Laracor.

He spent the following years between Ireland and England, becoming ever more involved in affairs of state as well as of the Church. The period of his most intimate involvement in affairs of state was during the last years of Queen Anne, when he was on familiar terms with the leaders of the Tory administration, Harley and St John, though less in their confidence than he supposed at the time. The appointment as Dean of St Patrick's was on Harley's recommendation; it was 'no great prize', as Leslie Stephen says. The death of Anne brought in the Whigs who were to dominate the century.

The rest of Swift's life was spent in virtual exile in Ireland. He knew the country from top to bottom, as few knew it. He had acquaintance in the best circles; he took long solitary journeys across the countryside and was familiar with the condition of the people at large. He became a hero in Dublin for his opposition to the rapacity of the Whig administration and the forces of money. He was punctilious and unobtrusive in his duties as a churchman, and exercised charity with a rough tongue. He died in 1745 and was buried in St Patrick's Cathedral where, as the epitaph he wrote for himself says, 'savage indignation could no longer tear his heart to pieces', *ubi saeva indignatio cor ulterius lacerare nequit.*

ON BROTHERLY LOVE
Hebrews 13:1.
Let Brotherly Love continue.

THIS SERMON was preached in St Patrick's on 1 December 1717. Swift's mind was by no means free from the mortification of his affairs in England. He was fifty—very much, though he would not have used Yeats's dramatic expression, 'the finished man among his enemies'. The Whigs were making the most of the alarm over the Pretender to push the Tories out of the way wherever they could. There were spies about. 'It seems there is a trade going of carrying stories to the government and many honest folks turn the penny by it', he wrote to his friend Knightley Chetwode (28 June 1715). He was under suspicion himself. 'If I had been called before them, I would not have answered one syllable or named one person', he said (letter of 21 June 1715), and one can believe him. He preached, some time during the early years of George I's reign, a sermon on Exodus 20:16, 'Thou shalt not bear false Witness against thy Neighbour'. It was no academic lesson; the practitioners of 'this abominable Trade and Sin' were at large around him. His advice to his hearers bears all the weight of his disillusion. 'Let me advise you to have nothing at all to do with that which is commonly called Politics, or the Government of the World; in the nature of which it is certain you are utterly ignorant;'— Swift was not given to flattering his congregation—'and when your Opinion is wrong, although it proceeds from Ignorance, it shall be an accusation against you. Besides, Opinions in Government are right or wrong just according to the Disposition of the Times; and, unless you have Judgment to distinguish, you may be punished at one Time for what you would be rewarded for in another.'

In the sermon *On Brotherly Love* there is a similar sharpness of tone. It is not merely on the politics of his contemporaries that Swift looks with anger. He knows that one age is as bad as another. 'The last legacy of *Christ*', he says, 'was Peace and mutual Love; but he foretold that he came to send a Sword upon the Earth: The primitive Christians accepted the Legacy, and their Successors, down to the present Age, have been largely fulfilling this prophecy.'

It is in the application of these generalities to his own times that Swift may be thought partisan. Swift's truthfulness is so habitual, not to say constitutional, that one should at least consider carefully what he says before dismissing it as mere political controversy. His position turns on a conception of moderation which had deep justification in English history. He saw the Church of England as the legitimate heir, in these islands, of the primitive Christians. There is a world of controversy which this view sets aside, and does not resolve. More immediately, there were the undoubted legal rights of the national church, and the proven loyalty of its adherents, which could be set against the record of the other two contenders. Behind the association of Roman Catholics with treason was the Bull of Pius V against Queen Elizabeth, which claimed to deprive her of her right and to absolve all her subjects from their oath and from all duties whatsoever towards her. The Presbyterians, to say nothing of more extreme Protestants, had proved their disloyalty to the Crown in the troubles which ended in 1660. Swift's view of 'a Man truly Moderate' was of one 'steady in the Doctrine and Discipline of the Church, but with a due Christian Charity to all who dissent from it out of a Principle of Conscience.' There was to be freedom of conscience, but no question of trusting papists or Protestant dissenters with political power. 'He hateth no Man for differing from him in Political Opinions.' Swift's humanity was profound; but so was his sense of the authority and order needed for government. He was no Jacobite, and supported the Revolution of 1689 as the only possible settlement. But he saw—to use some words from his sermon *Upon the Martyrdom of King Charles I*—that 'since the late Revolution, men have sate much looser in the true fundamentals both of religion and government', Swift had an instinct for the losing side. Since 1715, Toryism in his sense—which was also Dr Johnson's—has been a more or less obscure opposition doctrine. The 'new Meaning of the Word "moderate" ' to which Swift points in this sermon *On Brotherly Love* is the one that has since become general. The centre has shifted further and further from the objective realities of the Constitution to the world of opinion, in which one opinion is as good as another. In the 'new Meaning of the Word' in 1717, a moderate man was 'one to whom all Religion is indifferent'. It is this that Swift is here preaching against.

IN THE early times of the gospel, the Christians were very much distinguished from all other bodies of men, by the great and constant love they bore to each other; which, although it was done in obedience to the frequent injunctions of our Saviour and his apostles, yet, I confess, there seemeth to have been likewise a natural reason, that very much promoted it. For the Christians then were few and scattered, living under persecution by the heathens round about them, in whose hands was all the civil and military power; and there is nothing so apt to unite the minds and hearts of men, or to beget love and tenderness, as a general distress. The first dissensions between Christians took their beginning from the errors and heresies that arose among them; many of those heresies, sometimes extinguished and sometimes reviving, or succeeded by others, remain to this day; and having been made instruments to the pride, avarice, or ambition of ill-designing men, by extinguishing brotherly love, have been the cause of infinite calamities, as well as corruptions of faith and manners, in the Christian world.

The last legacy of Christ was peace and mutual love; but then he foretold, that he came to send a sword upon the earth: the primitive Christians accepted the legacy, and their successors down to the present age have been largely fulfilling his prophecy. But whatever the practice of mankind hath been, or still continues, there is no duty more incumbent upon those who profess the gospel, than that of brotherly love; which, whoever could restore in any degree among men, would be an instrument of more good to human society, than ever was, or will be, done by all the statesmen and politicians in the world.

It is upon this subject of brotherly love, that I intend to discourse at present, and the method I observe shall be as follows:

I. *First*, I will enquire into the causes of this great want of brotherly love among us.

II. *Secondly*, I will lay open the sad effects and consequences, which our animosities and mutual hatred have produced.

III. *Lastly*, I will use some motives and exhortations, that may persuade you to embrace brotherly love, and continue in it.

I. *First*, I shall enquire into the causes of this great want of brotherly love among us.

This nation of ours hath, for an hundred years past, been infested by two enemies, the papists and fanatics, who, each in their turns, filled it with blood and slaughter, and, for a time, destroyed both the church and government. The memory of these events hath put all true protestants equally upon their guard against both these adversaries, who, by consequence, do equally hate us. The fanatics revile us, as too nearly approaching to popery; and the papists condemn us, as bordering too much on fanaticism. The papists, God be praised, are, by the wisdom of our laws, put out of all visible possibility of hurting us; besides, their religion is so generally abhorred, that they have no advocates or abettors among protestants to assist them. But the fanatics are to be considered in another light; they have had, of late years, the power, the luck, or the cunning, to divide us among ourselves; they have endeavoured to represent all those, who have been so bold as to oppose their errors and designs, under the character of persons disaffected to the government; and they have so far succeeded, that now-a-days, if a clergyman happens to preach with any zeal and vehemence against the sin or danger of schism, there will not want too many, in his congregation, ready enough to censure him as hot and high-flying, an inflamer of men's minds, an enemy to moderation, and disloyal to his prince. This hath produced a formed and settled division between those who profess the same doctrine and discipline, while they who call themselves moderate are forced to widen their bottom, by sacrificing their principles and their brethren to the encroachments and insolence of dissenters, who are therefore answerable, as a principle cause of all that hatred and animosity now reigning among us.

Another cause of the great want of brotherly love is the weakness and folly of too many among you of the lower sort, who are made the tools and instruments of your betters to work their designs, wherein you have no concern. Your numbers make you of use, and cunning men take the advantage, by putting words into your mouths, which you do not understand; then they fix good or ill characters to those words, as it best serves their purposes: and thus you are taught to love or hate, you know not what or why; you often suspect your best friends and nearest neighbours, even your teacher himself, without any reason, if your leaders once taught you to call him by a name, which they tell you signifieth some very bad thing.

A third cause of our great want of brotherly love seemeth to be, that this duty is not so often insisted on from the pulpit, as it ought to be in such times as these; on the contrary, it is to be doubted, whether doctrines are not sometimes delivered by an ungoverned zeal, a desire to be distinguished, or a view of interest, which produce quite different effects; when, upon occasions set apart to return thanks to God for some public blessing, the time is employed in stirring up one part of the congregation against the other, by representations of things and persons, which God, in his mercy, forgive those who are guilty of.

The last cause I shall mention of the want of brotherly love is, that unhappy disposition towards politics among the trading people, which hath been industriously instilled into them. In former times, the middle and lower sort of mankind seldom gained or lost by the factions of the kingdom, and therefore were little concerned in them, further than as matter of talk and amusement; but now the meanest dealer will expect to turn the penny by the merits of his party. He can represent his neighbour as a man of dangerous principles, can bring a railing accusation against him, perhaps a criminal one, and so rob him of his livelihood, and find his own account by that much more than if he had disparaged his neighbour's goods, or defamed him as a cheat. For so it happens, that, instead of enquiring into the skill or honesty of those kind of people, the manner is now to enquire into their party, and to reject or encourage them accordingly; which proceeding hath made our people, in general, such able politicians, that all the artifice, flattery, dissimulation, diligence, and dexterity in undermining each other, which the satirical wit of men hath charged upon courts; together with all the rage and violence, cruelty and injustice, which have been ever imputed to public assemblies; are with us (so polite are we grown) to be seen among our meanest traders and artificers in the greatest perfection. All which, as it may be matter of some humiliation to the wise and mighty of this world, so the effects thereof may, perhaps, in time, prove very different from what, I hope in charity, were ever foreseen or intended.

II. I will therefore now, in the second place, lay open some of the sad effects and consequences, which our animosities and mutual hatred have produced.

And the first ill consequence is, that our want of brotherly love hath almost driven out all sense of religion from among us, which cannot well be otherwise: for since our Saviour laid so much weight upon his disciples loving one another, that he gave it among his last instructions; and since the primitive Christians are allowed to have chiefly propagated the faith by their strict observance of that instruction, it must follow that, in proportion as brotherly love declineth, Christianity will do so too. The little religion there is in the world, hath been observed to reside chiefly among the middle and lower sort of people, who are neither tempted to pride and luxury by great riches, nor to desperate courses by extreme poverty: and truly I, upon that account, have thought it a happiness, that those who are under my immediate care are generally of that condition; but where party hath once made entrance, with all its consequences of hatred, envy, partiality and virulence, religion cannot long keep its hold in any state or degree of life whatsoever. For, if the great men of the world have been censured in all ages for mingling too little religion with their politics, what a havoc of principles must they needs make in unlearned and irregular heads; of which indeed the effects are already too visible and melancholy all over the kingdom!

Another ill consequence from our want of brotherly love is, that it increaseth the insolence of the fanatics; and this partly ariseth from a mistaken meaning of the word *moderation*; a word which hath been much abused, and banded about for several years past. There are too many people indifferent enough to all religion; there are many others, who dislike the clergy, and would have them live in poverty and dependence; both these sorts are much commended by the fanatics for moderate men, ready to put an end to our divisions, and to make a general union among protestants. Many ignorant well-meaning people are deceived by these appearances, strengthened with great pretences to loyalty: and these occasions the fanatics lay hold on, to revile the doctrine and discipline of the church, and even insult and oppress the clergy, wherever their numbers or favourers will bear them out; insomuch, that one wilful refractory fanatic hath been able to disturb a whole parish for many years together. But the most moderate and favoured divines dare not own, that the word *moderation*, with respect to the dissenters, can be at all applied to their religion, but is purely personal or prudential. No good man repineth at the liberty of conscience they enjoy; and, perhaps, a very moderate divine may think better of their loyalty than others do; or, to speak after the manner of men, may think it necessary, that all protestants should be united against the common enemy; or out of discretion, or other reasons best known to himself, be tender of mentioning them at all. But still the errors of the dissenters are all fixed and determined, and must, upon demand, be acknowledged by all the divines of our church, whether they be called, in party phrase, high or low, moderate or violent. And further, I believe it would be hard to find many moderate divines, who, if their opinion were asked whether dissenters should be trusted with power, could, according to their consciences, answer to the affirmative; from whence it is plain, that all the stir, which the fanatics have made with this word *moderation*, was only meant to increase our divisions, and widen them so far as to make room for themselves to get in between. And this is the only scheme they ever had (except that of destroying root and branch) for the uniting of protestants, they so much talk of.

I shall mention but one ill consequence more, which attends our want of brotherly love; that it hath put an end to all hospitality and friendship, all good correspondence and commerce between mankind. There are indeed such things as leagues and confederacies among those of the same party; but surely God never intended, that men should be so limited in the choice of their friends: however, so it is in town and country, in every parish and street; the pastor is divided from his flock, the father from his son, and the house often divided against itself. Men's very natures are soured, and their passions enflamed, when they meet in party clubs, and spend their time in nothing else but railing at the opposite side; thus every man alive among us is encompassed with a million of enemies of his own country, among which his oldest acquaintance and friends, and kindred themselves, are often of the number: neither can people of different parties mix together without constraint, suspicion and jealousy, watching every word they speak for fear of giving offence, or else falling into rudeness and reproaches, and so leaving themselves open to the malice and corruption of informers, who were never more numerous or expert in their trade. And as a further addition to this evil, those very few who, by the goodness and generosity of their nature, do in their own hearts despise this narrow principle of confining their friendship and esteem, their charity and good offices, to those of their own party, yet dare not discover their good inclinations for fear of losing their favour and interest. And others again, whom God had formed with mild and gentle dispositions, think it necessary to put a force upon their own tempers, by acting a noisy, violent, malicious part, as a means to be distinguished. Thus hath party got the better of the very genius and constitution of our people; so that whoever reads the character of the *English* in former ages, will hardly believe their present posterity to be of the same nation or climate.

III. I shall now, in the last place, make use of some motives and exhortations, that may persuade you to embrace brotherly love, and to continue in it. Let me apply myself to you of the lower sort, and desire you will consider, when any of you make use of fair and enticing words to draw in customers, whether you do it for their sakes or your own. And then for whose sakes do you think it is, that your leaders are so industrious to put into your heads all that party rage and virulence? Is it not to make you the tools and instruments, by which they work out their own designs? Has this spirit of faction been useful to any of you in your worldly concerns, except to those who have traded in whispering, backbiting, or informing, and wanted skill or honesty to thrive by fairer methods? It is no business of yours to enquire, who is at the head of armies, or of councils, unless you had power and skill to choose, neither of which is ever like to be your case; and therefore to fill your heads with fears, and hatred of persons and things, of which it is impossible you can ever make a right judgment, or to set you at variance with your neighbour, because his thoughts are not the same as yours, is not only in a very gross manner to cheat you of your time and quiet, but likewise to endanger your souls.

Secondly, In order to restore brotherly love, let me earnestly exhort you to stand firm in your religion, I mean the true religion hitherto established among us, without varying in the least either to popery on the one side, or to fanaticism on the other; and in a particular manner beware of that word, *moderation*; and believe it, that your neighbour is not immediately a villain, a papist, and a traitor, because the fanatics and their adherents will not allow him to be a moderate man. Nay, is is very probable, that your teacher himself may be a loyal, pious, and able divine, without the least grain of moderation, as the word is too frequently understood. Therefore, to set you right in this matter, I will lay before you the character of a truly moderate man, and then I will give you the description of such an one, as falsely pretendeth to that title.

A man truly moderate is steady in the doctrine and discipline of the church, but with a due Christian charity to all who dissent from it out of a principle of conscience; the freedom of which, he thinketh, ought to be fully allowed, as long as it is not abused, but never trusted with power. He is ready to defend with his life and fortune the protestant succession, and the protestant established faith, against all invaders whatsoever. He is for giving the crown its just prerogative, and the people their just liberties. He hateth no man for differing from him in political opinions; nor doth he think it a maxim infallible, that virtue should always attend upon favour, and vice upon disgrace. These are some few lineaments in the character of a truly moderate man: let us now compare it with the description of one, who usually passeth under that title.

A moderate man, in the new meaning of the word, is one, to whom all religion is indifferent; who, although he denominates himself of the church, regardeth it no more than a conventicle. He perpetually raileth at the body of the clergy, with exceptions only to a very few, who, he hopeth, and probably upon false grounds, are as ready to betray their rights and properties as himself. He thinks the power of the people can never be too great, nor that of the prince too little; and yet this very notion he publisheth, as his best argument to prove him a most loyal subject. Every opinion in government, that differeth in the least from his, tends directly to popery, slavery, and rebellion. Whoever lieth under the frown of power, can, in his judgment, neither have common sense, common honesty, nor religion. Lastly, his devotion consisteth in drinking gibbets, confusion, and damnation; in profanely idolizing the memory of one dead prince, and ungratefully trampling upon the ashes of another.

By these marks you will easily distinguish a truly moderate man from those, who are commonly, but very falsely, so called; and while persons thus qualified are so numerous and so noisy, so full of zeal and industry to gain proselytes and spread their opinions among the people, it cannot be wondered that there should be so little brotherly love left among us.

Lastly, It would probably contribute to restore some degree of brotherly love, if we would but consider, that the matter of those disputes, which enflame us to this degree, doth not, in its own nature, at all concern the generality of mankind. Indeed as to those, who have been great gainers or losers by the changes of the world, the case is different; and to preach moderation to the first, and patience to the last, would perhaps be to little purpose: but what is that to the bulk of the people, who are not properly concerned in the quarrel, although evil instruments have drawn them into it? for, if the reasonable men on both sides were to confer opinions, they would find neither religion, loyalty, nor interest, are at all affected in this dispute. Not religion, because the members of the church, on both sides, profess to agree in every article: not loyalty to our prince, which is pretended to by one party as much as the other, and therefore can be no subject for debate: nor interest, for trade and industry lie open to all; and, what is further, concern only those who have expectations from the public: so that the body of the people, if they knew their own good, might yet live amicably together, and leave their betters to quarrel among themselves, who might also probably soon come to a better temper, if they were less seconded and supported by the poor deluded multitude.

I have now done with my text, which I confess to have treated in a manner more suited to the present times, than to the nature of the subject in general. That I have not been more particular in explaining the several parts and properties of this great duty of brotherly love, the apostle to the *Thessalonians* will plead my excuse. 'Touching brotherly love,' saith he, 'ye need not that I write unto you, for ye yourselves are taught of God to love one another.' So that nothing remains to add, but our prayers to God, that he would please to restore and continue this great duty of brotherly love or charity among us, the very bond of peace and of all virtues.

DOING GOOD
Galatians 6:10.
As we have therefore opportunity, let us do Good unto all men.

IN WRITING this sermon, in 1724, Swift was directing his mind—and those of his congregation—to a particular manner of doing good. It was the time of the controversy about Wood's half-pence. William Wood, an English manufacturer, had been given a patent to put his coins into circulation in circumstances which gave reason to suppose that he would make a large profit at the expense of the inhabitants of Ireland. There had been no consultation with the Parliament in Dublin. Swift, with an acerbity which sprang from his recollection of former times, approached Lord Carteret, who was to be the new Lord Lieutenant. 'I have long been out of the world, but have not forgotten what used to pass among those I lived with, while I was in it.' But his main contribution to the battle was to write, under the name of M. B. Drapier, the *Letters*, which were printed at the cheapest rate and circulated among the shopkeepers, tradesmen, farmers and 'Common-People of Ireland' to rouse them to the danger of the project. The *Letters* spread like wild-fire. As the argument developed, it was not only Wood's patent which was in question but the principle that Ireland was in some sort a dependent kingdom. The Drapier denied that there was any such thing. 'I declare, next under God, I *depend* only on the King my Sovereign,' he said, 'and on the Laws of my own Country. And I am so far from *depending* upon the People of *England*, that, if they should ever *rebel* against my Sovereign, (which GOD forbid) I would be ready at the first Command from his Majesty to take Arms against them.' The excuses and recriminations of Wood and his associates are 'no more than the last Howls of a Dog dissected alive.' The language of the sermon on *Doing Good* has not quite this brutality, but it is outspoken enough. Swift speaks of 'an open attempt' 'to make a great kingdom one large poor-house'. He knew that some of his congregation might think this way of talking 'not so proper from the pulpit'. But 'to turn our cities and churches into ruins, to make the country a desert for wild beasts and robbers, to destroy all arts and sciences, all trades and manufacture, and the very tillage of the ground, only to enrich one obscure, ill-designing projector, and his followers'! It was 'time for the pastor to cry out', and Swift cried.

The affair of Wood's half-pence was only an episode in Swift's campaign against the exploitation of Ireland. There is a brilliant sheaf of pamphlets, spread over a number of years. It was fortune—ill fortune, he would have said—which kept Swift penned in the country, but it gave him a subject which evoked his most sombre wit. It was not only in the sermon on *Doing Good* that he took the subject into the pulpit. There is a withering sermon on the *Causes of the Wretched Condition of Ireland*, preached on a text from Psalm 144: 'That there be no Complaining in our Streets. Happy is the People that is in such a case.' He thought it his duty in his place in the Church to denounce the situation of a country which was 'capable of producing all Things necessary' but in which, none the less, there was 'the heaviest Load of Misery and Want, our Streets crowded with Beggars, so many of our lower Sort of Tradesmen, Labourers and Artificers, not able to find Clothes and Food for their Families.' His personal disappointment had brought him face to face with the realities about which politicians, including those with whom he had formerly been familiar, care so little, in comparison with the fantasies of their own careers.

NATURE DIRECTS every one of us, and God permits us, to consult our own private good before the private good of any other person whatsoever. We are, indeed, commanded to love our neighbour as ourselves, but not as well as ourselves. The love we have for ourselves is to be the pattern of that love we ought to have towards our neighbour: but, as the copy doth not equal the original, so my neighbour cannot think it hard, if I prefer myself, who am the original, before him, who is only the copy. Thus, if any matter equally concern the life, the reputation, the profit of my neighbour, and my own; the law of nature, which is the law of God, obligeth me to take care of myself first, and afterwards of him. And this I need not be at much pains in persuading you to; for the want of self-love, with regard to things of this world, is not among the faults of mankind. But then, on the other side, if, by a small hurt and loss to myself, I can procure a great good to my neighbour, in that case his interest is to be preferred. For example, if I can be sure of saving his life, without great danger to my own; if I can preserve him from being undone without ruining myself, or recover his reputation without blasting mine; all this I am obliged to do: and, if I sincerely perform it, I do then obey the command of God, in loving my neighbour as myself.

But, beside this love we owe to every man in his particular capacity under the title of our neighbour, there is yet a duty of a more large extensive nature incumbent on us; which is, our love to our neighbour in his public capacity, as he is a member of that great body the common-wealth, under the same government with ourselves; and this is usually called love of the public, and is a duty to which we are more strictly obliged than even that of loving ourselves; because therein ourselves are also contained, as well as all our neighbours, in one great body. This love of the public, or of the commonwealth, or love of our country, was in ancient times properly known by the name of *Virtue*, because it was the greatest of all virtues, and was supposed to contain all virtues in it: and many great examples of this virtue are left to us on record, scarcely to be believed, or even conceived, in such a base, corrupted, wicked age as this we live in. In those times, it was common for men to sacrifice their lives for the good of their country, although they had neither hope nor belief of future rewards; whereas, in our days, very few make the least scruple of sacrificing a whole nation, as well as their own souls, for a little present gain; which often hath been known to end in their own ruin in this world, as it certainly must in that to come.

Have we not seen men, for the sake of some petty employment, give up the very natural rights and liberties of their country and of mankind, in the ruin of which themselves must at last be involved? Are not these corruptions gotten among the meanest of our people, who, for a piece of money, will give their votes at a venture, for the disposal of their own lives and fortunes, without considering whether it be to those who are most likely to betray or defend them?

But, if I were to produce only one instance of a hundred wherein we fail in this duty of loving our country, it would be an endless labour; and therefore I shall not attempt it.

But here I would not be misunderstood: by the love of our country, I do not mean loyalty to our king, for that is a duty of another nature; and a man may be very loyal, in the common sense of the word, without one grain of public good at his heart. Witness this very kingdom we live in. I verily believe, that, since the beginning of the world, no nation upon earth ever showed (all circumstances considered) such high constant marks of loyalty, in all their actions and behaviour, as we have done: and, at the same time, no people ever appeared more utterly void of what is called a Public Spirit. When I say the people, I mean the bulk or mass of the people, for I have nothing to do with those in power.

Therefore I shall think my time not ill spent, if I can persuade most or all of you who hear me, to show the love you have for your country, by endeavouring, in your several stations, to do all the public good you are able. For I am certainly persuaded, that all our misfortunes arise from no other original cause than that general disregard among us to the public welfare.

I therefore undertake to show you three things.

First, That there are few people so weak or mean, who have it not sometimes in their power to be useful to the public.

Secondly, That it is often in the power of the meanest among mankind to do mischief to the public.

And *lastly*, That all wilful injuries done to the public are very great and aggravated sins in the sight of God.

First, There are few people so weak or mean, who have it not sometimes in their power to be useful to the public.

Solomon tells us of a poor wise man, who saved a city by his counsel. It hath often happened that a private soldier, by some unexpected brave attempt, hath been instrumental in obtaining a great victory. How many obscure men have been authors of very useful inventions, whereof the world now reaps the benefit? The very example of honesty and industry in a poor tradesman will sometimes spread through a neighbourhood, when others see how successful he is; and thus so many useful members are gained, for which the whole body of the public is the better. Whoever is blessed with a true public spirit, God will certainly put it into his way to make use of that blessing, for the ends it was given him, by some means or other: and therefore it hath been observed, in most ages, that the greatest actions, for the benefit of the commonwealth, have been performed by the wisdom or courage, the contrivance or industry, of particular men, and not of numbers; and that the safety of a kingdom hath often been owing to those hands from whence it was least expected.

But, *secondly*, it is often in the power of the meanest among mankind to do mischief to the public: and hence arise most of those miseries with which the states and kingdoms of the earth are infested. How many great princes have been murdered by the meanest ruffians! The weakest hand can open a floodgate to drown a country, which a thousand of the strongest cannot stop. Those who have thrown off all regard for public good, will often have it in their way to do public evil, and will not fail to exercise that power whenever they can. The greatest blow given of late to this kingdom, was by the dishonesty of a few manufacturers; who, by imposing bad ware at foreign markets, in almost the only traffic permitted to us, did half ruin that trade; by which this poor unhappy kingdom now suffers in the midst of sufferings. I speak not here of persons in high stations, who ought to be free from all reflection, and are supposed always to intend the welfare of the community: but we now find, by experience, that the meanest instrument may, by the concurrence of accidents, have it in his power to bring a whole kingdom to the very brink of destruction, and is at this present endeavouring to finish his work; and hath agents among ourselves, who are contented to see their own country undone, to be small sharers in that iniquitous gain, which at last must end in their own ruin as well as ours. I confess, it was chiefly the consideration of that great danger we are in, which engaged me to discourse to you on this subject, to exhort you to a love of your country, and a public spirit, when all you have is at stake; to prefer the interest of your prince and your fellow subjects before that of one destructive impostor, and a few of his adherents.

Perhaps it may be thought by some, that this way of discoursing is not so proper from the pulpit. But surely, when an open attempt is made, and far carried on, to make a great kingdom one large poor-house, to deprive us of all means to exercise hospitality or charity, to turn our cities and churches into ruins, to make the country a desert for wild beasts and robbers, to destroy all arts and sciences, all trades and manufactures, and the very tillage of the ground, only to enrich one obscure ill-designing projector and his followers; it is time for the pastor to cry out that the wolf is getting into his flock, to warn them to stand together, and all to consult the common safety. And God be praised for his infinite goodness in raising such a spirit of union among us, at least in this point, in the midst of all our former divisions; which union, if it continue, will, in all probability, defeat the pernicious design of this pestilent enemy to the nation.

But, from hence, it clearly follows how necessary the love of our country, or a public spirit, is in every particular man, since the wicked have so many opportunities of doing public mischief. Every man is upon his own guard for his private advantage; but, where the public is concerned, he is apt to be negligent, considering himself only as one among two or three millions, among whom the loss is equally shared, and thus, he thinks, he can be no great sufferer. Meanwhile the trader, the farmer, and the shop-keeper, complain of the hardness and deadness of the times, and wonder whence it comes; while it is, in a great measure, owing to their own folly, for want of that love of their country, and public spirit and firm union among themselves, which are so necessary to the prosperity of every nation.

Another method, by which the meanest wicked man may have it in his power to injure the public, is false accusation, whereof this kingdom hath afforded too many examples: neither is it long since no man, whose opinions were thought to differ from those in fashion, could safely converse beyond his nearest friends, for fear of being sworn against, as a traitor, by those who made a traffic of perjury and subornation; by which the very peace of the nation was disturbed, and men fled from each other as they would from a lion or a bear got loose. And it is very remarkable, that the pernicious project now in hand, to reduce us to beggary, was forwarded by one of these false accusers, who had been convicted of endeavouring, by perjury and subornation, to take away the lives of several innocent persons here among us: and, indeed, there could not be a more proper instrument for such a work.

Another method by which the meanest people may do injury to the public, is the spreading of lies and false rumours, thus raising a distrust among the people of a nation, causing them to mistake their true interest, and their enemies for their friends: and this hath been likewise too successful a practice among us, where we have known the whole kingdom misled by the grossest lies, raised upon occasion to serve some particular turn. As it hath also happened in the case I lately mentioned, where one obscure man, by representing our wants where they were least and concealing them where they were greatest, had almost succeeded in a project of utterly ruining this whole kingdom; and may still succeed, if God doth not continue that public spirit, which he hath almost miraculously kindled in us upon this occasion.

Thus we see the public is many times, as it were, at the mercy of the meanest instrument, who can be wicked enough to watch opportunities of doing it mischief, upon the principles of avarice or malice; which, I am afraid, are deeply rooted in too many breasts, and against which there can be no defence, but a firm resolution in all honest men, to be closely united and active in showing their love to their country, by preferring the public interest to their present private advantage. If a passenger, in a great storm at sea, should hide his goods that they might not be thrown overboard to lighten the ship, what would be the consequence? The ship is cast away, and he loses his life and goods together.

We have heard of men, who, through greediness of gain, have brought infected goods into a nation, which bred a plague, whereof the owners and their families perished first. Let those among us consider this and tremble, whose houses are privately stored with those materials of beggary and desolation, lately brought over to be scattered like a pestilence among their countrymen, which may probably first seize upon themselves and their families, until their houses shall be made a dunghill.

I shall mention one practice more, by which the meanest instruments often succeed in doing public mischief; and this is by deceiving us with plausible arguments, to make us believe that the most ruinous project they can offer is intended for our good, as it happened in the case so often mentioned. For the poor ignorant people, allured by the appearing convenience in their small dealings, did not discover the serpent in the brass, but were ready, like the *Israelites*, to offer incense to it; neither could the wisdom of the nation convince them, until some, of good intentions, made the cheat so plain to their sight, that those who run may read. And thus the design was to treat us, in every point, as the *Philistines* treated *Samson* (I mean when he was betrayed by *Delilah*), first to put out our eyes, and then bind us with fetters of brass.

I proceed to the last thing I proposed, which was, to show you that all wilful injuries done to the public, are very great and aggravated sins in the sight of God.

First, It is apparent from Scripture, and most agreeable to reason, that the safety and welfare of nations are under the most peculiar care of God's providence. Thus he promised *Abraham* to save *Sodom*, if only ten righteous men could be found in it. Thus the reason which God gave to *Jonah* for not destroying *Nineveh* was, because there were six score thousand men in that city.

All government is from God, who is the God of order; and therefore, whoever attempts to breed confusion or disturbance among a people, doth his utmost to take the government of the world out of God's hands, and to put it into the hands of the devil, who is the author of confusion. By which it is plain, that no crime, how heinous soever, committed against particular persons, can equal the guilt of him who does injury to the public.

Secondly, All offenders against their country lie under this grievous difficulty, that it is impossible to obtain a pardon, or make restitution. The bulk of mankind are very quick at resenting injuries, and very slow in forgiving them: and how shall one man be able to obtain the pardon of millions, or repair the injuries he hath done to millions? how shall those, who, by a most destructive fraud, got the whole wealth of our neighbouring kingdom into their hands, be ever able to make a recompense? how will the authors and promoters of that villainous project, for the ruin of this poor country, be able to account with us for the injuries they have already done, although they should no farther succeed? The deplorable case of such wretches must entirely be left to the unfathomable mercies of God: for those who know the least in religion are not ignorant that, without our utmost endeavours to make restitution to the person injured, and to obtain his pardon, added to a sincere repentance, there is no hope of salvation given in the Gospel.

Lastly, All offences against our own country have this aggravation, that they are ungrateful and unnatural. It is to our country we owe those laws, which protect us in our lives, our liberties, our properties, and our religion. Our country produced us into the world, and continues to nourish us, so that it is usually called our mother; and there have been examples of great magistrates, who have put their own children to death for endeavouring to betray their country, as if they had attempted the life of their natural parent.

Thus I have briefly shown you how terrible a sin it is to be an enemy to our country, in order to incite you to the contrary virtue, which at this juncture is so highly necessary, when every man's endeavour will be of use. We have hitherto been just able to support ourselves under many hardships; but now the axe is laid to the root of the tree, and nothing but a firm union among us can prevent our utter undoing. This we are obliged to, in duty to our gracious king, as well as to ourselves. Let us therefore preserve that public spirit, which God hath raised in us for our own temporal interest. For, if this wicked project should succeed, which it cannot do but by our own folly; if we sell ourselves for nought, the merchant, the shop-keeper, the artificer, must fly to the desert with their miserable families, there to starve or live upon rapine, or at least exchange their country for one more hospitable than that where they were born.

Thus much I thought it my duty to say to you, who are under my care, to warn you against those temporal evils, which may draw the worst of spiritual evils after them; such as heart-burnings, murmurings, discontents, and all manner of wickedness which a desperate condition of life may tempt men to.

I am sensible that what I have now said will not go very far, being confined to this assembly; but I hope it may stir up others of my brethren to exhort their several congregations, after a more effectual manner, to show their love for their country on this important occasion. And this, I am sure, cannot be called meddling in affairs of state.

I pray God protect his most gracious majesty, and this kingdom, long under his government, and defend us from all ruinous projectors, deceivers, suborners, perjurers, false accusers, and oppressors; from the virulence of party and faction; and unite us in loyalty to our king, love to our country, and charity to each other. And this we beg, for *Jesus Christ* his sake: To whom, &c.

ON MUTUAL SUBJECTION
I Peter 5:5.
—*Yea, all of you be subject one to another.*

THE THIRD sermon chosen from Swift's work is less dramatic than the other two. The date of it is unknown, and it is not related to any particular set of public circumstances. Only eleven or twelve of Swift's sermons remain, altogether, so one cannot generalize as to his ordinary manner of discourse. It is to be assumed, however, that much of what he said in the pulpit dealt with the ordinary doctrinal topics, as in the sermon *On the Trinity*, a subject he says he was 'invited to' 'by the Occasion of this Season'—apparently it was for Trinity Sunday. There was no question of handling the subject abstrusely. He drove home the point that 'it would be well, if People would not lay so much Weight on their own Reason in Matters of Religion, as to think everything impossible and absurd which they cannot conceive.' There was a Mystery; arguments to show that Three cannot be One, or One Three, had nothing to do with the matter and divines who tried to answer such arguments were 'mistaken too, by answering Fools in their Folly'. Swift had no time for finicky talk, and did not want his congregation to be distracted by such matters. It would be surprising, from what we know of Swift, if this were not his ordinary pulpit manner.

The sermon *On Mutual Subjection* deals with a fundamental point of conduct. The argument is that 'there must be some kind of Subjection due from every Man to every Man, which cannot be made void by any Power, Pre-eminence, or Authority whatever.' Swift brings the point home—literally. 'For', he says, 'if our neighbour who is our inferior'—and it is no use cavilling at this expression, for it is a commonplace of eighteenth-century society—'comes to see us, we rise to receive him, we place him above us, and respect him as if he were better than ourselves; and this is thought both decent and necessary, and is usually called *good manners*.' That is how we should behave on all occasions, for every man is our neighbour, and Christ washed his disciples' feet.

THE APOSTLE having, in many parts of this epistle, given directions to Christians concerning the duty of subjection or obedience to superiors; in the several instances of the subject to the prince, the child to his parent, the servant to his master, the wife to her husband, and the younger to the elder; doth here, in the words of my text, sum up the whole by advancing a point of doctrine, which at first may appear a little extraordinary; 'Yea, all of you,' saith he, 'be subject one to another.' For it should seem, that two persons cannot properly be said to be subject to each other, and that subjection is only due from inferiors to those above them; yet St. *Paul* hath several passages to the same purpose. For he exhorts the *Romans*, 'in honour to prefer one another'; and the *Philippians*, that in 'lowliness of mind they should let each esteem other better than themselves'; and the *Ephesians*, that they should 'submit themselves one to another in the fear of the Lord.' Here we find these two great apostles recommending to all Christians this duty of mutual subjection. For we may observe by St. *Peter*, that having mentioned the several relations, which men bear to each other, as governor and subject, master and servant, and the rest which I have already repeated, he makes no exception, but sums up the whole with commanding 'all to be subject one to another.' From whence we may conclude, that this subjection, due from all men, is something more than the compliment of course, when our betters are pleased to tell us they are our humble servants, but understand us to be their slaves.

I know very well, that some of those, who explain this text, apply it to humility, to the duties of charity, to private exhortations, and to bearing with each other's infirmities; and it is probable the apostle may have had a regard to all these. But, however, many learned men agree, that there is something more understood, and so the words in their plain natural meaning must import; as you will observe yourselves, if you read them with the beginning of the verse, which is thus: 'Likewise ye younger submit yourselves unto the elder; yea, all of you be subject one to another.' So that, upon the whole there must be some kind of subjection due from every man to every man, which cannot be made void by any power, pre-eminence, or authority whatsoever. Now what sort of subjection this is, and how it ought to be paid, shall be the subject of my present discourse.

As God hath contrived all the works of nature to be useful,

and, in some manner, a support to each other, by which the whole frame of the world, under his providence, is preserved and kept up; so, among mankind, our particular stations are appointed to each of us by God Almighty, wherein we are obliged to act, as far as our power reacheth, towards the good of the whole community. And he, who doth not perform that part assigned him towards advancing the benefit of the whole in proportion to his opportunities and abilities, is not only an useless, but a very mischievous member of the public: because he takes his share of the profit, and yet leaves his share of the burden to be borne by others, which is the true principal cause of most miseries and misfortunes in life. For a wise man, who does not assist with his counsels, a great man with his protection, a rich man with his bounty and charity, and a poor man with his labour, are perfect nuisances in a commonwealth. Neither is any condition of life more honourable in the sight of God than another; otherwise he would be a respecter of persons, which he assures us he is not: for he hath proposed the same salvation to all men, and hath only placed them in different ways or stations to work it out. Princes are born with no more advantages of strength or wisdom than other men; and, by an unhappy education, are usually more defective in both than thousands of their subjects. They depend for every necessary of life upon the meanest of their people: besides, obedience and subjection were never enjoined by God, to humour the passions, lusts, and vanities of those who demand them from us; but we are commanded to obey our governors, because disobedience would breed seditions in the state. Thus servants are directed to obey their masters, children their parents, and wives their husbands; not from any respect of persons in God, but because otherwise there would be nothing but confusion in private families. This matter will be clearly explained by considering the comparison, which St. *Paul* makes between the church of Christ and the body of man: for the same resemblance will hold, not only to families and kingdoms, but to the whole corporation of mankind. 'The eye,' saith he, 'cannot say unto the hand, I have no need of thee; nor again the hand to the foot, I have no need of thee. Nay, much more, those members of the body which seem to be more feeble, are necessary: and whether one member suffer, all the members suffer with it; or one member be honoured, all the members rejoice with it.' The case is directly the same among mankind. The prince cannot say to the merchant, I have no need of thee; nor the merchant to the labourer, I have no need of thee. Nay, much more those members, which seem to be much more feeble are necessary. For the poor are generally more necessary members of the commonwealth than the rich: which clearly shows, that God never intended such possessions for the sake and service of those, to whom he lends them; but because he hath assigned every man his particular station to be useful in life, and this for the reason given by the apostle, 'that there may be no schism in the body'.

From hence may partly be gathered the nature of that subjection, which we all owe to one another. God Almighty hath been pleased to put us into an imperfect state, where we have perpetual occasion of each other's assistance. There is none so low, as not to be in a capacity of assisting the highest; nor so high, as not to want the assistance of the lowest.

It plainly appears from what hath been said, that no human creature is more worthy than another in the sight of God, farther than according to the goodness or holiness of their lives; and that power, wealth, and the like outward advantages, are so far from being the marks of God's approving or preferring those, on whom they are bestowed, that, on the contrary, he is pleased to suffer them to be almost engrossed by those, who have least title to his favour. Now, according to this equality wherein God hath placed all mankind with relation to himself, you will observe, that in all the relations between man and man, there is a mutual dependence, whereby the one cannot subsist without the other. Thus, no man can be a prince without subjects, nor a master without servants, nor a father without children. And this both explains and confirms the doctrine of the text: for where there is a mutual dependence, there must be a mutual duty, and consequently a mutual subjection. For instance, the subject must obey his prince, because God commands it, human laws require it, and the safety of the public makes it necessary (for the same reasons, we must obey all that are in authority, and submit ourselves not only to the good and gentle, but also to the froward, whether they rule according to our liking or no). On the other side, in those countries that pretend to freedom, princes are subject to those laws which their people have chosen; they are bound to protect their subjects in liberty, property, and religion, to receive their petitions, and redress their grievances: so that the best prince is, in the opinion of wise men, only the greatest servant of the nation; not only a servant to the public in general, but in some sort to every man in it. In the like manner, a servant owes obedience, and diligence, and faithfulness to his master; from whom, at the same time, he hath a just demand for protection, and maintenance, and gentle treatment. Nay, even the poor beggar hath a just demand of an alms from the rich man, who is guilty of fraud, injustice, and oppression, if he does not afford relief according to his abilities.

But this subjection we all owe one another is nowhere more necessary, than in the common conversations of life; for without it there could be no society among men. If the learned would not sometimes submit to the ignorant, the wise to the simple, the gentle to the froward, the old to the weaknesses of the young, there would be nothing but everlasting variance in the world. This our Saviour himself confirmed by his own example; for he appeared in the form of a servant, and washed his disciples' feet, adding those memorable words, 'Ye call me Lord and master, and ye say well, for so I am. If I then your Lord and master wash your feet, how much more ought ye to wash one another's feet?' Under which expression of washing the feet, is included all that subjection, assistance, love, and duty, which every good Christian ought to pay his brother, in whatever station God hath placed him. For the greatest prince, and the meanest slave, are not by infinite degrees so distant, as our Saviour and those disciples whose feet he vouchsafed to wash.

And although this doctrine of subjecting ourselves to one another may seem to grate upon the pride and vanity of mankind, and may therefore be hard to be digested by those, who value themselves upon their greatness or their wealth; yet it is really no more than what most men practise upon other occasions. For if our neighbour, who is our inferior, comes to see us, we rise to receive him, we place him above us, and respect him as if he were better than ourselves; and this is thought both decent and necessary, and is usually called *good manners*. Now, the duty required by the apostle is only, that we should enlarge our minds, and that what we thus practise in the common course of life, we should imitate in all our actions and proceedings whatsoever; since our Saviour tells us, that every man is our neighbour, and since we are so ready in the point of civility to yield to others in our own houses, where only we have any title to govern.

Having thus shown you, what sort of subjection it is, which all men owe one another, and in what manner it ought to be paid, I shall now draw some observations from what hath been said.

And *first*; A thorough practice of this duty of subjecting ourselves to the wants and infirmities of each other would utterly extinguish in us the vice of pride.

For if God has pleased to entrust me with a talent, not for my own sake, but for the service of others, and, at the same time, hath left me full of wants and necessities which others must supply; I can then have no cause to set any extraordinary value upon myself, or to despise my brother, because he hath not the same talents, which were lent to me. His being may, probably, be as useful to the public as mine, and therefore, by the rules of right reason, I am in no sort preferable to him.

Secondly; 'Tis very manifest from what has been said, that no man ought to look upon the advantages of life, such as riches honour, power, and the like, as his property, but merely as a trust, which God hath deposited with him to be employed for the use of his brethren; and God will certainly punish the breach of that trust, though the laws of man will not, or rather indeed cannot; because the trust was conferred only by God, who has not left it to any power on earth to decide infallibly, whether a man makes a good use of his talents or no, or to punish him where he fails. And therefore, God seems to have more particularly taken this matter into his own hands, and will most certainly reward or punish us in proportion to our good or ill performance in it. Now, although the advantages, which one man possesseth more than another, may, in some sense, be called his property with respect to other men, yet, with respect to God, they are, as I said, only a trust; which will plainly appear from hence; if a man does not use those advantages to the good of the public, or the benefit of his neighbour, it is certain he doth not deserve them, and, consequently, that God never intended them for a blessing to him; and, on the other side, whoever does employ his talents as he ought, will find, by his own experience, that they were chiefly sent him for the service of others; for to the service of others he will certainly employ them.

Thirdly; If we could all be brought to practise this duty of subjecting ourselves to each other, it would very much contribute to the general happiness of mankind: for this would root out envy and malice from the heart of man; because you cannot envy your neighbour's strength, if he makes use of it to defend your life, or carry your burden; you cannot envy his wisdom, if he gives you good counsel; nor his riches, if he supplies you in your wants; nor his greatness, if he employs it to your protection. The miseries of life are not properly owing to the unequal distribution of things; but God Almighty, the great King of heaven, is treated like the kings of the earth, who, although perhaps intending well themselves, have often most abominable ministers and stewards, and those generally the vilest, to whom they entrust the most talents. But here is the difference, that the princes of this world see by other men's eyes, but God sees all things; and therefore, whenever he permits his blessings to be dealt among those who are unworthy, we may certainly conclude, that he intends them only as a punishment to an evil world, as well as to the owners. It were well, if they would consider this, whose riches serve them only as a spur to avarice, or as an instrument to their lusts; whose wisdom is only of this world, to put false colours upon things, to call good evil, and evil good, against the conviction of their own consciences; and lastly, who employ their power and favour in acts of oppression or injustice, in misrepresenting persons and things, or in countenancing the wicked to the ruin of the innocent.

Fourthly; The practice of this duty of being subject to one another, would make us rest contented in the several stations of life, wherein God hath thought fit to place us; because it would in the best and easiest manner bring us back as it were to that early state of the gospel, when Christians had all things in common. For if the poor found the rich disposed to supply their wants; if the ignorant found the wise ready to instruct and direct them; or if the weak might always find protection from the mighty; they could none of them, with the least pretence of justice, lament their own condition.

From all that hath been hitherto said, it appears, that great abilities of any sort, when they are employed as God directs, do but make the owners of them greater and more painful servants to their neighbour, and the public: however, we are by no means to conclude from hence, that they are not really blessings, when they are in the hands of good men. For first, what can be a greater honour than to be chosen one of the stewards and dispensers of God's bounty to mankind? What is there, that can give a generous spirit more pleasure and complacency of mind, than to consider, that he is an instrument of doing much good? that great numbers owe to him, under God, their subsistence, their safety, their health, and the good conduct of their lives? The wickedest man upon earth takes a pleasure in doing good to those he loves; and therefore surely a good Christian, who obeys our Saviour's commands of loving all men, cannot but take delight in doing good even to his enemies. God, who gives all things to all men, can receive nothing from any; and those among men, who do the most good, and receive the fewest returns, do most resemble their Creator: for which reason St. *Paul* delivers it as a saying of our Saviour, that 'it is more blessed to give than receive.' By this rule, what must become of those things, which the world values as the greatest blessings, riches, power, and the like, when our Saviour plainly determines, that the best way to make them blessings is to part with them? Therefore, although the advantages, which one man hath over another, may be called blessings, yet they are by no means so in the sense the world usually understands. Thus, for example, great riches are no blessing in themselves; because the poor man, with the common necessaries of life, enjoys more health, and has fewer cares, without them: how then do they become blessings? No otherwise, than by being employed in feeding the hungry, clothing the naked, rewarding worthy men, and, in short, doing acts of charity and generosity. Thus likewise, power is no blessing in itself, because private men bear less envy, and trouble, and anguish without it. But when it is employed to protect the innocent, to relieve the oppressed, and to punish the oppressor, then it becomes a great blessing. And so, lastly, even great wisdom is, in the opinion of *Solomon*, not a blessing in itself: for 'in much wisdom is much sorrow'; and men of common understandings, if they serve God and mind their callings, make fewer mistakes in the conduct of life than those who have better heads. And yet wisdom is a mighty blessing, when it is applied to good purposes, to instruct the ignorant, to be a faithful counsellor either in public or private, to be a director to youth, and to many other ends needless here to mention.

To conclude: God sent us into the world to obey his commands, by doing as much good as our abilities will reach, and as little evil as our many infirmities will permit. Some he hath only trusted with one talent, some with five, and some with ten. No man is without his talent; and he that is faithful or negligent in a little, shall be rewarded or punished, as well as he that hath been so in a great deal.

Consider what hath been said, &c.

George Berkeley

BERKELEY WAS born in 1685 in County Kilkenny, where he went to school, and entered Trinity College, Dublin, at the age of fifteen. In 1707 he became a Fellow and Tutor. He held various posts in the college in the years that followed, including those of lecturer in Greek and lecturer in Hebrew. Meanwhile, as his *Commonplace Book* shows, he had from the age of twenty, or earlier, been preoccupied with certain intuitions about the nature of reality to which he gave a philosophical turn. Trinity College had changed since Swift was there twenty years before. The impact of Locke and Newton had been felt. The speculative mind of Berkeley quickly absorbed these new influences. He was, however, a man of a different kind. Although he developed the empiricism of Locke and is a link in the chain between Locke and Hume, he has affinities with the Traherne of the *Centuries of Meditations*. He was a visionary for whom the external world was important. In his speculations, he quickly went to the point of convincing himself that to exist means to perceive or to be perceived. This notion he developed in philosophical writing of elegance and luminous clarity, unlike any other in the language.

The *Essay towards a New Theory of Vision* was published in 1709; the *Treatise concerning the Principles of Human Knowledge* in 1710; and the *Three Dialogues between Hylas and Philonous*—the most seductive exposition of his philosophy—in 1713. After that there were several years during which Berkeley travelled extensively, particularly in Italy and Sicily, and spent some time intermittently in London. He was appointed Dean of Londonderry in 1724. For some years after that his main energies were devoted to a scheme for a missionary college in Bermuda—first in London, where he looked for contributions and support, and 1728-31 in America. It was a fundamental part of his scheme that 'the children of savage Americans, brought up in such a Seminary, and well instructed in religion and learning, might make the ablest and properest missionaries for spreading the gospel among their countrymen'. There is more than a touch of Berkeley's vivid delight in the external world in his recommendation of the islands: 'no part of the world enjoys a purer air, or a more temperate climate, the great ocean which environs them at once moderating the heat of the south winds, and the severity of the north-west.' The project failed, through lack of support from the home government. After a year or two back in London, Berkeley was appointed Bishop of Cloyne, and spent the years 1734-52 there, in intelligent and charitable care of his diocese. To this period belongs *The Querist*, a fascinating series of economic questions, the outcome of Berkeley's concern for the condition of Ireland and in particular for the poor of his secluded diocese. To this period also belongs the development of his interest in the merits of tar-water as a cure for and preventive against all manner of diseases. He not only used it himself and recommended it in the most practical manner to the people of his diocese, but made it the subject of a chain of reflections and inquiries, *Siris*, a work of Platonic and Neo-Platonic character. Berkeley retired in 1752 and spent the last year of his life in Oxford.

Swift said that Berkeley was 'an absolute Philosopher with respect to Money Titles or Power'—meaning that he cared nothing for them—and there is a debonair unworldliness about him which would itself be very engaging, even if he did not make so many other claims on our admiration. He lived simply and when he says, in the course of his reflections on the South Sea Bubble, 'Frugality of manners is the nourishment and strength of the body politic', he is saying what he means. 'The same atheistical narrow spirit', he goes on, 'centering all our cares upon private interest, and contracting all our hopes within the enjoyment of this private life, equally produce a neglect of what we owe to God and our country.' Berkeley is deeply aware of the Erastianism of his century, and with a single puff blows it away.

A SERMON PREACHED BEFORE THE INCORPORATED SOCIETY FOR THE PROPAGATION OF THE GOSPEL IN FOREIGN PARTS

John 17: 3.
This is Life Eternal, that they may know Thee the only true God, and Jesus Christ whom Thou hast sent.

THE S. P. G. was founded in 1701, three years after the S. P. C. K., the missionary work of which it was designed to assist. The following sermon was preached by Berkeley at the Society's anniversary meeting in 1732. Berkeley had just returned from America, which no doubt accounts for the choice of him as preacher on that occasion.

Berkeley's opening remarks are about the essential duty of 'bringing other men to the Knowledge of the only true God, and of Jesus Christ'. There is nothing speculative or scholastic about this knowledge. 'To know God as we ought, we must love him; and love him so as withal to love our brethren, his creatures and his children.' Yet this knowledge, so practical in its manifestations, is the same with that which Berkeley's philosophical speculations were designed to promote. The *Three Dialogues* were specifically written 'in opposition to sceptics and atheists', and *Alciphron, or the Minute Philosopher*, which appeared in the same year as this sermon, contained 'an apology for the Christian Religion, against those who are called Free-thinkers'. Berkeley's religion and his philosophy are inseparable.

Much in this sermon comes directly out of Berkeley's recent experience of what went on in the colonies. He has no illusions about the state of affairs at home where 'it is surmised the Christian religion is in a declining state', and he fully understands that 'it is hardly to be expected that, so long as Infidelity prevails at home', things should be different in the colonies. Still this does not lead him to be complacent about colonists who 'rival some well-bred people of other countries in a thorough indifference for all that is sacred'. He notes the 'old antipathy' for the Indians, the 'irrational contempt of the blacks, as creatures of another species, who had no right to be instructed or admitted to the sacraments'. All this is far from Berkeley's own temper. 'The likeliest step towards converting the heathen would be to begin with the English planters.' And the likeliest way of making progress with the planters, he concludes, would be to start at home; though with the practical sense which is never far from him he makes it clear that foreign attempts should not 'wait for domestic success'.

THAT HUMAN kind were not designed merely to sojourn a few days upon this earth: that a being of such excellence as the soul of man, so capable of a nobler life, and having such a high sense of things moral and intellectual, was not created in the sole view of being imprisoned in an earthly tabernacle, and partaking a few pains and pleasures which chequer this mortal life, without aspiring to anything either above or beyond it, is a fundamental doctrine as well of natural religion as of the christian. It comes at once recommended by the authority of philosophers and evangelists. And that there actually is in the mind of man a strong instinct and desire, an appetite and tendency towards another and a better state, incomparably superior to the present, both in point of happiness and duration, is no more than everyone's experience and inward feeling may inform him. The satiety and disrelish attending sensual enjoyments, the relish for things of a more pure and spiritual kind, the restless motion of the mind, from one terrene object or pursuit to another, and often a flight or endeavour above them all towards something unknown, and perfective of its nature, are so many signs and tokens of this better state, which in the style of the gospel is termed life eternal.

And as this is the greatest good that can befall us, the very end of our being, and that alone which can crown and satisfy our wishes, and without which we shall be ever restless and uneasy; so every man, who knows and acts up to his true interest, must make it his principal care and study to obtain it: and in order to this, he must endeavour to live suitably to his calling, and of consequence endeavour to make others obtain it too. For how can a christian show himself worthy of his calling, otherwise than by performing the duties of it? And what christian duty is more essentially so, than that of charity? And what object can be found upon earth more deserving our charity, than the souls of men? Or, how is it possible for the most beneficent spirit to do them better service, than by promoting their best and most lasting interest, that is, by putting them in the way that leads to eternal life.

What this eternal life was, or how to come at it, were points unknown to the heathen world. It must be owned, the wise men of old, who followed the light of nature, saw even by that light, that the soul of man was debased, and borne downwards, contrary to its natural bent, by carnal and terrene objects; and that, on the other hand, it was exalted, purged, and in some sort assimilated to the Deity, by the contemplation of truth and practice of virtue. Thus much in general they saw or surmised. But then about the way and means to know the one, or perform the other, they were much at a loss. They were not agreed concerning the true end of mankind; which, as they saw, was mistaken in the vulgar pursuits of men; so they found it much more easy to confute the errors of others, than to ascertain the truth themselves. Hence so many divisions and disputes about a point which it most imported them to know, insomuch as it was to give the bias to human life, and govern the whole tenor of their actions and conduct.

But when life and immortality were brought to light by the gospel, there could remain no dispute about the chief end and felicity of man, no more than there could about the means of obtaining it, after the express declaration of our blessed Lord in the words of my text; 'this is life eternal, that they may know thee, the only true God, and Jesus Christ whom thou hast sent.' For the right understanding of which words we must observe, that by the knowledge of God, is not meant a barren speculation, either of philosophers or scholastic divines, nor any notional tenets fitted to produce disputes and dissentions among men; but, on the contrary, an holy practical knowledge, which is the source, the root, or principle of peace and union, of faith, hope, charity, and universal obedience. A man may frame the most accurate notions, and in one sense attain the exactest knowledge of God and Christ that human faculties can reach, and yet, notwithstanding all this, be far from knowing them in that saving sense. For St. *John* tells us, that 'whosoever sinneth, hath not seen Christ, nor known him.' And again, 'he that loveth not, knoweth not God.' To know God as we ought, we must love him; and love him so as withal to love our brethren, his creatures and his children. I say, that knowledge of God and Christ, which is life eternal, implies universal charity, with all the duties ingrafted thereon, or ensuing from thence, that is to say, the love of God and man. And our Lord expressly saith, 'he that hath my commandments, and keepeth them, he it is that loveth me.' From all which it is evident, that this saving knowledge of God is inseparable from the knowledge and practice of his will; the explicit declaration whereof, and of the means to perform it, are contained in the gospel, that divine instrument of grace and mercy to the sons of men. The metaphysical knowledge of God, considered in his absolute nature or essence, is one thing, and to know him as he stands related to us as Creator, Redeemer, and Sanctifier, is another. The former kind of knowledge (whatever it amounts to) hath been, and may be, in Gentiles as well as Christians, but not the latter, which is life eternal.

From what has been said, it is a plain consequence, that whoever is a sincere christian, cannot be indifferent about bringing over other men to the knowledge of God and Christ; but that every one of us, who hath any claim to that title, is indispensably obliged in duty to God, and in charity to his neighbour, to desire and promote, so far as there is opportunity, the conversion of heathens and infidels, that so they may become partakers of life and immortality. For, 'this is life eternal, to know thee the only true God, and Jesus Christ whom thou hast sent.'

In my present discourse upon which words; I shall,

First, consider in general, the obligation that christians lie under, of bringing other men to the knowledge of the only true God, and of Jesus Christ. And,

Secondly, I shall consider it in reference to this laudable society, instituted for the propagation of the gospel. And under each head; I propose to obviate such difficulties as may seem to retard, and intermix such remarks as shall appear proper to forward so good a work.

Now although it be very evident, that we can really have neither a just zeal for the glory of God, nor a beneficent love of man, without wishing and endeavouring, as occasion serves, to spread the glad tidings of salvation, and bring those who are benighted in the shadow of death, to life eternal, by the knowledge of the only true God, and of Jesus Christ whom he hath sent. Yet this duty, plain and undoubted as it seems, happens to be too often overlooked, even by those whose attention to other points would make one think their neglect of this, not an effect of lukewarm indifference, so much as of certain mistaken notions and suppositions. Two principal considerations occur, which, in this particular, seem to have slackened the industry of some, otherwise zealous and serious christians.

One I apprehend to be this, that it is surmised, the christian religion is in a declining state, which by many symptoms seems likely to end either in popery, or a general infidelity. And that of course a prudent person has nothing to do, but to make sure of his own salvation, and to acquiesce in the general tendency of things, without being at any fruitless pains to oppose what cannot be prevented, to steer against the stream, or resist a torrent, which as it flows, gathers strength and rapidity, and in the end, will be sure to overflow, and carry all before it. When a man of a desponding and foreboding spirit hath been led, by his observation of the ways of the world, and the prevailing humour of our times, to think after this manner, he will be inclined to strengthen this his preconceived opinion, as is usual in other the like cases, by misapplication of holy scripture: for instance, by those words of our blessed Saviour, 'when the Son of man cometh, shall he find faith on the earth?' which have been applied to this very purpose, as importing that before the final judgment, christian faith should be extinguished upon earth; although these words do, from the context, seem plainly to refer to the destruction of *Jerusalem*, and the obstinate blindness of the *Jews*, who even then when they felt the hand of God, should not acknowledge it, or believe the *Roman* army to be the instrument of divine vengeance, in the day of their visitation, by him whom they had injuriously treated, rejected, and put to death.

But, granting the former sense might be supported by no absurd hypothesis, or no improbable guess; yet shall the endeavours of christian men for propagating the gospel of Christ be forestalled by any suppositions or conjectures whatsoever? Admitting, I say, those words regard the future advent of Jesus Christ, yet can anyone tell how near or how far off that advent may be? Are not the times and seasons foreknown only to God? And shall we neglect a certain duty today, upon an uncertain surmise of what is to come hereafter? This way of thinking might furnish as strong reasons against preaching at home, as abroad, within, as without the pale of the church. It would be as specious an argument against the one as the other, but in reality can conclude against neither. For, as we know not when that supposed time of general infidelity is to be, or whether it will be at all; so, if it were ever so sure, and ever so near, it would nevertheless become us to take care, that it may not be an effect of our own particular indifference and neglect.

But if we take our notions, not from the uncertain interpretation of a particular text, but from the whole tenor of the divine oracles, from the express promise and reiterated predictions of our blessed Lord and his apostles, we shall believe, that 'Jesus Christ is highly exalted of God, to the end; that at his name every knee shall bow, and every tongue confess that he is the

Lord, to the glory of God the Father.' That 'he must reign till he hath put all enemies under his feet.' That 'he is with us alway, even unto the end of the world.' And that, the church of the living God, the pillar and ground of truth, is so far from being destroyed by human means, 'that the gates of hell' (all the infernal powers) 'shall not prevail against it.' Let us therefore banish all such conceits as may seem to justify our indolence, as may reason us out of all courage and vigour in the race that is set before us; let us not, I say, slacken our own hands, nor enfeeble our own knees, by preconceived fancies and suppositions, considering that as the success of all enterprises in great measure depends on the spirit of the undertakers, so nothing is more apt to raise a spirit than hope; nor to depress it, than despondency. We ought therefore to shake off every vain fear in our spiritual warfare. The number, the presumption, and the abilities of those, who take counsel together against the Lord and against his anointed, should not dishearten, but rather excite and encourage us to stand in the gap.

Another consideration, that may possibly withhold divers sincere believers from contributing their endeavours for bringing men to the knowledge of God and Christ, and thereby to eternal life, is the want of miracles in the present age. Men naturally cast about for reasons to countenance the part they take. And as the gift of miracles was of mighty influence and help to those, who were commissioned to spread abroad the light of the gospel in its first promulgation, so no pretence offers itself more naturally to excuse a man from executing any purpose, than the want of authority, which, in the opinion of men, cannot be without a just commission, nor this unless distinguished by those proper means and powers that have been known to attend it. Now, with regard to this defect of miracles, I shall beg leave to make two observations.

First, It is to be observed, that if we have not miracles, we have other advantages which make them less necessary now, than in the first spreading of the gospel: whole nations have found the benefit of Christ's religion, it is protected by princes, established and encouraged by laws, supported by learning and arts, recommended by the experience of many ages, as well as by the authority and example of the wisest and most knowing men. Certainly, if the greatest part of mankind are Gentiles or Mahometans, it cannot be denied that the most knowing, most learned, and most improved nations, profess christianity; and that even the Mahometans themselves bear testimony to the divine mission of Jesus Christ. Whereas therefore, in the beginning, a few illiterate wanderers, of the meanest of the people, had the prejudices, the learning, and the power of their own, as well as other nations, in one word, the whole world, to oppose and overcome: those who at this day engage in the propagation of the gospel, do it upon terms in many respects far more easy and advantageous. It is power against weakness, civility against barbarism, knowledge against ignorance, some or other, if not all these advantages, in the present times, attending the progress of the christian religion, in whatever part of the world men shall attempt to plant it.

In the second place we may reflect, that if we have not the gift of miracles, this is a good reason why we should exert more strongly those human means which God hath put in our power; and make our ordinary faculties, whether of the head, or the hand, or the tongue, our interest, our credit, or our fortune, subservient to the great giver of them; and cheerfully contribute our humble mite towards hastening that time, wherein 'all nations whom thou hast made, shall come and worship before thee, O Lord, and shall glorify thy name.' It is at least a plain case, that the want of apostolical gifts should not be pleaded as a bar to our doing that, which in no respect, either of difficulty or danger, equals, or approaches the apostolical office. What pretence can this supply for men's being quite unconcerned about the spreading of the gospel, or the salvation of souls? for men's forgetting that they are christians, and related to human kind? How can this justify their overlooking opportunities which lie in their way, their not contributing a small part of their fortune towards forwarding a design, wherein they share neither pains nor peril; the not bestowing on it, even the cheap assistance of their speech, attention, counsel, or countenance, as occasion offers? How unlike is this worldly, selfish indifference, to that account which St. *Paul* gives of himself, that 'he sought not his own profit, but the profit of many, that they may be saved.' And yet herein he expected the *Corinthians* (and the same reason will hold for us) should be like him; for he subjoins 'be ye followers of me as I also am of Christ.'

Having considered the duty in general, I come now to treat of it with reference to *America*, the peculiar province of this venerable society; which I suppose well informed of the state and progress of religion in that part of the world, by their correspondencies with the clergy upon their mission. It may nevertheless be expected that one who had been engaged in a design upon this very view, who hath been upon the place, and resided a considerable time in one of our colonies, should have observed somewhat worth reporting. It is to be hoped, therefore, that one part of my audience will pardon, what the other may, perhaps, expect, while I detain them with the narrative of a few things I have observed, and such reflections as thereupon suggested themselves; some part of which may possibly be found to extend to other colonies.

Rhode Island, with a portion of the adjacent continent, under the same government, is inhabited by an *English* colony, consisting chiefly of sectaries of many different denominations, who seem to have worn off part of that prejudice, which they inherited from their ancestors, against the national church of this land; though it must be acknowledged at the same time, that too many of them have worn off a serious sense of all religion. Several indeed of the better sort are accustomed to assemble themselves regularly on the Lord's day for the performance of divine worship. But most of those, who are dispersed throughout this colony, seem to rival some well-bred people of other countries, in a thorough indifference for all that is sacred, being equally careless of outward worship, and of inward principles, whether of faith or practice. Of the bulk of them it may certainly be said, that they live without the sacraments, not being so much as baptized: and as for their morals, I apprehend there is nothing to be found in them that should tempt others to make an experiment of their principles, either in religion or government. But it must be owned, the general behaviour of the inhabitants in those towns where churches and meetings have been long settled, and regularly attended, seems so much better, as sufficiently to show the difference, which a solemn regular worship of God makes between persons of the same blood, temper, and natural faculties.

The native Indians, who are said to have been formerly many thousands, within the compass of this colony, do not at present amount to one thousand, including every age and sex. And these are either all servants or labourers for the *English*, who have contributed more to destroy their bodies by the use of strong liquors, than by any means to improve their minds, or save their souls. This slow poison, jointly operating with the small-pox, and their wars (but much more destructive than both) hath consumed the *Indians*, not only in our colonies, but also far and wide upon our confines. And having made havoc of them, is now doing the same thing by those who taught them that odious vice.

The negroes in the government of *Rhode Island* are about half as many more than the *Indians*; and both together scarce amount to a seventh part of the whole colony. The religion of these people, as is natural to suppose, takes after that of their masters. Some few are baptized; several frequent the different assemblies: and far the greater part none at all. An ancient antipathy to the *Indians*, whom, it seems, our first planters (therein as in certain other particulars affecting to imitate Jews rather than christians) imagine they had a right to treat on the foot of *Canaanites* or *Amalekites*, together with an irrational contempt of the Blacks, as creatures of another species, who had no right to be instructed or admitted to the sacraments, have proved a main obstacle to the conversion of these poor people.

To this may be added, an erroneous notion, that the being baptized, is inconsistent with a state of slavery. To undeceive them in this particular, which had too much weight, it seemed a proper step, if the opinion of his majesty's attorney and solicitor-general could be procured. This opinion they charitably sent over, signed with their own hands; which was accordingly printed in *Rhode Island*, and dispersed throughout the plantations. I heartily wish it may produce the intended effect. It must be owned, our reformed planters, with respect to the natives and the slaves, might learn from those of the church of *Rome*, how it is their interest and duty to behave. Both *French* and *Spaniards* have intermarried with *Indians*, to the great strength, security and increase of their colonies. They take care to instruct both them and their negroes, in the popish religion, to the reproach of those who profess a better. They have also bishops and seminaries for clergy; and it is not found that their colonies are worse subjects, or depend less on their mother country, on that account.

It should seem, that the likeliest step towards converting the heathen would be to begin with the *English* planters; whose influence will for ever be an obstacle to propagating the gospel, till they have a right sense of it themselves, which would show them how much it is their duty to impart it to others. The missionaries employed by this venerable society have done, and continue to do, good service, in bringing those planters to a serious sense of religion, which, it is hoped, will in time extend to others. I speak it knowingly, that the ministers of the gospel, in those provinces which go by the name of *New England*, sent and supported at the expense of this society, have, by their sobriety of manners, discreet behaviour, and a competent degree of useful knowledge, shown themselves worthy the choice of those who sent them; and particularly in living on a more friendly foot with their brethren of the separation; who, on their part, were also very much come off from that narrowness of spirit, which formerly kept them at such an unamicable distance from us. And as there is reason to apprehend, that part of *America* could not have been thus distinguished, and provided with such a number of proper persons, if one half of them had not been supplied out of the dissenting seminaries of the country, who, in proportion as they attain to more liberal improvements of learning, are observed to quit their prejudice towards an episcopal church; so I verily think it might increase the number of such useful men, if provision were made to defray their charges in coming hither to receive holy orders; passing and repassing the ocean, and tarrying the necessary time in *London*, requiring an expense that many are not able to bear. It would also be an encouragement to the missionaries in general, and probably produce good effects, if the allowance of certain missionaries were augmented, in proportion to the services they had done, and the time they had spent in their mission. These hints I venture to suggest, as not unuseful in an age, wherein all human encouragements are found more necessary, than at the first propagation of the gospel. But they are, with all due deference and respect, submitted to the judgment of this venerable audience.

After all, it is hardly to be expected, that so long as infidelity prevails at home, the christian religion should thrive and flourish in our colonies abroad. Mankind, it must be owned, left to themselves, are so much bewildered and benighted, with respect to the origin of that evil which they feel, and from which they are at a loss about the means of being freed; that the doctrines of the lapsed state of man, his reconciliation by Christ, and regeneration by the Spirit, may reasonably be hoped to find an easy admission, as bringing with them light and comfort, into a mind not hardened by impenitency, nor foreclosed by pride, nor biased by prejudice. But, such is the vanity of man, that no prejudice operates more powerfully than that in favour of fashion; and no fashions are so much followed by our colonies, as those of the mother country, which they often adopt in their modes of living, to their great inconvenience, without allowing for the disparity of circumstance or climate. This same humour hath made infidelity (as I find it too credibly reported) spread in some of our wealthy plantations; uneducated men being more apt to tread in the steps of libertines and men of fashion, than to model themselves by the laws and institutions of their mother country, or the lives and professions of the virtuous and religious part of it.

But this is not all; while those abroad are less disposed to receive, some at home are, perhaps, less disposed to propagate the gospel, from the same cause. It is to be feared, I say, that the prevailing torrent of infidelity, which staggers the faith of some, may cool the zeal and damp the spirit of others, who, judging from the event and success of those who impugn the church of Christ, may possibly entertain some scruple or surmise, whether it may not be, for the present at least, abandoned by Providence, and that human care must ineffectually interpose, till it shall please God, 'yet once more to shake not the earth only, but also the heavens.' This point hath been touched before, but deserves farther consideration: to the end, that the peculiar impiety of a profane age, may not be a bar to those very endeavours, which itself renders more necessary, and calls for more loudly now than ever.

Whatever men may think, the arm of the Lord is not shortened. In all this prevalency of atheism and irreligion, there is no advantage gained by the powers of darkness, either against God, or godly men, but only against their own wretched partisans. The christian dispensation is a dispensation of grace and favour. The christian church a society of men entitled to this grace, on performing certain conditions. If this society is diminished, as those who remain true members of it suffer no loss to themselves, so God loseth no right, suffereth no detriment, forgoeth no good; his grace resisted or unfruitful, being no more lost to him, than the light of the sun shining on desert places, or among people who shut their eyes.

Besides, this excess, this unstemmed torrent of profaneness, may possibly, in the conclusion, defeat itself, confirm what it meant to extirpate, and instead of destroying, prove a means of preserving our religion; the evil fruits and effects thereof being so notorious and flagrant, and so sensibly felt, as in all likelihood to be able to open the eyes, and rouse the attention of those, who may be blind and deaf to every other argument and consideration. Or, who knows but the christian church corrupted by prosperity, is to be restored and purified by adversity? which may prove aught we can tell, as salutary in future, as it hath been in past ages. Many insolent and presumptuous foes have set themselves against the church of God; whose hook nevertheless may be in their nostrils, and his bridle in their lips, managing and governing, even their rage and folly, to the fulfilling of his own wise purposes; and who may not fail in the end, to deal by them as he did by the king of *Assyria*, when he had 'performed his work upon Sion and upon Jerusalem, punishing their stout heart and high looks.' This presumptuous conqueror was, without knowing it, a tool or instrument in the hands of that God whom he blasphemed. 'O Assyrian, the rod of mine anger! I will send him against an hypocritical nation, and against the people of my wrath will I give him a charge to take the spoil, and to take the prey, and to tread them down like the mire of the streets. Howbeit he meaneth not so, neither doth his heart think so, but it is in his heart to destroy and cut off nations not a few.'

Thus much at least is evident: it is no new thing, that great enormities should produce great humiliations, and these again noble virtues, which have often recovered both single men, and whole states, even in a natural and civil sense. And if the captivities, distresses, and desolations of the Jewish Church, have occasioned their return to God, and reinstated them in his favour; nay, if it was actually foretold, whenever they lay under the curse of God, at the mercy of their enemies, peeled and scattered in a foreign land, that nevertheless upon their calling his covenant to mind, and returning to him, 'the Lord their God would turn their captivity, and have compassion upon them.' I say, if things were so, why may we not in reason hope for something analogous thereto, in behalf of the christian church. It cannot be denied, that there was a great analogy between the Jewish institutions, and the doctrines of the gospel; for instance, between the Paschal Lamb, and the Lamb of God slain from the foundation of the world; between the *Egyptian* bondage, and that of sin; the earthly *Canaan*, and the heavenly; the fleshly circumcision, and the spiritual. In these and many other particulars, the analogy seems so plain, that it can hardly be disputed. To be convinced that the law of *Moses*, and the Jewish economy were figures and shadows of the evangelical, we need only look into the epistle to the *Hebrews*. May we not therefore, in pursuance of this same analogy, suppose a similar treatment of the Jewish and christian church?

Let us then see, on what terms the former stood with God, in order to discover what the latter may reasonably expect. The solemn denunciation to the Jews was, 'If thou shalt hearken diligently unto the voice of the Lord thy God, to observe and to do all his commandments, which I command thee this day, that the Lord thy God will set thee on high above all the nations of the earth.' But in case of disobedience, it is added among many other threats and maledictions: 'The Lord shall smite thee with blasting and with mildew: and thy heaven that is over thy head shall be brass, and the earth that is under thee shall be iron.' And again, 'The Lord shall smite thee with madness, and blindness, and astonishment of heart.' Have not the people of this land drawn down upon it, by more ways than one, the just judgments of heaven? Surely we have felt in a metaphor the first of the forementioned judgments; and the last hath been literally fulfilled upon us. Is it not visible that we are less knowing, less virtuous, less reasonable, in proportion as we are less religious? Are we not grown drunk and giddy with vice and vanity and presumption, and free-thinking, and extravagance of every kind? to a degree that we may truly be said to be 'smitten with madness, and blindness, and astonishment of heart.'

As anciently most unchristian schisms and disputes, joined with great corruption of manners, made way for the Mahometan in the east, and the papal dominion in the west; even so here at home in the last century, a weak reliance upon human politics and power on the one hand, and enthusiastic rage on the other, together with carnal mindedness on both, gave occasion to introduce atheism and infidelity. If the temporal state, and outward form of the Jewish church was, upon their defection, overturned by invaders; in like manner, when christians are no longer governed by the light of evangelical truth, when we resist the Spirit of God, are we not to expect, that 'the heaven above will be as brass,' that the divine grace will no longer shower down on our obdurate hearts, that our church and profession will be blasted by licentious scorners, those madmen, who in sport 'scatter firebrands, arrows and death'? As all this is no more than we may reasonably suppose will ensue upon our backsliding, so we may, with equal reason, hope it will be remedied upon our return to God.

From what hath been said it follows, that in order to propagate the gospel abroad, it is necessary we do it at home, and extend our charity to domestic infidels, if we would convert or prevent foreign ones. So that a view of the declining state of religion here at home, of those things that produced this declension, and of the proper methods to repair it, is naturally connected with the subject of this discourse. I shall therefore beg your patience, while I just mention a few remarks or hints, too obvious, perhaps, in themselves to be new or unknown to any present, but too little visible in their effects, to make one think they are, by all, much attended to.

Some, preferring points notional or ritual to the love of God and man, consider the national church only as it stands opposed to other christian societies. These generally have a zeal without knowledge, and the effects are suitable to the cause; they really hurt what they seem to espouse. Others more solicitous about the discovery of truth, than the practice of holiness, employ themselves, rather to spy out errors in the church, than enforce its precepts. These, it is to be feared, postpone the great interests of religion to points of less concern, in any eyes but their own. But surely they would do well to consider, that an humble, though confused or indistinct faith in the bond of charity, and productive of good works, is much more evangelical than any accurate disputing and conceited knowledge.

A church which contains the fundamentals, and nothing subversive of those fundamentals, is not to be set at naught by any particular member; because it may not, in every point, perhaps, correspond with his ideas, no not, though he is sure of being in the right. Probably there never was, or will be, an established church in this world, without visible marks of humanity upon it. St. *Paul* supposeth, that 'on the foundation of Jesus Christ, there will be human superstructures of hay and stubble,' things light and trivial, wrong or superstitious, which indeed is a natural consequence of the weakness and ignorance of man. But where that living foundation is rightly laid in the mind, there will not fail to grow and spring from thence those virtues and graces, which are the genuine effects and tokens of true faith, and which are by no means inconsistent with every error in theory, or every needless rite in worship.

The christian religion was calculated for the bulk of mankind, and therefore cannot reasonably be supposed to consist in subtle and nice notions. From the time that divinity was considered as a science, and human reason enthroned in the sanctuary of God, the hearts of its professors seem to have been less under the influence of grace. From that time have grown many unchristian dissentions and controversies, of men 'knowing nothing, but doating about questions and strifes of words, whereof cometh envy, strife, railings, evil surmises, perverse disputings of men of corrupt minds and destitute of truth.' Doubtless, the making religion a notional thing, hath been of infinite disservice. And whereas its holy mysteries are rather to be received with humility of faith, than defined and measured by the accuracy of human reason; all attempts of this kind, however well intended, have visibly failed in the event; and instead of reconciling infidels, have, by creating disputes and heats among the professors of christianity, given no small advantage to its enemies.

To conclude, if we proportioned our zeal to the importance of things: if we could love men whose opinions we do not approve: if we knew the world more, and liked it less: if we had a due sense of the divine perfection and our own defects: if our chief study was the wisdom from above, described by St. *Paul*: and if, in order to all this, that were done in places of education, which cannot so well be done out of them: I say, if these steps were taken at home, while proper measures are carrying on abroad, the one would very much forward or facilitate the other. As it is not meant, so it must not be understood, that foreign attempts should wait for domestic success, but only that it is to be wished they may cooperate. Certainly if a just and rational, a genuine and sincere, a warm and vigorous piety, animated the mother country, the influence thereof would soon reach our foreign plantations, and extend throughout their borders. We should soon see religion shine forth with new lustre and force, to the conversion of infidels, both at home and abroad, and to 'the casting down imaginations, and every high thing that exalteth itself against the knowledge of God, and bringing into captivity every thought to the obedience of Christ.'

To whom with the Father, and the Holy Ghost, be ascribed all praise, might, majesty, and dominion, now and for ever.

Joseph Butler

BUTLER WAS born at Wantage, in Berkshire, of Presbyterian parents. His father was a retired linen merchant. As a dissenter, Butler was debarred from the universities, and went to an academy at Tewkesbury. At the age of twenty-one he was conducting a philosophic correspondence with Samuel Clarke, a divine noted for his talents as a reasoner. He conformed to the Church of England, and in 1714 entered Oriel College, Oxford, where divinity was treated rather differently. Indeed he thought of leaving Oxford, where he had to 'mis-spend so much time' 'in attending frivolous lectures and unintelligible disputations', in favour of Cambridge, but was prevented by various procedural difficulties. He took his B. A. in 1718 and was ordained the same year. The father of one of the friendlier Oriel Fellows was a bishop, and through his patronage Butler became preacher at the Rolls Chapel, an appointment he retained until 1726. Some of the sermons he preached there he himself described as 'very abstruse and difficult'; he evidently felt free to develop his ethical analysis before an intelligent audience. He published *Fifteen Sermons Preached at the Rolls Chapel* in 1726. About the same time he was given a wealthy living in Co. Durham. His influential friends did not neglect him. He spent seven years at Stanhope, and there wrote his most famous work, *The Analogy of Religion*. He was also said to have discharged conscientiously 'every obligation appertaining to a good parish priest', although the 'retirement was too solitary for his disposition, which had in it a natural cast of gloominess'. Once again his friends—this time Secker, an old school-friend from Tewkesbury, who later became Archbishop of Canterbury—came to his rescue. He became chaplain to the Lord Chancellor and later Clerk of the Closet to Queen Caroline, on whom he was in frequent attendance. He was given the 'mean' bishopric of Bristol in 1738, but it was only on being made Dean of St Paul's in 1740 that he resigned the living at Stanhope. He was an accomplished pluralist, and must have moved with discretion among the rather bloated hierarchy of the mid-eighteenth century. In 1750 he was translated to the see of Durham, which was extremely rich. He died in 1752.

Through all his excessive number of preferments Butler proceeded in a singular spirit. He was of an ascetic temper, and his benefactions were immense. There is no question of his having lived indulgently on his considerable fortune nor of having kept much of it for himself. Yet he seems to have thought the appointment to Bristol rather beneath him, and one might say that he never refused a preferment, but for a story that he was offered the see of Canterbury in 1747 and replied that it was 'too late for him to try to support a falling Church'. Butler had immense intellectual endowments, yet there is something commonplace about him, so far as commonplaceness can be said to go with so much distinction. The *Analogy* itself is so directed to the mind of the eighteenth century that it proves little now except that religion might have been invented by analogy with the world of nature. The objectives Butler proposed were modest and timely. It had, he said, come to be 'taken for granted, by many persons, that Christianity is not so much as a subject of inquiry; but that it is, now at length, discovered to be fictitious.' That was as clear in the eighteenth century as it is now, for those to whom such things are clear. Butler aimed to show simply 'that it is not, however, so clear a case, that there is nothing in it'. There is a 'cool self-interest'—Butler's own phrase—about much of his writing which is entirely that of the more well-fed part of his amiable century.

Yet Butler was in some respects far from that complacency. Apart from his endless charities he has left evidence—slight, as such things are often the better for being—of personal devotion and care for religion. Despite his Presbyterian beginning he belongs rather among the High Churchmen. One of his most interesting pieces of writing, to those who are concerned with him as a churchman rather than as a philosopher, is his *Charge to the Clergy of the Diocese of Durham*, in which he laments 'the general decay of religion' in this nation and pleads for the *forms of godliness* to be kept up, not for their own sake, but for what they may bring. It says something of the extraordinary state to which the Whig supremacy and the spread of deistic rationality had brought opinion by the mid-eighteenth century that this charge, together with a marble cross which Butler had erected in Bristol, were thought, a few years after his death, to be bases on which a charge of popery could be brought against him; and still more that such a charge could be seriously enough regarded for Secker, by then Archbishop of Canterbury, to intervene in defence of his memory.

UPON THE GOVERNMENT OF THE TONGUE
James 1:26.
If any man among you seem to be religious, and bridleth not his tongue, but deceiveth his own heart, this man's religion is vain.

OF THE fifteen sermons preached at the Rolls Chapel, of which this is one, Butler says, in his quietly high-handed way, that the reader 'is not to look for any particular reason for the choice of the greater part . . . their being taken from among many others, preached in the same place, through a course of eight years, being in great measure accidental.' Nor is the reader to look for any connection between them, except 'what will always be found in the writings of the same person, when he writes with simplicity and in earnest'. Butler certainly writes in that manner, and in fact the sermons do set out his ethical theory, which is at once an attempt to make the best of the epicureanism of the eighteenth century and a correction of the cruder of the current psychologies as found, for example, in Mandeville. The first three of the published sermons are an analysis of human nature, in terms of self-love, the social nature of man and the natural supremacy of conscience. It is because he believes that 'men are so much one body', that 'they feel for each other', that he is able to speak so approvingly of self-love. For true self-love cannot ignore this social element in man's make-up. A man should act in accordance with his whole nature, and this means setting aside the powerful impulse of the moment. All this is in accordance with the text from Romans 12 Butler has chosen for this sermon, except that, in his bland eighteenth-century way, he skates somewhat lightly over Paul's qualification, that 'we, being many, are one body *in Christ*'.

The sermon given follows immediately, in the published series, on the three *Upon Human Nature*. It is an application of Butler's general morality, and stands perfectly well by itself. There could be no more useful topic, for no one can deny that 'unrestrained volubility and wantonness of speech is the occasion of numberless evils and vexations in life'. With the lucidity which distinguishes his work he makes it clear that it is not 'Evil-speaking from Malice, nor Lying or bearing false Witness' that he is talking about, but the folly of mere chatter. From the shrewdness and variety of his observations on the subject one cannot doubt that Butler had suffered a great deal of it. 'The thing is', he says scathingly, 'to engage your attention; to take you up wholly for the present time.' So long as they can do that people do not care what they say. In an aside—made on an impulse no doubt too powerful for even the imperturbable Butler to resist—he says 'one may just mention that multitude, that endless number of words, with which business is perplexed; when a much fewer would, as it should seem, better serve the purpose.' He commends silence, the occasions for which, he says, are 'obvious'; the first being, 'when a man has nothing to say'.

THE TRANSLATION of this Text would be more determinate by being more literal, thus: 'If any Man among you seemeth to be religious, not bridling his Tongue, but deceiving his own Heart, this Man's Religion is vain.' This determines that the Words, 'but deceiveth his own Heart,' are not put in Opposition to, 'seemeth to be religious,' but to, 'bridleth not his Tongue.' The certain determinate Meaning of the Text then being, that he who seemeth to be religious, and bridleth not his Tongue, but in that particular deceiveth his own Heart, this Man's Religion is vain; we may observe somewhat very forcible and expressive in these Words of St. *James*. As if the Apostle had said, No Man surely can make any Pretences to Religion, who does not at least believe that he bridleth his Tongue: If he puts on any Appearance or Face of Religion, and yet does not govern his Tongue, he must surely deceive himself in that Particular, and think he does: And whoever is so unhappy as to deceive himself in this, to imagine he keeps that unruly Faculty in due Subjection, when indeed he does not, whatever the other Part of his Life be, his Religion is vain; the Government of the Tongue being a most material Restraint which Virtue lays us under: Without it no Man can be truly religious.

In treating upon this Subject, I will consider,

First, What is the general Vice or Fault here referred to: Or what Disposition in Men is supposed in Moral Reflections and Precepts concerning 'bridling the Tongue.'

Secondly, When it may be said of any one, that he has a due Government over himself in this Respect.

I. Now the Fault referred to, and the Disposition supposed, in Precepts and Reflections concerning the Government of the Tongue, is not Evil-speaking from Malice, nor Lying or bearing false Witness from indirect selfish Designs. The Disposition to these, and the actual Vices themselves, all come under other Subjects. The Tongue may be employed about, and made to serve all the Purposes of Vice, in tempting and deceiving, in Perjury and Injustice. But the Thing here supposed and referred to, is Talkativeness: A Disposition to be talking, abstracted from the Consideration of what is to be said; with very little or no Regard to, or Thought of doing, either Good or Harm. And let not any imagine this to be a slight Matter, and that it deserves not to have so great Weight laid upon it; till he has considered, what Evil is implied in it, and the bad Effects which follow from it. It is perhaps true, that they who are addicted to this

Folly would choose to confine themselves to Trifles and indifferent Subjects, and so intend only to be guilty of being impertinent: But as they cannot go on for ever talking of Nothing, as common Matters will not afford a sufficient Fund for perpetual continued Discourse: when Subjects of this Kind are exhausted, they will go on to Defamation, Scandal, divulging of Secrets, their own Secrets as well as those of others, any thing rather than be silent. They are plainly hurried on in the Heat of their Talk to say quite different Things from what they first intended, and which they afterwards wish unsaid; or improper things, which they had no other End in saying but only to afford Employment to their Tongue. And if these People expect to be heard and regarded, for there are some content merely with talking, they will invent to engage your Attention: and, when they have heard the least imperfect Hint of an Affair, they will out of their own Head add the Circumstances of Time and Place, and other Matters to make out their Story, and give the Appearance of Probability to it: Not that they have any Concern about being believed, otherwise than as a Means of being heard. The Thing is, to engage your Attention; to take you up wholly for the present Time: What Reflections will be made afterwards, is in Truth the least of their Thoughts. And further, when Persons, who indulge themselves in these Liberties of the Tongue, are in any Degree offended with another, as little Disgusts and Misunderstandings will be, they allow themselves to defame and revile such an one without any Moderation or Bounds; though the Offence is so very slight, that they themselves would not do, nor perhaps wish him an Injury in any other Way. And in this Case the Scandal and Revilings are chiefly owing to Talkativeness, and not bridling their Tongue; and so come under our present Subject. The least Occasion in the World will make the Humour break out in this particular Way, or in another. It is like a Torrent, which must and will flow; but the least thing imaginable will first of all give it either this or another Direction, turn it into this or that Channel: Or like a Fire; the Nature of which, when in a Heap of combustible Matter, is to spread and lay waste all around; but any one of a thousand little Accidents will occasion it to break out first either in this or in another particular Part.

The Subject then before us, though it does run up into, and can scarce be treated as entirely distinct from all others; yet it needs not be so much mixed or blended with them as it often is.

Every Faculty and Power may be used as the Instrument of premeditated Vice and Wickedness, merely as the most proper and effectual Means of executing such Designs. But if a Man, from deep Malice and Desire of Revenge, should meditate a Falsehood with a settled Design to ruin his Neighbour's Reputation, and should with great Coolness and Deliberation spread it; nobody would choose to say of such an one, that he had no Government of his Tongue. A Man may use the Faculty of Speech as an Instrument of False-witness, who yet has so entire a Command over that Faculty, as never to speak but from Forethought and cool Design. Here the Crime is Injustice and Perjury: and strictly speaking, no more belongs to the present Subject, than Perjury and Injustice in any other Way. But there is such a Thing as a Disposition to be talking for its own Sake; from which Persons often say anything, good or bad, of others, merely as a Subject of Discourse, according to the particular Temper they themselves happen to be in, and to pass away the present Time. There is likewise to be observed in Persons such a strong and eager Desire of engaging Attention to what they say, that they will speak Good or Evil, Truth or otherwise, merely as one or the other seems to be most hearkened to: And this, though it is sometimes joined, is not the same with the Desire of being thought important and Men of Consequence. There is in some such a Disposition to be talking, that an Offence of the slightest Kind, and such as would not raise any other Resentment, yet raises, if I may so speak, the Resentment of the Tongue, puts it into a Flame, into the most ungovernable Motions. This Outrage, when the Person it respects is present, we distinguish in the lower Rank of People by a peculiar Term: And let it be observed, that though the Decencies of Behaviour are a little kept, the same Outrage and Virulence, indulged when he is absent, is an Offence of the same Kind. But not to distinguish any further in this Manner: Men run into Faults and Follies, which cannot so properly be referred to any one general Head as this, that they have not a due Government over their Tongue.

And this unrestrained Volubility and Wantonness of Speech is the Occasion of numberless Evils and Vexations in Life. It begets Resentment in him who is the Subject of it; sows the Seed of Strife and Dissension amongst others; and enflames little Disgusts and Offences, which if let alone would wear away of themselves: It is often of as bad Effect upon the good Name of others, as deep Envy or Malice: And, to say the least of it in this Respect, it destroys and perverts a certain Equity of the utmost Importance to Society to be observed; namely, that Praise and Dispraise, a good or bad Character, should always be bestowed according to Desert. The Tongue used in such a licentious Manner is like a Sword in the Hand of a Madman; it is employed at random, it can scarce possibly do any Good, and for the most Part does a World of Mischief; and implies not only great Folly and a trifling Spirit, but great Viciousness of Mind, great Indifference to Truth and Falsity, and to the Reputation, Welfare, and Good of others. So much Reason is there for what St. *James* says of the Tongue, 'It is a Fire, a World of Iniquity, it defileth the whole Body, setteth on Fire the Course of Nature, and is itself set on Fire of Hell.' This is the Faculty or Disposition which we are required to keep a Guard upon: These are the Vices and Follies it runs into, when not kept under due Restraint.

II. Wherein the due Government of the Tongue consists, or when it may be said of any one in a moral and religious Sense that he 'bridleth his Tongue,' I come now to consider.

The due and proper Use of any natural Faculty or Power, is to be judged of by the End and Design for which it was given us. The chief Purpose, for which the Faculty of Speech was given to Man, is plainly that we might communicate our Thoughts to each other, in order to carry on the Affairs of the World; for Business, and for our Improvement in Knowledge and Learning. But the good Author of our Nature designed us not only Necessaries, but likewise Enjoyment and Satisfaction, in that Being he hath graciously given, and in that Condition of Life he hath placed us in. There are secondary Uses of our Faculties: They administer to Delight, as well as to Necessity: And as they are equally adapted to both, there is no Doubt but he intended them for our Gratification, as well as for the Support and Continuance of our Being. The secondary Use of Speech is to please and be entertaining to each other in Conversation. This is in every Respect allowable and right: It unites Men closer in Alliances and Friendships; gives us a Fellow-feeling of the Prosperity and Unhappiness of each other; and is in several Respects serviceable to Virtue, and to promote good Behaviour in the World. And provided there be not too much Time spent in it, if it were considered only in the Way of Gratification and Delight, Men must have strange Notions of God and of Religion, to think that He can be offended with it, or that it is any way inconsistent with the strictest Virtue. But the Truth is, such sort of Conversation, though it has no particular good Tendency, yet it has a general Good one: It is social and friendly, and tends to promote Humanity, Good-nature and Civility.

As the End and Use, so likewise the Abuse of Speech, relates to the one or other of These; either to Business, or to Conversation. As to the former; Deceit in the Management of Business and Affairs does not properly belong to the Subject now before us: Though one may just mention that Multitude, that endless Number of Words, with which Business is perplexed; when a much fewer would, as it should seem, better serve the Purpose: But this must be left to those who understand the Matter. The Government of the Tongue, considered as a Subject of itself, relates chiefly to Conversation; to that Kind of Discourse which usually fills up the Time spent in friendly Meetings, and Visits of Civility. And the Danger is, lest Persons entertain themselves and others at the Expense of their Wisdom and their Virtue, and to the Injury or Offence of their Neighbour. If they will observe and keep clear of these, they may be as free, and easy, and unreserved, as they can desire.

The Cautions to be given for avoiding these Dangers, and to render Conversation innocent and agreeable, fall under the following Particulars: Silence; Talking of indifferent Things; and, which makes up too great a Part of Conversation, Giving of Characters, Speaking well or evil of others.

The wise Man observes, that 'there is a Time to speak, and a Time to keep silence.' One meets with People in the World, who seem never to have made the last of these Observations. And yet these great Talkers do not at all speak from their having anything to say, as every Sentence shows, but only from their Inclination to be talking. Their Conversation is merely an Exercise of the Tongue: No other human Faculty has any Share in it. It is strange these Persons can help reflecting, that unless they have in Truth a superior Capacity, and are in an extraordinary Manner furnished for Conversation; if they are entertaining, it is at their own Expense. Is it possible, that it should never come into People's Thoughts to suspect, whether or no it be to their Advantage to show so very much of themselves? 'O that you would altogether hold your Peace, and it should be your Wisdom.' Remember likewise there are Persons who love fewer Words, an inoffensive Sort of People, and who deserve some Regard, though of too still and composed Tempers for you. Of this Number was the Son of *Sirach*: For he plainly speaks from Experience, when he says, 'As Hills of Sand are to the Steps of the Aged, so is one of many Words to a quiet Man.' But one would think it should be obvious to every one, that when they are in Company with their Superiors of any Kind, in Years, Knowledge, and Experience; when proper and useful Subjects are discoursed of, which they cannot bear a Part in; that these are Times for Silence: when they should learn to hear, and be attentive; at least in their turn. It is indeed a very unhappy Way these People are in: They in a Manner cut themselves out from all Advantage of Conversation, except that of being entertained with their own Talk: Their Business in coming into Company not being at all to be informed, to hear, to learn; but to display themselves; or rather to exert their Faculty, and talk without any Design at all. And if we consider Conversation as an Entertainment, as somewhat to unbend the Mind; as a Diversion from the Cares, the Business, and the Sorrows of Life; it is of the very Nature of it, that the Discourse be mutual. This, I say, is implied in the very notion of what we distinguish by Conversation, or being in Company. Attention to the continued Discourse of one alone grows more painful often, than the Cares and Business we come to be diverted from. He therefore who imposes this upon us, is guilty of a double Offence; arbitrarily enjoining Silence upon all the rest, and likewise obliging them to this painful Attention.

I am sensible these Things are apt to be passed over, as too little to come into a serious Discourse: But in Reality Men are obliged, even in Point of Morality and Virtue, to observe all the Decencies of Behaviour. The greatest Evils in Life have had their Rise from somewhat, which was thought of too little Importance to be attended to. And as to the Matter we are now upon, it is absolutely necessary to be considered. For if People will not maintain a due Government over themselves, in regarding proper Times and Seasons for Silence, but *will* be talking; they certainly, whether they design it or not at first, will go on to Scandal and Evil-speaking, and divulging Secrets.

If it were needful to say anything further, to persuade Men to learn this Lesson of Silence; one might put them in mind, how insignificant they render themselves by this excessive Talkativeness: insomuch that, if they do chance to say anything which deserves to be attended to and regarded, it is lost in the Variety and Abundance which they utter of another Sort.

The Occasions of Silence then are obvious, and one would think should be easily distinguished by every Body: Namely, when a Man has nothing to say; or nothing, but what is better unsaid: Better, either in regard to the particular Persons he is present with; or from its being an Interruption to Conversation itself; or to Conversation of a more agreeable Kind; or better, lastly, with regard to himself. I will end this Particular with two Reflections of the wise Man: One of which, in the strongest Manner, exposes the ridiculous Part of this Licentiousness of the Tongue; and the other, the great Danger and Viciousness of it. 'When he that is a Fool walketh by the Wayside, his Wisdom faileth him, and he saith to every one that he is a Fool.' The other is, 'In the Multitude of Words there wanteth not Sin.'

As to the Government of the Tongue in respect to talking upon indifferent Subjects: After what has been said concerning the due Government of it in respect to the Occasions and Times for Silence, there is little more necessary, than only to caution Men to be fully satisfied, that the Subjects are indeed of an indifferent Nature; and not to spend too much Time in Conversation of this Kind. But Persons must be sure to take heed, that the Subject of their Discourse be at least of an indifferent Nature: That it be no way offensive to Virtue, Religion, or good Manners; that it be not of a licentious dissolute Sort, this leaving always ill Impressions upon the Mind; that it be no way injurious or vexatious to others; and that too much Time be not spent this way, to the neglect of those Duties and Offices of Life which belong to their Station and Condition in the World. However, though there is not any Necessity, that Men should aim at being important and weighty in every Sentence they speak: Yet since useful Subjects, at least of some Kinds, are as entertaining as others, a wise Man, even when he desires to unbend his Mind from Business, would choose that the Conversation might turn upon somewhat instructive.

The last Thing is, The Government of the Tongue as relating to Discourse of the Affairs of others, and giving of Characters. These are in a Manner the same: And one can scarce call it an indifferent Subject, because Discourse upon it almost perpetually runs into somewhat criminal.

And first of all, it were very much to be wished that this did not take up so great a Part of Conversation; because it is indeed a Subject of a dangerous Nature. Let any one consider the various Interests, Competitions, and little Misunderstandings which arise amongst Men; and he will soon see, that he is not unprejudiced and impartial; that he is not, as I may speak, neutral enough, to trust himself with talking of the Character and Concerns of his Neighbour, in a free, careless, and unreserved Manner. There is perpetually, and often it is not attended to, a Rivalship amongst People of one Kind or another, in respect to Wit, Beauty, Learning, Fortune, and that one Thing will insensibly influence them to speak to the Disadvantage of others, even where there is no formed Malice or ill Design. Since therefore it is so hard to enter into this Subject without offending, the first Thing to be observed is, that People should learn to decline it; to get over that strong Inclination most have to be talking of the Concerns and Behaviour of their Neighbour.

But since it is impossible that this Subject should be wholly excluded Conversation, and since it is necessary that the Characters of Men should be known: The next Thing is, that it is a Matter of Importance what is said; and therefore, that we should be religiously scrupulous and exact to say nothing, either good or bad, but what is true. I put it thus, because it is in Reality of as great Importance to the Good of Society, that the Characters of bad Men should be known, as that the Characters of good Men should. People, who are given to Scandal and Detraction, may indeed make an ill use of this Observation: But Truths, which are of Service towards regulating our Conduct, are not to be disowned, or even concealed, because a bad Use may be made of them. This however would be effectually prevented, if these two Things were attended to. *First*, That, though it is equally of bad Consequence to Society, that Men should have either good or ill Characters which they do not deserve, yet, when you say somewhat Good of a Man which he does not deserve, there is no Wrong done him in particular; whereas, when you say Evil of a Man which he does not deserve, here is a direct formal Injury, a real piece of Injustice done him. This therefore makes a wide Difference; and gives us, in Point of Virtue, much greater Latitude in speaking well than ill, of others. *Secondly*, A good Man is friendly to his Fellow-creatures, and a Lover of Mankind, and so will, upon every Occasion, and often without any, say all the Good he can of every Body: But, so far as he is a good Man, will never be disposed to speak Evil of any, unless there be some other Reason for it, besides barely that it is true. If he be charged with having given an ill Character, he will scarce think it a sufficient Justification of himself to say it was a true one, unless he can also give some farther Account how he came to do so: A just Indignation against particular Instances of Villainy, where they are great and scandalous; or to prevent an innocent Man from being deceived and betrayed, when he has great Trust and Confidence in one who does not deserve it. Justice must be done to every Part of a Subject, when we are considering it. If there be a Man, who bears a fair Character in the World, whom yet ye know to be without Faith or Honesty, to be really an ill Man, it must be allowed in general, that we shall do a Piece of Service to Society, by letting such an one's true Character be known. This is no more, than what we have an Instance of in our Saviour himself; though he was mild and gentle beyond Example. However, no Words can express too strongly the Caution which should be used in such a Case as this.

Upon the whole Matter: If People would observe the obvious Occasions of Silence, if they would subdue the Inclination to Tale-bearing, and that eager Desire to engage Attention, which is an original Disease in some Minds; they would be in little Danger of offending with their Tongue; and would, in a moral and religious Sense, have due Government over it.

I will conclude with some Precepts and Reflections of the Son of *Sirach* upon this Subject. 'Be swift to hear: and, if thou hast Understanding, answer thy Neighbour; if not, lay thy Hand upon thy Mouth. Honour and Shame is in Talk. A Man of an ill Tongue is dangerous in his City, and he that is rash in his Talk shall be hated. A wise Man will hold his Tongue, till he see Opportunity; but a Babbler and a Fool will regard no Time. He that useth many Words shall be abhorred; and he that taketh to himself Authority therein, shall be hated. A back-biting Tongue hath disquieted many; strong Cities hath it pulled down, and overthrown the Houses of great Men. The Tongue of a Man is his Fall; but if thou love to hear, thou shalt receive Understanding.'

PREACHED IN THE PARISH CHURCH OF CHRIST-CHURCH, LONDON
Proverbs 22:6.
Train up a child in the way he should go: and when he is old, he will not depart from it.

THIS SERMON was delivered on 9 May 1745, 'being the time of the yearly meeting of the children educated in the charity-schools in and about the cities of London and Westminster'. To promote the erection of charity schools had been one of the primary objectives of the S.P.C.K., which had been founded in 1698, and the first quarter of the eighteenth century had seen the establishment of over thirteen hundred such schools in England and Wales. Religious instruction, reading and writing, a little arithmetic and needlework, might seem a modest enough curriculum, in the twentieth century, but it remains a sensible one, as far as it goes. There was of course a multitude of private schools and grammar schools and there was no question of education being confined to the rich, but for the vast hordes of the really poor little had hitherto been done, and it has to be remembered that the eighteenth century, in which the rich grew so fat, was, as the Hammonds showed (J. L. and Barbara Hammond, *The Village Labourer*, London, 1911), a time of expropriation and increasing poverty for a large section of the population. By the middle of the century, as the grip of Whig enlightenment tightened, the rate of increase in the number of such schools became less marked.

The charity schools were managed by local committees of subscribers, with the S.P.C.K. in a promotional and advisory role, and it is to such local committee members, it may be assumed, that the following sermon is largely addressed. They must be supposed to be largely middle-class people filled with the prejudices of their times. No doubt there was talk of the dangers of the poor being educated above their station. Butler takes account of this, and if the inculcation of habits of industry and subordination was a self-interested pursuit, for the well-to-do classes, it has also to be remembered that the possession of these qualities was, for the recipients of this education, virtually a condition of employment and the possibility of a regular livelihood.

Given the audience and the preconceptions of the times, and Butler's almost excessive discretion, the sermon is in places extremely outspoken. 'Children have as much Right', he says, 'to some proper Education, as to have their Lives preserved; and when this is not given them by their Parents, the Care of it devolves on all Persons, it becomes the Duty of all, who are capable of contributing to it, and whose Help is wanted.' Butler's own benefactions were large, so he had a right to speak. One might admonish grown persons, he says, with a coolness which comes from having some experience of so doing, but the care of children, their *education*, is 'a distinct Duty, from the particular Danger of their Ruin, if left to themselves, and the particular Reason we have to expect they will do well, if due Care be taken of them.' Some are so poor that they must be clothed, before they can come to school; very well, they must be clothed. It is 'poorly objected', he says, no doubt with some sinister example of well-to-do talk in mind, that clothing them might give them a 'little Vanity'. To this he provides an answer in which one can detect a certain warm-hearted indignation: 'it is scarce possible but that it will have even a quite contrary Effect when they are grown up, and ever after remind them of their Rank.' To those who are afraid the poor may get above themselves he answers: 'What about the rich?' People 'do not appear at all apprehensive of the like Danger for themselves or their own Children, in Respect of Riches or Power.'

HUMAN CREATURES, from the Constitution of their Nature and the Circumstances in which they are placed, cannot but acquire Habits during their Childhood, by the Impressions which are given them, and their own customary Actions. And long before they arrive at mature Age, these Habits form a general settled Character. And the Observation of the Text, that the most early Habits are usually the most lasting, is likewise everyone's Observation. Now whenever Children are left to themselves, and to the Guides and Companions which they choose, or by Hazard light upon, we find by Experience, that the first Impressions they take, and Course of Action they get into, are very bad; and so consequently must be their Habits, and Character, and future Behaviour. Thus if they are not trained up in the Way they *should go*, they will certainly be trained up in the Way they *should not go*; and, in all Probability, will persevere in it, and become miserable Themselves, and mischievous to Society: which, in Event, is worse, upon Account of Both, than if they had been exposed to perish in their Infancy. On the other hand, the ingenuous Docility of Children before they have been deceived, their Distrust of themselves, and natural Deference to grown People, whom they find here settled in a World where they themselves are Strangers; and to whom they have recourse for Advice, as readily as for Protection; which Deference is still greater towards those who are placed over them: These Things give the justest Grounds to expect, that they may receive such Impressions, and be influenced to such a Course of Behaviour, as will produce lasting good Habits; and, together with the Dangers beforementioned, are as truly a natural Demand upon us to 'train them up in the way they should go,' as their bodily Wants are a Demand to provide them bodily Nourishment. Brute Creatures are appointed to do no more than this last for their Offspring, Nature forming them by Instincts to the particular Manner of Life appointed them; from which they never deviate. But this is so far from being the Case of Men, that, on the contrary, considering Communities collectively, every successive Generation is left, in the ordinary Course of Providence, to be formed by the preceding one; and becomes good or bad, though not without its own Merit or Demerit, as this Trust is discharged or violated, chiefly in the Management of Youth.

We ought, doubtless, to instruct and admonish grown Persons; to restrain them from what is Evil, and encourage them in what is Good, as we are able: But this Care of Youth, abstracted from all Consideration of the parental Affection, I say, this Care of Youth, which is the general Notion of *Education*, becomes a distinct Subject, and a distinct Duty, from the particualr Danger of their Ruin, if left to themselves, and the particular Reason we have to expect they will do well, if due Care be taken of them. And from hence it follows, that Children have as much Right to some proper Education, as to have their Lives preserved; and that when this is not given them by their Parents, the Care of it devolves upon all Persons, it becomes the Duty of all, who are capable of contributing to it, and whose Help is wanted.

These trite, but most important Things, implied indeed in the Text, being thus premised as briefly as I could express them, I proceed to consider distinctly the general Manner in which the Duty of Education is there laid before us: which will further show its Extent, and further obviate the idle Objections which have been made against it. And all this together will naturally lead us to consider the Occasion and Necessity of Schools for the Education of poor Children, and in what Light the Objections against them are to be regarded.

Solomon might probably intend the Text for a particular Admonition to educate Children in a Manner suitable to their respective Ranks, and future Employments: but certainly he intended it for a general Admonition to educate them in Virtue and Religion, and good Conduct of themselves in their temporal Concerns. And all this together, in which they are to be educated, he calls 'the way they should go,' i. e. he mentions it not as a Matter of Speculation but of Practice. And conformably to this Description of the Things in which Children are to be educated, he describes Education itself: For he calls it 'training them up'; which is a very different Thing from merely teaching them some Truths, necessary to be known or believed. It is endeavouring to form such Truths into practical Principles in the Mind, so as to render them of habitual good Influence upon the Temper and Actions, in all the various Occurrences of Life. And this is not done by bare Instruction; but by that, together with admonishing them frequently as Occasion offers; restraining them from what is Evil, and exercising them in what is Good. Thus the Precept of the Apostle concerning this Matter is, to 'bring up children in the nurture and admonition of the Lord'; as it were by way of Distinction from acquainting them merely with the Principles of Christianity, as you would with any common Theory. Though Education were nothing more than informing Children of some Truths of Importance to them, relating to Religion and common Life, yet there would be great Reason for it, notwithstanding the frivolous Objections concerning the Danger of giving them Prejudices. But when we consider, that such Information itself is really the least Part of it; and that it consists in endeavouring to put them into right Dispositions of Mind, and right Habits of Living, in every Relation and every Capacity; this Consideration shows such Objections to be quite absurd: since it shows them to be Objections against doing a Thing of the utmost Importance at the natural Opportunity of our doing it, Childhood and Youth; and which is indeed, properly speaking, our only one. For when they are grown up to Maturity, they are out of our Hands, and must be left to themselves. The natural Authority on One Side ceases, and the Deference on the Other. God forbid, that it should be impossible for Men to recollect Themselves, and reform at an advanced Age: but it is in no sort in the Power of Others to gain upon them; to turn them away from what is Wrong, and enforce upon them what is Right, at that Season of their Lives, in the Manner we might have done in their Childhood.

Doubtless Religion requires Instruction, for it is founded in Knowledge and Belief of some Truths. And so is common Prudence in the Management of our temporal Affairs. Yet neither of them consist in the Knowledge or Belief even of these fundamental Truths; but in our being brought by such Knowledge or Belief to a correspondent Temper and Behaviour. Religion, as it stood under the Old Testament, is perpetually styled 'the Fear of God: under the New, 'Faith in Christ'. But as that Fear of God does not signify literally being afraid of Him, but having a good Heart, and leading a good Life, in Consequence of such Fear; so this Faith in Christ does not signify literally *believing* in Him in the Sense that Word is used in common Language, but becoming his real Disciples, in Consequence of such Belief.

Our Religion being then thus practical, consisting in a Frame of Mind and Course of Behaviour, suitable to the Dispensation we are under, and which will bring us to our final Good; Children ought, by Education, to be habituated to this Course of Behaviour, and formed into this Frame of Mind. And it must ever be remembered, that if no Care be taken to do it, they will grow up in a direct contrary Behaviour, and be hardened in direct contrary Habits. They will more and more corrupt themselves, and spoil their proper Nature. They will alienate themselves farther from God; and not only neglect, but *trample under foot*, the Means which He in his infinite Mercy has appointed for our Recovery. And upon the whole, the same Reasons which show, that they ought to be instructed and exercised in what will render them useful to Society, secure them from the present Evils they are in Danger of incurring, and procure them that Satisfaction which lies within the Reach of human Prudence; show likewise, that they ought to be instructed and exercised in what is suitable to the highest Relations in which we stand, and the most important Capacity in which we can be considered; in that Temper of Mind and Course of Behaviour, which will secure them from their chief Evil, and bring them to their chief Good. Besides that Religion is the principal Security of Men's acting a right Part in Society, and even in respect to their own temporal Happiness, all Things duly considered.

It is true indeed, Children may be taught Superstition, under the Notion of Religion; and it is true also, that, under the Notion of Prudence, they may be educated in great Mistakes as to the Nature of real Interest and Good, respecting the present World. But this is no more a Reason for not educating them according to the best of our Judgment, than our knowing how very liable we all are to err in other Cases, is a Reason why we should not, in those other Cases, act according to the best of our Judgment.

It being then of the greatest Importance, that Children should be thus educated, the providing Schools to give this Education to such of them as would not otherwise have it, has the Appearance, at least at first Sight, of deserving a Place amongst the very best of good Works. One would be backward, methinks, in entertaining Prejudices against it; and very forward, if one had any, to lay them aside, upon being shown that they were groundless. Let us consider the whole State of the Case. For though this will lead us some little Compass, yet I choose to do it; and the rather, because there are People who speak of Charity Schools as a new-invented Scheme, and therefore to be looked upon with I know not what Suspicion. Whereas it will appear, that the Scheme of Charity Schools, even the Part of it which is most looked upon in this Light, teaching the Children Letters and Accounts, is no otherwise new, than as the Occasion for it is so.

Formerly not only the Education of poor Children, but also their Maintenance, with that of the other Poor, were left to voluntary Charities. But great Changes of different Sorts happening over the Nation, and Charity becoming more cold, or the Poor more numerous, it was found necessary to make some legal Provision for them. This might, much more properly than Charity Schools, be called a new Scheme. For without question, the Education of poor Children was all along taken Care of, by voluntary Charities, more or less: but obliging us by Law to maintain the Poor, was new in the Reign of Queen *Elizabeth*. Yet, because a Change of Circumstances made it necessary, its Novelty was no Reason against it. Now in that legal Provision for the Maintenance of the Poor, poor Children must doubtless have had a Part in common with grown People. But this could never be sufficient for Children, because their Case always requires more than mere Maintenance; it requires that they be educated in some proper Manner. Wherever there are Poor who want to be maintained by Charity, there must be poor Children who, besides this, want to be educated by Charity. And whenever there began to be Need of *legal* Provision for the *Maintenance* of the Poor, there must immediately have been Need also of some *particular* legal Provision in Behalf of poor Children for their *Education*; this not being included in what we call their Maintenance. And many whose Parents are able to maintain them, and do so, may yet be utterly neglected as to their Education. But possibly it might not at first be attended to, that the Case of poor Children was thus a Case by itself, which required its own particular Provision. Certainly it would not appear, to the Generality, so urgent an one as the Want of Food and Raiment. And it might be necessary, that a Burden so entirely new as that of a Poor-Tax was at the Time I am speaking of, should be as light as possible. Thus the legal Provision for the Poor was the first settled; without any particular Consideration of that additional Want in the Case of Children; as it still remains, with scarce any Alteration in this Respect. In the mean Time, as the Poor still increased or Charity still lessened, many poor Children were left exposed, not to perish for want of Food, but to grow up in Society and learn every Thing that is Evil and nothing that is Good in it; and when they were grown up, greatly at a Loss in what honest Way to provide for themselves, if they could be supposed inclined to it. And larger Numbers, whose Case was not so bad as this, yet were very far from having due Care taken of their Education. And the Evil went on increasing, till it was grown to such a Degree, as to be quite out of the Compass of separate Charities to remedy. At length some excellent Persons, who were united in a *Society* [Society for Promoting Christian Knowledge] for carrying on almost every good Work, took into Consideration the neglected Case I have been representing; and first of all, as I understand it, set up Charity Schools; or however promoted them, as far as their Abilities and Influence could extend. Their Design was not in any sort to remove poor Children out of the Rank in which they were born, but, keeping them in it, to give them the Assistance which their Circumstances plainly called for, by educating them in the Principles of Religion, as well as civil Life; and likewise making some sort of Provision for their Maintenance: under which last I include Clothing them, giving them such Learning, if it is to be called by that Name, as may qualify them for some common Employment, and placing them out to it, as they grow up. These two general Designs coincide, in many Respects, and cannot be separated. For teaching the Children to read, though I have ranked it under the latter, equally belongs to both: And without some Advantages of the latter sort, poor People would not send their Children to our Charity Schools: Nor could the poorest of all be admitted into any Schools, without some charitable Provision of Clothing. And Care is taken, that it be such as cannot but be a Restraint upon the Children. And if this, or any Part of their Education, gives them any little Vanity, as has been poorly objected, whilst they are Children, it is scarce possible but that it will have even a quite contrary Effect when they are grown up, and ever after remind them of their Rank. Yet still we find it is apprehended, that what they here learn may set them above it.

But why should People be so extremely apprehensive of the Danger, that poor Persons will make a perverse Use of every the least Advantage, even the being able to read, whilst they do not appear at all apprehensive of the like Danger for themselves or their own Children, in Respect of Riches or Power, how much soever; though the Danger of perverting these Advantages is surely as great, and the Perversion itself of much greater and worse Consequence? And by what odd Reverse of Things has it happened, that such as pretend to be distinguished for the Love of Liberty, should be the only Persons who plead for keeping down the Poor, as one may speak; for keeping them more inferior in this Respect, and, which must be the Consequence, in other Respects, than they were in Times past? For till within a Century or two, all Ranks were nearly upon a Level as to the Learning in question. The Art of Printing appears to have been providentially reserved till these latter Ages, and then providentially brought into Use, as what was to be instrumental for the future in carrying on the appointed Course of Things. The Alterations which this Art has even already made in the Face of the World, are not inconsiderable. By means of it, whether immediately or remotely, the Methods of carrying on Business are, in several Respects, improved, 'Knowledge has been increased,' and some sort of Literature is become general. And if this be a Blessing, we ought to let the Poor, in their Degree, share it with us. The present State of Things and Course of Providence plainly leads us to do so. And if we do not, it is certain, how little soever it be attended to, that they will be upon a greater Disadvantage, on many Accounts, especially in populous Places, than they were in the dark Ages: for they will be more ignorant, comparatively with the People about them, than they were then; and the ordinary Affairs of the World are now put in a Way which requires, that they should have some Knowledge of Letters, which was not the Case then. And therefore, to bring up the Poor in their former Ignorance, now this Knowledge is so much more common and wanted, would be, not to keep them in the same, but to put them into a lower Condition of Life than what they were in formerly. Nor let People of Rank flatter themselves, that Ignorance will keep their Inferiors more dutiful and in greater Subjection to them: for surely there must be Danger, that it will have a contrary Effect, under a free Government such as ours, and in a dissolute Age. Indeed the Principles and Manners of the Poor, as to Virtue and Religion, will always be greatly influenced, as they always have been, by the *Example* of their Superiors, if that would mend the Matter. And this Influence will, I suppose, be greater, if they are kept more inferior than formerly in all Knowledge and Improvement. But unless their Superiors of the present Age, Superiors, I mean, of the Middle, as well as higher Ranks in Society, are greater Examples of public Spirit, of dutiful Submission to Authority, human and divine, of Moderation in Diversions, and proper Care of their Families, and domestic Affairs; unless, I say, Superiors of the present Age are greater Examples of Decency, Virtue and Religion, than those of former Times; for what Reason in the World is it desirable, that their Example should have this greater Influence over the Poor? On the contrary, why should not the Poor, by being taught to read, be put into a Capacity of making some Improvement in moral and religious Knowledge, and confirming themselves in those good Principles, which will be a great Security for their following the Example of their Superiors if it be good, and some sort of Preservative against their following it if it be bad? And serious Persons will farther observe very singular Reasons for this amongst us; from the Discontinuance of that religious Intercourse between Pastors and People in private, which remains in Protestant Churches abroad, as well as in the Church of *Rome*; and from our small public Care and Provision for keeping up a Sense of Religion in the lower Rank, except by distributing religious Books. For in this Way they have been assisted; and any well-disposed Person may do much Good amongst them, and at a very trifling Expense, since the worthy *Society* beforementioned has so greatly lessened the Price of such Books. But this pious Charity is an additional Reason why the Poor should be taught to read, that they may be in a Capacity of receiving the Benefit of it. Vain indeed would be the Hope, that anything in this World can be fully secured from Abuse. For as it is the general Scheme of divine Providence to bring Good out of Evil; so the Wickedness of Men will, if it be possible, bring Evil out of Good. But upon the whole, Incapacity and Ignorance must be favourable to Error and Vice; and Knowledge and Improvement contribute, in due Time, to the Destruction of Impiety as well as Superstition, and to the general Prevalence of true Religion. But some of these Observations may perhaps be thought too remote from the present Occasion. It is more obviously to the Purpose of it to observe, that Reading, Writing and Accounts, are useful, and, whatever Cause it is owing to, would really Now be wanted in the very lowest Stations: And that the *Trustees* of our *Charity Schools* are fully convinced of the great Fitness of joining to Instruction easy Labour, of some Sort or other, as fast it is practicable; which they have already been able to do in some of them.

Then as to placing out the poor Children, as soon as they are arrived at a fit Age for it; this must be approved by everyone, as it is putting them in a Way of Industry under domestic Government, at a Time of Life, in some Respects, more dangerous than even Childhood. And it is a known Thing, that Care is taken to do it in a Manner which does not set them above their Rank: though it is not possible always to do it exactly as one would wish. Yet, I hope it may be observed without Offence, if any of them happen to be of a very weakly Constitution, or of a very distinguished Capacity, there can be no Impropriety in placing these in Employments adapted to their particular Cases; though such as would be very improper for the Generality.

But the principal Design of this Charity is to educate poor Children in such a Manner, as has a Tendency to make them good, and useful, and contented, whatever their particular Station be. The Care of this is greatly neglected by the Poor: nor truly is it more regarded by the Rich, considering what might be expected from them. And if it were as practicable to provide Charity Schools, which should supply this shameful Neglect in the Rich, as it is to supply the like, though more excusable, Neglect in the Poor, I should think certainly, that Both ought to be done for the same Reasons. And most People, I hope, will think so too, if they attend to the Thing I am speaking of; which is the moral and religious Part of Education; what is equally necessary for all Ranks, and grievously wanting in all. Yet in this Respect the Poor must be greatly upon a Disadvantage, from the Nature of the Case; as will appear to any one who will consider it.

For if poor Children are not sent to School, several Years of their Childhood, of course, pass away in Idleness and Loitering. This has a Tendency to give them, perhaps a feeble Listlessness, perhaps an headstrong Profligateness of Mind; certainly an Indisposition to proper Application as they grow up, and an Aversion afterwards, not only to the Restraints of Religion, but to those which any particular Calling, and even the Nature of Society, require. Whereas Children kept to stated Orders, and who many Hours of the Day are in Employment, are by this Means habituated, both to submit to those who are placed over them, and to govern Themselves; and they are also by this Means prepared for Industry, in any Way of Life in which they may be placed. And all this holds abstracted from the Consideration of their being taught to read; without which, however, it will be impracticable to employ their Time: not to repeat the unanswerable Reasons for it before mentioned. Now Several poor People cannot, Others will not be at the Expense of sending their Children to School. And let me add, that such as can and are willing, yet if it be very inconvenient to them, ought to be eased of it, and the Burden of Children made as light as may be to their poor Parents.

Consider next the Manner in which the Children of the Poor, who have vicious Parents, are brought up, in Comparison with other Children whose Parents are of the same Character. The Children of dissolute Men of Fortune may have the Happiness of not seeing much of their Parents. And this, even though they are educated at Home, is often the Case, by Means of a customary Distance between them, which cannot be kept amongst the Poor. Nor is it impossible, that a rich Man of this Character, desiring to have his Children better than himself, may provide them such an Education as may make them so, without his having any Restraint or Trouble in the Matter. And the Education which Children of better Rank must have, for their Improvement in the common Accomplishments belonging to it, is of course, as yet, for the most Part, attended with some Sort of religious Education. But the Poor, as they cannot provide Persons to educate their Children; so from the Way in which they live together in poor Families, a Child must be an Eye and Ear-witness of the worst Part of his Parents' Talk and Behaviour. And it cannot but be expected, that his own will be formed upon it. For as Example in general has very great Influence upon all Persons, especially Children, the Example of their Parents is of Authority with them, when there is nothing to balance it on the other Side. Now take in the Supposition, that these Parents are dissolute, profligate People; then, over and above giving their Children no Sort of good Instruction, and a very bad Example, there are more Crimes than one in which, it may be feared, they will directly instruct and encourage them; besides letting them ramble abroad wherever they will, by which, of course, they learn the very same Principles and Manners they do at Home. And from all these Things together, such poor Children will have their Characters formed to Vice, by those whose Business it is to restrain them from it. They will be disciplined and trained up in it. This surely is a Case which ought to have some public Provision made for it. If it can't have an adequate one, yet such an one as it can: unless it be thought so rare as not to deserve our Attention. But in reality, though there should be no more Parents of this Character amongst the Poor, in Proportion, than amongst the Rich, the Case which I have been putting will be far from being uncommon. Now notwithstanding the Danger, to which the Children of such wretched Parents cannot but be exposed, from what they see at Home; yet by instilling into them the Principles of Virtue and Religion at School, and placing them soon out in sober Families, there is Ground to hope, they may avoid those ill Courses, and escape that Ruin, into which, without this Care, they would almost certainly run. I need not add how much greater Ground there is to expect, that those of the Children who have religious Parents will do well. For such Parents, besides setting their Children a good Example, will likewise repeat and enforce upon them at Home, the good Instructions they receive at School.

After all, we find the World continues very corrupt. And it would be miraculous indeed, if Charity Schools alone should make it otherwise: or if they should make even all who are brought up in them Proof against its Corruptions. The Truth is, every Method that can be made use of to prevent or reform the bad Manners of the Age, will appear to be of less Effect, in Proportion to the greater Occasion there is for it: As Cultivation, though the most proper that can be, will produce less Fruit, or of a worse Sort, in a bad Climate than in a good one. And thus the Character of the common People, with whom these Children are to live, in the ordinary Intercourse of Business and Company when they come out into the World, may more or less defeat the good Effects of their Education. And so likewise may the Character of Men of Rank, under whose Influence they are to live. But whatever Danger may be apprehended from either or both of these, it can be no Reason why we should not endeavour, by the likeliest Methods we can, to better the World, or keep it from growing worse. The good Tendency of the Method before us is unquestionable. And I think myself obliged to add, that upon a Comparison of Parishes where Charity Schools have been for a considerable Time established, with neighbouring ones, in like Situations, which have had none, the good Effects of them, as I am very credibly informed, are most manifest. Notwithstanding I freely own, that it is extremely difficult to make the necessary Comparisons in this Case, and form a Judgment upon them. And a Multitude of Circumstances must come in to determine, from Appearances only, concerning the positive Good which is produced by this Charity, and the Evil which is prevented by it; which last is full as material as the former, and can scarce be estimated at all. But surely there can be no Doubt, whether it be useful or not, to educate Children in Order, Virtue and Religion.

However, suppose, which is yet far from being the Case, but suppose it should seem, that this Undertaking did not answer the Expense and Trouble of it, in the civil or political Way of considering Things. What is this to Persons who profess to be engaged in it, not only upon mere civil Views, but upon moral and christian ones? We are to do our Endeavours to promote

Virtue and Religion amongst Men, and leave the Success to God: The Designs of his Providence are answered by these Endeavours, *whether they will hear, or whether they will forbear*; i.e. whatever be the Success of them: And the least Success in such Endeavours is a great and valuable Effect.

From these foregoing Observations, duly considered, it will appear, that the Objections which have been made against Charity Schools, are to be regarded in the same Light with those which are made against any other necessary Things; for Instance, against providing for the Sick and the aged Poor. Objections in this latter Case could be considered no otherwise than merely as Warnings of some Inconvenience which might accompany such Charity, and might, more or less, be guarded against, the Charity itself being still kept up; or as Proposals for placing it upon some better Foot. For though, amidst the Disorder and Imperfection in all human Things, these Objections were not obviated, they could not however possibly be understood as Reasons for discontinuing such Charity; because thus understood, they would be Reasons for leaving necessitous People to perish. Well-disposed Persons therefore will take Care, that they be not deluded with Objections against this before us, any more than against other necessary Charities; as though such Objections were Reasons for suppressing them, or not contributing to their Support, unless we can procure an Alteration of That to which we object. There can be no possible Reasons for leaving poor Children in that imminent Danger of Ruin, in which many of these must be left, were it not for this Charity. Therefore Objections against it, cannot, from the Nature of the Case, amount to more than Reasons for endeavouring, whether with or without Success, to put it upon a right and unexceptionable Foot, in the particular Respects objected against. And if this be the Intention of the Objectors, the Managers of it have shown themselves remarkably ready to second them: for they have shown even a Docility in receiving Admonitions of anything thought amiss in it, and Proposals for rendering it more complete. And, under the Influence of this good Spirit, the Management of it is really improving; particularly in greater Endeavours to introduce Manufactures into these Schools; and in more particular Care to place the Children out to Employments in which they are most wanted, and may be most serviceable, and which are most suitable to their Ranks. But if there be any thing in the Management of them, which some particular Persons think should be altered, and others are of a contrary Opinion, these Things must be referred to the Judgment of the Public, and the Determination of the Public complied with. Such Compliance is an essential Principle of all charitable Associations; for without it they could not subsist at all: and by charitable Associations, Multitudes are put in mind to do Good, who otherwise would not have thought of it; and infinitely more Good may be done, than possibly can by the separate Endeavours of the same Number of charitable Persons. Now he who refuses to help forward the good Work before us, because it is not conducted exactly in his own Way, breaks in upon that general Principle of Union; which those who are Friends to the Indigent and distressed Part of our Fellow-Creatures, will be very cautious how they do in any Case: but more especially will they beware, how they break in upon that necessary Principle in a Case of so great Importance as is the present. For the Public is as much interested in the Education of poor Children, as in the Preservation of their Lives.

This last, I observed, is legally provided for. The former is left amongst other Works of Charity, neglected by many who care for none of these Things, and to be carried on by such only as think it their Concern to be doing Good. Some of you are able, and in a Situation, to assist in it in an eminent Degree, by being *Trustees*, and overlooking the Management of these Schools; or in different Ways countenancing and recommending them; as well as by contributing to their Maintenance: Others can assist only in this latter Way. In what Manner and Degree then it belongs to You, and to me, and to any particular Person to help it forward, let us all consider seriously, not for one another, but each of us for himself.

> And may the Blessing of Almighty God accompany this Work of Charity, which He has put into the Hearts of his Servants, in Behalf of these poor Children: that being now *trained up in the way they should go, when they are old they may not depart from it.* May He, of his Mercy, keep them safe amidst the innumerable Dangers of this bad World, through which they are to pass, and preserve them unto his heavenly Kingdom.